WISDOM
from World Religions

✦

pathways toward
HEAVEN ON EARTH

Sir John Templeton

TEMPLETON FOUNDATION PRESS
PHILADELPHIA & LONDON

Templeton Foundation Press
Five Radnor Corporate Center, Suite 120
100 Matsonford Road
Radnor, Pennsylvania 19087

Designed and typeset by Gopa & Ted2
Printed by Sheridan Books

Library of Congress Cataloging-in-Publication Data available
ISBN: 1-890151-91-2

Printed in the United States of America

02 03 04 05 06 07   10 9 8 7 6 5 4 3 2 1

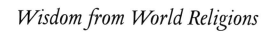

Wisdom from World Religions

Contents

Week Four

Week Five

Week Six

Week Seven

Week Eight

Week Nine

Introduction

WHO AM I? Why am I here on planet Earth? What does the future hold? How can I set out on my own into a world that sometimes seems filled with conflict and strife? How can I get along better with the people in my life? How do I cope with day-to-day pressures? How can I be successful in my work? How do I find peace in the midst of turmoil? How can my life be useful and happy?

These are questions often asked by many people today. Do you want to be a constructive participant in building "heaven on earth"? Well, we *can* help create a more meaningful and fruitful world—by our thoughts, feelings, consciousness, and actions. In addition, we *can* reflect that inner realization of unlimited love, compassion, kindness, honesty, integrity, strength, and a sense of our purpose in life to every person and situation in our area of experience. Fortunately, there are positive responses and definite and helpful guidance that can enrich the life of every individual who is sincerely seeking to learn. And many people have a deep, inner desire to live life in a manner that can bring body, mind, and spirit into a harmonious alignment with everyday experiences.

Evidences are increasing that "There's more to why you're here than what you presently know!" Your search for that "something more" can be a sacred adventure into new insights, provocative choices, unexpected turning points, an enthusiasm to enter the unknown. Daily living can become more joyful, successful, and useful. Our spiritual lessons are often the myriad life situations that come our way, especially the ones we may not immediately comprehend. These are times when knowing, understanding, and practicing the *laws of life* can be of important assistance in helping a person to be happy and to contribute to life in effective ways.

These laws are simply a "set of rules" by which we can guide the way we live. They are found in a vast array of sources, such as: the major religions of the world; various schools of philosophical thought, both ancient and modern; storytellers from all nations; scientists; and historians, to name a few. There seem to be literally hundreds of such laws, and most families and religions seek to teach the laws they were taught. Some laws are so clear that most people can agree that they are true. For example, honesty and truthfulness rank high as values in cultures and societies around the world.

Followers of the ancient Chinese sage Lao Tzu understood spiritual law as the *Tao Teh Ching*. The simplest interpretation of the Tao, or spiritual law, is: "This is how things work." One way to comprehend this law is to realize that it expresses the relationship between a person's mind and the thoughts and ideas of the mind, a person's emotions and how they are expressed, and the physical activities that give expression to those thoughts, feelings, and ideas. A definite relationship exists between the invisible thoughts and feelings of our mind and heart and the visible actions we take because of them.

Finding effective words to speak of universal spiritual truths may be somewhat difficult. How *do* we express the unconditional, the ultimate, the source, the inconceivable within which all things are created? God, Buddha, Allah, Brahma,

Muhammad, Wakantanka, the Divine, the Creator? The words and the understanding of the words may vary in different spiritual traditions and, in some instances, may not be simply interchanged. Yet, cannot the universal language of unlimited love perceive the basic goodness that is the essence of every living being?

The world operates on spiritual principles just as it operates on the laws of physics and gravity. It is up to us as individuals to learn what these laws or principles are, and then choose to live by them. Let's look at understanding this idea more clearly. You might ask, "What is a spiritual law?" We may answer that it is a timeless law or principle and, being of spirit, is not visible. However, spiritual law is quite real. Spiritual law is not shaped or determined by any person's current opinion or whim. Spiritual laws are impartial in that they apply equally to everyone, everywhere throughout our world. They work without prejudices or bias at *all* times and in *all* places. These laws are self-enforcing and are not dependent on human authority or commandments.

Our stay on this small planet called Earth is a brief one and we have an excellent opportunity to leave the world a better place than we found it through our choice of how we live our life. One way to accomplish lasting improvement is to master the laws of life.

We often create our own realities by the choices we make in perceiving and interacting with the world around us. Certainly, many of these choices may be made unconsciously through conditioned responses. Yet, we are the only ones who can choose to move in a different direction. How can we grow through various inputs of knowledge to become wise by working through the ways of wisdom? As we begin to work with the laws of life where we are, in the situations in which we find ourselves, to ask for understanding, to try to be loving in our thoughts, in our words, and in our actions, we can find our understanding increasing. It becomes easier for us to look beyond the *appearances* of a situation to the *heart*

of the situation to the *heart* of another person.

While we are attending school, whether it is grade school, high school, public school, private school, college, graduate school, or the school of life, we can have a wonderful time. We can take pleasure in learning, in improving our minds, and in preparing ourselves for a useful future. On the other hand, we can be discontented and complain and cause ourselves and others around us to be uncomfortable. It is up to us. The physical world with its work, duties, laws, opportunities, obligations, relationships, and responsibilities is a *school* for our spiritual being. It is the place where we come for an education. Ask yourself these questions: What kind of student am I? Do I learn my lessons well? Do I apply myself to "homework" such as prayer or meditation or expressions of gratitude? Am I working at keeping my relationships with other people happy and harmonious? Do I fulfill whatever duties may be mine to do effectively and with a spirit of humility? Do I take advantage of opportunities to be a responsible person?

When we deny our personal responsibilities and attribute to external causes the limits we may place on ourselves, we can make the process of learning more difficult. Perhaps one of humanity's greatest challenges is to acknowledge our individual responsibility for our lives. Growth is often synonymous with accepting responsibility—perhaps a bit at a time—as we become more able to handle situations. Each individual can be sincerely accountable for performing with honesty and integrity and in a sound, prompt, and conscientious manner.

One of my favorite poets—first read in high school—is Henry Wadsworth Longfellow. I particularly like the poem "A Psalm of Life." In these verses, we can learn what the young man said to the Psalmist as he moved through his process of "growing in wisdom."

Tell me not in mournful numbers,
Life is but an empty dream!—
For the soul is dead that slumbers,
And things are not what they seem.

Life is real! Life is earnest!
And the grave is not the goal:
Dust thou art, to dust returnest,
Was not spoken of the soul.

Not enjoyment and not sorrow,
Is our destined end or way;
But to act, that each to-morrow
Finds us farther than to-day.

Art is long, and Time is fleeting,
And our hearts though stout and brave,
Still, like muffled drums, are beating
Funeral marches to the grave.

In the world's broad field of battle,
In the bivouac of Life,
Be not like dumb, driven cattle!
Be a hero in the strife!

Trust no Future, howe'er pleasant!
Let the dead Past bury its dead!
Act,—act in the living Present!
Heart within, and God o'erhead!

Lives of great men all remind us
We can make our lives sublime,
And, departing leave behind us
Footprints on the sands of time.

Footprints, that perhaps another,
Sailing o'er life's solemn main,
A forlorn and shipwrecked brother,
Seeing, shall take heart again.

Let us, then, be up and doing,
With a heart for any fate;
Still achieving, still pursuing,
Learn to labor and to wait.

The truth of this poem can be demonstrated if we look to the lives of some of the famous people as well as the unsung heroes of the past and present. Here we can find many models for useful, happy living. Moreover, when we examine their words and deeds, we can often discover the principles that inspired and sustained their benefits to present and future generations. It is my belief that the basic laws or principles for leading a "sublime life," to paraphrase Longfellow, can be examined and tested just as science examines and tests natural laws of the universe.

Wisdom from World Religions: Pathways toward Heaven on Earth is designed to offer people of all ages and all nations an opportunity to learn a little more about the spiritual laws, principles, and teachings of a variety of great spiritual practices. I hope that in this book we can offer a Scripture verse or story or parable or discipline or quote that may show you the world in a way more helpful than you have seen it before. The materials presented in this book can provide an opportunity for learning and "growing in wisdom."

There are clear scriptural and philosophical bases for advocating the need for an inquiring and open mind. For example, according to the Gospel of Luke, Jesus said: "Ask, and it shall be given you; seek, and you shall find; knock, and it shall be opened unto you. For every one who asks, receives, and he who seeks, finds; and to him who knocks, it shall be opened" (Luke 11:9-10). Can the value in learning to see a different world lie not in replacing the one you have, but in providing a basis for an opportunity to see from a different, or larger, perspective? Can the timeless universal principles of life that transcend modern times or particular cultures help people in all parts of the world live happier and more useful lives?

GROWING IN WISDOM

What is "wisdom"? Webster's Dictionary defines "wisdom" as "the quality of being wise . . . [it] implies the ability to judge and deal with persons, situations, etc. rightly, based on a broad range of knowledge, experience, and understanding." In other words, a wise person may be one who has the ability to look for the deeper, inner meaning of things. There is a definite difference between *acquiring* knowledge and information and *possessing* wisdom. A person may acquire knowledge and meaningful information from attending a university, through travels, through relationships, through books that are read and studied, and through a variety of activities in which one may participate. But is the person also gaining wisdom?

How happy are you in your life right now? How are you working with the "tools" you presently have? For example, how do you perceive the people and situations around you? Is your outlook positive? Are you open and receptive to the ideas of others? Are you willing to make progressive changes? Do you take time to come apart from daily activities, even for a few minutes, and be still and *listen* to your thoughts and feelings? Are you a seeker—after greater understanding and wisdom?

Wisdom, as a personal quality, can be a mental and behavioral activity that can require a depth of understanding, such as perception—or how you "see" or perceive what is happening around you. Wisdom can also be a quality of everyday behavior, such as performance—or how you conduct your daily life. Can emotions also constitute a substantial component of a capacity for practical wisdom? Perhaps, if we consider that through our emotions we track what is meaningful to us and communicate to others what we morally care about.

Achieving wisdom is a journey that can emphasize learning how to be observant about life, to be open and receptive to situations around you, to ask questions, to have patience, to be willing to learn, and to be humble. In the process of this journey, there are opportunities to learn through studying the laws of life, the world's religions, and the lessons they offer.

Evidence indicates that the rate of spiritual development is accelerating. Throughout the two hundred thousand years of our history as a species, there have been periods of gradual growth followed by rapid development in the physical and intellectual periods. Now, a new vision of our place and our purpose in the cosmos is unfolding. Possibly, we may be setting the stage for a giant leap forward in our spiritual understanding.

Many of these recent discoveries in fields such as physics, cosmology, neural science, and evolutionary biology have been so phenomenal that they have changed the way we think about ourselves and our place in the universe. Certainly, through these discoveries, many scientists have been brought to a state of wonderment and humility and serious consideration to basic philosophical and theological questions.

The two hundred laws of life that were chosen from many religions for this book can be important and helpful as well as possible to apply in your life. Each law is presented in an essay format, with applications, opinions, stories, examples, Scripture verses, and quotations offered to examine the validity of the law. Each quotation that titles an essay points to a particular law that holds true for most people worldwide under most circumstances. The material is designed to inspire as well as to encourage you, to help you consider more deeply the laws you personally live by; and to reap the rewards of their practical application.

The laws herein may be used as *effective, practical,* and *workable* tools. When you apply them consistently, you can draw forth the power to transform your life into a more deeply useful and joyful experience. Even if your life is already working well, it is possible that it can work even better as you incorporate more of the wisdom from the great religions contained in these pages. If I had found a book of two hundred basic laws of life during my educational years, I could have been far more productive then as well as in the years that have followed.

Although *Wisdom from World Religions: Pathways toward Heaven on Earth* may be read like any other inspirational book, its organization follows that of an academic study program. The laws are arranged into the forty weeks of a typical school year. Alongside each essay, you will find wisdom quotes pertaining to the topic. At the end of each week are highlights from the material presented in the essays, guideline exercises for "Living the Various Spiritual Laws," and space to note the personal ideas and examples you may perceive for working with the law. At the conclusion of the recommended study process, you will have read and become familiar with the meanings of the two hundred laws of life contained in this book. The book's format can provide useful guidance and a meaningful study program for individuals, families, study groups, business and professional organizations, schools, and colleges.

Ways You Can Use This Book

Let's look for a moment at some possible ways you may benefit from the laws by applying them to various activities in your life.

◆ An informal discussion group could be formed with friends, family, or a school, church, or social group. People often benefit by coming together with others to study useful topics of mutual interest. If this approach is chosen, you might select a single essay, read it aloud as a group, then spend an hour or so discussing the key ideas. This kind of participation often develops trust and allows the group members to deepen their relationship to the concepts presented and to each other by sharing personal experiences as you apply the laws to your life. In addition to exploring a variety of points of view on the verification, importance, and meaning of the laws of life, support and encouragement for individual members of the group may be provided as different ones begin to make improvements in their lives and attitudes.

◆ Another approach is to ponder some of the spiritual laws individually and privately. Set aside a block of time when you are unlikely to be dis-

turbed. As you relax and allow your thoughts and feelings to become peaceful and settled, think about something that may be paramount at the present moment in your life. This could be a tough decision of some kind you may be making, a situation or circumstance that could be troubling you, a time for giving thanks for your blessings, or you may simply be open and receptive for guidance. Choose your focus and formulate a question. Scan the listing of essays in the table of contents until a particular one catches your attention. Then, open the book to that particular essay and listen, with inner perception and prayer, to the message that may help to bring insight into your life.

◆ Individually or in the group context, you might select and study all of the essays relative to a particular theme. For example, you may choose "humility" and concentrate intensively upon that particular subject. Or, choose "love," "peace," "values," "gratitude," "giving," etc. Then, discuss various ways of demonstrating this law.

◆ Another idea is to keep a spiritual journal in which you record your responses to what you have read and to what is happening in your life. In fact, keeping a journal is *highly recommended,* because activities will be offered in the "Spotlights" and "Living the Various Spiritual Laws" sections which can serve as a bridge to take you from the teachings of the essays to their adventures in your everyday life. Writing encourages you to focus your thoughts and, more precisely, to identify your feelings. They—your thoughts and feelings—are a vitally important part of your life. The more clarity and understanding you have in these areas, the richer your experiences will be.

◆ Make a list of questions that may come to mind as you read the essays. Asking questions can be a most rewarding avenue toward finding answers! Make a note of "first responses" that come to mind as the questions are asked. Plan further research into the theme of your questions and note this information in your journal.

You can probably find other ways to use this wisdom of the ages. Indeed, we would welcome and encourage the submission of ideas and evidence for verification of any law that supports, illustrates, or disproves any of the two hundred laws of life in this book. Can you also help discover other spiritual laws in different countries that are not in conflict with any Scripture or prophet? The reward of this book for the author is the joy of receiving letters from readers about how the book may have helped them learn the joy of becoming helpers in the acceleration of divine creativity. Your communications may be sent to:

John Templeton Foundation (WWR)
5 Radnor Corporate Center, Suite 100
100 Matsonford Road
Radnor, PA 19087

Several years ago, I began offering support for a Laws of Life Essay Contest in my boyhood home of Franklin County, Tennessee, in the United States. Mr. and Mrs. Handly Templeton assist in operating the program. Prizes for the essays—averaging one hundred to fifteen hundred words —are awarded semi-annually, with a first prize of $2,000, a second prize of $800, and a number of runner-up prizes. The response has been gratifying. The number of entries continues to increase. It would be heartwarming to learn that your locality would like to embark on its own version of the Franklin County program. The John Templeton Foundation can provide information on the various essay contest methods that have become beneficial for teenagers in more than one hundred localities of several nations.

The limitless potentials of wisdom from world religions can be so powerful when shared. Can you perceive what an effective investment in the spiritual development of human beings this could be? Let's make a loving commitment to share the benefits of our increasing spiritual awareness with others, because sharing our most prized possessions can be the highest form of "Love thy neighbor." Let's study enthusiastically the glorious highlights of the world's spiritual teachings, and with a spirit of humility recognize that no one will ever comprehend all that God is. Let's permit and encourage each prophet to proclaim the best of truth as it is revealed to him or her. There is no conflict unless the restrictive idea of exclusiveness enters in.

This book can be read, considered, absorbed, and practiced until it begins to clarify and enhance your personal interpretation of these laws of life and wisdom from around the world. The purpose of this book is not to make a profit, but rather to help humanity. Therefore, the U.S. publisher can make available copies of *Wisdom from World Religions: Pathways toward Heaven on Earth* in lots of one hundred or more at a greatly reduced price. Also, publishers in other languages are encouraged to send proposals to publish this volume. Please contact tfp@templeton.org for further information.

It is my desire that this book may encourage some of you to begin, or to continue, the exploration into a deeper understanding of the ways of God with all His creatures in the long history of this cosmos. Be loving and gentle with yourself and let your heart, mind, and spirit guide you in a fulfilling experience in your search for expanding truth.

God loves you and so do I.

—John Marks Templeton

In Appreciation

The publishing of this book is accomplished with reverence and appreciation for the world religions that purify a person's mind and heart, elevate his emotions, and offer guidance for a spiritual way of life. Much of the material contained herein has been made possible by the sincere light of the prophets, teachers, and traditions of the world's great religions that, through the ages, have expressed sacred insights and wisdom to humanity.

I must also credit that ordering principle—the cosmic creative intelligence, the pulse of evolution within the universe—that manifests itself to us as synchronicity. In many conversations and readings, I often find the same ideas and insights expressed through different minds around the planet.

Also, without the help of many individuals, employees, colleagues in business and charities, and family members who shared their ideas and wisdom with me, this book would not have been possible. To each of you I extend my thanks.

Wisdom from World Religions

Week One

✦ LAW I

When you rule your mind, you rule your world. —Bill Provost

The mind is everything; what you think, you become.
—*Buddha*

By the mind one is bound, by the mind one is freed . . . He who asserts with strong conviction, "I am not bound, I am free," becomes free.
—*Ramakrishna*

ARE YOU AWARE that there is presently within you a tremendous energy available to be harnessed and utilized to guide you into the joys of more satisfying and successful living? Do you also realize this same energy can assist you in living a life filled with meaningful contributions to your personal world, your family, and your community? This easily accessible and usable energy is often referred to as "the power of the mind," or "the law of mind action." And it works for both male and female genders, in all areas of a person's life, and in all nations and countries of the world.

Some of the elements of the power of the mind may be familiar to you: *desire, vision, imagination, intent, belief, positive* or *negative thinking,* to name a few. Everyone uses these elements of mind frequently throughout the day. But many people may not realize the important contribution these aspects of the mind make toward defining the character and personality of an individual. So, understanding the quote, "When you rule your mind, you rule your world," can provide powerful insight into some of the ways you function as an individual. Let's take a look at how it works.

In his book, *The Revealing Word,* Charles Fillmore describes our mind in the following manner: "The mind is the seat of perception of the things we see, hear, and feel. It is through the mind that we see the beauties of the earth and sky, of music,

of art, in fact, of everything. That silent shuttle of thought working in and out through cell and nerve weaves into one harmonious whole the myriad moods of mind, and we call it life."

Within the mind of every individual abides the starting point of a person's thoughts, spoken words, actions, and even one's feelings. What you think about the Creator of all, yourself, your family, your neighbors, your acquaintances, your work associates, or others makes a great deal of difference in your daily life. In fact, every aspect of your life can be affected by the way you think! As Joseph Addison once said, "One of the most difficult things for a powerful mind is to be its own master!"

Throughout the period of one day, a person may fluctuate between confidence and uncertainty, decision and indecision, peaceful calmness and frustration, or being happy or sad. Your life may appear to be governed by people, events, and circumstances. But is this observation correct? It *is* important to be aware of the situations and circumstances around you. It is also important and helpful to possess certain qualities in life: sincerity of purpose, dedication to ideals, commitment to integrity, and a continual thirst for knowledge.

Your true anchorage is not in things temporary, but in things eternal; not in things of the outer world, but in the sacred inner awareness and truth of your own being. To know this truth and to stand firm in this awareness may be difficult on occasion, especially in today's busy and expanding world. But it is possible to be centered and focused! How can this be done? A good way is to become the master of your thoughts.

A universal law or principle called the *law of mind action* plays its role in every person's life. How does the law of mind action affect a person and his world? One answer offers the premise that thinking is the connecting link between the universal mind of God and man. Awareness of this law and its application can help you shepherd your thoughts and ascertain that they are positive and

and ideas that are like its own nature. Energy from your thoughts flows forth through time and space to touch others, like a ripple in a pond, affecting all it touches.

As you become more aware of the truth that "thoughts are things" and that thoughts are equally as important as actions, you may take a giant step forward toward becoming the master of your mind. In other words, you become aware of your thinking process and begin to focus on thoughts that are positive and productive. The way you think paves the way for how you respond to daily situations and thereby profoundly influences your world.

All that is comes from the mind; it is based on the mind, it is fashioned by the mind.

— The Dhammapada

productive. Thinking is also the movement of ideas within your mind, or your intellect in action. From these ideas, mental images or pictures are formed in your mind, based on your acquired understanding. These images may then be brought forth as desires and actions.

The thinking process is a creative force that is constantly at work in humanity. A mental atmosphere is produced by the kind of thoughts you think, and this energy draws unto itself thoughts

When you understand the universal *law of cause and effect*—what you give forth, so you get back— you receive and develop positive, workable, affirmative truths that are useful and beneficial in your daily life. The law of cause and effect, often referred to as "the balance wheel of the universe," is closely aligned with the law of mind action. In a sense, we live in two worlds: the world of cause (the within) and the world of effect (the without).

✦ LAW 2

Where there is no vision, the people perish.—Proverbs 29:18

AN ANCIENT PROVERB tells us: "Where there is no vision, the people perish." This is one way of saying that it is important to have a dream, a goal, a particular focus, or a vision of what is desired in order to live life fully and fruitfully. When we have no goal, or when our vision of the goal is

obscured, we may lose our sense of purpose and direction. Even when we've prepared ourselves well and have an aptitude for a given activity, poorly directed efforts can rob us of the vital energy necessary for achievement. Establishing goals, along with establishing guidelines on how to achieve them, can keep us focused and energized and often make our lives more interesting, useful, and successful.

Occasionally, there may be little difference between where a person presently is in life and where he would like to be. Often, the moment we add an additional purpose to what we presently have, an opportunity is presented to move toward our goal. As little as a 10 percent increase in energy or commitment can make a difference. However, the real accomplishment lies in the fact that a person becomes inspired to do better and refuses to accept complacency. Unless we create specific goals that match our purposes in life, and unless we keep a clear vision of these goals, we may eventually falter and fail.

Sometimes, particular aspects of life may seem to be routine, and a *certain* amount of routine can help to keep the momentum going. However, inspiration often comes to those who work toward a definite goal. There is always room for improvement. Can you visualize how you can put your inspiration to work through the power of your thoughts? Your intellect is both a product and a producer of creativity. This strength is already within you and can be stimulated by a desire to achieve beneficial goals.

One of the quickest and most thorough ways to increase your vision and to unfold spiritually is to be of as much help as possible to others. "An idle life is a wasted life." How can this statement be true for you?

A story is told of a Christian monk who earnestly prayed that a vision of Jesus Christ might be revealed to him. After praying for many hours, the monk heard a voice telling him the vision would occur the next morning at daybreak. Before the first rays of dawn appeared the following morning, the monk was on his knees at the altar.

A fierce storm was brewing, but the monk paid

> But the bravest are surely those who have the clearest vision of what is before them, glory and danger alike, and yet notwithstanding go out to meet it.
> — Thucydides

it no heed. He watched and prayed and waited for the vision. As the storm broke in great fury, a soft knock came at the door. Interrupted in his devotions, the monk turned away from the altar to open the door. He knew some poor wayfarer was seeking shelter from the raging storm. As he turned toward the door, he caught a glimpse of the vision for which he had prayed.

Torn between his desire to stay and experience the vision—one that he felt would last but for a moment—and his desire to help a brother in distress, the monk quickly decided that duty must come first. Upon opening the door, he gazed into the bright blue eyes of a small child who had apparently lost her way. She was tired, shivering from the cold, and hungry.

The monk gently reached out his hand and led the child into the warm room. He placed a bowl of milk and some fresh bread before her and did everything he could think of to make her comfortable. Warm, fed, and comfortable, the child fell asleep in a chair.

Then, with a heavy heart, he turned back toward his altar, fearing that the vision had vanished. To his joy and surprise, it was there—clear and bright and shining with radiant glory! As the monk gazed rapturously upon the precious vision for a long time, he heard a voice gently speak: "If thou had not attended to my little one, I could not have stayed."

It has been said that life is but a day. Can we reverse this statement and affirm with a greater awareness that every day is a life? When you awaken each morning, will you resolve that your day be filled with faithful purpose, a high vision, loving service, and gentle growth? It can happen! Then, as the day progresses, throw a glance backward and observe how well you have kept the morning's resolution.

The present moment is the action moment. You may have heard the following statement many times: "Do not put off until tomorrow what you can accomplish today." Let your interest and focus be in the *now* moment, the action moment. Where there is interest, there can be activity, vision, and transformation. How beautifully the Apostle Paul said this when he declared: "Do not be conformed to this world but be transformed by the renewal of your mind, that you may prove what is the will of God, what is good and acceptable and perfect" (Romans 12:2).

Will you accept the challenge and the change —and transform yourself? The earnest person is one who is completely dedicated to his or her chosen purposes. There is simplicity in what we seek to do when we dedicate ourselves to the doing. At this moment, accept only the vision that uplifts, but do not reject what you may not understand. In a definite change of attitude, embrace all things that are part of you. Then, release—release all and everything.

Become still and know. Know that order, *divine order*, can be the high vision expressing itself through an expanded conscious awareness of you, your world, and your purpose and place in it.

✦ LAW 3

Why were you created? —John Marks Templeton

DOESN'T IT SEEM LOGICAL that if we really *know* something, we can walk forward with a higher level of confidence, greater assurance, and increased capacity to achieve our goals in life? Have we not all, at some point in our lives, been caught up in wonder and perhaps, searching for a resolution to a particular situation, asked the questions, "Why am I here? . . . What is life *really* all about? . . . Why was I created as this particular individual?"

You may have heard the expression that mankind came into the world to bring forth his God-likeness, to express his own true nature, to unfold his glorious divine blueprint, or as divinity's ideal creation of the productive person. Certainly this can be "food for thought." And Scripture tells us: "I say, 'You are gods; children of the Most High, all of you'" (Psalms 82:6).

When we live as earth-plane beings, with only our human faculties to draw upon, we present to the world and to each other a human self-hood: human qualities and human awareness. This human self can be limited, finite, and consisting mostly of what we have learned through education, personal experiences, environment, and other exterior influences. Hidden behind this personal self, however, abides the reality of our being. We are more than the physical and mental person. We have a spiritual identity and the physical is included within the spiritual.

Could our relation to the Creator be like that of the sunbeam to the sun? Nothing can separate the sun from one of its rays. Made of the sun's substance, partaking of its nature, each sunbeam has a particular mission, a certain spot of the earth to caress and warm and light. Like the sunbeam, we, too, have our own special spot to fill. We have our own special work to do. Thus, we are a part of the divine plan and necessary to the perfect whole.

Think about this idea. Can you imagine anything more meaningful or more powerful than realizing our true heritage, and then stepping forward to attain it? What does it mean to be a "child of God"? And to what are we heirs? One response could be that to be an heir of God means we, as his children, share abundantly in the infinite purpose of our Creator.

Humanity's fascination with a spiritual dimension, a hidden sphere of power, an underlying ordering principle that lies unseen behind everyday events as well as behind gigantic happenings, has grown and taken on new importance.

Science is constantly unveiling more of the fundamental structure of matter. Yet, each new discovery and explanation lures us on to ever deeper and expanding research. The penetration of each mystery opens more profound situations that challenge our intellectual capacity. As we follow the path of investigation, like an explorer climbing a rugged mountain, new vistas of knowledge unfold. As each mountain peak is crested, another peak, loftier still, appears on the horizon.

The more we know about the universe and our place in it, the more we realize how little we know. So in our ongoing search, we often look to the spiritual teachings of the world religions to provide assistance in helping us understand more of who and what we are and why we are here.

Our souls long for God—by whatever name we call the Creator of all there is. We long to know God in magnificent expressions of love, life, power, peace, beauty, compassion, companionship, and more. However, in many instances, we may interpret this longing for God as a desire for things, and things in themselves can never bring satisfaction. Satisfaction comes when we gain a clear, vivid consciousness of the indwelling presence of the Creator.

We are told in Matthew 6:33, "Seek first his kingdom and his righteousness, and all these things shall be yours as well." Can it be that the

Our Birth is but a sleep; and a forgetting:
The soul that rises with us, our life's star,
Hath had elsewhere its setting,
And cometh from afar:
Not in entire forgetfulness, and not in utter nakedness,
But trailing clouds of glory do we come
From God, who is our home.
— William Wordsworth

soul is longing for something that is hidden within itself? Are we already imbued with the divine power to achieve the goals we desire? Is our life an adventure to *realize our divinity*? Could this be the reason we were created? Does the urge to live creatively come from the urge of the divine imagination that pushes itself out through us into self-expression? Is it possible that the true reality of each of us is the *spirit* that is the great *light* of our being? Are we in embodiment to work out our destiny?

We live, knowingly or unknowingly, under the laws of life. These laws or spiritual principles reflect the energy of the Creator moving through each person, prompting us to bring forth the highest from within. Thus, as God works, we work.

As we stay poised and balanced, doing our best every day, we can make wonderful progress toward noble goals. If we utilize the understanding that under all circumstances it is meaningful to be compassionate, kind, honest, loving, and generous with those we meet on life's journey, then life becomes a joyful experience. If we continue doing our best work and thinking our best thoughts every day, we gradually wear away concern over problems. We learn how to meet new situations, and this awareness can help us take correct and beneficial action.

We can scatter the clouds that obscure the light so our way forward becomes clear. Channels open for greater fruitfulness. The divine idea for our life is fantastic and is so much greater that we can imagine. Divinity's plan for us is so great that we glimpse it only occasionally, but those glimpses are the light that leads us through the seeming darkness.

When the great poet Tagore was working

among the poor in India, he experienced what he thought was an overpowering vision of God. He was so deeply moved by this vision that he made immediate plans to leave the city and retire in the mountains of the high Himalayas. He felt that he needed a period of solitude in which to reflect on the vision and to try to understand it more deeply. But as he walked out of the gates of the teeming city to go up into the uninhabited mountains, he looked at his people, and the vision left him.

Tagore remained in the city—*with* his people.

Often the opportunity to be of service is right where the vision occurs! Insights can come quickly and easily when we commit ourselves to the action of the spirit, when we have committed ourselves to the awakening of our soul faculties. The spiritual life has its foundation in the realization that "I and my Father are one" (John 10:30). With this awareness, we can take strong strides in understanding ourselves and why we were created.

✦ LAW 4

Infinite in all directions. —Freeman Dyson

> The most beautiful and profound emotion we can experience is the sensation of the mystical. It is the sower of all true science. He to whom this emotion is a stranger, who can no longer wonder and stand rapt in awe, is as good as dead. To know that what is impenetrable to us really exists, manifesting itself as the highest wisdom and the most radiant beauty which our dull faculties can comprehend only in their most primitive forms—this knowledge, this feeling, is at the center of true religiousness.
> —*Albert Einstein*

HUMANITY HAS OFTEN allowed itself to think in terms of limitations, boundaries, and restrictions. Fences surround our properties, traffic signals and speed limits slow us down, lines on a map and differing cultures separate states and countries, and religious beliefs can cause separations and misunderstandings between individuals. However, obstacles or limitations are relative and can be surmounted as humanity progresses.

For example, the edge of the world was pushed back and finally eliminated by courageous explorers who dared to venture into the "unknown." Astronomers pushed back the earlier belief in a dome-shaped firmament covering the world and gave us knowledge of galaxies millions of light-years away. Present-day physicians assure us that a life span over one hundred years is conceivable. In fact, one-hundredth birthday celebrations are doubling every ten years! Athletic records are being surpassed so rapidly that one wonders if there are any limits left!

> We need no ladders to the sky, we need only . . . observe the structure and functions of man's bodily organs . . . to know that the Creator exists. Job said, "From my flesh shall I see God."
> — *Abba Mari ben Eligdor, fourteenth-century French Talmudist and philosopher*

It may be difficult for us to imagine the small quantity of knowledge and the limited concept of the cosmos that was prevalent when the Scriptures of the major religions were written. This thought raises a question: Do our wonderful Scriptures need to be supplemented by further information about the universe and humanity?

Teilhard de Chardin called for a new theology that would incorporate the modern scientific discoveries of the "immensity of space, which imbues our accustomed way of looking at things with a strain of Universalism," and the progressive "duration of time which . . . introduces . . . the idea of a possible unlimited Progress [futurism]." Because of these two concepts, universalism and futurism, de Chardin believed we now possess a higher and more organic understanding of the cosmos, which could serve as a basis for new spiritual information.

Life is consciousness! When our consciousness is

focused on lack or limitation, then these conditions tend to manifest in our life. The great prophets and teachers of the ages taught us to search for an unseen power and activity far greater than the self.

Many people may think someone, some condition, some circumstance, some event, or some joy controls their prosperity. We can agree that our supply comes to us through people and conditions acting as channels for good. But can we look deep within and *know*, beyond a doubt, that we were created without limitations—regardless of outer appearances? When we understand God as the source, we do not panic if the channel for our supply changes. Instead, we can search for opportunities, ask for guidance and direction, and be receptive to new avenues for our good.

This speaks of the truth of another law of life:

"There is no limit in the universe." In fact, we may say there is a law of no limitation! Instead of focusing on shortcomings, limitations, or thoughts of lack, would it seem wise to focus on thoughts of abundance?

Observe the many "people-made" objects—buildings, bridges, automobiles, ships, computers, high-tech equipment, lasers, etc. Now, look beyond those creations. Can you visualize the vastness of the resources from which these things are created—and comprehend that the greatest of these human resources is the intelligent mind? Our minds are filled with ideas and thoughts that show us how to build or create the things our imaginations can conceive. If our attitude is open for new understanding, fresh stimulation, and acceleration of discovery, we currently have no idea of what discoveries can be accomplished!

Most people live, whether physically, intellectually, or morally, in a very restricted circle of their potential being. They make use of a very small portion of their possible consciousness, and of their soul's resources in general, much like a man who, out of his whole bodily organism, should get into a habit of using and moving only his little finger. Great emergencies and crises show us how much greater our vital resources are than we had supposed.
— William James

We live in a world of change, and nowhere is that more profound than in the sciences. Indeed, a textbook unrevised for several years is practically useless in some fields, and a laboratory with ten-year-old equipment is like a museum. But most scientists are quick to point out that some things in science are far more secure—the periodic table, the laws of thermodynamics, relativity, the genetic code, biological evolution—and that we are steadily building a foundation of unchanging face from which a more complete picture of physical reality is emerging. . . . It has become apparent that we can no longer talk about scientific concepts and even mechanisms as though they were literal descriptions of objective reality.
— John Marks Templeton

◆ Law 5

As you give, so shall you receive. —Matthew 7:12; Luke 6:31

THE BASIC LAW of increase is "As you give so shall you receive" or "Sow and you shall reap." These statements are various ways of expressing what we call The Golden Rule: "So whatever you wish that men would do to you, do so to them; for this is the law and the prophets" (Matthew 7:12).

In Christian scriptures, Jesus described The Golden Rule in his own words, and this workable wisdom is expressed in various forms in every major world religion. Similar ideas of conduct are found in the literature of Hinduism, Buddhism, Islam, Confucianism, Judaism, Taoism, Persia, and in the writings of Aristotle, Plato, Seneca, as well as other great philosophers and teachers. In Jewish literature, The Golden Rule is expressed as: "What you hate, do not do to anyone."

The guidance of The Golden Rule offers a pattern or a plan for living that we can read, understand, and utilize to bring all manner of good into our lives. To treat others as you wish to be treated

THE GOLDEN RULE AS EXPRESSED IN MAJOR WORLD RELIGIONS:

BAHÁ'Í: Blessed is he who preferreth his brother before himself. — *Bahá'u'lláh*

BRAHMANISM: This is the sum of duty: do naught unto others which would cause you pain if done unto you.

BUDDHISM: Hurt not others in ways that you yourself would find hurtful. — *Udnaa-Varga*

CHRISTIANITY: All things whatsoever ye would that men should do to you, do ye even so to them. — *Matthew 7:12*

CONFUCIANISM: Do not unto others what you would not have them do unto you. — *Analects*

HINDU: This is the sum of duty: do naught unto others which would cause you pain if done to you. — *Mahabharata*

ISLAM: No one of you is a believer until he desires for his brother that which he desires for himself. — *Sunnah*

JAINISM: In happiness and suffering, in joy and grief, we should regard all creatures as we regard our own self.
  — *Lord Mahavira, 24th Tirthankara*

JUDAISM: What is hateful to you, do not to your fellowman. That is the law, all the rest is commentary. — *Talmud*

NATIVE AMERICAN: Respect for all life is the foundation. — *The Great Law of Peace*

PERSIA: Do as you would be done by.

TAOISM: Regard your neighbor's gain as your own gain and your neighbor's loss as your own loss.

SIKHISM: Don't create enmity with anyone as God is within everyone. — *Guru Arjan devji 259, Guru Granth Sahib*

ZOROASTRIANISM: That nature only is good when it shall not do unto another whatever is not good for its own self.
  — *Dadistan-I-Dinik*

is a plan that works wonderfully from every perspective for everyone involved. And it requires something of us!

Many people are familiar with the fable of Aladdin and his wonderful lamp. A marvelous genie that eagerly awaited Aladdin's bidding lived in the lamp. (Could we analogize this with the light within ourselves?) Yet, in the story, the genie didn't simply appear whenever Aladdin wished her to appear. He had to *do something* to invoke the genie's presence—he had to rub the lamp! When Aladdin took the necessary steps for putting in order that which had been placed in his custody, his good appeared. This same activity is true for us. How?

We can begin where we are to use the attributes we already possess, whether these are talents and abilities, material possessions, or opportunities for service to ourselves and others. There is a reward so tremendous that is greater than any money or appreciation we might receive in the outer world. This reward is the awareness that we have done our work and given our service in the best way possible. This is the feeling of happiness and satisfaction that comes from the real giving of our inner selves. So, what is an effective guideline for daily living? *Do the most you know how to do with what you have to do it with.*

It doesn't matter *who* benefits from the service we give, but it does matter what *kind* of service we give and how we give it. Take one step at a time; begin by taking the step immediately before you. *Rub your lamp!* Someone said, "What we are is God's gift to us; what we become is our gift to God!" Now is the time to give our best efforts. Life responds to us in the way we approach it. If we act in ways that are abusive to others, we may find ourselves abused. Our life may not work well and others may not trust our integrity. Let's identify with the gifts of the universe—such as abundance, wellness, joy, beauty, love, faith, or wisdom—and these attributes will become the energy we can draw into our experiences. People will respond to our efforts because they recognize when we are giving our best.

Kindness, compassion, and consideration have often been described as "love in action." Isn't this what The Golden Rule is about? Each day offers many opportunities for everyone to do some kindness for another and to be considerate, understanding, and supportive. Look at your life for a moment. Do you rush from one thing to another, perhaps from one appointment or meeting to another, and fail to notice how others may be feeling or responding? Do you take the time to observe what may be happening in another person's life? Are you willing to help bring about a positive change by shifting your awareness from your personal desires to the needs of others? Surely, someone whose life you touch today can use your gift of kindness. Surely, your sincere caring would be greatly appreciated by some person in your world. And the whole world needs our consideration and support.

Again, the greatest reward is the inner reward, the happiness that comes from a job well done. Will we recognize the opportunity to give when it tugs at our sleeve?

Spotlights ✦ ✦

1. Universal principles or laws of life are self-enforcing spiritual truths—applicable to everyone, everywhere, at all times—providing guidelines for living a useful and fulfilling life.

2. The laws of life work for the highest good of everyone.

3. One primary law of how things work is: "As within, so without!"

4. The mind is the seat of perception of the things we see, hear, and feel.

5. A mental atmosphere is produced by the kind of thoughts you think.

6. Establishing goals and guidelines to achieving them can help you live a more interesting, useful, and successful life.

7. Small, persistent efforts can lead to big accomplishments.

8. Life is consciousness! We have the ability to exercise free will in making choices.

9. How do you perceive yourself? Can you comprehend that your physical identity is included in your spiritual identity?

10. The Golden Rule is a pattern or a plan that you can read, study, and put into application in your daily life toward building a sound "house of living."

11. Kindness, compassion, and consideration have often been described as "love in action."

Living the Various Spiritual Laws ✦ ✦

One of the best ways to make changes in your life is to make daily affirmative changes in the way you think, feel, speak, and act. A sincere and enthusiastic commitment to bring out the best in yourself and your world can bring about tremendous results. Perhaps the following excerpt from the Nobel lecture of the Dalai Lama, given in 1989, can offer some "food for thought" toward making changes.

Because we all share this small planet Earth, we have to learn to live in harmony and peace with each other and with nature. That is not just a dream, but a necessity. We are dependent on each other in so many ways that we can no longer live in isolated communities and ignore what is happening outside those communities. We need to help each other when we have difficulties, and we must share the good fortune that we enjoy.
I speak to you as just another human being, as a simple monk. If you find what I say useful, then I hope you will try to practice it.

◆ LAW 1

Your life becomes what you think. —Marcus Aurelius

THOUGHT—or the act of thinking—is one of the greatest powers we possess and, like most powers, it can be used positively or negatively, as we choose. Many people have never been taught how to use the power of thought, the master power of the mind. And in today's world, it is equally important to learn how to think correctly as it is to speak or act correctly. Ernest Holmes, founder of Science of Mind, explains why he believes this is so. He said, "Life is a mirror and will reflect back to the thinker what he thinks into it."

With modern scanning equipment, we can see the brain, but we cannot see the brain working. We see only the results of the brain's activity. The mind, which is invisible, directs the thinking process. It tells the brain how to sort experience and fact and how to give shape and form to new ideas. The indirect action of thought is easy to understand, because obviously a person thinks before he does anything. Thought is the motivating power behind an action, just as electricity is the motivating power behind lighting homes. Thought also has a direct action on matter. Regardless of whether or not we translate our thought into actual performance, the thought itself has already produced some kind of result.

Have you ever had an original idea and wondered where it came from? It's as if your mind planted a seed of the idea in the brain. From your past experiences and accumulated knowledge, your brain developed the idea in a way that could be expressed by you in a coherent and persuasive manner. The idea may have improved as you tested or expressed it under various conditions.

In a similar way, the mind can tell the brain what to think. It may be tempting to believe that we have no control over what comes into our heads, but in reality we do. If a thought comes to us that may not be in our best interest, we can, with very alert practice, begin thinking about something else so that the undesirable thought will be squeezed out.

Sound difficult? Try the following experiment. If someone says to you, "Don't think about bananas," what happens? Most people will immediately have a mental picture of a banana right in the middle of their consciousness! So, to tell yourself to stop thinking about something doesn't do a great deal of good, does it? Replace the undesirable thought with a desirable thought. If you don't want to think about bananas, turn your focus to something else—such as apples, oranges, or coconuts! Once you bring another image to the forefront of your mind, the image of bananas is gone. How? It is because the mind cannot focus on too many different images at the same moment.

This is called the "crowding-out technique." If you fill your mind to capacity with positive and productive thoughts, there's no room left for negative ones. In essence, you release or "crowd out" the undesirable thoughts and fill the created vacuum with desirable thoughts. The responsibility for setting the law of mind action into motion belongs to each of us. Our personal world is of our own making. Creating the kind of life we want depends greatly on the managing of our minds. As has been said, "Change your thinking; change your life."

When we change our thinking, it is important that we continue with beneficial thought processes.

"expert" at something before we can accomplish the desired goal. Because of this type of thinking, we may read all kinds of books, attend various seminars, classes, and workshops, seek out "expert" advice, etc. Do these avenues of opportunity make a difference? Certainly! Any increased knowledge has an affect on our overall consciousness.

Could the way of the "beginner" be more effective at times than the way of the "expert"? Think for a moment. One of the best examples of a "beginner's" mind is that of a baby learning to walk. Babies don't read books about how to walk

It is not enough to have a good mind. The main thing is to use it well.
— René Descartes

Little is accomplished if, after a few days of effort, we revert to the old way of thinking and to old habits.

In altering our present way of thinking, perhaps the first requirement is to pause and ask some pertinent questions. How do I desire my life to differ from this present moment? Do I wish for greater energy? When do I feel focused? What am I thinking during those moments? Do I want to make a difference in my world? How can I make a difference? How can I be of meaningful service? What do I wish to accomplish?

As responses come to these questions, the next step involves becoming a constant shepherd of your thoughts. Guard the gates of your mind to insure you think those thoughts, and speak only those words, that are congruent with your goals and desires.

So often we may think we have to become more

or attend walking seminars! They pull themselves up, take a step, and fall down. Then they do it all over again! A baby may get frustrated when he falls, but he doesn't get discouraged. A baby doesn't say, "Look what happened! I fell! I'll never learn to walk!" A baby simply keeps on keeping on until the day arrives when those first precious steps are taken. Then, "practice makes perfect" and those hesitant first steps eventually become stronger strides. Fantastic!

We can learn to walk forward in life mindfully by learning how to flow with the energy around us, by learning how to smile in growing awareness, at home, at work, at play, and throughout the day. Mindfulness can be the foundation for a happy life. Remember, the Creator's spirit within you can guide you to your perfect expression when you open your mind and heart. Meet each day with confidence and faith and joy in living.

✦ LAW 2

Love given is love received. —John Marks Templeton

A MAN WAS APPROACHING a florist shop to order a bouquet of roses to be sent to his mother for her birthday. As the man approached the door to the florist shop, he noticed a small boy sitting on the curb in front of the shop, crying. When the man inquired what the problem was, the little boy said he had come to buy a rose for his mother. However, he had only seventy-nine cents and a rose cost one dollar. With compassion, the man took the little boy inside the shop and bought him a rose. He then asked if the boy would like a ride home. The child replied, "I would appreciate it, Sir, if you would take me to my mother." The boy then directed the man to a cemetery where he placed the rose on his mother's grave.

After the man took the boy home, he went back to the florist shop and canceled his order. Instead, he bought the bouquet and took it with him in his car as he drove two hundred miles to visit his mother! During the trip, the man reflected deeply on the power of love and the many blessings that flow through the "hands" of love.

It is easy to talk about love. There are pretty songs about love and lengthy books have been written about love. But how do we *understand* love? A minister friend once said, "All the protestations in the world that God is love mean nothing unless we have our arms sincerely around one another!" What a transcending thought!

In some manner of expression, love seems to be the ideal and the dream of every person. Could our souls have been conceived in the Creator's love? We seem to be more fulfilled when we are in a state of *spiritual* love, and somehow emptied when our focus moves elsewhere. Is it possible that love—unlimited love—becomes the purpose for our existence? Could the reason love is considered the treasure of life be that it is the true nature of our souls?

Scholars throughout the ages have defined love as the power that joins and bonds the universe and everything in it; love is often called the greatest harmonizing principle known to humanity. How do we discern these descriptions? No one ever saw love, or heard love, or touched, smelled, or tasted love—literally! How can a person physically touch a thought, an idea? Certainly, we can see the *effects* of love, but not the divine energy creating the effects. We can *hear* the sound of compassion and caring in a voice. But how can we *taste* the sweetness of inner peace and spontaneous joy? We may *see* love in the actions of others as they express this innate energy from within themselves to another person. We may *smell* love through the dinner so lovingly prepared by one who "loves to cook." And loves us! We may *touch* love in the embrace of dear ones as they open their hearts and let their love flow toward us. The five senses can only perceive love from within, outward. But when we express love, we are the first to receive love. How? We begin to recognize in others that which we are.

One fundamental of psychology is that a great need of humanity is to be loved. We may nod our heads in agreement with that thought. "Yes, I agree. Life can seem empty and meaningless unless we're loved." Do we need to look at this concept from a different perspective? Could it be that the most important way a person can be loved is to *give* love? As long as we're looking for love outside ourselves, we may be frustrating the love inside!

Giving love doesn't mean contrived sentimentality or flattery. Pure love is a natural attitude and demeanor of good will, kindness, compassion, caring, support, and benevolence. It is a willingness to do what you can to be helpful and to make things a little better for someone. When we live in love, making a conscious choice to experience and express love, we participate in a most powerful active force.

What would happen in our world if we decided

Love the person not their acts.

to "look with the eyes of love"? Would we behold beauty and truth in every person we meet? Would we be more receptive to the thoughts and feelings of others? Would we applaud and be joyous supporters of other people's "divine ideas"? Would we be forgiving and compassionate in our relationships? An interesting thing happens when we "look with the eyes of love."

We begin to notice the sparkle in the other person's eyes. Situations can change when we are learning to give unlimited love and be non-resistant. What are some of the results of giving love?

+ You can become fearless, because "perfect love casts out fear."
+ You can be happy, because disharmony cannot enter where love abides.

+ You will never be lonely, because love fills your world with loving companions.
+ You will not be sad, because love is the greatest bearer of happiness.
+ You can be more successful, because "love never fails."
+ You will be beloved, because like attracts like, and love is a tremendous attracting power.
+ You will be alive, alert, and increasingly aware, because love sharpens all the faculties.

Fill your mind and heart with love and life will pour its richest blessings upon you. The result is that when you begin to bless others in love, you are also enfolded in love. Through unlimited love, you touch the real kingdom of heaven on earth and great good is added to your life.

✦ LAW 3

To be forgiven, you must first forgive. —John Marks Templeton

IN HIS BOOK *You'll See It When You Believe It,* Dr. Wayne Dyer talks about deeply moving instances of forgiveness he has experienced. He said, "One of the most poignantly memorable covers of a national magazine appeared several years back. It was a picture of Pope John Paul II, sitting in a dungeon with the man who attempted to assassinate him. That portrait of forgiveness left a lasting impression on me. People whom we consider . . . role models of decency always are able to forgive without qualification or doubt. They do not cloud their consciousness with thoughts of anger, hatred, and revenge toward those who have attempted to wrong, or harm, them. Rather, they provide us with a role model of forgiveness that we can use in our daily lives."

When Mahatma Gandhi was assassinated, he instinctively threw up his hand in the Hindu gesture of forgiveness. Gandhi understood what truth was about or he could never have said, "The weak can never forgive. Forgiveness is an attribute of the strong." Another important law of life states that we must forgive ourselves and others if we wish to overcome certain difficulties and make real spiritual progress. The significance of forgiveness may not be obvious at first, but surely it isn't by happenstance that every great spiritual teacher has strongly insisted on the attribute of forgiveness.

Developing the ability to forgive others when wrongdoings occur can be crucial to our health as well as to the quality of our human relationships. The accumulation of resentments and the buildup of the urge to revenge are among the most destructive tendencies to abide in the human mind. We

The spirit of Buddha is that of great loving kindness and compassion.
— Buddha

The highest wisdom is loving kindness.
— Talmud

He that cannot forgive others breaks the bridge over which he must pass himself; for every man has need to be forgiven.
— Lord Herbert

can develop the spiritual habit of cleansing our personalities of these emotional toxins as soon as they are experienced. If we harbor the memory of some hurt or wrong, real or imagined, it is time to release it! Let it go!

We can speak of releasing or letting go from two perspectives. One perspective recommends that we immediately release any upsetting feelings of the moment. Sometimes we judge others and put them into a prison of our own mind. If we review our own life, we may have committed similar offenses in the past. Since life is constantly changing, there is no need to hold on tightly to anything. For example, trying to grasp or hold on to happiness does not bring happiness, but can be a sure way to be miserable.

Another perspective is to let go of or surrender attachment to the ego. From the perspective of universal oneness, the ego struggles to maintain the illusion of a separate existence. In truth, letting go of the ego and releasing any sense of struggle could be the same. When we give up the struggle to prove that we are worthy of love or approval, we allow the life energy to flow clear and clean within us. When we let go of the struggle to justify our existence, we often find meaningful and fulfilling avenues of service. When we release the struggle to hold on to limited beliefs and concepts of how things "should be," we free ourselves to enjoy life in its many expressions. The spiritual power of forgiveness can vanquish any tendency to resent being wronged. Resentment is self-centered and rooted in our wounded feelings.

We have a wonderful model of forgiveness available when we look at how often and how fully the Creator forgives us. During his ministry,

Jesus was asked, "How often should we forgive?" He responded, "Seventy times seven" (Matthew 18:22). In other words, there is no limit to forgiving. It is an ongoing process!

In another gospel Jesus makes the statement, "Father, forgive them for they know not what they do" (Luke 23:34). Can you perceive that people who are inflicting harm on others, really and truly, may not know what they are doing? What they may be directing toward others says nothing about the other people. But their actions can speak volumes about their own anger, hatred, blame, or desire for revenge. From this example, we can learn an important lesson about forgiveness. People who have behaved toward us in a disagreeable or hurtful manner may not realize that everyone is connected. Once we know within our hearts that we are connected to all others, including those who may behave in unseemly ways, we have a key to the power of forgiveness. This awareness can prompt an increasing ability to forgive.

Forgiveness has been described as a process similar to peeling an onion—it is done in layers! When we come upon a new layer or aspect of our being where some resentment appears, there is more work to do. This does not mean our previous work with forgiveness was not effective. All effort is meaningful. We simply need to continue the forgiving process.

Do we want an inner poise and grace that cannot be disturbed, a gentleness that cannot be hurt, a deep, abiding comfort, and a rest so perfect that it can never be upset? Forgiveness, giving up the false for the true, offers the fulfillment of these desires and more!

He who forgives
ends the quarrel.
— *African proverb*

To forgive is
the highest,
most beautiful
form of love.
In return, you will
receive untold peace
and happiness.
— *Robert Muller*

If those around us make mistakes,
we can easily offer them our compassion,
since God is constantly showering
His Compassion upon us.
— *Sri Chinmoy*

✦ Law 4

An attitude of gratitude creates blessings. —John Marks Templeton

Great is the man who
has not lost his
childlike heart.
— *Mencius*

Gratitude is the sign
of noble souls.
— *American proverb*

To give thanks is
good, and to forgive.
— *Charles Swinburne*

TODAY, let's sing a song of praise and thanksgiving for our innumerable blessings! Can the secret of a grateful heart be an attitude of gratitude that lifts us into a continual high consciousness where we know that life is good and blessings abound? It is a law of life that if we develop an *attitude of gratitude,* our happiness increases. How? The virtue of gratitude can directly touch the ultimate foundation of a person's existence and the reasons for being grateful can begin to multiply.

Just what is "an attitude of gratitude"? And how can it be developed? An attitude of gratitude is a conscious decision to look for the good and the blessing in every person we meet and in every situation we experience. It is the natural result of our belief in the possibility of a giver of good and our willingness to experience the good. Whether we call the giver by the name of God, Allah, Spirit, or whatever, we can achieve the attitude in which we prepare to give of ourselves and to receive of the bounty of good in which we dwell.

Whatever we give our attention and belief to becomes our experience. So, in order to develop an attitude of gratitude, wouldn't it seem logical to focus our attention on the present blessings in our lives? We can begin by appreciating our families, our loved ones, our homes, and our communities. We can expand our attitude of gratitude to include being grateful for our talents and abilities by accepting them as opportunities to be invested for the common good. We can appreciate our opportunities by accepting them as challenges to achievement. Being grateful can open the door to creative ideas that enrich life and help us contribute to human progress.

Two powerful words—"Thank you!"—sincerely spoken or silently realized, can open the door to an expanding world of good. Appreciation is acknowledgment. It is a recognition and affirmation that something positive and meaningful has

occurred. And do we not all feel pleased when we hear a word of praise or approval sincerely given? Through our tone of voice, our facial expression, or a certain choice of words, we can communicate our appreciation to another. Surely there can be as much greatness in acknowledging a good turn as in doing it!

As our souls grow in compassion and caring, we become increasingly interested in our fellow human beings who endure the joys and sorrows, successes and challenges, experienced through daily living on planet Earth. We can empathize with our fellow travelers and seek to cheer and encourage those whom we meet. We are not separate and apart. We are one in spirit. What affects one affects all. Every firm handclasp that is offered in assistance can bring a greater humbleness in the joy of true and selfless service. We long for more and deeper illumination and wisdom.

We begin to realize one of the greatest antidotes for any seeming lack, limitation, or negative experience is to count our daily blessings. It is impossible for anyone to be aware of the abundance present in life and feel deprived at the same time. Regardless of whatever situation that may be present, the factor of life—god-life moving through all—is cause for thanksgiving and rejoicing.

An attitude of gratitude can help us break free from self-imposed limitations. We begin to see the necessary ingredients for joyful living and know that a new day always follows the night. We begin to understand that only in appearances could anything be impossible. Our positive attitude provides the inner assurance and sustenance that can rise victorious over any circumstance.

The path to becoming more grateful can be as simple and powerful as the following story. A group of neighborhood children would gather frequently and share what was happening in their lives. The friendship among the children was beautiful to

Critical must cosmic consciousness

behold and surprising knowledge flowed from these young minds. The mother of one of the children would occasionally join the gathering and tell stories to the group. When she spoke of her "jewel box," which was her most prized possession, she could send the children's imaginations soaring. She emphasized that the jewel box was so secure its contents could never be stolen! Of course, the children's minds filled with dazzling pictures of diamonds, emeralds, rubies, pearls, and other priceless items of adornment. They daydreamed that she must be an heiress of a rich family, although her simple, everyday life did not indicate vast material wealth.

One day the children asked the woman what was in the jewel box. As the children's eager, upturned faces waited expectantly for her reply, she smiled at each child individually. Then she beckoned them to gather around her and sit on the grass. "Let me tell you a wonderful secret," she whispered. "The jewel box is not a material box!" The children's eyes were big with expectation. The mother continued, "In reality, it is the treasure chamber of your heart. And everyone has one! Its contents are the feelings of love, joy, peace, gratitude, and the faith that we are heirs to the Creator's kingdom . . . truly a divine inheritance.

> Gratitude opens our consciousness to receive more.
> — *Elizabeth Sand Turner*

O Great Spirit, I awake to another sun,
Grateful for gifts bestowed, granted one by one.
Grateful for the greatest gift, the precious breath of life.
Grateful for abilities to guide me day and night.
As I walk my chosen path of lessons I must learn,
Spiritual peace and happiness, rewards of life I learn.
Thank you for your spiritual strength, and for my thoughts to pray;
Thank you for your infinite love that guides me through the day.
— *Twylah Nitsch*

God's presence in your heart is an inner experience, a treasure of knowing, that abides forever." The children asked many questions that day. Most of them never forgot the story of jewel box and appreciated it more as they grew into adulthood.

Perhaps more than you know, you can be a power for good. More than you may ever know, you can help, bless, appreciate, and inspire others. Through your own attitude of gratitude, you can bring strength, comfort, and peace to the hearts of those around you. And perhaps, like the mother in the story, you can be an unconscious influence in the lives of those about you.

An ancient proverb states, "A donkey may carry a heavy load of precious sandalwood on its back and never know its preciousness, only its weight." Without an attitude of gratitude, we may feel the weight of circumstances and lose sight of the precious nature of the gift before us.

✦ LAW 5

You fear what you do not understand. — Anonymous

> Nothing is terrible except fear itself.
> — *Francis Bacon*

EMOTION, in its many expressions, can form the crux of how we experience life. Properly used, our emotions can elevate us to new heights of joyous living. When ignored or wrongly directed, they can make daily living a miserable experience.

Perhaps one of the most influential and destructive emotions is fear. An old Moorish proverb brings to mind an important truth: "He who is

I believe that anyone
can conquer fear
by doing the thing
he fears to do.
— Eleanor Roosevelt

What a new face
courage puts on
everything.
— Ralph Waldo
Emerson

Your fears can be
overcome if you deal
with them properly.
Fear is an emotion.
Emotions come
wholly from within,
and have only the
strength we allow
them. As human
beings, we enjoy the
possession of an
intellect, and it is the
intellect, not the
emotions, that must
be the supreme guid-
ing force of our lives
if we are to know
any measure of
happiness here.
Emotions are the
color of life; we
would be drab crea-
tures indeed without
them. But we must
control those emo-
tions or they will
control us. This is
particularly true of
the emotion of fear,
which if allowed free
rein, would reduce
all of us to trembling
shadows of men, for
whom only death
could bring release.
— John M. Wilson

afraid of a thing gives it power over him." Here is the description of the power of fear in a nutshell! Could fear be the source of many of the mistakes we make? In a state of fear, which has been described as the emotional nature trying to rid itself of some threat, a person may find it difficult to concentrate his or her thoughts in a positive manner. Fear is a painful emotion, identified by alarm, dread, disquiet; its corollary is depression. If we choose to remain in fear, then one fear can lead to another and there can always be something to be afraid of.

What have you done today that took courage?

The fear of God (unknown) is the creaturely knowledge of the darkness to which none of our spiritual powers can reach, and out of which God reveals himself.

Therefore, "the fear of God" is rightly called "the beginning of knowledge" (Psalm 111:10). It is the dark gate through which man must pass if he is to enter into the love of God.

— Martin Buber

Many scientists can tell us that the proper definition of any problem is the biggest single step toward its solution. The divine nature of the soul can be the opposite of anxiety or fear of anything. It is creative. It is positive. And it offers certain knowledge, wisdom, and inspiration to overcome fearful thoughts. Many fears are "educated" into us and can be educated out! How can we overcome fear? One way is by seeking greater understanding of the source of the fear. When we increase our understanding of ourselves and others, fear is less likely to take root.

It has been said that when we are at the end of our rope, we can do one of three things. We can let go. We can tie a knot and hang on. Or we can splice the rope and begin again! If we can learn to look beyond the end of any fear, we can always see an exciting, fresh beginning. At the end of every fearful storm is calm. At the end of every argument, there is silence. At the end of a long night, the sun appears over the horizon.

Understanding is a foundation of progress, and introspection can often provide greater self-understanding. Some more commonly expressed fears

include fear of the unknown, fear of bodily harm, fear of failure, fear of being unloved, and fear of being ridiculed. At some point in life, everyone has fears of different sizes and shapes. It is important to learn what they are and face them directly.

Do you remember an earlier essay about the power of the mind that discussed the truism "When you rule your mind, you rule your world"? When we understand the reality of thoughts and the power they have to create and to change the world around us, we come to a supremely important realization: *we can bless and we can heal!* And this pertains to our fears as well as to other aspects of life. Blessing and healing are a right—and a responsibility—of every single human being. And as soon as we begin to admit to ourselves that we can be instruments for the healing love of the Creator, we can begin releasing fears and making the kinds of changes in our lives and in the world we may have always wanted to make!

Friedrich Nietzsche described a three-fold process in the maturation of consciousness. The analogy could also apply to letting go of fear. He said that in the first stage, we are like a *camel* bending down to have hoisted upon us the load of social conditioning, habit, and convention. In the second stage, we are like a *lion* roaring against the "thou shalts" of society. Only after we have completed the work of the lion do we become the *child*, which is to say, a fully human being, capable of spontaneously, intuitively, and competently responding to the world. The courage of the lion is the courage to find our own path in life.

One definition of courage is the ability to conquer fear. The measure of our courage can be reflected in the vision we choose for our life and

> Be not afraid of life. Believe that life is worth living, and your belief will help create the fact.
> — *William James*

how fearlessly we march toward that vision. As our fears are overcome, one by one, we know that our light is not a weak candle that can be blown out by a wind of alarm or disappointment. Rather, we are like a blazing bonfire offering light and warmth to others.

Spotlights ✦ ✦

1. Thought—the act or process of thinking—is one of the greatest powers you can possess and, like almost all powers, it can be used positively or negatively.

2. Should a negative thought arise, replace it immediately with a positive thought.

3. Love is "the spiritual glue" that holds everything together.

4. Look within your own heart to find the treasure of love.

5. The first step in being forgiven is to forgive!

6. Look around you. In appreciation, find beauty, blessings, and joy and invite them to be permanent guests in your house.

7. Emotion has been described as the essence of impulse and activity in humanity. Perhaps one of the most influential and destructive emotions is fear.

8. One definition of courage is the ability to conquer fear.

9. "[C]all upon me in the day of trouble; I will deliver you, and you shall glorify me" (Psalm 50:15).

10. Shinto saying: "Both heaven and hell come from one's own heart."

Living the Various Spiritual Laws ✦ ✦

For many years, Persian poetry has been the chief interpreter of Persian thought, both in the East and in the West. In his work the *Mathnawi*, the poet Jalalu'ddin Rumi sets the matter of his discourse within a framework of stories, which introduce and exemplify various topics and are frequently interwoven with explanations of their inner meaning. One example is the poem/story "The Unseen Elephant," which indicates that religions are many, but God is one. As individuals, we may perceive the same object or topic from a variety of perspectives.

The intellect, groping in the dark, cannot form any true conception of the Creator's nature.

The Unseen Elephant

The Elephant was in a dark house: some Hindus
    had brought it for exhibition.
As seeing it with the eye was impossible, every-
    one felt it in the dark with the palm of his hand.
The hand of one fell on its trunk: he said, "This
    creature is like a water-pipe."

Another touched its ear: to him it appeared like a fan.

Another handled its leg: he said, "I found the Elephant's shape to be like a pillar."

Another laid his hand on its back: he said, "Truly this Elephant resembles a throne."

Had there been a candle in each one's hand, the difference would have gone out of their words.

If we look intimately at the wisdom in this story, we may find guidance about areas of our own lives we need to develop. How open are we to new ideas? Are we willing to observe the things around us from a variety of perspectives? Can we be flexible in our thinking and listen and learn from another person's viewpoint? Can we allow ourselves to explore multiple definitions and roles in our progress toward always enlarging our concepts about the infinity of divinity?

Week Three

✦ LAW 1

Nothing can bring you peace but yourself. — Ralph Waldo Emerson

Do not lose your inward peace for anything whatsoever, even if your whole world seems upset.
— *St. Francis de Sales*

Do your duty, always, but without attachment. This is how a man reaches the ultimate Truth: by working without anxiety about results.
— *Hindu saying*

Thou dost keep him in perfect peace, whose mind is stayed on thee.
— *Isaiah 26:3*

THE PROCESS OF LIVING is not aimless; it is directional. Each day offers a challenging new stretch of road to travel. When we make the *conscious* decision to uplift our ordinary activities with spiritual inspiration, we can enter into an entirely different way of living. The most fleeting interaction with another person can become an opportunity for sharing unlimited love.

Perhaps one of the most meaningful and useful qualities in our daily lives is an inner awareness of peace and calm. When tensions and pressures arise, possibly creating inner irritations that can build up, a means of releasing this tension becomes necessary. It appears obvious that if we are not centered and poised, if we do not have control over our emotional nature, then something else is in control of us. And an "explosion" often occurs. That "out of control" something could be the very thing that is blocking us from our highest fulfillment and self-expression!

It is important to keep in mind the basic truth that what we hold persistently in our consciousness tends to manifest itself in our lives. If our inner consciousness is filled with harmony and peace, this is what we can bring to every situation and to every person we meet through our words

and actions. Being centered and focused helps create the harmony and happiness we desire.

Our first step to inner peace can be the realization that when anger, irritation, or feelings of upset arise within us, it is not the fault of some other person or thing. Rather, these feelings are prompted by our own improper response to others. It is important to realize that change needs to occur within us. This can be a situation where negative thoughts may be blocking the unfolding of good in our lives.

The wise can direct their thoughts, subtle and elusive, wherever they choose: a trained mind brings health and happiness. — *The Dhammapada*

How?

Making the decision to no longer point a finger of blame and realizing there is a better way to handle life's situations readies us to control our thoughts and do the work of prayer in building a consciousness of the perfect peace of God.

There is great power in the peaceful response, and today is the day to put it into practice in each experience until our habitual way of life is peaceful. Our entire consciousness of mind, body, and spirit can be more harmonious when, in the present moment, we respond with peace to whatever may be happening. If we can be peaceful right now, we can be peaceful in each unfolding moment, until our nature is that of peace.

It could be helpful to take a reflective look at our responses to life at the end of a day. We can look at our actions and reactions objectively and allow time to review and focus on positive results. Should a conflict occur, the first step on the path of peace is to shift our attitudes. The way we perceive a situation can be more important than the circumstances of the situation. We know that by transforming ourselves, we transform our world. Reaching out from our center of peaceful power, we can create new solutions, new possibilities. In peace, our entire being becomes a place of prayer, a holy temple set upon a hill.

A man or woman who smiles with ease possesses one of God's greatest gifts—peace of mind.

— George W. Cummins Sr.

✦ LAW 2

Listen to learn. — Alcoholics Anonymous

THERE IS AN OLD SAYING that God gave us two ears and one mouth so we may hear more and talk less. How well we use our ears can play an important part in determining what we learn as we go through life. In many instances, we may be so busy planning our response that we don't give ourselves an opportunity to really *hear* what another person may be saying. It is important to allow our minds the opportunity to assimilate what we have heard before we respond. Some people may mistake sharing as a request for advice and think that they must dispense their wise guidance to the person who is speaking.

Wrong! When people are sharing with us, what they are doing is sharing. *Period!* We don't have to say anything, simply be fully present and *listen* to what *they* have to say. Listening is an excellent way to keep the lines of communication open. The good listener can add immensely to the art of true communication and to the enjoyment of those around him. Effective communication is certainly one of the most important skills for successful and useful living.

Learning from others is a law of life. A successful businessman began his journey of progress and discovery as a young child. He observed his classmates as well as the adults with whom he came in contact. He listened to farmers, shopkeepers, business and community leaders, and others and learned from each of them which things led to success, happiness, and productivity and which things did not. He learned what to emulate as well as what to avoid. He observed how a closed mind could tend to be self-centered and "preachy," while an open mind provided fertile territory for progress and discovery. Most important, he learned to assimilate the wisdom of many lives. Each of us can do the same. If we are alert and maintain an open mind, we can learn from each person we meet.

A major reason why some relationships break down could be that one or more of the parties involved have not learned to listen! Listening is a *learned* skill. When we develop it to the fullest, we increase our capacity to learn, we expand our creative talents, and we enhance our ability to maintain healthy relationships. A true conversation can be an exciting opportunity to learn something *about* one another *from* one another!

Active listening necessitates staying focused on what the person speaking is saying. In active listening, we use our ears in the same way a photographer uses a camera. To get the best pictures, the photographer adjusts the lens of the camera until the settings are correct. As active listeners, we must adjust the focus of our attention to remain aware of what the speaker is telling us. The more we listen and learn, the better able we become to develop the potential we possess. In school, who learns more, the child who listens intently or the child who talks the most? Is this law the same in the great school of life?

A young father had relaxed into his easy chair to read the evening newspaper. The man's five-year-old son was excited to see his father and kept asking him endless questions while he was trying to read the newspaper. Finally, seizing on an idea to have some quiet time, the father found a picture of the Earth in the newspaper and cut it out and into little pieces. He spread the pieces on the floor and asked the child to reassemble the pieces as a jigsaw puzzle.

The child eagerly settled on the floor to begin the task of arranging the pieces of paper into a picture. To the father's astonishment, the child returned a little later with the picture perfectly intact.

"Look, Daddy," the child exclaimed, "The world is back together again!"

The father was amazed at how quickly the child completed the puzzle. "How did you do it so fast?" he asked.

The child smiled. "It was easy, Dad. I couldn't get the pieces of the Earth to fit together. Then I looked on the other side of the pieces, and there were pictures of parts of a man. It was easy to put the man together, so that's what I did. And when the man came together, so did the Earth!"

Could part of our time on Earth be about putting into action our growing understanding of our place in the cosmos and how we all "fit" together to form the completed picture? Could it also be about practicing living in harmony and unity with all people—our family, our friends, our work associates, our community, our government, and the nations of the world? It is important to take every opportunity, on whatever scale, to affirm togetherness, family, and community. In reality, when we understand our unity as a family of humankind, we accept the joys and sufferings of humanity as our own. Could *listening to learn* be a key factor in human progress?

✦ ## LAW 3

Don't ever think you are wise enough. —Proverbs 3:7

IN ANTIQUITY, philosophers walked along the shores of the Mediterranean, pondering the mysteries of life as they looked into starlit skies. Today, people gather in churches, classrooms, retreats, workshops, and discussion groups to ponder the same perennial questions. What is the best way to live? How large is God? How are finite beings related to the infinite? What was God's purpose in creating the universe? How can we be helpful? These ageless questions can inspire people today just as they have inspired people throughout the ages, linking the human soul to philosophy and to the love of wisdom.

Some have likened the desire for greater wis-

Wisdom, thoroughly learned, will never be forgotten.
— *Pythagoras*

Ponder a while thereon, that with both your inner and outer eye, ye may perceive the subtleties of Divine wisdom and discover the gems of heavenly knowledge.
—*Bahá'u'lláh*

If therefore you are intent upon wisdom a lamp will not be wanting and a shepherd will not fail, and a fountain will not dry up.
—*Anonymous*

dom to an ancient inner urge, similar to the longing of the lost for the return home. Or to the desire of the unfulfilled for spiritual sustenance. The genius of the universe created us and seems to have instilled a portion of that genius within each one. When we dare to reach beyond our comfort zone in life and declare that a great drama may be being enacted through us, are we glad to be helpers in the acceleration of divine creativity? And are we wise enough to assist this genius in whatever way possible? Life builds its center of focus around rhythms, changes, times of rest, times of activity, growing, unfolding, listening, searching, and producing.

As intelligent beings, included in our makeup is an ability to listen, to notice what is happening around us, and to be in tune with the rhythm and flow of our lives. We are continually in the process of growth. Things happen. Life changes. And we might ask, "What do I do now? What's the next step?" An important thing to remember is that we are never wise enough. There is always something to learn.

A businessman set himself the goal to learn something new each day. He felt it was important to let not a day pass without learning the meaning of an unfamiliar word, without a new insight, without experiencing a fresh taste, thought, or sensation. He felt that among those who achieved success would be the ones who used their time wisely for self-improvement, greater productivity, and continued learning. He also felt that successful people sought information and advice more frequently than they gave it!

Can you imagine what it would be like to improve on all levels of your being and in all aspects of your life? How would it feel to know you were making a real contribution to your world? Would it be uplifting to feel that because of you and your work, someone's life was blessed? Or that the whole universe was positively ampli-

Learn to be wise! Train your senses; be contented.
— *The Dhammapada*

fied because you are a part of it? These are not unrealistic questions.

The Talmud asks, "Who is a wise man?" and answers, "He who learns of all men." To increase in wisdom, we must be willing to suspend our personal beliefs about something, to set aside our prejudices, and to think with an open mind. It is important to expand our awareness parameters and learn in many different areas, from a variety of sources, even at the risk of looking foolish or being embarrassed. Are we ready to admit that we may not know the answers to everything and become willing to learn? Learning is a desirable process that might include making mistakes along the road to greater knowledge. But the overall results can be life changing! True wisdom acknowledges that the more we learn about a subject, the more interesting it becomes and the more there is to learn!

We may have heard someone say, "I learned my lesson! I'll never do that again!" But how often do we hear the comment, "That was a wonderful lesson. And even though I was uncomfortable at the time, I learned a great deal. With this new awareness, I can choose differently so I won't make the same mistake again." The sincere willingness to take a reflective look at experiences that may have seemed like mistakes can be the first, perhaps most important step we take to make future experiences more beneficial. The fruitfulness of our day-to-day lives, especially in rapidly changing world situations, can very much depend on making wise decisions. Greater wisdom is necessary for every person who considers himself or herself, first and foremost, a helper of the human family, and who desires to see things in larger perspectives.

Norman Cousins once said, "Fortunately or otherwise, we live at a time when the average individual has to know several times as much in order to keep informed as he did only thirty or forty years ago. Being 'educated' today requires not only more than a superficial knowledge of the arts and sciences, but a sense of inter-relationship such as is taught in few schools. Finally, being 'educated' today, in terms of the larger needs, means preparation for world citizenship; in short, education for survival."

 # LAW 4

Humility leads to prayer as well as progress and brings you in tune with the infinite. —John Marks Templeton

Do not treat men with scorn, nor walk proudly on the earth. God does not love the arrogant and the vainglorious. Rather let your gait be modest and your voice low . . . Do not walk proudly on the earth. You cannot cleave the earth, nor can you rival the mountain in stature.

— Qur'an

As we vision and work toward a more meaningful and fruitful way of life, we may need some way to check up on ourselves to determine two things: how are we using the *laws of life* with which we are familiar, and whether or not we are improving. A good way to perform this checkup is to mentally stand aside and watch yourself! In other words, stop and review what you have been saying, doing, and thinking. How was your last contact with another person? Did you feel "in tune" with the person? How did you feel about what you said or did? Were you honest and sincere or did your ego/personality come into play? Would you act in the same way again if you had the chance? Such an analysis of your actions can provide an evaluation to use in making changes and improvements. And the ability to learn is one of the greatest strengths of human personality.

Humility is a tremendous key to progress. Humility helps us become more receptive to others and it can open wondrous doors to the realms of spirit and to research and progress in all fields of endeavor. Humility is an individual's gateway to deeper understanding and knowledge. Without the virtue of humility, we may become too self-satisfied with past glories to launch boldly into new challenges. Without humility, we may not be enthusiastic enough to discover new areas for research. If we are not humble, we may be unable to admit mistakes, seek advice, or avoid pride, intolerance, and religious strife.

The humble approach is for everyone who is not satisfied to allow life to simply drift along. The humble approach is for every person who desires to channel that inner creative restlessness toward helping build heaven on earth. The word "humil-

There is no holiness without humility.

— Thomas Fuller

ity" is used in these concepts to indicate the understanding that the Creator infinitely exceeds anything anyone has ever thought or said about divinity. Is the creative source of all infinitely beyond human comprehension and understanding? As we realize this and become more humble, can we reduce the stumbling blocks placed in our paths by our own misguided egos?

Because it is self-centered and nonproductive, egotism has been a major cause of many mistaken notions in the past. Our outlook is tremendously broadened when we approach life from an awareness of how little we yet know. Humility can guide us into the joy and thrill of diligent, rigorous research for accelerating progress and usefulness.

That one I love who is incapable of ill will, who is friendly and compassionate.

Living beyond the reach of "I" and "mine" and of pleasure and pain,

patient, contented, self-controlled, firm in faith, with all his heart

and all his mind given to me—with such a one I am in love.

— *Bhagavad Gita*

And progress can accelerate forever. Mysteries solved lead to even more mysteries. Forces still undreamed of are probably present within and around us. The more we learn about our world, the more humble we can be, realizing how ignorant we have been in the past and how much more is waiting to be discovered.

One lesson to learn is that building heaven is up to each of us. Emanuel Swedenborg wrote, "we will not be in heaven until heaven is in us." So how may we begin to build that heaven within? True humility can lead us into a prayerful attitude and prayer helps bring us in tune with the infinite. There is a real, mystical power in prayer, and it works! Through our times of prayer and conscious attunement with spiritual energy, we are increasing our own spiritual light. A daily review of our lives can indicate a growing expression of life in every way. We are attracting the energies and virtues of

what we are building! Are we touching a larger power? Are we building a more productive and fruitful life?

Think for a moment on an analogy. As a furnace purifies gold, so may life purify souls. When a person is born into the world, he may be likened to a piece of charcoal. Charcoal is soft and amorphous, so when sunlight falls on it, nothing is reflected. Then, in the crucible of time, the charcoal becomes subjected to such intense heat and pressure that it is transformed into a diamond "in the rough." The stone's natural inner design is determined and marked. The diamond is then carefully cut with many facets to emerge into the precious and radiant jewel. Then, when rays of sunlight fall upon it, the colors of the rainbow are reflected, creating a magnificent symphony of beauty and radiance.

So it is with each person born into the material world. We may feel "pressed and cut" by life's experiences and by the choices we make. Then, however, we are "born" to greater understanding: the humility our soul has achieved begins to reflect the light of divinity. Perhaps this could be one reason why the God of Unlimited Love created the crucible called earth!

◆ LAW 5

Failing to plan is planning to fail. — Benjamin Franklin

A BUSINESSMAN had planned and worked for many years to build a flourishing company in household furniture. He was a man of vision and was also blessed with the ability to bring the vision into manifestation. His business prospered and the man was an asset to the community where he lived. After a particularly busy season, the man decided to take his family on vacation. However, he returned from the holiday only to find that, during

his absence, his shop and house had caught fire.

As the businessman stood before his burned-out property with bowed head, all kinds of thoughts raced through his mind. What could he do? Complain? To whom? Blame the god he remembered in prayers every day? Blame the fire department for being slow to respond? Shed tears?

The man took a deep breath, squared his shoulders, slowly lifted his head, and quietly whispered,

I think the necessity
of being ready
increases. Look to it.
— Abraham Lincoln

"Lord, what would you have me do next?"

Then he waited for a response. After a short time, a soft smile touched his face. The next day, over the ruins of what had once been the scene of a booming business, he put up a sign that read:

SHOP BURNED! HOUSE BURNED!

MERCHANDISE BURNED!

FAITH STILL INTACT!

PLANS ARE UNDERWAY TO REBUILD BUSINESS!

Here was a man who had learned how to meet the challenges of life in a positive and productive way! The same planning methods that had stood him in good stead in his "burned out" business would lay the foundation for another successful venture. He knew he could "begin again," and prayerful planning is an excellent starting place.

Those who reach
greatness on earth
reach it through con-
centration.
— The Upanishads

If we decide to take a trip to a new location, one of the first things we are most likely to do is to study a road map and plan the direction to reach our destination. There are probably several possible routes for the journey. If we're in a hurry, we may choose the "shortest distance between two points." If we have plenty of time, we may choose a more leisurely, scenic, perhaps longer, excursion.

What holds true for taking a trip or rebuilding a business may be equally true for the accomplishment of any goal. Without a "road map" or a plan, our minds can wander aimlessly and be ineffective and nonproductive. To formulate a plan to achieve desired goals, a good beginning is to study systematically the various alternatives in a scientific manner. When goals are pursued in this way, success occurs more often than failure.

Life can be pulled by
goals just as surely
as it can be pushed
by drives.
— Viktor Frankl

As human beings, we are made up of many things. Among the most effective of these in daily living are our thoughts and feelings. Every single thought and feeling can contribute toward bringing us closer to our sincere desires, or can build a roadblock in our path. Can you perceive why

awareness and planning can play such an important role in our lives? Well thought-out plans are guideposts along the road to a meaningful life. In his book *How to Succeed*, Brian Adams wrote: "Poorly devised plans will never harvest riches. Achievements can be no greater than the undertakings. If your plans are sketchy and your aims low, you can never hope to achieve high rewards."

Perhaps it would be helpful to think of our attitudes in various situations as commitments toward long-term investments in life! We receive greater benefits from our life's endeavors if we are as constant as possible. If we are able to calm our minds and remain relaxed as we pursue our life's goals, we will find them far more attainable. Shall we invest our talents wisely, with careful forethought and planning, in our work, relationships, and spiritual life?

Nothing splendid has ever been achieved except by those who dared believe that something inside them was superior to circumstance.
— John Barton

The human mind is rich in unseen resources. When there is intent, desire, motivation, incentive, and purpose for the way we live life and accomplish our goals, there are riches in every opportunity that comes our way. Most overcoming, recouping from a perceived failure, or getting a good start, can be accomplished through a step-by-step process. Maintaining constancy, based on wisdom and planning, while pursuing life's goals, brings peace of mind and eventual rewards.

Those who reach greatness on earth reach it through concentration.
— The Upanishads

Spotlights ✦ ✦

1. We live and interact with a variety of happenings every day that can be stressful. How we handle ourselves in these situations can determine the fruitfulness of lives.

2. The process of living should be purposeful, not aimless.

3. Keep in mind the basic truth that what we hold persistently in our consciousness tends to manifest itself in our lives.

4. Communication and sharing are necessary parts of any relationship.

5. Be glad to listen and learn! Open minds are ready to grow.

6. Be willing to look at yourself honestly and courageously every day.

7. "Wisdom is not to be obtained from textbooks, but must be coined out of human experience in the flame of life" (Morris Raphael Cohen).

8. The universal *law of choice* affirms that if we wish to change our lives, we must change our *choices.*

9. *Humility is a tremendous key to progress.* It opens the door to realms of spirit, and to research and progress in all fields of endeavor.

10. Noble purpose creates fruitful, happy lives.

Living the Various Spiritual Laws ✦ ✦

Great teachers have always known that a little story can ignite the soul. You are invited to reflect on the wisdom contained in this story from the book *The Good You Do Returns,* by the honored Indian spiritual teacher J. P. Vaswani.

LEARN OF ME!

A merchant, an old man, and his little daughter met by the side of a fountain of clear, sparkling waters. On the fountain was an inscription that read, "Learn of me!"

The merchant said he learned a great lesson from the fountain. It started as a trickle of water, but as it wended its way to the sea, it was joined by streams and brooks and creeks and, in due course, became a roaring river. We should do our work likewise, start with little beginnings and soon develop big businesses.

The old man said that the lesson he learned from the fountain was to serve silently, friends and strangers alike.

The little girl said that the lesson she learned was that the water is useless unless it is pure. Therefore, we should live a clean and chaste life.

The teacher is one. Everyone learns according to his or her aptitude and capacity. In this school of life the day on which we have not learned something new is a lost day indeed.

Week Four

③ How important is beauty to you?

✦ LAW 1

① *Beautiful thoughts build a beautiful soul.* –John Marks Templeton

> Every year of my life I grow more convinced that it is wisest and best to fix our attention on the beautiful and the good, and dwell as little as possible on the evil and the false.
>
> — Richard Cecil

② ③

IF YOU WERE ASKED the question, "How would you describe a beautiful thought?" what would be the first image that comes to your mind? You may say, "What a beautiful day," and mean that the day is sunny, warm, and pleasant outside. Or, your response might be, "This is a gorgeous day!" because this day has ushered love, opportunity, creativity, enthusiasm, humor, and beauty into your life.

How much beauty is in your life? In the use of the word "beauty," is much more meant than an outer or surface appearance? The meaning of "beauty" being considered here means the radiant inner qualities of honesty, humility, gratitude, love, creativity, and spiritual wealth that glow from the depths of a person's soul. ④ what meant by?

Do we need to expand our perception of beauty? Have you ever considered the possibility that the need for beauty may overarch a person's higher needs because it encompasses the others? Does beauty, as an aspect of *universal creative energy*, lie inherent within the soul of each person and can it become more apparent in all areas of life? A key is to discipline our thoughts to focus more clearly and succinctly. For example, observe the effects that a beautiful environment can have on a person. Feeling more positive about our world can help us see more beauty. Individuality is beautiful. Compassion, beneficial work, scientific research,

noble purpose, a life of service, and, yes, physical beauty, help us bring beauty to the lives of others.

In his novel *La Réponse du Seigneur*, Alphonse de Châteaubriant compares the human mind to one of those butterflies that assume the color of the foliage they settle on. He said, "We become what we contemplate." If our mind is occupied with worry, concern, gossip, resentment, or other nonproductive thoughts, it will assume their hue. If our focus is maintained on thoughts of unlimited love, joy, purpose, enthusiasm, diligence, usefulness, and other positive traits, the mind's hue will again respond. Years earlier, Marcus Aurelius made much the same observation when he said, "Such as are thy habitual thoughts, such also will be the character of thy soul—for the soul is dyed by thy thoughts."

Our thoughts do a great deal more than color our minds! A universal fundamental principle at work is the idea: *our thoughts define our world.* Far from being ethereal and remote from life, our thoughts act upon our world in tangible and profound ways. A person can be born in seeming poverty and unenlightened, but by directing his thoughts in a positive manner, he can rise over apparent limitations. By the end of his life on earth, he may pass on as a more beautiful soul. Isn't this potential worth the effort to "think beautiful thoughts"?

what colors? colors vibration blend

How can we think beautiful thoughts? See the goal. Comment on good - compliment on good - introduce good - Bring out good in others - Talk to your plants - a new book - a flower

By practice, can we create, visualize, and strengthen a particular idea by focusing upon it? As we observe the possibilities, dimensions, and applications of an idea, can it become more clearly defined in our minds? Thus, by thinking about love, strength, humility, or joy, we can *create* love, strength, humility, and joy within ourselves. Using the mind for higher purposes is a fruitful experience. Such positive mental qualities may take time to develop. However, continued reflective focus and attention can be a simple and effective key toward beautiful thoughts building a beautiful soul!

Noble purpose and concentrated thinking can be found functioning among creative people of all kinds—artists, inventors, scientists, business people, religious leaders, political leaders, and so on. One beautiful description of developing the mind for higher purposes may be found in Evelyn Underhill's book, *Mysticism*. The words of St. Teresa of Avila are given in the form of an instruction. She said, "As soon as you apply yourself to reflection, you will feel at once your senses gather themselves together; they seem like bees which return to the hive and there shut themselves up to work at the making of honey."

People should be beautiful in every way—

in their faces, in the way they dress, in their thoughts,

and in their innermost selves."

— *Anton Chekhov*

Is your life beautiful? Do you live in surroundings, mentally and physically, that you have made beautiful through your own loving, creative ideas? There is always something beautiful to be found, right where you are, if you look for it.

✦ LAW 2

Progress depends on diligence and perseverance. –John Marks Templeton

IF OUR DAILY EXPERIENCES are not producing the progress or results we desire, then do we need to take a good look at how we view life? What is our basic perspective? How diligent are we in pursuing our goals? What are our goals? What talents can we build to assist in reaching our goals? Is our creativity accelerating? How can we enhance our productivity? Are we able to focus mentally on the tasks at hand and block extraneous influences that might distract us from our higher purposes in life?

Success is something that nearly everyone seeks, whether professional or personal. Yet occasionally, obstacles arise, and adversity may seem to stand between our goals and us. Should we be faced with a difficulty, where do we place our focus? Do we blame others or do we seek new opportunities? Do we look for evidences of new good that may be emerging? If we assess the situation realistically, we may find we are doing better than we think. Life is a creative endeavor. In every moment, there resides the seed of greater expansion, opportunities, and effectiveness. Our progress may depend on diligence, resourcefulness, and perseverance toward our goals.

The ancient Chinese sage Lao Tzu set down laws of effective living that he developed after years of meditation and careful observations of the varieties of lives around him. He called his invaluable teaching the *Tao Te Ching* or *How Things Work*. Many of his teachings reflected the effects of diligence and perseverance. One meaningful example is described in "The Ripple Effect" from the *Tao*:

Do you want to be a positive influence in the world? First get your own life in order. Ground yourself in the universal principle so that your behavior is wholesome and effective. If you do that, you will earn respect and be a powerful influence.

Your behavior influences others through a ripple effect. A ripple effect works because everyone influences everyone else. Powerful people are powerful influences. If your life works, you influence your family. If your family works, your family influences the community. If your community works, your community influences the nation. If your nation works, your nation influences the world. If your world works, the ripple effect spreads through the cosmos. Remember that your influence begins with you and ripples outward. So be sure that your influence is both potent and wholesome. How do I know that this works? All growth spreads outward from a fertile and potent nucleus. You are a nucleus.

oceans in a similar manner. If we would compare a single stroke of a pickax or one impression in the ground with a spade, with the general plan of the desired end result for a building or a canal, we might feel overwhelmed. Yet, small, persistent operations can surmount great difficulties and achieve the desired goal.

Occasionally, we may be tempted to spend valuable time pursuing those interests that provide entertainment, while neglecting our long-range goals. For real progress to occur, a person needs a set of standards to follow, a goal to shoot for, a set of ultimate values to affirm. Hard work and diligent research can put a person in position to exercise his powers of discernment and good judgment to the fullest. Could it be that love, compassion, and the desire to truly be of service are key components in our progress, and diligence and perseverance are the "icing on the cake"?

Can this "bigger picture" offer inspiration for greater diligence and perseverance? An old adage states, "nothing worth doing ever comes easily." Can enthusiasm and determination, combined with diligence and optimism, help us achieve success? Many avenues of opportunity are available for developing our many and unique talents and abilities. This can mean making a commitment to developing self-discipline and persisting until the goal is met.

A stone quarry becomes a skyscraper by the perseverance of the workers. Canals connect

Whenever an opportunity comes our way that will allow us to express our talent, let's welcome that opportunity with open arms! Unquestionably, every one of us is capable of achievement. The primary requirement is that we commit ourselves with determination to develop our talents, one moment at a time, one day at a time. Perseverance is the plus that helps assure us of the completion of a goal. Among our many rewards will be accomplished goals, higher self-esteem, happiness, and a secure sense of productivity and creativity.

◆ LAW 3

Love thy neighbor as thyself. —Matthew 19:19

UNLIMITED LOVE has been called the unifying, harmonizing, creative energy wherein the entire universe lives and moves and has existence. This pure, unlimited love may be the basic reality from which all else is only fleeting perceptions by transient creatures! While "love" may be difficult to define, it may be experienced by anyone who is willing to open his or her mind and heart and soul to its powerful

The light which shines in the eye is really the light of the heart. The light which fills the heart is the light of God.
—Jalalu'ddin Rumi

Love is not a possession. It is the flow of God's energy.
—Swami Chidvilasananda

Show love to all creatures and you will be happy; for when you love all things, you love the Lord, for He is all in all.
—Tulsidas

energy. Many of us may know from personal experience and observation that love has the ability to bring a sparkle to the eyes and vitality to life.

Unlimited love can forgive shortcomings; it keeps no score of wrongs, and is patient and kind. Unlimited love is not jealous, boastful, irritable, or resentful, and does not rejoice in what is wrong. It finds pleasure in the truth and fulfills every law. It eliminates fear, guilt, condemnation, unhappiness, and transforms the individual or situation in which it is permitted to be expressed. So, on the basis of experience and evidence, it seems essential to become thoroughly acquainted with unlimited love.

Love accents the completeness of life. Is it the ever-present potential through which we can find the fulfilling action or the harmonious attitude? Through unlimited love, can we enter the dimension of spiritual unity, wholeness, and maturity? Mature spiritual love can unite us more closely with the Creator and with those around us—our neighbors! The universe is not isolated from us, nor are we from it! Divine love expresses itself through all phases of creation.

When we allow the eyes of the heart to be opened in unlimited love, can we see more of the realities hidden behind the outer forms of this world? When the ears of the heart are open, can we hear words of truth that may be hidden behind other words? A teacher once said, "The heart is a temple that can house God. All hearts are temples, and to open our hearts is to allow in the divine presence . . . All wisdom is already within us; all love is already within us; all joy. Yet they are hidden within us until the heart opens."

The Bible speaks often about the meaning of love. In Jesus' Sermon on the Mount, we are advised to "love our enemies." We are told to love

Love is to see what is good and beautiful in everything. It is to learn from everything, to see the gifts of God and the generosity of God in everything.

It is to be thankful for all God's bounties.
—Sheikh Muzaffer

those who hate us. We are instructed to turn the other cheek! While some people may scoff at this advice and call it impractical, pure, unlimited love can be the most fruitful way to lead a truly successful life! The *Tejabindu Upanishad* tells us, "To be united with the Lord of Love is to be freed from all conditioning. This is the state of Self-realization, far beyond the reach of words and thoughts." And Lahiji, from the Sufi teachings, says, "The heart is the treasury in which God's mysteries are stored. Seek the purpose of both the worlds through the heart, for that is the point of it."

To "love your neighbor" is to go beyond the call of duty, the burden of obligation, the narrow code of conviction, and the rigid rules of half-living into the joyous expression of a new way of life. To prepare to love your neighbor is to take a new and joyous (and sometimes painfully honest) look at God, yourself, your neighbor, your world, and everything in it! And who is our neighbor? Is it not every other person living on the planet?

When we practice unlimited love, it becomes easier to love our "enemies," to tolerate those who may annoy us, and to find something to appreciate in every person, place, and experience. The great paradox of unlimited love may be that it calls on us to be fully ourselves and honor our individual truth, releasing self-centeredness and then giving with nothing held back. Love, as with any other spiritual virtue, doesn't simply fall into our life as manna from heaven. Like an inquiring mind, it needs to be cultivated.

The important element in anything we do is our personal attitude toward it. Is this not a perfect moment to take the time to establish an attitude of joy and anticipation in possibly the greatest assignment life may give us—loving our neighbors as ourselves?

✦ LAW 4

To be wronged is nothing unless you continue to remember it. —Confucius

FIRMIN ABAUTIZ was known as a man of serene disposition. Nobody in his town could recall his having lost his temper at any time during his eighty-seven years. One man, who doubted the possibility that a person could be so unflappable, made a deal with a housekeeper, offering her money if she could provoke him to anger.

The housekeeper knew that Abautiz was very fond of a comfortable, orderly bed, so one day she neglected to make his bed. The next morning, Abautiz kindly reminded her of the undone chore. The next night, Abautiz again found an unmade bed and the following morning, he again called it to her attention. She made a lame excuse, which he kindly accepted.

On the third morning, Abautiz said, "You still have not made my bed; it is evident you are determined not to do it. Well, I suppose you find the job troublesome, but it is of little consequence, for I begin to get used to it already." Moved by such goodness of temper, the woman called off the deal and never again failed to make his bed as comfortable as possible!

Not everything can be the way we like it all the time, but criticism and harsh words rarely bring about a lasting and peaceful cooperation or fulfillment of our desire. Patience and kindness, on the other hand, do.

Occasionally, we may allow another person's angry outbursts or critical remarks to "bore a hole" in our good nature and rob us of an otherwise sunny disposition. It can take some work on our part to rise above the situation and refuse to allow the perceived "wrong" to take up permanent residence in our consciousness.

> Learning to forgive is much more useful than merely picking up a stone and throwing it at the object of one's anger, the more so when the provocation is extreme. For it is under the greatest adversity that there exists the greatest potential for doing good, both for oneself and others.
>
> —Dalai Lama

Yes, it hurts to be wronged, but does isolating ourselves, or repeatedly reliving an event that transpired a day, a week, a month, or even years ago bring the needed healing? When we continue to pick at emotional scars, are we not indulging in useless, unnecessary suffering instead of getting on with our lives?

Sometimes the challenges in our lives can actually become revealing sources of light and optimism. Regardless of what "wrongs" or dilemmas we may experience, can we move forward through the help of friends, hard work, diligence, loving service, prayer, and allowing unlimited love to be a directive energy?

What can we do to convert a hurtful experience into an opportunity to practice love? How about using the loving energy of forgiveness as a powerful progressive agent? The process of forgiveness may involve increasing our depth perception—the desire to understand the influences that may have shaped the oppressor's behavior. If we seek to understand, to the best of our ability, where another person may be coming from, and observe what problems may be prevalent in his life, are we not putting forth a sincere effort to "walk a mile in his shoes"?

Are human relationships like a living laboratory within which we make progress toward greater maturity and usefulness? Through our positive response to perceived wrongs, do we create a useful personal arena for developing many desired noble qualities or virtues? Once we can begin to comprehend the dynamics behind the perceived "wrong" or abuse, we may more easily and quickly forgive the offender. An old African proverb says,

"He who forgives ends the quarrel." Are you willing to be the instigator of such a positive action?

Understanding, forgiving, and forgetting a hurt does not mean condoning another person's words or actions. However, can the process of love and forgiving help us reframe the experience, release our pain from the event, and renew our allegiance to life? On a deeper level, could the action of releasing or "letting go" of perceived wrongs be an indication of releasing attachment to the ego's illusions of separateness? Are "letting go" of the ego and "letting go" of offense one and the same?

Our world is always in a state of flux and change. Sometimes, we may have little time for preparation or reflection regarding an unfolding event. On such occasions, can our ability to be prepared for the challenges we may face be linked to our spiritual strength? Is this a good time to pause for a moment to take a personal inventory and monitor and strengthen your spiritual assets to assist you in adapting to life's changes? Does forgetting and forgiving flow automatically from pure, unlimited love for every human without any exceptions?

✦ Law 5

Enthusiasm facilitates achievement. —John Marks Templeton

THE WORD "enthusiasm," which is derived from the Greek word "entheos," means to be inspired, to have zeal or fervor, to be joyful, to be filled with spirit, or "full of God." Doesn't this sound like a recipe for a happy and useful life? Surely, most people desire a particular quality of life, perhaps a combination of special interests: research, achievement, progress, and usefulness. In addition, in our heart of hearts, is there an inner longing to experience beauty, love, and noble purpose? And what about possessing the energy and vitality necessary to meet daily responsibilities with vigor to spare? Can life be a joyous daily adventure?

Enthusiasm is considered one of life's greatest qualities, but for it to become a dominant factor in a person's life, it must be *practiced* regularly! If we observe the activities of a small child, what is the outstanding characteristic that often catches our attention? Is it not enthusiasm? Everything fascinates the child. He is interested in whatever is happening in his world. He asks questions! He is eager to learn! He thinks the world is terrific and he

loves it! Thomas Huxley said that the secret of genius is to carry the spirit of the child into old age, which of course means never to lose our enthusiasm. What a powerful consideration!

If we feel we would like to get more out of life, would a good starting place be to examine the state of our enthusiasm? How can a person become more enthusiastic? One way is to make effective use of the "as if" principle. William James, who taught this principle, said, "If you want a quality, act as if you already have it." Shakespeare tells us in Act III of *Hamlet*, "Assume a virtue, if you have it not." If we wish to become a different type of person, could the first step be to decide specifically what particular characteristic we wish to possess? The next logical step would be to firmly hold that image in our consciousness. Then, we can proceed to develop it by *acting as if* we already possess the desired characteristic.

Can you visualize starting your day with a plan for developing more enthusiasm? A story is told that author Henry David Thoreau, upon awakening, would lie in his bed for a while and recount to himself all the good news that he could think of. Then, he arose to meet the day in a world filled with good things, wonderful people, and great opportunities! He used this practice of spiritual motivation at the start of each day to infuse himself with new zeal and enthusiasm.

Another helpful consideration is to develop the habit of expressing only hopeful, enthusiastic ideas. Can we make a deliberate decision to look at the positive side of every situation, experience, and person? If we express enthusiasm freely and openly upon all occasions, isn't it logical that our lives can strongly tend to become more joyful and fruitful? It becomes natural to expect the good, the positive.

How does enthusiasm facilitate achievement? Have you heard the familiar expression, "If life gives you a lemon, make lemonade"? Can enthusiasm help us look at the positive side of every situation? Does the enthusiastic individual constantly release maximum potential because of the outgoing attitude that accompanies enthusiasm?

How does enthusiasm make a definite difference in a person's performance? For example, if someone becomes apathetic, recognizes it, desires to change the situation, and begins to act more enthusiastically, would this energy begin to show as new vitality? This process can require commitment, perseverance, and self-discipline, but it can also help a person achieve a new, positive, and productive attitude.

A boy who did not know what an echo was cried across a valley, "Who is there?"

The echo answered, "Who is there?"

The child could not see who spoke those words and he asked, "Who are you?"

Back came the words, "Who are you?"

The boy thought someone was trying to tease him. So he shouted, "Please stop it!"

The echo repeated, "Please stop it!"

Just as the child was becoming bewildered by the echo, his mother explained to him that no one was trying to tease him, that it was only an echo of his own voice that came back to him. The child thought about this for a moment, then cried out, "I love you!"

Back came the words, "I love you!"

The child enthusiastically shouted, "You are so good!"

The compliment was returned to him and the child became happier and more enthusiastic about life. The moral of the story is that what we give to this world comes back to us. So, if we express enthusiasm, unlimited love, kindness, assistance, compassion, and service, according to spiritual principles, would they not return to us?

The words of Norman Vincent Peale in *Treasury of Joy and Enthusiasm* offer a challenging formula for better living: "Those persons who consistently live by the joy and enthusiasm pattern of thinking seem to achieve a remarkable mastery over circumstances."

Can you resolve to double the amount of enthusiasm that you have been putting into your life? If you can and do make that resolve, be prepared to see astonishing results.

Spotlights ◆ ◆

1. What are some ways you can develop a loving, empowering attitude?

2. Do we need to expand our perception of beauty? How?

3. How would you describe beautiful thoughts as building a beautiful soul?

4. How are diligence and perseverance important ingredients in progress?

5. How can enthusiasm and determination, combined with diligence and perseverance, help us achieve the success that we earn through sincere effort?

6. How does unlimited love accent the completeness of life?

7. Who is our neighbor? ("Love thy neighbor. . ." [Matthew 19:19])

8. Forgiveness is a process of giving up the false for the true, erasing error concepts from mind and body, and continuing with a fruitful life. How can you relate this statement to your daily life?

9. How can we relegate a hurtful experience to an appropriate and constructive place in our lives?

10. How may enthusiasm be considered one of life's greatest qualities? *Inspiration*

11. Why is *practicing* enthusiasm regularly meaningful to daily living? *Energy peace*

12. How would you consider researching spiritual principles an important tool in improving your life? How would you go about your research?
Becoming more aware

Living the Various Spiritual Laws ◆ ◆

Theodore Gaster, a professor of comparative religion at Dropsie College, found in this summation by Yehuda Halevi an expression of a "central, unique, and tremendous idea . . . that God and man are partners in the world, and that for the realization of His plan . . . God needs a committed, dedicated group of men and women."

. . . [T]o experience God means to be touched by the Divine Spirit in one of a variety of ways. That experience may be of a Spirit that inspires and encourages; a Spirit that unleashes creative energy; a Spirit that feeds motivation and dedication; a Spirit that extends love and is repaid by love; a Spirit that strives for peace and welcomes reconciliation; or a Spirit that reaches for God by appreciating nature.

The beauty of nature
a Presence; an answer to a prayer —
a realization

Spiritual satisfaction comes when one finds the unique way in which one personally feels God.

A popular story offers the answer. In this tale an adult, sitting on a park bench, is watching a child play with a kite. The kite soars upwards and disappears into the clouds.

The man approaches the child and asks, "What are you doing?"

She answers, "I am flying a kite."

"I don't see a kite," says the man. "How do you know it's up there?"

"I know it's up there because I feel the pull of it!"

How does the kite story depict the child's, or our way of "experiencing God"? What are some ways you experience a connection with the Creator?

◆

Week Five

✦ LAW 1

By giving you grow. —John Marks Templeton

GEORGE HERBERT, the great English poet, was on his way to a concert when he found a huckster whose horse had fallen down, apparently beneath the burden of a heavy weight. Herbert helped the huckster unload the horse, lift it up, and reload it. In the process, his clothes were spoiled, soiled with mud. When he arrived at the concert, some of his friends were shocked to see the condition of his clothes. When he explained to them what had happened, they said to him, "How could you condescend to do such a thing?"

Herbert answered, "What I did will be as music at midnight, but if I had not done anything, there would have been a discordant note sounding within me all the time."

In today's world, opportunities abound for the soul who is alert and awake and open to give and receive. How often do we take advantage of these

> He who sows sparingly will also reap sparingly, and he who sows bountifully will also reap bountifully . . . for God loves a cheerful giver.
>
> *–2 Corinthians 9:6–7*

opportunities? What is an opportunity? Could one description be that it is heaven's call for us to fulfill our highest destiny? Could an opportunity also be a chance to do and to become something splendid?

Oftentimes an occasion that may seem to be fraught with difficult elements of human necessity can prove to be an occasion of tremendous divine opportunity. Would the greater wisdom be not to turn away from *any* experience, but rather to look for the lesson or gift that the experience may bring? At every moment during our lives, hidden perhaps from our human view, are universal energies being released into the area where we meet our daily tasks? Could these energies contain the essence of the Creator's love and simply await our attention and creativity? How does the principle of *giving and receiving* relate to our life experiences?

Giving is more important than getting, and those who give freely will experience the return on their generosity. How can we give? Can we give our assistance in whatever area our "touch" may make a difference? Do we offer our encouragement and carefully reasoned advice in appropriate situations? Are the abilities, talents, intelligence, and material success with which we are blessed returned to the world in some meaningful way that will benefit humanity? Does investing our talents and abilities for the good of humankind bring dividends, both materially and spiritually? Are giving to meaningful charities, useful research organizations, and religious education, for example, an important contribution to the progress of humanity? Is giving a greater percentage of our time and energy to worthwhile causes an investment that will pay off on many levels?

Let's consider an analogy. A farmer does not dispose of his entire crop but keeps some of the grain for seed. When we give a tithe to God's work, do we consider this tithe as a seed that can produce another harvest? If we sow nothing, what do we reap? And do we accept the good that comes into our life with gratitude?

Giving brings a sense of joy and accomplishment. Giving can lead to greater giving and become a fruitful way of life. It is a cycle that feeds on itself in a positive way. And throughout this process, our sense of gratitude and enthusiasm can grow as well. Are we actually trustees of all that we receive? If we use well what we have received, as did the man in the parable of the talents, can we, too, hear the inner rewarding words, "You have

been faithful over a little, I will set you over much" (Matthew 25:21)?

Can giving also be a test of our maturity? From one perspective, those who are truly "grown up" give. The immature do not. Scripture teaches us that if anyone would be first among us, let him first become the servant of all. Is there any greater gift than to help another person? How can we understand the deep meaning of the words, "We can never out-give God"? Is life without giving a hollow existence? How are spiritual progress and material success closely connected?

Is true success the result of a well-developed consciousness of all good? Could one of the best ways to develop this consciousness be to recognize the Creator as the *source* of all good? One of our greatest privileges may be in taking the initiative in how we live our lives. Consider looking around you from the perspective of determining opportunities to express your talents and abilities. Find some ways to give, and then do it with a loving heart. One of the keys to prosperity is realizing that true prosperity does not come from *getting* more; it comes from *giving* more. We can prosper by trying to give better quality and lower costs rather than by focusing only on what we will get.

You can never have a greater or a less dominion than that over yourself.
—Leonardo da Vinci

All God's creatures are His family; and he is the most beloved of God who doeth most good to God's creatures.
—Islamic saying, Hadith of Burkhari

Giving of yourself, learning to be tolerant, giving recognition and approval to others, remaining flexible enough to mature and learn—yields happiness, harmony, contentment, and productivity. These are qualities of a rich life.
—Jack C. Yewell

I don't know what your destiny will be, but one thing I know: the only ones among you who will be really happy are those who have sought and found how to serve.
—Albert Schweitzer

✦ LAW 2

Does the word "religion" imply authority,
whereas the word "spiritual" may imply progress? —John Marks Templeton

In his book *Reaching High: The Psychology of Spiritual Living,* Dr. Marvin Gawryn wrote:

Religion is a most controversial subject. Its critics have described it as a major source of war and hatred between men, as a psychological crutch that encourages man to be weak and unrealistic about life, . . . an outmoded relic, a superstitious left-over from pre-scientific times.

Religion's supporters, on the other hand, claim that it can bring happiness to the individual and peace among nations, that it is a guiding light in an unstable world, that life is empty without it, and that man's hopes for survival and progress depend on his accepting religious principles of living.

How is it that people can hold such opposite opinions on the single phenomenon of religion?

An interesting insight is that culture, race, and religion, are often the things that most typically separate us into various camps.

Could one possible answer derive from the realization that "religion" and "spirituality" are not necessarily one and the same? In some instances, could the word "religion" imply authority, whereas the word "spirituality" might imply *progress?* How? The terms "religion" and "religious" often refer to social organizations created by groups of like-minded believers. As an example, some religious organizations may require total loyalty toward the institution and its human leaders in authority. Dedication may be directed first to the institution, and secondarily to God.

The term "spiritual" can refer to the inner personal experience an individual may have with divinity. "Spirituality" means the unique divine experience of the individual believer. It encourages sharing of meaningful research insights between people. Spirituality can act as a vehicle of the higher urges for expressions of useful service. Would "spirituality" then be dedicated first to divinity rather than to organizational, individual, or material aims?

Can one primary purpose of religion, with its pageantry and traditions, be to get our attention and help open our minds and hearts so that God's spirit can be revealed within us? Do the beneficial principles developed by human religions offer evidences of basic invisible realities and infinite wisdom? Marcus Bach wrote decades ago that each religious tradition offers a different path up the mountain, at the top of which a deeper, fuller union with God occurs—a spiritual awareness that goes beyond whatever "religion" one started out with. Do not these differences distinguish the religious heritage of our world? Is each religion a showcase for one more way in which man can learn aspects of infinite divinity? From this perspective, can we welcome the religious varieties between people? In one sense of the word, could the diversity of our religious traditions, the cultural richness of our spiritual history, be cause for

Great men are they who see that spiritual is stronger than any material force, that thoughts rule the world. —*Ralph Waldo Emerson*

celebration, an opportunity to learn from others and to gain enthusiasm for more research?

The Divine Creator is sometimes referred to as "Infinite Intelligence." Can a person's consciousness become activated through spiritual practices such as prayer? And can this activation in a person's consciousness generate greater expressions of spirituality? Could this be what some people describe as "living the spiritual life," rather than being "religious"? Could progress in religion increase if additional research were directed toward evidences of varieties of manifestations of infinite intelligence?

Spiritual information seems to be multiplying in our modern world. In the midst of social and cultural progress, can religious research provide an arena of progress for the spiritually motivated individual? Could religious institutions offer a larger avenue for progress by adjusting the focus from ritual and doctrine to the personal experience of blessings from spiritual living? Does "religion" need to give up the struggle of competing doctrines and search for the seminal truths that underlie the traditions of all the world's great religions? How can a community of individuals with spiritual goals and visions be powerfully supportive in the search to live by higher values and noble purpose?

One of the most common misconceptions of our times is that science and religion conflict. Can a mature religion expand and become even more beneficial through science and statistical research?

Will there always be higher truths to be discovered? Our present religious views, while worthy, may be neither final nor complete. Developing spirituality means constantly adding new insights to our present understandings.

◆

◆ Law 3

The family that prays together, stays together. — Common saying

Would a person intentionally go for a week or two weeks without food? Not likely! The ingestion of food on a regular basis is important for the physical body to stay healthy and functional. Without the necessary nutrients provided by food, we would lose energy, our mind would cease to function clearly, and our bodies would eventually die.

As physical food on a regular basis is necessary to sustain bodily energy, do we also need regular spiritual nourishment to maintain spiritual vigor? Does one foundation of an active, healthy, and purposeful life lie in developing the habit of being aware of our place in divine infinity? Without ongoing spiritual study, would our personalities become depleted and undernourished? Would we feel isolated, fearful, and inadequate? Without spiritual sustenance, can our attitudes change, causing us to become emotionally unstable and intolerant? How is spiritual inspiration and insight a re-energizing factor? The bottom line is that prayer is a powerful activity.

A daily period of intimate communion with the unlimited, eternal Creator can provide us with increasing spiritual strength and enthusiasm to meet the challenges of everyday living.

Prayer can become a major benefit for every aspect of daily life. A prayer of gratitude and thanksgiving can lift us to greater heights of performance and insight. Prayer can help us realize that we are only a tiny fraction of God's creation, and yet it can help move us into a greater feeling of oneness with the Creator. If we become humble tools in the Creator's hands and clear channels for his purposes, are we able to accomplish more than if we fail to realize that oneness? What can happen when our prayer becomes: "Let the words I speak and the actions I take be offered in harmony with God's purpose and for the benefit of humanity"? If this is our sincere prayer, will our accomplishments be more successful and likely to endure? Is prayer a cause for experiencing greater joy in life? Does persistent prayer elevate the personality?

Often throughout his day, a businessman prays simply, "Thy will be done." He feels this approach helps him empty his mind of all preconceptions so he may give himself more completely to his perception of divine guidance. When we pray in this manner, our minds are no longer in conflict with any person or situation. Does our ability to make decisions improve tremendously when we seek to bring our mind and heart into more intimate contact with divinity and oneness with universal purpose? Can prayer offer a channel for increased clarity of mind and depth of insight that can be key factors for fruitful living?

What is our reaction when carefully outlined plans fall by the wayside? How do we respond when someone disagrees with us? What is our response when thoughtless words may hurt our feelings? When uncomfortable situations arise, can we remember that even in the stress and strain of daily living, we are first and foremost spiritual beings? Can we comprehend that we live, move, and have our existence in divine creation, and act accordingly?

When we pray with our family, whether the "family" consists of parents, grandparents, brothers, sisters, or a group of close friends, we desire to enter a silent place of wisdom and peace. This experience can mend hurt feelings, calm anger, encourage love and forgiveness, and help us remember how important we are to one another.

For a family, prayer can even happen when general words are no longer effective. If you have ever returned home feeling hurt, disillusioned, or fearful, and someone quietly held your hand and spoke sincere words of comfort, you entered into a place of prayer together. If we are experiencing difficulty with another person or handling a tough situation, prayer better equips us to improve the relationship. We can pray for the welfare of others. As a family begins to make the choice to pray together in their own way, conflict can begin to

resolve itself and love increases. Feelings of separateness can be resolved.

Is the major effect of prayer on the person who prays? How does prayer help us to become more sensitive to spiritual guidance? How can prayer strengthen our spiritual values and noble purpose? How is prayer a generator for sensitivity to others and to high ideals? How is prayer a key ingredient in the spiritual life of an active, growing personality? Why is it necessary for *effective* prayer to be an expression of our heartfelt spiritual desires?

Prayer has been called a way of life rather than a series of isolated acts. It is an attitude of the soul that at times expresses itself in words, but may be best when offered silently from within. Prayer has also been called the "home-life of the soul." It is the work and goal of the soul that dwells in divinity. Its eloquence may be expressed in deeds and its breath as aspiration. Prayer can be as unceasing as breathing and, like breathing, can be an inhalation of pure heaven on earth!

The Creator is a boundless source of spiritual sustenance. Living in an attitude of prayer is like having a divine companion traveling with us wherever we go, one with whom we can talk things over whenever we desire. Over time, this realization can develop into a habit, and our days are filled with joyous awareness of, and interaction with, divinity.

✦ LAW 4 *The Law of Goal setting —*

If at first you don't succeed, try, try again. —William Edward Hickson

HOW ENTHUSIASTIC are we about *planning* our goals? How would we describe the maxim that "success is a journey, rather than a destination?" If, on occasion, we become exposed to frustrations, delays, disappointments, or what might seem like

a "failure," how do we get back on course and continue with diligence and purpose? How can optimism be described as a tremendous source of energy behind progress and success?

When progress may seem slow, or not immediately visible, how important is it to "keep on keeping on?" Are delays in your life purpose an opportunity to review the details of the original goal that was so stimulating at its inception? Could patience and, perhaps, expert guidance be helpful ingredients for the next breakthrough to occur? Positive action and perseverance do pay off in the long run. Many successful people can attest to the multitude of difficulties that were overcome on their journey to a goal's achievement.

An aspect of humanity that sets us apart from other creatures has been called "imaginative wisdom." We have an ability to perceive things as they *can be!* Does our ability to transform "mountains into molehills" stem from the truth that each of us lives, moves, and has our being in an unlimited, eternal Creator? What can better stimulate motivation than an exciting vision or goal, coupled with the opportunity to bring it into reality? Is there a particular "attracting" energy around a person who is dedicated to a useful and noble purpose? Could it be the wonder of creativity? Are there any limits to what can be realistically achieved when our talents, energies, and goals are directed toward loving service?

Do you remember times when as a child, teenager, or adult, you had opportunities to "try again"? If you wanted to accomplish something, like ice-skating, for example, you probably got a little smarter and better with every turn on the ice. In fact, as you learned to skate, the first thing your body probably figured out was how to *fall down* on the ice without getting hurt! Learning how to relax and tuck your legs under, or roll or slide, became important so you that didn't bang your head against the ice. You most likely came up laughing and ready to try again. Failure was not a consideration because of the enjoyment of the sport and perhaps your instinctive knowledge that with perseverance the feat could be mastered!

The twists and turns of life can call upon us to

be flexible. How do we *choose* to meet the requirements, options, and invitations of each new day? Do we follow an exciting avenue toward experiencing greater personal and spiritual growth and expanding boundaries? Are the people who more often succeed in reaching goals the ones who are adaptable, creative, resourceful, diligent, and who welcome the varieties of life's rich opportunities?

In his book, *Companions of the Heart*, Alan Cohen describes the achievements of Dr. George Washington Carver:

When most of us look at a peanut, we see a peanut. When he looked deep into the peanut, Dr. Carver . . . saw over 300 uses for the tiny legume, including washing powder, shaving cream, bleach, salve, paper, ink, synthetic rubber, axle grease, linoleum, shampoo, wood filler, coffee, and pickles. He also discovered 118 uses for the sweet potato. In short, he accepted what he was given, recognized its preciousness, and served the world through it.

Was Dr. Carver an inspired genius or someone who held a high vision—or both? And what would be the difference, if any?

Any circumstance is a good starting point for creativity. The prompting of the "still, small voice within" is always speaking to us. Are we willing to listen to divine inspiration and then take action? Do we dare to venture into unknown territory and try new experiences? Can we "revitalize" an unfulfilled goal and make another run for success?

Do all the good you can, by all the means you can, in all the ways you can, in all the places you can, to all the people you can.

— *John Wesley*

Whatever our goal may be, have we sincerely committed to "give it all we've got" and press onward? Be aware that we can set new goals or change direction in our life journey without being failures! Let's not confuse what we do or how well we do it with our worth as human beings. Our worth as persons comes from within and is as much a part of us as our hearts or brains! Can we admit when we've made a mistake? If the checkbook is balanced incorrectly or we forget to do a repair job on our car, can we simply say, "I goofed!" and take steps to rectify the situation? "If at first you don't succeed, try, try again," is a useful thought to hold in mind when we care about what we originally set out to accomplish.

From investment counselor Gary Moore's book *Spiritual Investments,* we read:

As we hold the focus and work toward our goals, let's remember the powerful spiritual principle of service to others. All of the hard work, thought, preparation, and talent you can muster may not bring real success unless helping others is part of your plan. In your work, your relationships, and your spiritual life, maintaining an attitude of "What can I give?" rather than "What can you give to me?" will bring you bountiful dividends. . . .

The gifts and talents you have been given do not belong to you. You have them on loan—in trust—to make what you can of them for the betterment of humanity. Success follows directly behind each good deed, each act of kindness and generosity. If your life on every level is led foremost by a sense of doing good, you will find yourself more satisfied with its outcomes.

✦ LAW 5

See everyone in your own self and yourself in everyone. —adapted from *Isha Upanishad*

What kind of planet do you want to live on? How big are your dreams? What are some of the illusions that separate us from others? How can we assist a global society in encouraging altruism and noble purpose? This may be simpler said than done, yet look inside your heart. Seed ideas for the improvements we long for may be already within us, and that is a great beginning. The desire for a better future can progress through the efforts of each individual. Are we serving as useful tools in the hands of unlimited love?

We are naturally attracted to some people more than to others. These we often choose as our friends. In the greater perspective, can we comprehend that people throughout the world are our brothers and sisters, our friends? Are we willing to see ourselves in others and others in ourselves? This might

take some introspection and soul-searching. What are some ways we can assist this vision in becoming reality? How can we grow by looking at everyday situations with a new approach and from a higher point of view? Do we grow in consciousness when we become aware of the importance of sharing our loving concern with all of creation? Through becoming aware of the next larger context of life, are we, by the very nature of our being, impelled onward? Nurturing an awakening consciousness can be central in seeing a "bigger picture" of ourselves and also the enormity of divinity.

Einstein once said, "No problem can be solved from the same consciousness that created it." Could reframing how we view our world and expanding our individual and collective consciousness be an excellent starting point? To be bold enough to meet the challenges of our times, do we need to examine our most cherished assumptions, beliefs, and values, and be open to progress? How could research, educational programs, very personal and deep inner inquiry, and collective acts of service serve as common work to help unite us for heaven on earth?

It's amazing how powerful a personal philosophy can be. Developing our wider insights can help turn challenges into opportunities and, ultimately, lead us to greater prosperity and usefulness. Will we discover our purpose in the divine Infinite Intelligence?

Spotlights ✦ ✦

1. How does the principle of "giving and receiving" relate to life experiences?

2. How does giving lead to greater giving and become a fruitful way of life?

3. How would you personally describe "religion" and "spirituality"?

4. A daily period of intimate communion, through prayer, with the unlimited, eternal Creator, can provide us with increased spiritual strength and stamina to meet the challenges of everyday living.

5. Let the words I speak and the actions I take be offered in harmony with God's purpose and for the benefit of humanity.

6. What is your personal definition of "success"?

7. Any circumstance is a good starting point for creativity.

Living the Various Spiritual Laws ✦ ✦

As far as research provides, religion has existed in every society, from the most primitive to the most culturally advanced. Throughout the ages, people have established codes of behavior and clothed them with appropriate beliefs and ceremonies. Although these may differ from one another in practice, they are often similar in theory and often evolve from a common source—the search for basic purposes of life. Each of the major religions of the world honors particular practices and prophets. As we move through this book, an opportunity will be provided for the reader to become familiar with some of the important concepts of various religions. Let's take a look at the *Five Pillars of Islam,* which were mentioned earlier in the essays:

1. Recitation of the *Shahadah* (Testimony): There is no god but God. Muhammad is His messenger.
2. *Zakat* or Alms-Levy: The Compulsory Annual

Giving of a Portion of One's Holdings to Those in Need. (The alms-levy, an annual duty, is different from ordinary charity *[sadaqah]*, which the Muslim is enjoined to give generously and often.)

3. *Salat* or Daily Prayer: Fortify yourself with patience and prayer. This may indeed be an exacting discipline, but not to the devout, who know that they will meet their Lord and that to him they will return.

4. *Sawm* or Fasting during the Month of Ramadan: The month of Ramadan was the time in which the Qur'an was sent down as guidance for mankind.

5. *Hajj:* Pilgrimage to Mecca and the Ka'ba: For Muslims, the holiest place in creation is a cubical building, the Ka'ba, in the center of the Great Mosque at Mecca. Islamic tradition attributes the founding of the Ka'ba to the biblical Abraham and his son Ishmael. The culmination of the pilgrimage to Mecca is a ritual circumambulation of the Ka'ba.

Holmes: Rone is the givingness of life to it's self —

wholehearted acceptance — cure loving christian beyond surface meaning Total acceptance caring —

◆ LAW I

It is better to love than to be loved. —St. Francis of Assisi

The astrolabe of the mysteries of God is love.
—*Jalalu'ddin Rumi*

HOW WOULD YOU respond if someone suggested to you, "Unlimited love, working through you, could help divinity become more known to the world?" Some people might reply with astonishment, "Who, me?" and feel small and unimportant when comparing themselves and their service with the Creator and the divine plan of life. Yet, isn't it through every person and the expressions of every person's effort that the *divine plan* of human life is carried out?

Many opportunities occur in the course of a day for us to accomplish some kindness for others and to give love! Could divine, unlimited love, expressed through sincere and compassionate service, ever fail to help the Creator's purpose of blessing? Like a messenger straight from the heart of Creation, do our blessings of love fly before us as missives of joyful encouragement and assurance to bring gladness and enthusiasm to the hearts of those who may be touched by our love? How does giving more love bring increased dignity and meaning to our own lives?

A story is told about a man who turned his time of retirement into an opportunity to find ways to be of loving service to others. Since his house was near a bus stop, the man would invite people who were waiting for the bus to step up on his screened porch when it was raining. He even printed a small sign that said, "You are welcome to wait on the porch when it is raining." Many grateful people accepted the invitation. On occasion, the man would see bus passengers alight in a downpour and go out to meet them with an umbrella. "Here," he would say, "you may borrow this umbrella and return it the next time you pass by." The people would return the borrowed umbrellas and,

Love seeks no cause beyond itself and no fruit; it is its own fruit, its own enjoyment. I love because I love; I love in order that I may love . . . Of all the motions and affections of the soul, love is the only one by means of which the creature, though not on equal terms, is able to treat with the Creator and to give back something resembling what has been given to it.
—*St. Bernard*

through loving thoughtfulness, the man made many friends. More importantly, he was opening the way for the inner glow that comes when love is made active in the life of an individual. Can this be one of the capacities of unfolding love through which heavenly human beings are developed?

Could the dawning awareness of this concept of love be a divine purpose for our world?

The sun of our solar system has been described as a self-sustaining unit whose energy source is derived from internal thermonuclear reactions. Scientists tell us the energy released in these reactions is so vast that the sun could shine for millions of years with little change in its size or brightness.

Do you perceive how the power of unlimited love can be paralleled with the sun allegory? Unlimited love sustains itself. Even when the clouds of human emotions may hide it, unlimited love is as present as the sun is present, although clouds may hide it from the earth. Our lives thrive on love. Lying at the deep center of our spiritual being, unlimited love is self-sustaining and creates its own energy. Based on this awareness, why is it better to give love than to be loved? Can we think of our lives as a source of "sunshine" for humanity? Why is it important to love simply because we have love to give?

Love's energy is also described as a "healing balm." How does love begin its work first in the one who gives it? When we allow love to express itself through us as our basic nature, does it automatically radiate out to every aspect of our environment? As photosynthesis is the process by which the sun and plants together make food, does a similar process take place within us as we allow

the energy of love to transform our lives? Does unlimited love become meaningful sustenance for ourselves and others?

What are some ways we can love enough to find fulfilling and true closeness to others that satisfies the desire of our hearts to reach out and touch them?

Love is remembering to let our light shine. In fair weather and foul, unlimited love shines like the sun. How can we use this light to encourage and support the unfolding of divine potential within ourselves and others?

Love is remembering that there is no limit to its endurance, no end to its trust, and love never fails! Unlimited love can eliminate fear, resentment, and guilt. It bears no grudges. How can love help us to be receptive to the highest and best in all?

Love is remembering that "God is love." And although we may presently "look through a glass darkly," our vision of reality becomes clearer as we "see with the eyes of love." How can love help us perceive greater reality in all things and in all people?

Love is remembering that our neighbors are also extensions of infinite love, and that we are all created as sons and daughters of divinity. Can we treat everyone in this manner, especially in the tug and pull of everyday, ordinary, and extraordinary events?

What are some ways we can remember that we are extensions of infinite love?

✦ LAW 2

Thanksgiving leads to having more to give thanks for. —John Marks Templeton

Every time we take in a breath and then exhale, we engage in a process of giving and receiving that is vital to the natural and spiritual world. Every *inhalation* provides us with oxygen and nitrogen necessary for human existence. Each *exhalation* gives back the carbon dioxide necessary for the

plant world. The natural flow of the spiritual principle of "giving and receiving" can be as important to human well-being as the life-sustaining act of breathing!

Thanksgiving is an attitude of appreciation that centers on things for which to give thanks! It flows from a deep response of the full human heart's awareness of unity with everything in the universe. The grateful mind offers a continual and active response to the condition of things in life. The generous heart sings a celebration of an ever-present spiritual reality.

What is the connection between *thanksgiving* and *giving*? "Attitudes of gratitude" can open doors to an increased flow of abundance in a person's life. However, a deeper interpretation of thanksgiving focuses on the *level of consciousness* that enables us to perceive things from a higher perspective. When we contemplate the purpose of our life on the material plane, could an important accomplishment be giving a life of service to others?

Two of the finest qualities of giving thanks are that it is practical and that its instrument is everyday life! As we become increasingly aware of our numerous blessings, how do we begin to mold and change our responses to situations in life? How can an attitude of thanksgiving hold the potential for revolutionizing our lives? Is becoming more appreciative a surface sign of value changes that may be happening on a much deeper level of our personalities?

How do optimism and gratitude go hand in hand? Can you wake up every day and think of five new things for which you are overwhelmingly grateful? Try this experiment and notice if your day goes better, if relationships improve, and if your life seems more useful and successful.

Thanksgiving opens the door to spiritual growth. If there is any day in our life which is not thanksgiving day, then we are not fully alive. Counting our blessings attracts blessings. Counting our blessings each morning starts a day full of blessings. Thanksgiving brings God's bounty. From gratitude comes riches—from complaints, poverty. Thankfulness opens the door to happiness. Thanksgiving causes giving. Thanksgiving puts our mind in tune with the Infinite. Continual gratitude dissolves our worries.

Giving thanks can embrace the purpose of creation within itself. How may the person who gives thanks with his whole heart experience transformation? In what ways does giving thanks enrich a person on every level of his being? Could thoughts and feelings of "inner poverty" be the times when we fail to give thanks for what we have received? Can the depth of our inner happiness depend on the degree of our attitude of gratitude to the Creator? Once we find the first reason for giving thanks, other blessings will follow; ultimately, we can find ourselves giving endless thanks.

The gratitude ascending from man to God is the supreme transaction between earth and heaven.

—Albert Schweitzer

What are some of the results of living an appreciative and grateful life? Is a growing sense of joy and optimism part of the experience? When we realize that the Creator is making infinite knowledge and unlimited love available to us, how can we share the joy and love we feel with others? Do we search for unexplored ways to revel in the fulfillment of leading a life bursting with meaning and purpose? Do patterns of a more divine nature occur through our spiritual living? Are we continually reaching for higher values? Is living a life of gratitude a way of experiencing the world and our place in it through unlimited love rather than through judgment? Is thanksgiving part of the spiritual quickening of the life principle flowing in and through our "awakening" to the planet and its inhabitants? Does gratitude activate a desire to learn more about scientific and philosophic truth, aesthetic beauty, and spiritual goodness? How does our gratitude stimulate a fuller appreciation of the Creator's infinite universe? We stand, joyful and expectant, at the doorway opening into a new adventure of time and eternity.

Essential Sufism, edited by James Fadiman and

Robert Frager, includes a beautiful expression regarding gratitude.

Gratitude transforms us. It opens our hearts and brings us closer to God. Unfortunately most of us are unconscious of the many blessings we receive and rarely feel gratitude. Or if we do feel gratitude, it is often extremely short-lived.

I have been amazed by observing older dervishes serve one another. Even when serving a glass of water or a cup of tea, the one who is serving is attentive and grateful for the chance to serve. The dervish who is served receives whatever is served with real gratitude, as opposed to taking it for granted. This is all done quietly, with no outer show or fanfare.

For months after a serious car accident, I would wake up each morning in great pain. I would look out my bedroom window into my garden and weep—with gratitude. I was alive, and this world was filled with beauty.

◆ # LAW 3

You cannot be lonely if you help the lonely. —John Marks Templeton

THERE IS A SCENE in the marvelous movie *Lost Horizons*, in which a group of travelers become stranded in the Himalayas. They are met miraculously by a guide who provides them with warm clothing. The guide then leads the group on a journey that he describes as "not particularly far, but quite difficult." As the travelers trek up the steep, icy footpaths, they are all linked together by a long, well-knotted rope. This is done so that if one of them begins to slip toward the abyss, the combined strength of his fellow travelers would save him.

If we pause to review our lives, perhaps occasions may be recalled when we felt "stranded," lonely, or isolated—standing apart from others. We may have yearned for the company of a friend, or someone with whom to share our thoughts. And all the while, helping hands may have contributed loving, positive energy, in perhaps unexpected ways, to provide assistance or companionship.

The statement *"You cannot be lonely if you help the lonely"* speaks a great truth. If we aspire to serve others and make a useful contribution to humanity, is not the first step taken by letting go of any self-pity, fear, doubt, or loneliness? Loving service may result from directing our attention from self to others. For how could we assist another until we release our own feelings of loneliness?

We were not designed to stand alone as an isolated and independent creation, but rather to blend and interact with manifested life. A coursing stream of currents of dynamic energy flows within us, accounting for our vital processes, urges, impulses, thoughts, emotions, dreams, and visions. If we desire to create good effects with this energy, doesn't it become important to utilize the universal laws or principles in the highest way we presently understand? How can we do this? One way is through applying the "fruits of the Spirit"(Matthew 7:16) in our lives by acting with *love, joy, peace, patience, kindness, goodness, faithfulness, gentleness, and self-control.*

Life is an individual experience and requires effort on our part. Do you see how our attitudes can either help or hinder our participation in life events? Our negative or positive traits can determine whether, and by whom, we are liked or disliked. If we desire to become more likable, where must we make ourselves more attractive? From within? How can we engage those thoughts and actions that nurture the good qualities we desire?

A positive mental attitude can release detrimental thoughts that could hinder us from our highest good. Are not the differences in each man's character of his own cultivation?

The Duke of Norfolk, one of the greatest men in England, dwelt in a large castle. He was a simple, humble, gentle soul of great compassion. One day the Duke was at the railway station when a little Irish girl got off a train, carrying a heavy bag. She had arrived to work as a maidservant at the castle. The castle was situated about a mile's distance from the station. The little Irish girl had only a shilling and offered it to a porter, asking him to please carry the heavy bag to the castle. When the porter contemptuously refused, the Duke, who was simply dressed, stepped forward and offered to carry the bag.

Upon arriving at the castle, the Duke graciously accepted the shilling the girl offered. Not by a single sign did he reveal who he was. It was only the next day when she met her employer that the girl discovered that the man whom she had taken for a porter was none other than the Duke of Norfolk himself. Life fulfills itself in service. Are not the greatest those who greatly serve?

Opportunities are limitless when we seek to fill a need in humanity. Whatever we would choose for ourselves, we may offer to another. If we desire to be more successful, how can we help another to be successful? If we wish to experience joy and enthusiasm, how can these emotions be expressed to another in a stimulating manner? If an increase of love is our desire, then how can we give, give, and give unlimited love in such quantity that it must return to us magnified? Can we do these things not because we seek personal gain, but because we sincerely want to help others experience the joys of the spirit in their life? Can we perceive how consideration for others is a most wonderful quality? How is humbly providing service to others an assurance that we will never be lonely?

Think about the mirror principle: "What you see in the world is a reflection of yourself." Inasmuch as universal laws are the basis of order in the universe, we can begin to perceive that order as we make these principles a part of our daily lives. If we ask to be shown and become willing to accept a higher point of view, we can begin to see the principles at work in every event of our lives.

This growth in consciousness is available to each of us. Let's become like the tree planted by the river that brings forth its fruit in a vibrant, healthy, and joyous manner!

✦ LAW 4

*You are sought after if you reflect love, joy, peace, patience,
kindness, goodness, faithfulness, gentleness, and self-control.* —John Marks Templeton

WHAT DO YOU SEE reflected when you look into a mirror? Is there a light of joyous sparkle in your eyes? Is your smile warm and friendly, patient and understanding? Do you like the "self" looking back at you? To be admired and appreciated is a natural and deep-seated human desire. That is why millions of products like toothpaste, creams, and deodorants are sold! The advertising promises acceptance, beauty, and popularity. In poll after poll, the personal wish that appears most often is the desire to be liked and accepted.

So, the experience of getting along well with others is no small matter. Is this an important skill that needs developing if we are to be effective and happy in relationships? Do we have any manufactured notions that may impede our relationships with others? If so, are we creating a division between ourselves and others? Could we be the ones to whom Jesus was speaking when he said, "If you love those who love you, what credit is that to you?" (Matthew 5:46). Is our love unselfish or selfish?

Mother Teresa says that love is the central point of our existence. She has written: "For this purpose we have been created: to love and to be loved." When the focus of life is on enthusiasm for discovery, diligence in research and concepts that expand our awareness of who and what we are, do our lives become more about giving and serving? When our focus is on unlimited love, do we

Possess a pure, kindly, and radiant heart,

that thine may be a sovereignty ancient,

imperishable, and everlasting.

—Bahá'u'lláh

release expectations of others? When we deal with people honestly and with kindness, faithfulness, and gentleness, are we sending a loving message that we care? When we are patient, humble, and

trustworthy, are others drawn to us by the sincerity of our being? As we encounter circumstances in life that reflect the quality of our deeper consciousness, are we contributing toward the uplifting of the planet and its people? What are other ways we can radiate positive attributes and send a message that we care?

Is unlimited intelligence reflected by the creation of the universe? Intelligence flows through everything in the universe and has been called by many names. We may not be able to see or hold this invisible intelligence, but are we willing to listen to the inner promptings that whisper to us that we are part of this intelligent system and that we are here for some divine reason? Could part of that divine reason be to reflect, to the best of our ability and understanding, sacred principle and noble purpose?

According to author Ernest Holmes, "Life is a mirror and will reflect back to the thinker what he thinks into it." From this perspective, what do we see? How do we appear to ourselves? Have we created the positive, loving image that will draw others to us? Every act of helping another is a way of saying "yes" to life. And saying "yes" is a profound form of successful behavior. When we meet someone, do we ask, "What makes this person special?" Do we look for the glow of that person's nature? Obviously, all of us have a variety of personality habits. Do we look for the good in another and fill our minds with happiness? Do we use our time fruitfully and avoid wasting precious moments? In our relations with others, do we exemplify the attribute of "promptness is politeness and consideration"? Do we "go the extra mile" or "give the extra ounce"? Do we have a reputation for reliability? Do we continually try to surpass ourselves?

✦ LAW 5

A smile breeds a smile. —Ted Engstrom

Wear a smile
and have friends;
wear a scowl and
have wrinkles.
What do we live for
if not to make the
world less difficult
for each other.
—George Eliot

A smile
costs nothing,
but gives much.
—American proverb

You are not fully
dressed until you
put on a smile.
—American proverb

Better by far you
should forget and
smile than that you
should remember
and be sad.
—Christina Georgina
Rossetti

THE SAYING "Smile and the world smiles with you; weep and you weep alone" expresses an effective truth. Everyone likes to be around a person who smiles easily and sincerely. Have you ever passed a stranger on the street and your eyes met and you smiled at each other? A simple action, perhaps, but didn't you feel a lift to your spirit afterward? Could this happen because a smile reaches down inside of us and pulls to the surface reasons for rejoicing in our lives? Can there be a connection between the spontaneous action of one person and the immediate thought response of another? How does such an invisible connection exist?

A smile is contagious. Could it be that a smile stirs "something" within that tells us we have been given a gift? In choosing to return a smile, are we saying "yes" to the other person, to life, and to ourselves? Consider the people you know who have a positive attitude, a sense of humor, and a happy perspective on life. Then, ask yourself how *you* fit this pattern. How many times have you smiled today? And what brought the smile to your heart and face?

A smile is a gift we can easily pass on to everyone we meet through the sincere effort of giving. It is a gift we can offer ourselves as well, and it can be triggered by a thought, an idea, or remembrances of happy times past. Living life with a smile has been compared to combining yeast into a bowl of flour, adding warm water, and waiting for the flour to rise to make bread. It multiplies many times over.

Most of us are drawn to those who respond to life in a positive manner. Do we prefer the company of the optimist rather than the company of the pessimist? Why is this? The optimist has faith in life and its opportunities. His smile reflects this faith and enthusiasm for living. On the other hand, the pessimist may think he has no reason to smile and lives his life from a different perspective and is often alone. Has the pessimist, on some unconscious level, chosen to ignore the many blessings offered by life?

An old man who lived alone in his house never smiled and didn't go too far from his own front door. One day, while talking to a neighbor in his yard, he complained that his eyesight had grown weak. When he looked out his window, he could hardly see the trees in his yard! The neighbor came to visit and noticed that the windowpanes were covered with dust and dirt. Wanting to be helpful, she cleaned the windows with soap and water. When she finished the job, the old man looked out the window and a smile lit up his face. He was delighted to find he could see as clearly as ever.

The neighbor smiled at his excitement and said, "Your eyesight was all right; your windows were dirty!"

Should we try never to allow the "windows" of our soul to get dirty and obscure our smile? A sincere smile from the heart can kindle little lights of love and service wherever we go.

When we learn to smile in the face of life's adversities, are we better equipped to overcome problems more effortlessly? Ella Wheeler Wilcox wrote:

> *'Tis easy enough to be pleasant,*
> *When life flows along like a song;*
> *But the man worth while is the one who will smile*
> *When everything goes dead wrong.*

There are three simple words that can be of tremendous assistance for developing a positive attitude in our lives. *Feel supremely happy!* When we focus on feeling supremely happy—regardless of outer appearances—our mind and body experience metamorphosis! Our thoughts, emotions facial expressions, health, attitudes—in fact, everything about us—improve. If we persist with this feeling and with thanksgiving until it becomes a vital part of our lives, could we experience greater harmony in all areas of life? Does living life with a smile enable us to perceive the joy of life, regardless of the situation or experience?

Although there may be times when it is inappropriate to giggle or laugh aloud, a genuine smile is never out of place. Can you think of times or places where the world could use a little more light and love? The smile we bring to a difficult life situation can infuse the challenge with the light of understanding and love, which attracts harmonious solutions. It may also inspire those around us to respond in a similar manner. Our smile makes a difference!

> What's the use of worrying? It never was worthwhile, so, pack up your troubles in your old kit bag, and smile, smile, smile.
> —George Asaf (George H. Powell)

Spotlights ◆ ◆

1. Opportunities occur many times in the course of a day for us to express love and compassion to others.

2. How could the energy of unlimited love be described as a healing balm for one's spirit, soul, body, and affairs?

3. Thanksgiving is an attitude of appreciation that centers on things for which to give thanks!

4. How do optimism and gratitude go hand in hand?

5. What are some of the results of living an appreciative life?

6. See all the good you can and bless the good you can see!

7. What does the statement "You cannot be lonely if you help the lonely" mean to you?

8. Loneliness cannot be overcome by *getting* something; it must be overcome by *giving* something.

9. Opportunities are limitless when one seeks to fill a need in humanity. What are some of your resources, inner and outer, that you can share with others?

10. A smile is contagious!

11. When you *feel supremely happy*, everything about and around you changes for the better!

Living the Various Spiritual Laws ◆ ◆

In the book *Essential Sufism*, the editors share interesting insights on the world as mirror of the divine:

There are two approaches to the world in almost every tradition. One is that heaven is separate from this world, accessible only after death. The other is that heaven, (and hell), are here right now.

The Sufis say that this world can be heaven—when we love and bless one another, serve one another, and become the instruments for one another's inner growth and salvation. This world can also be a hell—in which we experience pain, betrayal, loss of love, and lack of caring.

Both aspects of the world are part of the divine order. This world is a place to taste the nectar of paradise and also to feel the coals of hell . . . All the world's beauty reminds us of the supreme Artist. The love found all around us—between parents and children, between lovers—is a sign of the Beloved.

A Bedouin was once asked how he could believe so strongly in a God he could not see. The man replied, "If you see the tracks of a camel in the desert, do you have to wait to see the camel itself before believing it exists?"

This world is our mirror. It mirrors our faults and failings as well as the Divine within each of us. As one sheikh has said, "Every rose is the reflection of a smile or a kind word, and every thorn the result of an unkind word or action."

The task for the Sufi is to polish the mirror of oneself so that one can catch the reflection of heaven during life—unmisted, undistorted, and in all its glory

What are your perspectives on the material shared here?

Week Seven

✦ LAW I

Great heroes are humble. —John Marks Templeton

One of integral virtue never sets about grandiose things, yet he is able to achieve great things.
—*Lao Tzu*

Is HUMILITY vastly undervalued in our modern western culture? Many people consider pride and aggressive behavior as virtues and humility as a weakness. Could this be because the true meaning of "humility" isn't clearly understood? Is it possible that some people may, through lack of understanding, equate "humility" with being passive and long-suffering, and with having a sense of inferiority?

The true meaning of humility is realizing that the personal self is a vehicle of higher power. Jesus of Nazareth said, "It is not I, but the Father within that does the work" (John 14:10). Other spiritual leaders have also recognized that true genius contains a deep sense of personal humility. The great scientist Albert Einstein maintained a strong sense of humility and was known for his childlike simplicity. Walter Russell, a genius in many fields, remarked, "Until one learns to lose oneself, he cannot find himself. The personal ego must be dissolved and replaced by the universal ego."

By not putting your own importance first in worldly affairs, you will not impede the natural growth of all things.
—*Lao Tzu*

What is the difference between the universal ego and the personal ego? The personal ego may be what many people consider the bodily "self." It identifies with appearance, achievements, possessions, separateness, and personal opinions. It can be overly competitive, controlling, and may feel hurt or angry if it doesn't get what it wants. The

The greater you are, the more you practice humility.
—*Ben Sira*

personal ego often tries to solve problems through human effort without seeking assistance in spiritual wisdom. Could rigid creeds also be a form of personal ego?

The universal ego, the spiritual self, is an individualized center of divine consciousness. We often don't "see" this higher self because we may be blinded by identification with the self-centered ego. It's like trying to see the stars in the blaze of the midday sun. They are present in the universe, but obscured by the light of the sun. Only with the setting of the sun do we see these heavenly lights. As we become more willing to release the selfish ego, can we open the door to greater communication with the universal ego or Divine Spirit?

Could humility be the real basis for developing the spiritual life? Humility has been considered a gateway to greater understanding. Can humility mark the beginning of a process helping you to becoming more productive and open-minded? Could humility develop an awareness of consecrated oneness with all of humanity? When we establish a feeling of oneness with others, do we immediately expand our consciousness and spirituality and happiness?

In his teachings about the paths of discipline essential for those who sought to know God, Jalalu'ddin Rumi told the story of the three pearls.

When God created the pure body of Adam, he drew it out of the earth and breathed into it His sacred breath and said to Gabriel, "Take from the sea of My Omnipotence three pearls, place them on a plate of light, and present them to Adam so he can choose one." The three pearls were reason, faith, and humility.

Gabriel presented the plate to Adam and told him what God wanted. Adam, illumined by the divine light, chose the pearl of reason. Gabriel wanted to take back the plate with the two pearls it still held to the sea of Omnipotence; but, because of their heaviness, he did not have the strength to lift them. The pearls of faith and humility then said to him, "We cannot separate ourselves from the holy company of our friend Reason; without him, we cannot establish ourselves firmly or even exist. During ancient times we were all three the jewels of the mine of Divine Glory; the pearls of the Sea of Omnipotence are inseparable."

Then the voice of God rang out, "Gabriel, leave the two pearls where they are and return!" So Reason installed itself at the peak of the human intellect; faith lodged itself in Adam's pure and sensitive heart; and humility reigned on his holy face.

These three pearls are the heritage of the children of Adam. Every child descended from Adam who is not adorned by these three pearls and does not shine with their

brilliance is shut off from the Light and deprived of authentic gnosis.

If we desire to grow spiritually, how much of the personal ego must be transcended by the divine universal ego? Do we become clearer channels for unlimited love and divine wisdom when we are not self-centered? Can there ever be a "loss" when we move to a higher level of usefulness and awareness? Or is growth simply taking place? How can learning to be humble lead to greatness in our lives? When a person truly has something to offer to the world, does that person become more humble? Through increasing daily awareness, could we discover that humility is its own reward? Does acknowledging humbly that we know only a little of God's truth indicate we are agnostic? If a medical doctor can admit, with an open mind, that no one has yet understood all diseases, symptoms, and cures, can we humbly admit we need to search for over one-hundred-fold more spiritual information? Through humility, we can begin to gain a deeper and truer perspective of the creative process, of our place in it, and of ways we can help.

✦ LAW 2

Love given grows; love hoarded dwindles. —John Marks Templeton

THE RICH VARIETY of world religions creates a tapestry of amazing beauty—a testimony to the essential spiritual nature of our human visit on earth. And yet, within this amazing and sometimes fascinating diversity can be found an equally amazing unity. Could the basis for this unity be agape love? Agape love means feeling and expressing pure unlimited love for every human being with no exception. It gives of itself and expects nothing in return. Can you imagine what our

world could be like if developing such divine ability was a goal for the people of our world? Does agape love come closest to describing the kind of love with which the Creator loves his creatures?

Among the greatest legacies of *Judaism* has been its focus on fulfilling responsibilities and duties. In this instance, agape becomes more than a warm feeling: it is also action. It entails being true to God, to the Ten Commandments, and to the responsibilities toward family and neighbor as set

What does the Lord require of you, but to do justice, love and kindness, and to walk humbly with your God?
—Micah 6:8

I met a hundred men on the road to Delhi, and they were all my brothers.
—Indian proverb

forth in these eternal precepts. It means turning to goodness, truth, mercy, and charity to direct our actions. Agape affirms living an ethical life according to the highest of traditions. The reality of love lives within all of us and often is found in that "still, small voice," of our sacred self.

Agape in the *Christian* context also means loving our enemies. In his Sermon on the Mount, Jesus told the people, "You have heard that it was said 'You shall love your neighbor and hate your enemy.' But I say to you, love your enemies and pray for those who persecute you." Christian love is not an isolated action; rather, it is a way of life, a habit in search of constant expression. No time for agape is too soon. No setting for agape is inappropriate. No recipient of agape is unworthy. Such is the nature of unlimited love eternal.

One does not have to look far to discover the call to agape in the *Islamic* context. The opening chapter of the Qur'an, in two of the first three lines, refers to Allah as "the Merciful, the compassionate." Indeed, mercy and compassion are primary manifestations of God, and followers of God are called upon to embrace these characteristics. Islam teaches that love for God is corroborated through love for neighbors and that it is impossible for those who do evil to love God.

The *Hindu* religion provides a basic rationale for the ethic prescribed by The Golden Rule, for it teaches that all reality is ultimately one in being and in function. Because all human beings are in some sense one and, indeed, because all of creation is one, the only way to treat others is with respect, kindness, justice, and compassion. Hindu spirituality recognizes that there is meaning beyond the individual self and beyond material possessions and earthly pleasures. This emphasis does not come at the expense of agape love, but rather as a supplement to it. In the Hindu context, agape is a by-product of *bhakti* yoga, the realization of God through love.

In a sense, the religion of *Buddhism* was born out of agape, out of a willingness to sacrifice on behalf of the suffering people of the world. Buddhists who are in touch with their religious heritage reflect the moral qualities of compassionate caring; they are full of love and are ready to sacrifice selfish desire for the benefit of others. Would it not be wonderfully beneficial for all of us to learn these spiritual values?

Seeing agape love in the *Tao* is like trying to separate a wave from the ocean. It is difficult to see either agape or the wave as separate from the whole. It is the source, the named and the unnamed, the first cause. The Taoist concept of agape love begins with an effort to address what is wrong. To the Taoist, addressing what is wrong is not so much a question of efficient problem solving as it is a matter of the heart.

To many people worldwide, the name *Confucius* is virtually synonymous with "wisdom." His was

Listen to the still, small voice.
It tells us to follow in the ways of holiness.
And asks us to sanctify our days with kindness.
The still, small voice is not in the wind, the shaking of the earth or in fire. The still, small voice is heard in the hearts of those who listen.
—Esta Cassway, adapted from 1 Kings 19:11—12

wisdom deeply rooted in love and respect for others. Does the world need more of this great wisdom? Some people treat love like a quantity that can be exhausted. They are careful not to use it up, perhaps in not loving others for fear there may be none left for family and friends. Agape, however, is unlimited. It cannot be "used up." In fact, to Confucius, agape was quite the opposite—the more we love, the more capable we become of loving.

Agape love is a deliberate choice that each of us can make. It resembles an exercise program. When a person signs up for a program like running or lifting weights, persistence and perseverance are necessary to successfully recognize the many benefits.

The same can be true of increasing our ability to love in an unlimited way. We "exercise" every day and, as we do, we become increasingly able to develop a habit of loving unconditionally and in an unlimited manner. Love given grows; love hoarded dwindles!

What could be the benefits if we no longer said "Hello" or "How are you?" as a greeting, but always said instead a simple "I love you"?

✦ LAW 3

Find good in everything. —John Marks Templeton

Life is like riding a bicycle. You don't fall off unless you stop pedaling.
—*Claude Pepper, former U.S. Congressman*

Those who wish to sing always find a song.
—*Swedish proverb*

Life is what we make it, always has been, always will be.
—*Grandma Moses*

IF A PERSON looks at the world in a narrow way, how narrow it seems! On the other hand, if a person looks at the world with a broad, generous, and friendly attitude, then everything seems to be lighter, lovelier, and more fulfilling. The optimistic person's life seems more progressive and useful. Have you ever noticed how some people seem to be happy regardless of what may be happening? Buoyancy beams from their spirit and a sparkle dances in their eyes! A wondrous glow radiates from their faces, their words sparkle with ideas and enthusiasm, and even their movements reflect joy, grace, and excitement.

There are others who seem to live in perpetual clouds of unhappiness or pessimism and reflect an attitude of gloomy, negative thoughts. Reginald B. Mansell, a business executive, remarked: "A pessimist is one who makes difficulties of his opportunities; an optimist is one who makes opportunities of his difficulties." Have you noticed that most great endeavors have an optimist at their helm? Could this be in part because a negative life dwells on problems, while an optimistic life promotes remedies?

Success depends to a great degree upon an optimistic and enthusiastic attitude. For example, think of yourself as a water faucet. If the faucet is completely open, the water flows through from the source and expresses a blessing to the person who drinks it or to the garden that needs it. If the faucet is turned off or is only slightly opened, then not much happens. Where is our focus? Where are we putting our attention?

A schoolteacher was driving home from work when he saw a Little League baseball game being played in a park near his home. Intrigued by the excited yells of the children, he stopped to watch the game. After seating himself behind the bench near home plate, he asked one of the children what the score was.

"Well, right now, we're behind six to nothing," was the enthusiastic reply.

"Really?" the teacher responded. "You don't look very discouraged."

"Oh, no, Sir," replied the Little Leaguer. "We haven't had our turn at bat yet!"

A successful and fruitful life can depend on how wisely and purposefully we utilize the twenty-four hours of each day. Can you find ways to make each day an adventure in living? Can you see the good in affirming that each day can be a life-enhancing seminar? As our lives become more productive, richer, and more interesting, we also become more interesting to others. To reach out and try something new is to accentuate the positive. Can you see how a successful person continues reaching for and experiencing new ideas, new goals, and new things? When you have a goal and begin to fulfill it, can you imagine the sense of accomplishment you can feel?

Now, what happens if our thoughts are not always positive and light-filled as we move toward our goal? First, don't worry! We keep moving and practice cheerfulness along the way. We pay attention to what is in front of us and find something there to appreciate! Most people's lives are a combination of positive and negative experiences. When we focus on the good that's already present, we feel better and life goes more smoothly. If we don't, it doesn't! Either way, life goes on! How would you describe focus, faith, and persistence as shaping our experiences?

Have you considered how seeing the good in everything and everyone can be an effective tool to bring family members and friends into a closer bond of greater love and harmony? How does speaking well of others and avoiding gossip help in "seeing the good in everything and every one?" Consider making a list of other areas of life where you can practice seeing the good. Some starters could be: reading inspirational literature, avoiding making comparisons, welcoming changes and the opportunity to try a new path, traveling more, and setting aside time each day for prayer and planning.

When we light a candle in the darkness that illuminates our life and the lives of those around us, that very light can lead us to our goals.

◆ LAW 4

What the mind can conceive, it may achieve. —Anonymous

IT HAS BEEN wisely said that each of us is the ruler of the greatest "nation" on earth—our imagi-"nation!" We are constantly creating mental images about our work, play, family, friends, associates, in fact, life in general. Do we have a choice regarding how we use our innate capacity to imagine? Yes, of course we do! Is imagination different from wishful thinking? Yes, it has often been referred to as the faculty of the mind that forms images. Does our imagination have the power to shape and form thought? Through using the faculty of our imagination, can we clothe our ideas with the vital mental energy necessary to bring them to fulfillment? Psychologists, philosophers, ministers, and others have often described imagination as one of the strongest powers of the mind. And perhaps you have heard the proverb, "What the mind can conceive, it may achieve."

Imagination has also been called "the cutting scissors of the mind" that shapes our heart's desire—the picturing power of the mind. Can you "imagine" the incredible impact this picture power applies to an idea? How does this work? If you

hold an image or picture of a desired goal in your thoughts daily, are you providing your mind with a creative opportunity to be productive?

In his book *You'll See It When You Believe It*, Wayne Dyer describes how his thoughts have always created his world. He tells about watching a favorite television program and picturing himself as a guest on that particular show. He practiced talking with the show's host and actually worked on routines he could use as a guest. Most of these "guest appearances" centered around his belief that he could chose his own destiny and he could make people laugh! Dr. Dyer described telling his friends about his ideas, how they would humor him and then direct the conversation to something more "realistic." However, his internal pictures were never damaged by the attitudes of others. He said, "For as long as I can remember, I have been able to enter this world of 'pure thought,' and it is as real for me as the world of form is to all of us."

You may recall seeing pictures of carvings on the walls of caves placed there by prehistoric man. He may have believed if he frequently looked at these pictures, an unseen power would bring food in the form of finding game, fish, or fowl. The Egyptians also used the picturing power of the mind to produce intricate artwork in the tombs of their pharaohs. When a royal child was born, in many cases his tomb was immediately started. In this tomb, pictures were painted depicting the many happy and victorious experiences the child would have throughout his life. The people of Greece often surrounded their prospective mothers with elegant statues, beautiful pictures, and lush scenery so that the unborn children would receive the benefits of health and beauty from the mind-pictures of the mother!

How do we direct our imagination to work for us? The French philosopher Simone Weil wrote,

> The primary imagination I hold to be the living power and prime agent of all human perception, and as a repetition in the finite mind of the eternal act of creation in the infinite I Am.
>
> —*Samuel Taylor Coleridge*

"Imagination and fiction make up more than three-quarters of our real life!" And American athlete Muhammad Ali said, "A man who has no imagination has no wings!" How important is it to be clear and concise in our picturing thoughts? This could be an excellent time to pause and ask some questions of ourselves. Am I thinking clearly, definitively, and wisely? Am I taking one step at a time in diligent progression? Am I staying on purpose toward my goal? Am I creating positive or negative picture patterns? Will what I am doing produce greater good for myself and for others?

The human mind is a remarkable creative tool. Could the faculty of imagination be a springboard for human activity and a principle source for human improvement? Could imagination be a little understood essence of progress? Is our imagination the seat of "divine discontent" that prevents us from ever being satisfied with our present condition or with past achievements?

Successful people frequently use the faculty of imagination to assist them in achieving useful results. Many stories are told about people from all walks of life who applied creative visualization techniques to help achieve their goals. Training programs designed to promote success in the work environment often emphasize positive imaging as a prime technique that produces results.

Being strong in our application of mental principles, if our mental image is a noble purpose, can be a fruitful act of humility. It is important to acknowledge the spiritual principle of the highest good for all involved. In other words, "Not my will, but Thine be done!"

✦ LAW 5

Be steadfast in prayer. —Qur'an

Prayer is the most powerful form of energy a person can generate.
—*William L. Fischer*

Prayer focuses thought on God the way a compass keeps its needle turned on North.
—*James Dillet Freeman*

When we pray we link ourselves with an inexhaustible motive power.
—*Alexis Carrel*

NO ONE REALLY KNOWS when, where, or how prayer began. Almost two thousand years ago, Plutarch, the Greek biographer and historian, was impressed by this fact. He observed, "If we traverse the world, it is possible to find cities without walls, without letters, without wealth, without coin, without schools or theaters; but a city without a temple, or that practices not worship, prayers, and the like, no one has ever seen."

Is the foundation of an active and healthy spiritual life established through developing a greater awareness of divine presence? And is there any better way to comprehend this realization than to start and maintain a "conversation" with that inner presence? Could there be a better way of life than to bring ourselves into a growing awareness of oneness with the infinity of divinity?

Most people throughout the world are convinced there exists a divine *power* of some sort, but are not sure of what it is. Nor do they know how to become helpers in accelerating the divine, eternal, infinite creativity. Some people could have a similar thought and feeling about the nuances of prayer. There are many kinds of prayers and many ways of praying. Scientists are now beginning to research the varieties, causes, and benefits of prayers.

Prayer has been described as being a concerted effort for the physical consciousness to become attuned to the *consciousness* of the Creator, either collectively, or individually. Some people have called prayer a "spontaneous conversation with God," an "attitude of the heart," while others refer to prayer as "getting in harmony with the Creator's purpose."

Since the beginning of time, prayer, in some form, has been observed in every culture recorded and studied by humanity. Could this be because the desire to attune oneself toward a higher intellect is an innate part of the human soul? As we grow from childhood to adulthood and our lives become more complex and our concerns more encompassing, prayer often becomes a source of strength. The Scripture guideline, "pray without ceasing," may be forgotten. When thoughts and feelings become self-centered, we may lose sight of our ideal and a state of disharmony results. This is an excellent time to refuse to be misled by appearances and to turn to sincere prayer for guidance.

The four words "Thy will be done" are probably the most difficult yet the most important part of any prayer. In C. S. Lewis's book *Letter to Malcolm: Chiefly on Prayer*, he notes that "Thy will be done" doesn't necessarily mean we must submit to disagreeable things that God has in store for us. Rather, there is a great deal more of the Creator's purpose to be accomplished! Does this petition, then, focus on both experiencing and expressing the Creator's purpose? Lewis also notes the human tendency to overlook the present good the universe offers us because we may have been expecting something else!

The inner spirit is constantly attempting to reach our minds with spiritual blessings. Prayer opens us up and enlarges our ability to be receptive and productive. So, could we affirm that prayer makes us more sensitive to spiritual guidance? And through prayer, is our disposition more able to receive spiritual energy? Does prayer become *more* effective when we are dedicated to *acting* on the spiritual insights we may have gained within times of prayer? Does prayer, then, become *most* effective when it results in noble human decision-making and growth?

In his book *My Favorite Quotations*, Norman Vincent Peale wrote this about prayer: "If you want to utilize the matchless power of prayer, begin praying immediately and continue at every opportunity. I have observed from a number of inquiries that the average person probably spends about five minutes a day in prayer. That is one-half of 1 percent of one's waking hours. . . . If you want to experience the heady energy of prayer, practice it often."

Prayer does not eliminate problems from occurring in our lives. However, it does provide us with a powerful spiritual tool to overcome tough situations. In fact, the person who has developed the habit of steadfast prayer can calmly and effectively take on any challenging new situation. From this perspective, does prayer heighten our sense of responsibility to review the problems of our world courageously? Are human industry and ingenuity positive side effects of a prayerful consciousness? So, when we wholeheartedly, "pray without ceasing" (1 Thessalonians 5:17), do we allow prayer to assist us in the privilege of assuming greater responsibility in the service of God and man? The heart that reaches out and touches the Creator taps a limitless reservoir of the universal spiritual substance created by the spirit. Our times of prayer are truly "food for the soul."

Spotlights ◆ ◆

1. Could humility be the real basis for developing the spiritual life?

2. Humility can provide a deeper and truer perspective of the creative process and our place in it.

3. Agape love means feeling and expressing pure unlimited love for every human being with no exception.

4. Agape love is a deliberate choice that each of us can make.

5. Pay attention to what is before you and find something there to appreciate!

6. When we light a candle in the darkness that illuminates our lives and the lives of those around us, that very light can lead us to our goals.

7. Could the faculty of imagination be a springboard for human activity and a principle source for human improvement?

8. Imagination has been called "the cutting scissors of the mind." Why? *change*

9. In your own words, how would you describe prayer? *Being w/ God —*

10. How can the Scripture guideline "pray without ceasing" be utilized in your daily life? *Being alive*

11. How is prayer a powerful assist to working with difficult situations?

12. How is the affirmation "Thy will be done" an open door for greater awareness and gratitude in any situation?

Communion

Living the Various Spiritual Laws ✦ ✦

The following story, "The Sincere Penitent," is a selection from the *Mathnawi* of Jalalu'ddin Rumi, translated by Reynold A. Nicholson. The stories in the *Mathnawi* primarily consider the problems and speculations bearing on the conduct, use, and meaning of life. As you read this story, how could you parallel some of the ideas presented in this week's essays with the characters and precepts of the story?

A man was going to attend the Friday prayers. He saw people leaving the mosque and asked one of them why they were departing so early.

He replied, "The Prophet has prayed with the congregation and finished his worship. How art thou going in,
O foolish person, after the Prophet has given his blessing?"

"Alas!" he cried; and it seemed as though the smell of his heart's blood issued, like smoke, from that burning sigh.

One of the congregation said, "Give me this sigh, and all my prayers are thine."

He answered, "I give thee the sigh and accept thy prayers." The other took the sigh that was so full of regret and longing.

At night, whilst he was asleep, a Voice said to him, "Thou hast brought the Water of Life and Salvation."

For the sake of that which thou hast chosen, the prayers of all the people have been accepted.

✦

Week Eight

◆ LAW 1

With God all things are possible. —Matthew 19:26

A YOUNG MAN on crutches who had been stricken with infantile paralysis was asked the question, "With a misfortune such as yours, how can you face the world so confidently and enthusiastically?" His instantaneous reply was, "Oh, easily! The disease didn't affect my heart! *And with God all things are possible!*" This young man had confidence in himself and in a *guiding inner power.* He mentally overcame a tough life situation and developed spiritual confidence. With spiritual confidence, the young man did not live a frustrated existence, but worked to develop his talents and abilities to the point where life was rewarding to him.

Can we reflect on how results in our personal world may be an expression of an idea, an opinion, or a concept? Can we see these elements as expressions of our consciousness? When our focus is on spiritual ideals, do we reflect a stronger, inner confidence that can pave the way for a fruitful life? If our focus is on outer appearances, believing material things can determine our health, wealth, and happiness, could our confidence be shaken and our way of life become uncertain?

In his book *Positive Thoughts for Successful Living,* Rev. Jim Lewis writes, "Growing up spiritually is a process of bringing forth order out of chaos. Divine Order is thinking, feeling, and acting in harmony with God's good plan and purpose for our life. It is working with His laws to bring forth the good He has for us. For every mess we get ourselves into, there is a plan to get us out. It is the good plan bringing release and freedom." What are some ways we can think, feel, and act as a spiritual being with inherent powers of creativity? How may we, as diligent individuals, utilize this power to be what we want to be, to do what we want to do, and to go where we wish to go? We may not have all the answers at any given time; however, we can discover a new relationship to life with this creative power.

Connecting with divine energy can be compared to tuning a radio dial to a powerful broadcasting station. The transmitting station is constantly emitting a clear, concise signal. Some radios pick up this signal and give off good, clear sound. Other radios may not be picking up the broadcast signal well, so the broadcast from that radio isn't as clear. If we are having problems receiving a good quality "sound," what do we need to do? Can we improve our "reception" by fine-tuning our "radio" to the broadcast station?

The world abounds with meaningful stories of wondrous connections between individuals and the divine. Many of these stories endure for long periods of time. Their truths stir the minds of people of all ages and speak effectively to the heart as nothing else can. So it is that great teachers such as Jesus, Buddha, Allah, Manu, Krishna, Mahatma Gandhi, Vaswani, Rumi, and others told stories to enlighten their followers. The stories of the great teachers are inspiring. Their wisdom is refreshing, and their truth beckons us to follow their guidance. Many of these stories carry the theme, "With God all things are possible." May the three included here bring you inspiration, introspection, wisdom, purpose, and love.

THE SAINTLY MERCHANT

Bahram was a wealthy merchant. Every year his caravans carried goods worth millions of dollars for sale to foreign lands. One day, robbers looted his caravans and Bahram lost several million dollars. One of his friends came to sympathize with him in his great loss. Because it was a time of famine, Bahram thought his friend had come in the hope of getting something to eat. Bahram asked the servant to prepare a meal. But the friend said, "I don't need any food. I came to sympathize with you in your loss."

Bahram said, "It is kind of you to come. But I'm not fretting about what has happened. I feel grateful to God that though the robbers looted my goods, I have looted none! Although the robbers stole a portion of my perishable wealth, they have not touched the Treasure Imperishable, the treasure of faith in Allah, the Compassionate. That is the true treasure of life!"

Tribulations can draw out the best that is in you. Do not run away from them, but greet them as friends. They will not sting you. They will lead you from success to greater success.

—told by J. P. Vaswani to his students in India

STRIKE ON THIS SPOT

Dhun-Nun the Egyptian explained graphically in a parable how he extracted knowledge concealed in Pharaonic inscriptions.

There was a statue with pointing finger, upon which was inscribed: "Strike on this spot for treasure." Its origin was unknown, but generations of people had hammered the place marked by the sign. Because it was made of the hardest stone, little impression was made on it, and the meaning remained cryptic.

Dhun-Nun, wrapped in contemplation of the statue, one day exactly at midday observed that the shadow of the pointing finger, unnoticed for centuries, followed a line in the paving beneath the statue.

Marking the place, he obtained the necessary instruments and prized up by chisel-blows the flagstone, which proved to be the trapdoor in the roof of a subterranean cave which contained strange articles of a workmanship which enabled him to deduce the science of their manufacture, long since lost, and hence to acquire the treasures and those of a more formal kind which accompanied them.

—excerpted from *The Tales of the Dervishes*

HE WAS IN NO OTHER PLACE

Cross and Christians, end to end, I examined. He was not on the Cross. I went to the Hindu temple, to the ancient pagoda. In none of them was there any sign. To the uplands of Herat I went, and to Kandahar. I looked. He was not on the heights or in the lowlands. Resolutely, I went to the summit of the [fabulous] mountain of Kaf. There only was the dwelling of the [legendary] Anqa bird. I went to the Kaaba of Mecca. He was not there. I asked about him from Avicenn, the philosopher. He was beyond the range of Avicenna.... I looked into my own heart. In that, his place, I saw him. He was in no other place.

—Jalalu'ddin Rumi

✦ Law 2

I shall allow no man to belittle my soul by making me hate him. —Booker T. Washington

WHO DOES hate change? What conditions does hate improve? The answers to these questions may be surprising. Hate, like prayer, can change the person involved in the activity, while the person who may be the target of the hate can be unaffected. If a person kicks a brick wall that is before him, he is the one who gets hurt, not the wall! Hate doesn't change the person to whom this energy is directed. In this context, it may diminish the person doing the hating!

For example, could an energy that begins as hate be redirected to reverse the direction toward learning the joy of unlimited love? Does a redirection of our attitudes by applying wisdom to the natural impulse of hating make it more beneficial than dangerous? In his book *Your Four Great Emotions*, David Seabury states, "In trying to understand hate and turn it into something useful— which it is not impossible to do—a most important principle relating to emotion should become common knowledge: the fact that most of the expression of hate is the result of fear . . . If we do not know that it is largely fear that makes us hate, we can be constantly acting unjustly without realizing it."

Certainly, we can individually control our personal outlook on life as well as our attitudes. We are gifted by the Creator with the tool of decision, our power of choice. The power to choose is a most enlivening human characteristic. So, could choosing to do research and education in the area of thought control benefit each individual and help us build a life that is safe, sane, and more productive? How can greater research and diligence

help us direct our emotions in positive and productive ways?

African American educator Booker T. Washington was keenly aware of the power of choice when he said, "I shall allow no man to belittle my soul by making me hate him." In his early years, Washington lived in poverty so severe that he went to work at the age of nine. He could easily have blamed his situation on difficult circumstances and

I have often thought that the best way to define a man's character would be to seek out the particular mental or moral attitude in which, when it came upon him, he felt most deeply and intensely active and alive. At such moments, there is a voice inside which speaks and says: "This is the real me!"
—William James

used these as an excuse for hatred. Instead, he managed to harness his energies and channel them into improving his personal life and that of others.

Booker T. Washington worked as a janitor to obtain an education—the method he believed would lead to self-improvement and eventual improvement of conditions for humankind. Rather than viewing himself as a victim of difficult circumstances, he took command of his life. After graduation, he accepted a position as the head of a new school for black people at Tuskegee, Alabama. The challenges inherent in a major new project—little money, no equipment, lack of appropriate buildings, etc.—did not deter a man with a goal and the determination to obtain that goal.

Rather than wasting valuable energies in unproductive arguments or resentments, he directed his inspiration and enthusiasm to fulfill a vision of education for many. Booker T. Washington allowed no man to belittle his soul because he remained responsible for his inward self. He knew that only he could control his inner being.

✦ LAW 3

Do your allotted task! Work excels idleness! —*Bhagavad Gita*

A BELOVED TEACHER once said, "Anything worth doing is worth doing well." There's a definite practicality as well as essential wisdom in this statement. If we're going to take the time and exert the effort to accomplish a particular task, wouldn't it make sense to utilize our time and energy wisely and productively? Wouldn't putting forth anything less than our full attention and best effort be a waste of valuable resources? Being the best in a single career can be more helpful than being second-best in several areas.

If we were to search for a dominant factor within ourselves that could represent us as unique individuals, what would we find? What characteristic could *individualize* an essence of what we are, and fortify us in the life process? If your name was mentioned among a group of friends, what trait or traits would they use to describe you? You might hear comments like, "She gives 100 percent of herself to whatever she does." "Give him the job and it will be done thoroughly and completely!" "She is a totally committed person!" Or, "He uses his talents wisely and effectively and with so much enthusiasm!" Comments of this kind speak of a life being lived fully and usefully. There is no waste of precious energies.

How can we lay a stronger foundation upon which to develop and build our talents and abilities? And what talents can we build? Constantly looking for ways to grow and become a better person is one "building block." Developing natural talents and abilities can offer possibilities for new vocations or can enlarge our present work. Another "tool" can be surrounding ourselves with quality people. These would be people who are industrious, honest, humble, have integrity, and can help us grow mentally and spiritually. We enhance our abilities by associating with people whose actions and beliefs we respect and admire. A lot can be learned from these experts.

Also, we can make important decisions based on open-minded, diligent research, rather than on popular trends. We learn to make more fruitful choices in life and to achieve better appreciation of people when we look beyond the surface elements. Being open to the ever-unfolding glory and wisdom of the universe can spark enthusiasm and excitement for life's possibilities. As we learn to respect the variety of the universe as it manifests around us, how could we not be touched by *humility*?

O Son of Man! I loved thy creation, hence I created thee. Wherefore, do thou love Me, that I may name thy name and fill thy soul with the spirit of life."
—*Bahá'u'lláh*

Fear of making mistakes can cause a person to hesitate. However, if we allow ourselves to become immobilized by a preoccupation of what might happen, we may deprive ourselves of many opportunities to move forward, invent, create, or try new things. Can precious time be lost through procrastination? Can fear be an excuse not to try? Can we accept that mistakes may come with various endeavors? But would not the greatest mistake be to not engage or fully participate in life? Can we study the lessons gleaned from past mistakes and use them to inspire wisdom for our future decisions and actions? Could humanity have achieved all that it has in the past century without some trial and error? Can we also think of situations where a person, giving full attention to research and discovery, made a real difference?

What are some ways that our productivity can be enhanced? Are we not more productive when we are purposeful, enthusiastic, and maintain a personal feeling of well-being? And, when we are engaged in doing something we enjoy, does not this creativity make our life more fruitful?

An idle life is a wasted life. A life without purpose is a life wasted. How can purpose produce productivity? Gary Moore, author of several books integrating spirituality and wealth management, says, "Research, plan, and analyze. Learning to look before you leap will not stop you from enjoying life, but will help you avoid unnecessary worry. There is something to be said for spontaneity—it certainly can add spice and a bit of the unexpected to life. But for major life-changing decisions, doing some preplanning is not only helpful, but essential. You cannot know what curves life is going to throw you, but you can prepare for many eventualities by arming yourself with good information."

Learning discernment is an important step in becoming a more responsible person. Through research, education, observation, and spiritual guidance we can learn to evaluate the essential aspects of every situation. Doing this requires taking a panoramic view of the whole situation, not just the part that may be easiest to deal with. This open-minded research and diligence can help us make the best possible choice, whether it is a job, a relationship, or a spiritual path. Once the direction is decided, can we make every minute count by giving our full attention and best effort? "Halfway attention wastes your life!"

◆ LAW 4

Enthusiasm is contagious. —John Marks Templeton

THE MAGNIFICENt sculptor and artist Michelangelo is credited with creating forty-four statues in his lifetime. Most people are familiar with some of the ones he finished—*David*, the *Pieta*, and *Moses*, to name a few. However, did you realize he only finished fourteen of his sculptures? And the thirty pieces Michelangelo didn't complete are quite interesting. For example, in one piece of marble, a person may see a sculptured elbow or the beginning of a wrist. The rest of the human form is still locked up in the marble. Another piece of marble shows a leg with the thigh, knee, calf, heel, and foot clearly chiseled out of the hard stone, but the rest of the body remains frozen inside.

Upon viewing these unfinished masterpieces in a museum in Italy, a person might think, "What a

The most severe bankruptcy is the soul that has lost its enthusiasm.
—Rebecca Clark

tragedy these pieces were never completed!" and continue on his journey. But wait a moment! Are you and I and all others not unfolding masterpieces in the hands of a master sculptor? We are "in the process of becoming" in this journey of life. Becoming what? What tremendous, unexplored possibilities are still encased within us?

There are always greater things we can do. When we may be tempted to stop along the path of life and enjoy the view, we should do it! We must never lose an opportunity for seeing something beautiful. But don't stand and stare too long! Give thanks for the blessing, then step forward and move on to new and greater heights. A world of joyousness and enthusiasm, of wonder and delight, unfolds all around us. As we liberate our imaginations and unleash our enthusiasm, who knows what can be accomplished?

Nothing great was ever achieved without enthusiasm.
—Ralph Waldo Emerson

In his book *Reach Out for New Life*, Dr. Robert Schuller wrote a little story in an effort to capture the meaning of enthusiasm:

Enthusiasm produces energy, and energy is life and power.
—Charles Roth

Enthusiasm is that mysterious something that turns an average person into an outstanding individual. It lifts us from fatigue to energy. It pulls us up from mediocrity to excellence. It turns on a bright light in our life until our face glows and our eyes sparkle. It's a spiritual magnet that draws happy people to us. It's a joyful fountain that bubbles and causes people to come to our side and share their joy. Out of this fountain there leaps self-confidence that shouts to the world, "I can! It's possible! Let's go!"

Enthusiasm is the long sought-after fountain of youth. . . . Drink from this fountain of enthusiasm, and you will experience a miracle. Discouragement will fade away like the morning's fog in the noonday sun. Suddenly, you will start laughing, whistling, singing, and you know you are a child of God. Enthusiasm—when someone offers it to you, take it, especially if you don't want it.

What a way to live! To live is to create. While consciously creating, how can we move in harmony with life and participate enthusiastically with divine creative power? The individual who takes up any useful activity as a positive adventure can inspire a similar attitude in others. In what ways can the person who enjoys his work and looks for new ways to be enthusiastic about it set the stage for others to follow his example? If we assume our tasks with enthusiasm, will those around us likely catch the spirit? Whatever a person does, for good or ill, can be contagious. A smile can be contagious, and so can a frown.

So, how do we experience real joy and enthusiasm? Perhaps becoming genuinely outgoing is one way. Could developing an attitude of goodwill be another? Or, how about making goodwill even stronger by allowing it to become unlimited love for all people? Many people desire to live a good life of physical strength and health, mental interest, moral and ethical values, and spiritual purpose. Is a "good life" partly based on a definitive value system in which joy and enthusiasm serve as both cause and effect?

The word "enthusiasm" is derived from the Greek and Latin words meaning "possessed by God."

To be properly expressed, a thing must proceed from within, moved by its form.
—Meister Eckhart

✦ LAW 5

Small attempts repeated will complete any undertaking. —Og Mandino

A YOUNG WOMAN tells the story about when she was a little girl. Her father, an artist, would be busy at his easel, mixing oils and painting on his canvases. She often sat nearby on the floor, working just as busily with her own set of crayons and a coloring book. Many a time, her father would set his brushes aside, reach down, and lift her up on his lap. Then he would curl her little hand around one of his brushes, enfolding it with his own larger and stronger hand. Ever so gently, he would guide her hand and the brush, dipping it into the palette and mixing the burnt umbers and raw siennas. Then he would stroke the wet, shiny paint onto the canvas before them.

The little girl watched in amazement as they painted something beautiful together. Possibly this loving father hoped that he was giving his daughter skills that would bring great fulfillment to her life. Today, that little girl, Joni Tada—a quadriplegic since a diving accident during her teen years—is still painting. However, now she holds the paintbrush in her mouth! Much of her earnings as an artist are channeled into ministry to help others. Her compassion is a reflection of that shown her by a loving, tender father.

Who can count the number of the small attempts made by Joni and her father that brought success to her artistry! The more we work toward improving something—a talent, a goal, a job, a relationship, whatever—the more success we achieve toward that purpose. Step-by-step we progress. If we are able to articulate our own sense of purpose, have we moved, to a degree, along the avenue of transcending self and reached out toward all humanity?

Years ago, the song "Little Things Mean A Lot" was quite popular. That theme remains important for living in today's world. Whether we seek to advance from turmoil to peace, from fear to love, from study to creativity, from striving to arriving, the small things along the way often propel us forward, one experience at a time, toward our goals. How have some of the "little things" in your life paved the way for greater things?

Do you remember memorizing the multiplication tables in school? How did you begin? With the first table—one times one equals one—and you continued all the way through the tables. How many times did you repeat the first table until it came easily and readily to your mind? Then you moved on to the second table, and so on. This is a good example of "small attempts repeated will complete any undertaking!" Through practice and repetition, undertakings of increasing complexity can be accomplished.

Life has often been called the schoolroom for spiritual wealth. Could the "small" experiences of life serve as a training ground to teach us to be alert to the opportunities that knock at our door? We are seldom presented with challenges we cannot meet, with obstacles we cannot overcome, or with problems that cannot be solved. Is approaching each situation with a positive attitude and proceeding to take one step at a time an effective way to reach a solution? Can you see the value of consistent daily application of attitudes and activities that serve to fulfill our goals?

Spotlights ✦ ✦

1. The impossible is the untried!

2. How may we utilize our inherent powers of creativity?

3. A wise person avoids negative emotions and destructive activities.

4. How does practicing unlimited love help us become more "awake"?

5. "They are never alone that are accompanied with noble thoughts" (Sir Philip Sidney).

6. "Success is a journey, not a destination, and half the fun is getting there!" (Wayne Dyer).

7. Can we remain strong in our values although opposition may be persuasive?

8. What tremendous unexplored possibilities are still encased within each of us?

9. If we assume our tasks with enthusiasm, will those around us likely catch the spirit?

10. How do we experience real joy and enthusiasm?

11. Step-by-step we progress.

12. How do the "little things" in life help advance us to the greater things?
    And how would we describe "greater things"?

> Practice is the best
> of all instructions.
> —Aristotle

Living the Various Spiritual Laws ✦ ✦

Positive mental qualities are frequently referred to as the "builders" of our advancement along the journey of life. We often hear the phrase, "our thoughts define our universe." Indeed, our thinking acts upon our lives in profound ways. Portraits of advanced mental development often underscore the point that there is little process of self-actualization without a well-trained mind. It is not only *what* we think, but also *how* we think that powerfully determines the patterns of our life. In his book *What We May Be*, Piero Ferrucci offers several attributes of a well-functioning mind. Could these attributes be interesting check points for us?

A well-functioning mind:

✦ *Can concentrate at will and examine in depth any given topic, even in distracting situations.*

✦ *Can organize ideas, memories, and images in inner files, which can be consulted instantly.*

✦ *Can become conscious of the grooves it is functioning in and choose to get out of them.*

✦ *Can see all sides of a question, not only those it is comfortable with.*

✦ *Can build tight, qualified environments.*

✦ *Can switch easily from one mental universe to another and be at home in all of them.*

✦ *Can evaluate and modify its own ways of functioning.*

✦ *Can examine details without getting lost in them and grasp general principles without forgetting the details.*

✦ *Never takes anything for granted.*

✦ *Is aware of its own limits and is able to transcend them.*

✦ *Experiences its own working as effortless delight.*

> The best inheritance
> a father can leave
> his children is a
> good example.
> —Anonymous

Week Nine

✦ Law I

Defeat isn't bitter if you don't swallow it. —Ted Engstrom

Success has many fathers, while failure is an orphan.
—*English proverb*

If at first you don't succeed, try, try, try again.
—*English proverb*

What steps do we take when we find ourselves in a seemingly "impossible" situation? Many people, at one time or another may experience some kind of "failure" or defeat. How do we overcome these experiences? How can we obtain an appropriate answer to the question, "What shall I do now?" Do challenges help us open our minds and learn to be more resourceful?

Okay. A person may recognize a guilt feeling from what might be considered a failure. What failed? The individual? If so, why did he "fail?" Was it because he perceived he didn't do what he "should" have done, or "could" have done? Why didn't he? We may not have a ready response to these question and say, "I don't know." Or, we might come up with a variety of reasons. A person might say he failed because he wasn't smart enough or didn't make good choices or didn't act effectively. If he had performed in a certain manner, he would have been a success, etc.! Do blame or guilt, directed toward ourselves or toward others, or harboring guilt feelings from past errors, improve a situation? Of course not! Such responses are not helpful or progressive. We can forgive ourselves for the things we may regret, accept the lesson learned, then continue on.

Every one of us can find room for self-improvement, regardless of our situation, place in life, or circumstances. However, it is important to prove to *ourselves*, through the discipline of our thoughts, feelings, and actions, that we all have the *ability to accomplish such progress as we make up our mind to accomplish*. Fear, hesitancy, and feelings of inadequacy can paralyze our mental action and feed the idea of defeat or failure.

Thomas Edison knew eight hundred ways not to build a light bulb! One of Madam Curie's "failures" was radium. Christopher Columbus thought he had discovered the East Indies. Rodgers and Hammerstein's first musical collaboration bombed so badly that they didn't get together again for years! But did "failure" stop the progress of these daring souls? The whole history of thought is filled with people who arrived at the "wrong" or "different" destination!

How many times have we been on "rock-bottom" and the kind thoughts and words of encouragement spoken by a friend provided the incentive for us to try again? How often have we continued extended effort because someone believed in us? Is the real courage necessary for overcoming adversity, a spiritual idea stemming from the mind of God? Courage to continue, desired with all the intensity of our heart, believed in, and sought after until it becomes an awakened part of our nature, can handle difficult situations. We develop the ability to "keep on keeping on."

Some of the greatest challenges often bring the

most profound opportunities! Now, can we consider the possibility that opportunities don't *just* happen? Could they be the result of practical vision? When something wonderful happens in a person's life, it is usually explained that the person was at the right place at the right time when the opportunity came along. Could it be that the person was able to perceive an opportunity from an inner perspective, to recognize it when it came along, and to proceed to *do* something about it?

Can we be willing to acknowledge that situations we may have considered "failures" were actually "training sessions" for greater growth? If we allow ourselves to swallow defeat, then isn't our ability to function effectively severely impaired? Almost every great leader, athlete, explorer, scientist, thinker, inventor, and businessperson has

made mistakes and experienced failure in some manner. These people did not blame themselves or anyone else for their failure. Instead, they used their mistakes as powerful lessons on how to improve themselves and their performance. They understood that failure was a momentary occurrence and did not necessarily mean defeat. They refused to swallow the bitterness of failure and were willing to persevere to the sweetness of success.

Self-confidence leads to happiness and success. With it, a person can accomplish almost anything he or she sets as a goal. One clue to developing greater self-confidence could lie in answering the question, "Where am I going to place my confidence? Will it be in outer perspectives, or will it be on the divinity within me?"

Life is either a daring adventure, or nothing.
—Helen Keller

Failure is the source of success.
—Japanese proverb

What is defeat? Nothing but education; nothing but the first step to something better.
—Wendell Phillips

✦ LAW 2

The unexamined life is not worth living. —Socrates

A STORY ascertained that the fame of Socrates had traveled beyond the borders of Athens to distant lands. From far and near came earnest seekers to have *darshana* of this man of God who kept away from pomp and power. One day, from a faraway place, a man arrived at the house of Socrates. Socrates himself opened the door and greeted the man. "Welcome, friend!" he said to the visitor.

Education is not filling a bucket but lighting a fire.
—William Butler Yeats

I know of no more encouraging fact than the unquestionable ability of man to elevate his life by a conscious endeavor.
—Henry David Thoreau

"Crossing hills and valleys have I come to have a *darshana* of Socrates," the man said. "Can you tell me where I may find him?"

"You have come to the wrong man," Socrates replied. "For, believe me, brother, I have been in search of Socrates for many years but have not yet been able to find him."

"What, you have searched for Socrates for many years and not found him yet! Are you not a citizen of this place?" the man asked.

"I was born here," Socrates replied. "And I have lived here all of my life. And though by day and night I have been in search of Socrates, he continues to elude me."

"Then there is no hope for me," the man answered in despair. "I must return to my country beyond the hills."

Socrates looked into the man's eyes and responded, "Verily the most difficult thing is to know oneself, one's true and real Self."

The study of human behavior actually began in ancient times. The phrase, "Man, know thyself," is attributed to the fifth-century B.C.E. Greek philosopher, Socrates. Socrates was a powerful teacher who urged his fellow Athenians to live noble lives, to think critically and logically, and to cultivate inquiring, probing minds. Along with Plato and Aristotle, he believed that evil arises from ignorance and the failure to investigate reasons why people behave as they do. He is also credited with saying, "The unexamined life is not worth living." What do you think he intended by these words? Or, more importantly, what do these words mean for us as individuals?

Surely most people sincerely desire to live noble and moral lives. It seems logical that in order to achieve these goals, we would seek to learn and understand more about *who* and *what* we are. *Who* and *what* are we as individuals? *Who* and *what* are we as physical/spiritual beings? *Who* and *what* are we as members of the human family? Until we study these questions carefully, how well can we *know ourselves*? Imelda Shanklin, author of the book *What Are You?* wrote: "The error in your mind which causes you to assume the who when you should recognize the what, is the source of every misunderstanding in life that perplexes you."

Let's examine this idea more closely. The *who*, or personal and visual part of each of us, is described as our body, our conduct, our situation. The *what*, or impersonal and unseen part of each of us, can be described as our mind and the spiritual essence of our being. An honest self-analysis on both levels can help us tremendously. Learning the reasons why we do certain things can help build integrity. As greater realization flows through our personality, certain definite, objective changes occur in our lives. Realization refines and sensitizes the codes of personal conduct. We learn what is *real* to us. And we learn what *matters* to us! We learn to be true to our spiritual natures and how to live our lives with dignity and humility.

What can happen when we take the time to examine our lives? Are we happy with our present circumstances? If not, why not? How do we feel about where we've been—physically, mentally, emotionally, and spiritually? How would we formulate the next step of our journey? Do we take helpful action on circumstances or do we only react to people and situations?

Is thoughtfulness an example of the refinement of our soul? Thoughtfulness has occasionally been referred to as one of life's overtones, something added to our work by which our soul is beautified and ennobled. One of the eight parts of the Buddhist path to the real is defined by the articles as *right thoughtfulness*. Can this term be richer in meaning than the phrase "right thinking"? Can there be any enlightened living without studying the reasons for living?

How does examining our lives assist us in becoming centered and focused in a greater awareness of our oneness with the Creator? What are ways we can explore our thinking and behavior and expunge attitudes or habits unworthy of a beloved child of God? How can we express more compassion and empathy for others through greater understanding of ourselves?

Many guidelines and disciplines expressed by Plato, Pythagoras, Socrates, Aristotle, and other great philosophers are still effective. The Buddhist monks of China, Siam, and Burma, the Brahman priests of India, and other world teachers continue to live these ancient disciplines. Their purpose is to release into manifestation the spiritual values in humanity. Now, living in a different time with new social experiences, how can we adapt these universal principles to modern life? Can diligent introspection, with an emphasis on growth and progress, help us achieve richer and more useful lives?

✦ LAW 3

An honest man's word is as good as his bond. —American proverb

A word fitly spoken is like apples of gold in a setting of silver.
—Proverbs 25:11

A YOUNG WOMAN came to Anjali. Her face was flushed and her whole body was trembling.

She said, *"I have spoken to a friend words that were as unkind as they were untrue. And my voice was terrible as the thunder of the sky. Tell me how I may undo the wrong I have committed."*

Anjali picked up a sheet of red paper. He tore it into sixty-four fragments and gave them to the girl, saying, "Go and scatter these in the street below."

The girl did as she was told. As soon as she had scattered the bits of paper, a strong gust of wind blew, and the pieces of paper flew hither and thither and were lost to view.

When the girl returned, Anjali said to her, "My child! Now go and bring back the little bits of paper."

The girl went into the street to look for the little bits of paper. But do what she would, she was unable find a single piece. After a futile search, she came back to Anjali. "I cannot find a single piece of paper," she said.

And Anjali said, "So it is with the words you speak. No sooner do they leave your lips than they are scattered and lost forever. Do what you will, you can never get them back again.

So take care of your words. Before you speak anything, make sure that what you are about to speak is better than silence; else remain silent. If you observe this simple rule, you will not have to repent."

Using our ability to think and to speak wisely offers a key to mastering many things. Through the power of constructive thinking, humanity has created newer and better tools, machines, medicines, and improved ways of doing things in many fields of endeavor. Because of our ability to think and speak, we are able to cooperate with one another, to build great cities, to grow, store, and distribute food, and to manufacture useful items. We can pool our talents with others to enhance many projects. We are able to record our thoughts

so that ideas may be preserved and others who come after us may benefit from them. Through the power of our words, we are able to communicate our ideas to others and oftentimes to establish cooperation among many minds.

When spiritual words abide in man's consciousness, the word or thought formed in intellectual and sense mind must give way to the higher principles of Being.
—Charles Fillmore

However, a deeper significance and power can be found in thinking and speaking. Our thoughts and words are *creative.* They take hold of the invisible universal substance that is present everywhere and they weave an invisible garment or atmosphere around the words we speak. Our words are the vehicles through which ideas come into manifestation and reflect the character of our thoughts. The words we speak are of supreme importance, because they make impressions on the conscious mind and on the subconscious mind. Do these impressions often shape the quality of our thinking and action?

Your words are the seed, your soul is the farmer, the world is your field: let the farmer look to the sowing, that the soil may abundance yield.
—Nasir-I-Khusraw

How do we shape our world with the use of our words? In many ways! And how important is it to follow through on what we say? Immensely! Could there be any substitution for keeping our

Omit needless words.
—William Strunk Jr.

The power of words is immense. A well-chosen word has often sufficed to stop a fleeing army, to change defeat into victory, and to save an empire.
—Emile DeGirardin

word? What happens when someone promises to give us a call and doesn't? How do we feel? Is our trust in that person somewhat shaken? What happens to our reputation for *dependability* and *responsibility* when we fail to follow through on our word? How may we cause someone unhappiness and harm ourselves when we fail to keep our word? If we are not good at keeping our word, do we lessen our integrity?

On the other hand, if we consistently follow through with what we say we will do, is our integrity enhanced? How can we go about training ourselves to think and speak only those things that will help us grow? How can loving and positive words given to another be described as a gift? How would this also be a gift to ourselves? Why is it important never to underestimate the power of the spoken word?

✦ LAW 4

Tithing often brings prosperity and honor. —John Marks Templeton

NEARLY ALL civilizations have practiced some form of philanthropy. Many ancient civilizations levied a tithe, or tax, for the poor. The Egyptians and the people of Greece gave money to establish libraries and universities. By encouraging members to tithe, medieval churches supported hospitals and orphanages. Under the Mosaic law, a tenth part of all the increase of the flocks, of the land, and of all income was to be given into the Lord's treasury. Long before Moses' day, however, Melchizedek, King of Salem, blessed Abraham and Abraham gave to Melchizedek a tithe of all he possessed.

What do we mean by "tithing"? The word "tithe" derives from the Anglo-Saxon *teotha*, which means a tenth part. To tithe means to give one-tenth or more of a person's earnings. There are many interpretations of the meaning of this kind of generous giving. Some might refer to the biblical principle that "the more you give, the more you'll receive." Second Corinthians 9:6–7, among other Scripture verses, supports this idea: "He who sows sparingly will also reap sparingly, and he who sows bountifully will also reap bountifully . . . for God loves a cheerful giver."

Upon researching the activity of tithing, we find that tithing establishes a conscious, consistent method for giving and for being good stewards for the bounty in our lives. Giving on a regular basis prompts the mind to build a growing awareness toward supply, abundance, and further giving. When we become givers in and to life, the divine presence can be felt moving through us as love, support, compassion, and additional blessings. This is one investment that can be suitable for all persons!

When we move into the practice of giving, we become conscious participants in the flow of life. We become part of the movement of life and the Creator's flow. The nature of God is to give and, as we align with this power, it moves through us and enhances our willingness to be part of the givingness of the universe. What inner responses do we receive when we ask ourselves: "How am I participating in the flow of life? How am I a source of giving in the world?

Why and how is success more likely to come to those who are willing to give some of their wealth away? Is giving a method whereby a person can grow and become truly a success? How could this be explained? The positive feeds on the positive.

Giving establishes a cycle that continually feeds on itself in a meaningful and helpful way. Giving leads to greater giving and becomes a way of life. And the natural "next step" is that our sense of gratitude and spiritual accomplishment grows as well!

In *The Seven Habits of Highly Effective People*, Stephen Covey describes seven predominant habits of many people. He calls one of these "inside-out" living. If we live "inside-out," the willingness to give can cause good things to happen. An example could be, "It is a joy to be nice to people because it makes me feel so good!" If we live "outside-in," then we're waiting for something "out there" to happen before we take a step. For example, "If you would be nicer to me, then I would be nicer to you!" We each have our own paradigm, the way we see our world. It's our own personal map of the way the world works. How does your model work? What would happen if we began to see things differently?

Malachi 3:10 states, "Bring the full tithes into

the storehouse." What is meant by the "full tithes"? In addition to the monetary tithe, could this also include giving from our whole self? Is it when we give of ourselves that we truly give? Could "bring the full tithes" describe a commitment to work with divine law in *every* aspect of life? For instance, the discipline of positive thinking, the will to give way to the flow of spirit in every thought and word to bless and love people, to give praise and appreciation to all whose lives touch ours.

Is giving a possible test of maturity? Would an immature attitude understand the blessing from the practice? Does the person who practices tithing soon have more to give than he or she ever thought possible? How does tithing clear away anything that could possibly obstruct the free flow of divine greater blessings? How does tithing help build an individual relationship with the Creator? How is true tithing a prayer of thanksgiving? How is tithing a healing activity?

The parable of those who spend their property in the way of Allah is as the parable of a grain growing seven ears with a hundred grains in every ear; and Allah is Ample-giving, Knowing.
—Qu'ran

◆ LAW 5

Wisdom is more blessed than riches. —John Marks Templeton

CONSIDERING the growing number of people enrolling in different institutions of learning, interest in education seems to be expanding. One area of growing awareness is *values* and *moral* education, sometimes referred to as the conscious attempt to help people acquire the knowledge skills, attitudes, and values that contribute to more personally satisfying and socially constructive and useful lives.

In *100 Ways to Enhance Values and Morality in Schools and Youth Settings*, Howard Kirschenbaum describes values and moral education as one endeavor with two goals. The first goal is helping people—young people in this instance—live more *personally satisfying* lives filled with meaning, direction, and joy. The second goal is to help people live more *constructive* lives through contributing to the good of the community. Love and compassion for all human beings plays a major role.

Some of the topics covered in this kind of education are exquisitely beneficial and form building blocks toward a useful and happy life. For example: knowing oneself, self-esteem, goal-setting ability, thinking skills, decision-making skills, communication skills, social skills, transcendental knowledge, academic and worldly knowledge, and character education are but a few areas of meaningful self-development. Discipline and self-control may be part of the learning experience, but a life of purpose, enthusiasm, and creativity is certainly worth the effort.

Think for a moment. Are there particular talents, abilities, or aspects of yourself where you would like to expand your knowledge? Are you using your own talents and abilities to the fullest degree? How do you feel about people who seem to accomplish much with seemingly little effort? Could they have exerted a lot of quiet perseverance and self-control to achieve their present status? History indicates there is little "instant success!" And *perseverance and self-control win the race!*

The most important function of education at any level is to develop the personality of the individual and the significance of his life to himself and to others.

—Grayson Kirk

People have dreams and heart's desires. What is the good news about our dreams and opportunities to learn? Well, when we pursue any one of our abilities, we can find fruitfulness. Can we also attain satisfaction in the active *learning* process while *pursuing* the dream? Once we discover how to fulfill personal dreams, are we then naturally inspired to reach for larger, global, and universal dreams? How can we do this? By learning! It has been said, "Life is for learning." And the process of learning can be *so* enjoyable. Could there ever be a time when we declare ourselves "done," when the

formal education is over? Renting a cap and gown and receiving a scroll isn't necessarily a stamp of completion. Graduation is called "commencement" because it also means a new beginning? The more we learn, the more we can accomplish. The more we accomplish, the more we can learn!

Only the curious will learn and only the resolute overcome the obstacles to learning. The quest quotient has always excited me more than the intelligence quotient.

—Eugene S. Wilson

A teacher, when asked by a child, "Why do we have to learn all this stuff?" responded with the story of "The Magic Pebbles." What does it teach you?

One night a group of nomads were preparing to retire for the evening, when suddenly, they were surrounded by a great light. They knew they were in the presence of a celestial being. With great anticipation, they awaited a heavenly message of great importance that they knew must be especially for them.

Finally, the voice spoke. "Gather as many pebbles as you can. Put them in your saddle bags. Travel a day's journey and tomorrow night will find you glad and it will also find you sad."

After having departed, the nomads shared their disappointment and anger with each other. They had expected the revelation of a great universal truth that would enable them to create wealth, health, and purpose for the world. But instead they were given a menial task that made no sense to them at all. However, the memory of the brilliance of their visitor caused each one to pick up a few pebbles and deposit them in their saddle bags while voicing their displeasure.

They traveled a day's journey and that night while making camp, they reached into their saddle bags and discovered every pebble they had gathered had become a diamond. They were glad they had diamonds. They were sad they had not gathered more pebbles.

Spotlights ✦ ✦

1. Each of us can find room for self-improvement, regardless of our situation, place in life, or circumstances.

2. What is meant by the quote, "The unexamined life is not worth living"? *Seeking is essential for satisfaction*

3. What can happen when we take the time to examine our lives? *unlimited horizons*

4. Some of the greatest challenges often bring the most profound opportunities! *always*

5. Are situations that may seem like "failures" actually "training sessions" for greater growth?

6. How do we literally shape our world with the words we speak? *Thoughts & words = our worlds*

7. What happens to our reputation for dependability and responsibility when we fail to follow through on our word?

8. Looking deep within, decide what "tithing" represents to you. *A part of life -*

9. Why and how is success more likely to come to those who are glad to give some of their wealth away? *Make room - good begets good -*

10. Why is learning so important? *Stimulation - no end in sight gives vitality -*

11. What area of learning would you like to pursue? *Wisdom; self-understanding*

12. Perseverance and self-control win the race! *takes me forward - get the job done -*

Living the Various Spiritual Laws ✦ ✦

GLEANINGS FROM THE WRITINGS OF BAHÁ'U'LLÁH *on Education*

He Who is the Eternal Truth hath, from the Day Spring of Glory, directed His eyes towards the people of Bahá, and is addressing them in these words: Address yourselves to the promotion of the well-being and tranquility of the children of men. Bend your minds and wills to the education of the peoples and kindreds of the earth, that haply the dissensions that divide it may, through the power of the Most Great Name, be blotted out from its face, and all mankind become the upholders of one Order, and the inhabitants of one City. Illumine and hallow your hearts: let them not be profaned by the thorns of hate or the thistles of malice. Ye dwell in one world, and have been created through the operation of one Will. Blessed is he who mingleth with all men in a spirit of utmost kindliness and love.

Regard man as a mine rich in gems of inestimable value. Education can, alone, cause it to reveal its treasures, and enable mankind to benefit therefrom.

◆ LAW 1

If God is infinite, then nothing can be separate. —John Marks Templeton

MODERN SCIENCE has revolutionized our understanding of the world. This is quite obvious. But what impact have these developments had on our knowledge of God? How do we see human beings fitting into the overall scheme? We know very little—probably less than 1 percent of what can be discovered—about God and fundamental spiritual principles. In recent years, scientific research has revealed that the universe is staggering in its immensity and intricacy, and some scientists are now suggesting that a much larger God than we previously had imagined may be its source. Yet many people, even highly trained theologians, seem to have various, restricted views of a description of the Creator and of what his purposes are for creating this amazing universe.

The Theology of Humility encourages open-minded thinking and conclusions that are qualified with the tentative word "maybe." It is important to rethink what is known and to revise the assumptions and preconceptions behind our current knowledge. This is one way that progress and increase in knowledge can occur. It is possible that through the gift of free will, God allows us to participate in this ongoing creative process. Perhaps a prerequisite on our part is to look beyond our biases and our fears, our personal hopes and aspirations, to see the glorious planning and the infinite majesty of the planner. Maybe we should also ask ourselves—whether we are students of the natural world or of the spiritual world—to study and experience the ultimate relationships between

We cannot in any better manner glorify the Lord and Creator of the universe than that in all things, however small they appear to our naked eyes, but which have yet received the gift of life and power of increase, we contemplate the display of his omnificence and perfection with the utmost admiration.
—Antonie van Leeuwenhoek

physical and spiritual realities in our own lives.

In his book *Coming of Age in the Milky Way,* Timothy Ferris talks about our ignorance in light of the enormous size of the universe. "And yet the more we know about the universe, the more we come to see how little we know. When the cosmos was thought to be but a tidy garden, with the sky its ceiling and the earth its floor and its history coextensive with that of the human family tree, it was still possible to imagine that we might one day comprehend it in both plan and detail. That illusion can no longer be sustained."

One of the major perspectives considered from

time to time is: *If God is infinite, then nothing can be separate.* What seems abundantly clear is that reality is much deeper and more profound than has been previously thought. Can we learn new aspects of the Creator by studying the deeper aspects of nature and by proposing new concepts to be verified or falsified? Some subjects for this kind of scientific study could easily include:

◆ Further evidence for purpose.
◆ Explanations for the comprehensibility (at least in part) of nature.
◆ Research into significance of the following scientific observations or inferences:
  1. That the creation is:
    –Mostly unseen.
    –Much larger than previously thought.
    –Apparently much older than previously thought.
    –Increasing and even accelerating in its diversity.
    –Increasing and even accelerating in its complexity.
    –Ruled by law.
  2. That human beings are:
    –Highly creative.
    –Dominated by purpose.
    –Accumulating knowledge at an accelerating rate.
    –Spiritual beings exhibiting love, prayer, thanksgiving, forgiveness, sacrifice, honesty, ethics, etc.
    –Probably not the only self-conscious, intelligent creatures in the universe.

There is a smorgasbord of "food for thought" in these considerations. It is my hope that these questions concerning God's ultimate relation to the visible world may promote greater interest on the part of students, scholars, and researchers into our true relation to the awesome and wonderful Creator of the universe.

◆ # LAW 2

Where there is a will, there is a way! —Aesop

FROM THE BEGINNING of his sojourn on earth, man has been a searching, inquiring, and creative creature. He has pondered the mystery of the stars above him and the world around him. Surely, it is a great day in man's life when he begins to discover himself. History is filled with the results of men who discovered something about their capacities. However, history has yet to record the man who fully discovered all he might have accomplished. Emerson commented, "Man is an inlet and may become an outlet for all there is in God." And we could add, "If he is willing to do so!" Is the real secret to being able to change our willingness to do so?

Our lives and affairs are influenced and shaped by the character of our thoughts. We are not limited by heredity, environment, fate, circumstance, or even by God's will! One writer states, "Because God is the epitome of free will, what was created in his image must also be given free will. We have the opportunity to choose between an unlimited expression of good and a limited expression of good. Man, through the gift of free will, is given the opportunity to master his consciousness by achieving a greater consciousness through attuning his mind with the Mind of God." We are blessed with the freedom of choice—to observe the world around us and to decide how we choose

A man should first direct himself in the way he should go. Only then should he instruct others.
—Buddha

In idle wishes fools supinely stay; be there a will, and wisdom finds a way.
—George Crabbe

Was it not said that the seeker will find the way?
—The Tao

to go forward. As Shakespeare voices through Julius Caesar, "The fault, dear Brutus, is not in the stars, but in ourselves, that we are underlings."

Our minds, in a sense, can be considered our world. Our thoughts are the tools with which we carve our life stories on the substance of the universe. When we rule our minds, we rule our world. When we choose our thoughts, we choose results. If we are willing to think straight, then life becomes straighter for us. Is the appropriate question: Are we *willing* to change our thinking and change our lives? Just as a generator at a waterfall captures natural energy, can an attitude of *willingness* catch spiritual energy? Creative energy surrounds us. How can we provide a useful channel through which it can flow? Could one of the laws of wisdom be: As we are willing to ask for guidance within ourselves, will it be given?

Let's look for a moment at our spiritual faculty of *will*. What do we mean by the "faculty of will?" Our will has been described as the ability to deliberate, decide, and act. It enables us to move directly in line with a decision, to enforce the decision, and to express what we decided! "Will" has been called the "executive faculty of the mind" because it *facilitates* how we make decisions, whether we say "yes" or whether we say "no" to a situation, person, place, or thing. Our thoughts can be used as powerful tools with which we make determinations, seize upon and move toward selected goals. How important is the process of making decisions?

Remember the story of a hungry donkey sitting between two bales of hay. Each bale of hay was an equal distance from the donkey. But the donkey couldn't decide which bale of hay to approach! He looked from one to the other. Back and forth, unable to decide; eventually, the donkey died of starvation in the midst of plenty!

Now, if we are focused too strongly in our

faculty of will, what happens? Is this where we can become stubborn and demanding in a selfish way? Certainly, this attitude doesn't get us very far. What happens if we fail to focus strongly enough on our faculty of will? Are the results "wishy-washy" and lacking in decisiveness? Where is the point of balance and effective ongoing in this kind of thinking?

Those who are willing to forget old grievances will gradually do away with resentment.
—Confucius

If life's occurrences are for training the soul, how does our free will fit into the picture? What is *free will*? Could free will mean we are free to take responsibility into our own hands? Can it also mean that at times we can give the outworking of a situation into the hands of the Creator and wait upon the outcome? Is it logical to expect everything to always go according to our personal wills? How do we respond when situations differ from our personal desires? Every individual is divinely and wondrously created. Could one of the great activities of life be the willing journey of self-discovery? How can we know our capacities and our potential until we know more about ourselves?

As human beings, we may not be able to see the unlimited possibilities of what we call our divine destiny, or that which we were meant to accomplish while on this earth. *Where there is a will* (or willingness to do our part), *there is a way!* When the universe opens its doors to us, how willing are we to receive? How do our thought patterns run? Where is our attention?

✦ LAW 3

Count your blessings and you will have an attitude of gratitude. —John Marks Templeton

Whoever does
not express his
gratitude to people
will never be able to
be grateful to God.
—Muhammad

Rest and be
thankful.
—Anonymous

A joyful and
pleasant thing it
is to be thankful.
—1662 Book of
Common Prayer

Gratitude is not
only the greatest
of virtues, but
the parent of all
the others.
—Cicero

HOW OFTEN during the day do we pause to count our blessings and give thanks for the abundance that is ours? Gratitude can be a powerful magnet that attracts increasing blessings to us—love, joy, opportunity, health, friends, material good. Those who are grateful experience the wonderful balance of being both givers and receivers. An interesting aspect of gratitude is that we can feel it when others do something for us *and* when we do for others. Edwin A. Robinson observed, "There are two kinds of gratitude—the sudden kind we feel for what we receive; and the larger kind we feel for what we give." Gratitude nurtures within us a positive, joy-filled consciousness and unifies us with the universal flow of life energy. In this manner, our feelings of gratitude can give birth to greater inner fulfillment. Is sincere gratitude a spiritual quality that is enhanced and expanded in the soul with each day's practice? The rewards of gratitude are rich and satisfying.

What are some different ways we can express gratitude? How does counting our blessings transform melancholy into a cheerful attitude? What are some powerful expressions of gratitude? Laughter? Joy? Benevolence? Praise? Expressed appreciation? Unlimited love? How do we become more attractive mentally, physically, and spiritually when we count our blessings and fill our hearts and minds with gratitude? Why is it that the more we look for good in everything, the more we find? How does counting our blessings awaken us to increased understanding and a larger richness of life? How does gratitude help us look at life with eyes wide open? How can we expect more from the universe if we don't appreciate what we already have? As we are appreciative of every blessing, life will open up to us in new and wondrous ways!

What would you think of starting a "gratitude journal"? It could be one way of "opening your inner eyes" and giving life a good, long look. The journal could begin with an inventory of your life's assets. List every blessing that comes to mind in the journal. Then, expand your perspective and begin giving thanks for more and more! The sun shining on a new day in your life, the smell of morning coffee or tea, a fragrant lilac bush outside your door, baked chicken and stuffing for Sunday supper, hearing the words, "I love you."

Only by cultivating the virtue of wholeness and by returning injury with kindness can there be true harmony. Therefore, one of deep virtue always gives without expecting gratitude.
—Lao Tzu

Can each day be alive with authentic moments of pleasure and adventure that are uniquely ours? For example, what if upon awakening each morning, we expressed our joy with an exclamation like, "Wow! I am alive again! I can see! I can think! What wondrous gifts will this day bring?" With this kind of beginning, your day will go better for you! Each night before going to bed, remind yourself of several things for which you are grateful, including having a roof over your head, a job, health, friends, and the comfortable bed that will give your body rest.

When we fill our minds with blessings and gratitude, an inner shift in consciousness can occur. As we focus on the abundance in our lives rather than on what we lack, a wonderful blueprint for the future begins to emerge. Our consciousness is changing; so are our habits. What really matters is that we create a space in our consciousness for appreciation of all that we presently have so we can live more joyously in the present moment. A

French proverb reminds us, "Gratitude is the heart's memory." Our heart's memory will set into motion an ancient spiritual law: the more we are grateful for what we have, the more will be given to us.

✦ LAW 4

We learn more by welcoming criticism than by rendering judgment. —J. Jelinek

How DO *we* respond when someone is expressing anger or criticism toward us? It seems we have two basic choices: we can attempt to defend ourselves, or we can learn from the conflict. A resentful attitude allows for emotions of anger, blame, and criticism to emerge, which only increase conflict.

On the other hand, if we are willing to learn whatever a life situation may be expressing, can we lift our consciousness above personality and human limitations? Can you think of a good way to start the learning process? How about listening to the other person's point of view and giving him an opportunity to express his feelings? Quiet listening can encourage calmness and patience under pressure. Emerson said, "There is one mind common to all individual men, and by lowly listening we shall hear the right word." Could asking informative questions be another positive way to learn more about the situation? Asking questions can help clarify a misunderstanding. We might find that we didn't really *hear* what our friend was saying! Clear communication is so important.

Welcoming criticism can offer an opportunity for a frank and honest examination of our virtues and vices! And taking this kind of personal inventory from time to time can be important to our spiritual growth. When we have the debits and credits of *character* before us, are we not in a better position to balance our spiritual budget? Is becoming aware of our shortcomings simply a way of discovering a program of improvement? No one expects anyone to live a life without some

faults or errors. However, isn't it most desirable that we learn by and profit by our mistakes? Where are our biases? Is ignorance a contributing factor? Are we most nearly balanced when our attitudes, ideals, and opinions are more equally developed?

Make it a practice to judge persons and things in the most favorable light at all times and under all circumstances.
—*St. Vincent de Paul*

What happens to us when we render judgment against another? What is the difference between judgment and discernment? Someone said that when we point a finger at another, there are three fingers pointing back at us! What does this mean? From one perspective, "judgment" may be described as a mental act of evaluation through comparison or contrasts. Cannot this process be effective in our lives? Is this the "discernment" aspect of judgment? Is this especially true when judgment is exercised through spiritual understanding rather than emotions?

I am reminded of the story of two old Dutchmen sitting on a park bench. Night was drawing near and the moon was shining overhead. A river flowed not far from the bench where the men sat. A chorus of crickets resounded from the banks of the river. Peter, the first gentleman, listened to the crickets and said, "Crickets sure do like to sing."

When someone
does something
good, applaud!
You will make two
people happy.
—Samuel Goldwyn

I never met a man
I didn't like.
—Will Rogers

John, sitting next to him, replied, "Yep, they sure know how to sing." At that moment, John heard the voices of the choir coming from a nearby church and remarked, "Beautiful music, isn't it?"

Pete listened and said, "Yeah, and to think they do it just by rubbing their legs together!"

Each man heard different music. One was listening to the crickets. The other heard the choir. Life is like that. The Creator gives us senses with which to perceive our world and yet, our perception of any given situation depends on where we stand personally. How are we listening? Does what

Judge thyself with the judgment of sincerity, and thou will judge others with the judgment of charity.
—John Mitchell Mason

we hear depend on where we're coming from and where we're going?

When times of conflict or misunderstandings arise, perhaps we could pause for a moment and reflect on the creative energy that made and sustains the universe and every living creature, including ourselves. When we focus on the greater reality, how could there be any room or desire for criticism or harsh judgment of another human being?

We are constantly molding the character and destiny of our lives. Part of being human is realizing we may not be perfect all the time. A disagreement with another person is not an attack on our worth as an individual. Could it be that we simply need to look at ourselves and our thoughts and feelings in a more open-minded way? It has been aptly said, "We can learn more by welcoming criticism than by rendering judgment."

◆ Law 5

What talents can you build? —John Marks Templeton

Hide not your
talents, they for
use were made.
What's a sun-dial
in the shade?
—Benjamin Franklin

HAVE YOU EVER felt a sense of limitlessness? Perhaps it came as a growing awareness that humans have comprehended only a tiny part of the vast, awesome realities of the universe. A sense of limitlessness can occur as we begin to understand that creativity is accelerating and our potential for growth and discovery is unlimited. Why has the Creator given us such opportunity? Could a key lie in recognizing that God has a superb purpose for our lives? Having the right of self-determination, what shall we choose to do with ourselves and our talents and abilities? Could one challenge in this life be to discover and extend our talents and abilities? So many opportunities can be within our reach. *What talents can we build?* Why would we

ever accept the mundane when we can experience the magnificent?

Valdas Adamkus proved to himself and to the world that a person could accomplish what he set his mind to accomplish. Valdas immigrated to the United States from Lithuania and, after years of hard work, rose to become a highly decorated government official. He implemented a massive environmental cleanup plan for the Great Lakes and received the nation's highest honor for government officials from President Ronald Reagan. In 1991, Lithuania became free, and Valdas realized he wanted to go back and help his home country the same way he had helped America.

In 1998, at the age of seventy-one, when many

people would be retiring, Valdas Adamkus became the president of Lithuania. When asked about his reasons that led him to run for such a demanding office at his age, Valdas replied, "There are no limits in life." He was inspired to make a contribution to humanity and found a way to do so!

Inspiration has been described as the moment in which divine infinite intelligence is accessed and comprehended. It often begins when something in our world, *inner* or *outer*, sparks a flame within and a divine idea is born. Is the next step, then, to give the idea the space to emerge into our consciousness? We have infinite permission to learn, to love, to grow, and to express.

So, where can we begin? Accomplishments do not have to be heroic or of major proportions to illustrate limitlessness. What do you *like* to do? Do you have a talent or ability that has not been fully expressed? Would you feel a sense of achievement and increased joy if you became more accomplished in this area? Do you *believe* you can do it? How could you arrange to further develop a particular talent? What *choices* can you make that

enhance your abilities? Have you prepared for what you want? Do you treat your talents and abilities with dignity and respect? Are you enthusiastic about expanding something you do well? Do you need to begin new behaviors? Have you given yourself every opportunity to succeed?

What abilities and activities bring us a sense of usefulness and positive outcome? Does progress toward our goals bring lightness to our heart and work wonders for our soul? If so, how? If not, why not?

To improve is to change; to be perfect is to change often.
—Winston Churchill

When our intent is deep and loving, divinity will afford us the opportunity to achieve our plans. Our yearnings for exploration, adventure, and invention are for a purpose. The exhilaration of masterful achievement through beneficial endeavors can characterize our path through eternity.

Spotlights ✦ ✦

1. How are our lives and activities shaped by our wills?

2. How would you describe the statement, "Aligning our will with God's will for us"?

3. Why is it helpful to be thankful for difficulties as well as blessings?

4. Welcoming criticism can offer an opportunity for a frank and honest examination of our virtues and vices!

5. How would you define "judgment" and "discernment"?

6. Do you have a talent or ability that has not been fully expressed?

7. Which of your talents and abilities bring you a sense of growth and fruitfulness?

Living the Various Spiritual Laws ✦ ✦

A Story of the Buddha

The Prince-turned-beggar wandered about from place to place for seven years in search of wisdom. He visited monasteries and discussed with other monks the truth as revealed in the *Vedas*. However, he could find no answers to the questions he put forth during this quest for enlightenment. At times he became discouraged. But he continued his search. He practiced asceticism, often fasting until he fainted. He grew weaker and weaker, but no wiser. Finally, he decided that self-immolation does not lead to wisdom. He began to eat and regained his strength. His mind became clearer, and he continued his search.

One day, he sat down under a wild fig tree to meditate. He vowed not to move from that spot until he found the wisdom he was seeking. Under the tree he remained, hour after hour, concentrating on all he had learned from the *Vedas*. He focused on what he accepted and what he rejected. Suddenly, his face lit up with joy and he exclaimed, "The first Law of Life is: From good must come good, and from evil must come evil. This is the Key to Wisdom."

The Prince knew this idea was nothing new. It was the Law of Karma taught by Hinduism. However, from the idea he drew new conclusions. For seven days, he remained under the fig tree (now called the Bo Tree: the Tree of Wisdom), preparing to answer any questions he might be asked upon the conclusions he had reached. Then he traveled to the City of Benares, gathered around him a number of monks, and presented to them his first sermon—remembered as "The Sermon at Benares."

When he finished his presentation, according to legend, one monk asked him,

"Are you a god?"

"No," answered Gautama.

"Then, are you a saint?"

"No," came the prompt reply.

"If you are not a god and not a saint, then what are you?"

"I am awake," answered Gautama, the Prince.

From that day on, his disciples and followers called him *Buddha*, which means *The Awakened*, or *The Enlightened*. Thus began what became a great religion.

—adapted from *What the Great Religions Believe*

Week Eleven

✦ LAW I

You will find what you look for: good or evil, problems or solutions. —John Marks Templeton

ONE MORNING a young woman was driving along a familiar street that she traveled almost every day to commute to her office in the downtown of a busy city. Usually she was impatient with the rush-hour traffic, anxious to arrive at her office to complete some unfinished task. On this particular morning, however, she felt more relaxed. As the traffic inched its way along the thoroughfare, she looked around at the vibrancy of color and variety displayed in the dazzling morning sun.

Suddenly, off to her left, the young woman noticed a three-story office building of exquisite architecture. Around the top of the neoclassic structure was a beautiful frieze of pastel-colored tiles. She exclaimed to her friend, who was a passenger in the car, "Look at that lovely building! When did it get there?" Immediately, the young woman knew this was a silly question; it was obvious the building must have been at that location for quite some time.

The friend mumbled a reply, "Well, uh, I think it's been there for quite a while."

The young woman smiled shyly and explained, "I've never noticed it before, and it's so beautiful!"

The two friends had a good laugh over the young woman's oversight, but the woman was chagrined to think she had neglected to see something that could have provided her with daily joy

and pleasure. She had been so preoccupied with thinking about where she was going that she had failed to enjoy the process of getting there!

All of us are in the process of living different realities and experiences. The reality we see is often a matter of personal perception as much as objective fact. Basically, *we find what we look for, good or evil, problems or solutions.* If people look for the bad, or evil, in the world around them—in their leaders, in their neighbors, in their personal situations—they will surely find the bad, and this can have destructive consequences. Dreams are not built on cynicism; optimism begets achievement. If people look for the good, they will find it; in countless ways, looking for the good will have constructive consequences. Enthusiasm breeds effort and success.

Where are we placing our attention? Do we look toward the "evil," or can we diligently focus on the idea of "good in all"? Are we caught up in "problems," or do we seek to be part of the solution? Are we focusing on external appearances, or do we take the time to look more deeply into a situation? Simply noticing our own behavior can bring us to greater awareness. When we observe our actions as objective spectators, can we allow ourselves to see the patterns we may be repeating? With every plan, we have an opportunity to look within and ask ourselves, "What is my noble purpose? How can I improve my outlook to achieve my goals?"

"I know I'm not seeing things as they are, I'm seeing things as I am," said singer Laurel Lee. And truly, our interpretations of events tell as much about ourselves as about those we may be describing! So, how do we *see* ourselves? Do we express a happy, positive acceptance of the good we now have? Do we focus on things that bring us joy, enthusiasm, creativity, and progress? How do our attitudes influence the day's events? What do we look for when we meet new people or find ourselves in a different type of experience? Can we search for silver linings in the darkest clouds because we are committed to a way of thinking that invites growth? How do we express our thoughts and feelings in various situations? When are some appropriate times to release preconceptions and allow receptivity to new ideas? Does unlimited love reflect its beauty through our being? Is it utopian to imagine we can have open and honest relationships with family, friends, asso-

ciates, and the community at large? *What are we looking for?* What a difference the focus of our attention can make in our lives!

As we progress on our spiritual journey, we may be likened to the butterfly seeking to break out of its own chrysalis. The various "layers" of our identities form a cocoon over the self that we are creating. The multiple steps and improvements of our journey represent the process of changing from a caterpillar to a butterfly, from a sleeper to an awakened soul. Have you ever noticed that the butterfly emerges from a cocoon a third its size? And remember, the cocoon is of the caterpillar's own making to provide a place of protection during its transformation into the butterfly! What do you think the butterfly must experience as it presses against the structure of the cocoon in its efforts to grow and be free?

If people look for the good, they will find it! In countless ways, this can have constructive consequences. If we look for the good, it is present in abundance to be seen and appreciated.

✦ LAW 2

Is creativity accelerating? —John Marks Templeton

FROM MANY vantage points, this is a wonderful time to be alive! In terms of our nutrition and health, our standards of living and working conditions, our political and economic freedoms, our educational facilities, and our ability to communicate with one another, we live in amazing, progressive, creative times. Our ease of movement and leisure are astounding. As we consider the broad outlook for humankind, perhaps most heartening is the recent improvement in our ability to get along with one another. Not unrelated is our increasing development of spiritual wealth. Evi-

dence of the speeding up of progress is widespread. We might ask if *creativity is* the mainspring for these benefits.

Nature's great scheme involves change. "The world alters as we walk in it," wrote nuclear physicist Robert Oppenheimer, "so that the years of man's life measure not some small growth or rearrangement or moderation of what he learned in childhood, but a great upheaval." Today, this great upheaval signals nothing less than the beginning of a new era in the story of the world, because with recent changes we have reached and begun to

Be brave enough to
live life creatively.
—Alan Alda

transcend the heretofore ultimate limits of nature and the earth itself. In the past, change was isolated, infrequent, and limited. Today it is becoming ubiquitous and universal.

In his book *Mastering Change*, Leon Martel described how we now have the capacity of communicating simultaneously with every person on earth. In the summer of 1982, nearly half of the earth's population could watch the World Cup Soccer finals—at the same time. Someone has noted that it took five months to get word back to Queen Isabella about the voyage of Columbus, two weeks for Europe to hear about Lincoln's assassination, and only 1.3 seconds to get the word from Neil Armstrong that a person can walk on the moon! Old eras of communications end and new ones begin.

God expresses
through his creation.
—Unknown

Are we products of an incredibly creative process that had us in mind? Have we been hampered in our creative development because of an unwillingness to fully explore human creative potential through empirical and statistical research methods? Could human brain functions be greatly enhanced if proper conditions could be found for mobilizing the remaining neural networks? Is this suggestion supported by the limited data on so-called idiot savants who exhibit remarkable abilities in mathematics or in music, although their general abilities may be quite limited? Does this imply that the human brain can perform incredible functions under certain conditions? How can we find these conditions? Could spiritual attributes also be greatly enhanced by diligent research, thus leading to accelerated spiritual development of humankind?

Creativity is so
satisfying, so
important,
not because
it produces
something, but
because the
process is
cosmological.
—Matthew Fox

I shook the habit off entirely and forever,
and again in Nature's presence stood, as now I stand,
a sensitive being, a creative soul.
—William Wordsworth

Data from Templeton Foundation-financed research programs frequently suggest that great

resources of mind may be accessible if methods are researched carefully and scientifically. Experiences of penetrating insight, the sudden appearance of solutions to seemingly intractable scientific problems, the incredible creativity that musical and mathematical inspiration often entails, and the sense of the presence of an awesome force are often seen as essential spiritual "happenings" by the people who experience them. How can these spiritual experiences, which are so valuable to the individuals involved, be extended to a much wider spectrum of society?

The higher forces and powers of the inner life,
those of the mind and spirit, always potential within,
become of actual value only as they are
recognized, realized, and used.
—Ralph Waldo Trine

Are our minds capable of helping in the creative activity of the universe as well as in the growth of the human soul? By following the humble approach to discovery, do we keep our minds as open and receptive as possible because we never know what opportunities await us? Should we also keep our minds strongly linked to our souls and our souls linked to the Creator? In this way, can the creative process in which we engage flow from the mind of God through our souls to our minds, where creative thinking can produce creative results in the physical world?

Through creative thinking, we can see the divine effecting changes in the visible culture we humans create within our homes, families, schools, churches, businesses, and governments. We can also be aware of spiritual evolution in our own personalities. Our minds are tremendously powerful. The mind can bring on physical illness as well as influence the rate of recovery! If our minds can produce such results within us, can you imagine what could be achieved with conscious effort in our exterior world!

In her poem "Attainment," Ella Wheeler Wilcox wrote: "Use all your hidden forces. Do not miss the purpose of this life, and do not wait for circumstances to mold or change your fate!" In "You Never Can Tell," she wrote:

> You never can tell what your thoughts will do in
> bringing you hate or love,
> For thoughts are things, and their airey wings
> Are swifter than carrier doves.
> They follow the law of the Universe,
> Each thing must create its kind,
> And they speed o'er the track to bring you back
> Whatever went on in your mind.

Yes, there is an intimate relationship between what we think and what we are. The creative process goes from thought to deed. Our words are our thoughts crystallized. The objects we build and the deeds we do emanate from our thoughts and our words. Even more awesome is the fact that thoughts build not only outwardly, but also inwardly. By our thoughts, we create not only our possessions but also our personalities and our souls. With this awareness, how can we direct our thoughts in such a manner that our personal creativity is accelerating? What evidences of accelerating creativity are we seeing in our daily lives?

How do we do it? What action do we take to utilize the great law of creativity to bring forth the beneficial life? What is it that can bring mind, heart, spirit, and soul together in a beneficial creativity? Could it be achieved by utilizing the simple teaching of so long ago: "Love one another"?

✦ Law 3

The only way to have a friend is to be a friend. —Ralph Waldo Emerson

> This same Spirit is in all people, and the spirit that is in you is the spirit that is in me. It is one Spirit, just one.
> —*Ernest Holmes*

Life sponsors a variety of courses on love. We begin learning about love as babies nestled in the arms of our parents. Family relationships can tutor us in intimacy and self-esteem. Early friendships and first love can open our eyes to the possibilities of new unions. Marriage and parenting can provide opportunities to continue growing in love through different family settings. As we learn from unlimited love, we begin to feel friendship for everyone. Love has power. Love gives of itself. Love guides us into the knowing that "the only way to have a friend is to be a friend."

The power of attraction, working through divine intention for our highest and greatest good, is constantly taking place. Love attracts love. Life attracts life. No one can keep us from meeting, blending, and *being* one with others in a happy, fulfilling friendship—except ourselves. Your attrac-

tive energy of friendship has its source within your own actions. What does a friend do? How does a friend act? What does a friend require of another friend? We are often called upon to be supportive of others in friendship. What are some ways

> He who has a thousand friends has not a friend to spare,
> and he who has one enemy will meet him everywhere.
> —*Ali ibn-Abi-Talib*

friends can be supportive of each other? Are we nonjudgmental, trustworthy, and loving? Do we bring joy to our relationships? Do we treat people not as they may appear, but as they really are in their deeper selfhood? Could behaving as a true friend serve as a catapult to help others discover

> From quiet homes and first beginning,
> Out to the discovered ends,
> There's nothing worth the wear of winning,
> But laughter and the love of friends.
> —*Hilaire Belloc*

Wherever you are,
it is your friends
who make your
world.
—*William James*

Ever been the
best of friends!
—*Charles Dickens*

more of their own talents and blessings? When healthy friendship reaches outward to involve another person, a wonderful exchange of energy occurs.

We may give money and time and service; we may write donation checks and do volunteer work—but do we also give sincere friendship? Underlying all the differences that we may perceive between ourselves and others, do we recognize the unity and unlimited love that binds all persons into one great whole? Is the unity of all humankind scientifically as well as spiritually verifiable? How?

A true friend is a friend, whether living next door or in another place. Nearness and distance are words whose most obvious meaning has to do with the physical plane of life. When we dwell in this plane—mentally, physically, and emotionally—it is natural for us to desire to be near those we love and call our friends. However, when conditions of the physical plane make this seemingly impossible, we can live above the sense of separation by centering our attention in the realm where there is no separation. We can become the master of our lives, the pilots of our souls.

A FRIEND OR TWO

There's all of pleasure and all of peace
In a friend or two;
And all your troubles may find release
In a friend or two;
It's in the grip of the sleeping hand
On native soil or in alien land,
But the world is made—do you understand—
Of a friend or two.

A song to sing, and a crust to share
With a friend or two;
A smile to give and a grief to bear
With a friend or two;
A road to walk and a goal to win,
An inglenook to find comfort in,
The gladdest hours that we know begin
With a friend or two.

A little laughter, perhaps some tears
With a friend or two;
The days, the weeks, and the months and years
With a friend or two;
A vale to cross and a hill to climb,
A mock at age and a jeer at time—
The prose of life takes the lilt of rhyme
With a friend or two.

The brother-soul and the brother-heart
Of a friend or two
Make us drift on from the crowd apart,
With a friend or two;
For come days happy or come days sad
We count no hours but the ones made glad
By the hale good times we have ever had
With a friend or two.

Then brim the goblet and quaff the toast
To a friend or two,
For glad the man who can always boast
Of a friend or two;
But fairest sight is a friendly face,
The blithest tread is a friendly pace,
And heaven will be a better place
For a friend or two.
—Wilbur D. Nesbit

✦ Law 4

Your thinking greatly affects your life. —John Marks Templeton

CONSIDER the thinking process and analyze its effects in your life and affairs. We are aware that there is a power within each person that can lift us out of ignorance and misery. Now, how do we continue to expand the attitude of mind that is positive, permanent, and progressive? One possibility may be discovered through turning our thoughts toward the spiritual aspects of life and letting them dwell on the infinite good within ourselves and others. We have the opportunity to control our thoughts and to view our lives in whatever way we choose. The bottom line is that *we find what we look for!*

If we believe it is within our ability to arrange our lives in a useful and orderly progression, what do we do? We look for the areas that may be improved. If we are looking for a closer relationship with the Creator of our world, would we not involve ourselves in activities such as prayer, gratitude, and loving service to bring this about? Each of us has the ability to select where we will focus our attention. When we ask the question, "What am I looking for?"—in whatever kind of situation, circumstance, or experience may be unfolding at the moment—we begin to be more creative and to put to good use our thinking and feeling faculties. Are we looking for blessings or for problems? Are we directing our attention toward worry or toward possible solutions? Are we focusing in a positive or in a negative frame of mind?

Author Horace Rutledge had this to say, "When you look at the world in a narrow way, how narrow it seems! When you look at it in a mean way, how mean it is! When you look at it selfishly, how selfish it is! But when you look at it in a broad, generous, friendly spirit, what wonderful people you find in it!" J. Kenfield Morley expressed his views on a positive versus a negative viewpoint in this aphorism: "I can complain because rosebushes have thorns, or rejoice because thorn bushes have roses. It's all how you look at it." Why not make a sincere effort to see our world and the people in it in the brightest and most positive perspective?

Nothing worthwhile is ever accomplished without *desire*. A man who does not desire to reach the other side of a chasm will not likely do so. Within every person resides the desire, intense or moderate, for a more abundant, more vigorous, richer life for the soul. It is up to each one of us to fan the flame of that desire to make it stronger. But desire alone is not enough. A distance runner who enters a race may have the desire to win, but he isn't likely to win unless he has committed himself to the experience of intensive training.

The quest of the spirit is also a training process. It requires steadfast effort. It requires *action* on our part. If we are looking for spiritual growth, we can begin right now to lay a strong foundation by seeing ourselves as loving, caring, and kind to every man, woman, and child we meet. We can see ourselves as patient and considerate. We can think of ourselves as focused and strong in all conditions and under all circumstances—strong with the ability to reach out a loving hand; strong with the ability to speak the right words, to take the right actions, and to become an unshakable tower of strength, love, and light.

Declare your life to be a seminar in living! This can be achieved by learning something new each day, no matter how small. Reach out to others by never passing up an opportunity for a new experience that will enlarge your knowledge. Travel as much as possible, so you can see new places and meet new people from different backgrounds. Read literature that inspires you. Inspiration is a core characteristic of the positive personality. Avoid comparisons. They have a way of making negatives out of positives. See your cup of blessings as full, rather than as half-empty. Be happy.

Happiness breeds success. And successful people are free to love.

As William Makepeace Thackeray, the author of *Vanity Fair*, said: "The world is a looking glass and gives back to every man the reflection of his own face. Frown at it and it will in turn look sourly upon you; laugh at it and with it and it is a jolly good companion."

♦ LAW 5

Learning is a lifelong activity. —John Marks Templeton

ARE WE PART of a grand program, moving forward in accordance with the unfolding of our expanding human concepts and discoveries? In the twenty-first century, due to astounding advances in various technologies, a greater emphasis on the learning process may be required of all of us. Humanity's discoveries are accelerating. *Learning is an exciting lifelong activity!*

Is learning an essential part of our human nature? What stimulates us through life is our ability to grow and to discover new possibilities in ourselves and in our world. Successful inventors, artists, musicians, doctors, scientists, or leaders in any field never lose the enthusiasm for discovery. When they don't know exactly what they are doing, they embrace the challenge, diligently seek to find answers, realize with every fiber of their beings that they are learning, and learning is what life is all about! Is the best way to explore any new territory to take one step at a time and to learn along the way? Is an openness to process a key to learning?

If we desire to learn more about where certain abilities may lie, we can take aptitude tests and learn more about ourselves. It is also possible to talk to teachers, family, and friends, asking them to assess our strengths, weaknesses, and possibilities.

People who are dedicated to continuous learning are often multifaceted individuals. They are able to meet a variety of challenges with strength of character and a vast reservoir of skills. Aware of the importance of process, they carefully research situations to bring about the best results. They are always learning, always growing in open-minded resourcefulness.

Those who know the needs of the people are fit to govern them. Those who responsibly meet life's conflicts can truly lead the world.
—The Tao

It is important to be patient with ourselves when we are learning something new. Learning can be an invitation to leave what may be familiar territory and cross the threshold into a new and wider world. When we leave the known for the unknown, we may encounter some resistance. However, we are never limited by what has been. Astronaut Chuck Yeager told how his aircraft and instruments began to shake violently as he approached the sound barrier. But when he broke *through* the barrier, the air was suddenly calm and smooth as glass!

As a person thinks, so is that person. This example is generally agreed upon by all religions. Increasing knowledge through stimulated thinking can provide beneficial learning experiences. The benefits of the power of the mind, if taught to young people, could provide the basis for future generations to become much more disciplined in the control and management of their minds and lives. What an aid to learning this could be!

More benefits may result in the domains of spirit if each individual were to draw up a personal list of the laws governing spiritual matters. Of course, this would be easier is he or she first studied the books and articles of philosophers, theologians, and scientists engaged in investigating powerful laws of the spirit. What could be more uplifting than for each human to write in his or her mind and heart, as well as on paper, the various laws by which he or she ought to live? And

In a free world, if it is likely to remain free, we must maintain . . .

the opportunity for a man to learn anything.

—*J. Robert Oppenheimer*

could each individual measure his or her spiritual growth if every year he or she revised and rewrote the personal list of laws? How beneficial could it be if every school, every day, devoted a few minutes to help each pupil study the laws of spirit as they are brought to light and formulated by great scientists, so that each person could improve his or her written list? Do the supreme moments of our growth occur when we grasp a new, inspiring truth and appropriate it so that it revitalizes our personalities and becomes a part of our lives?

Self-discipline is also a central teaching and learning experience of many religions. For example, the five million or so followers of Islam in the United States are taught to abstain from alcohol and tobacco. One notable practitioner of such teachings is Rashaan Salaam, a Heisman Trophy winner and Chicago Bears football team running back. Rashaan, who prays five times a day, claims that, beside abstinence, "Islam has taught me to be patient with people and to live life with a positive attitude." What are we doing to increase our store of knowledge—in our professions, in our personal lives, and in our communities? What are we doing to learn and grow more in matters of the spirit?

An old Zen Buddhist legend tells of an accomplished young man who came to a teacher seeking enlightenment. The young man introduced himself, and the master poured tea. The young man spoke effusively of his life and of his achievements. The master continued to pour tea. As the man talked on, the tea spilled over the sides of the cup.

"Stop," said the young man. "Don't you see what you're doing?"

The old master smiled, his eyes twinkling as he replied, "You cannot fill a cup that is already full."

The young man was full of himself. To learn, or to receive anything new, he would have to empty his cup. Likewise, to learn we may need to empty ourselves of preconceptions, to suspend judgment, and to clear away the clutter of our minds. Should we learn the vital lesson of *yohaku*, which is the Japanese term for "white space" or background in an ink painting? Because *yohaku* adds balance to the whole, the empty space is as important as the image itself.

As we continue to learn, we increase our knowledge base, our competence, our open-mindedness, and our joy in life. The next time we find ourselves attempting something new, we can affirm, "I'm learning!" and enjoy the process!

Spotlights ✦ ✦

1. Each morning upon awakening we have the opportunity to influence the day's events by our attitudes.

2. How alert and aware are we to our surroundings? Where are we placing our attention?

3. "I know I'm not seeing things as they are; I'm seeing things as I am" (Laurel Lee).

4. If we look for the good, we will find it!

5. Is there an intimate relationship between what we think and what we are?

6. What can we do to utilize the great laws of creativity to bring forth a fruitful life?

7. What are some indications that creativity is accelerating? *change*

8. Friendship not only involves us; it begins with us. How? *Put forward a good hand — it comes back*

9. How is learning an essential part of our human nature? *We need it —*

10. How is learning important to our well-being and progression in life? *you can't stand still forward or back*

11. How is learning sometimes an adventure into "the unknown"?

Living the Various Spiritual Laws ✦ ✦

Confucius has been described as a different kind of sage. He is not considered a prophet crying in the wilderness, . . . nor does he fit the classical profile of the Indian Yogi. Rather, Confucius is, unabashedly, an educator. He is a learner and a teacher, a person-in-community who encourages nothing less than the full moral maturity of the entire body politic.

—Philip Novak, *The World's Wisdom*

Following is a lesson on "goodness" taken from *The World's Wisdom.*

Our Original Capability Is Goodness

The disciple Kung-tu Tzu said: "Kao Tzu (a philosophical rival of Mencius) says that human nature is neither good nor bad. Some say that human nature can be turned to be good or bad. Thus when (sage-kings) Wen and Wu were in power, the people loved virtue; when (wicked kings) were in power the people indulged in violence. Some say that some natures are good and some natures are bad. . . . Now you say that human nature is good. Are the others then all wrong?"

Mencius replied: "When left to follow its natural feelings human nature will do good. This is why I say it is good. If it becomes evil, it is not the fault of our original capability. The sense of mercy is found in all people; the sense of shame is found in all people; the sense of respect is found in all people; the sense of right and wrong is found in all people. . . . Only we give them no thought. Therefore, it is said: 'Seek, and you will find them, neglect and you will lose them.' Some have these virtues to a much greater degree than others—twice, five times, and incalculably more—and that is because those others have not developed to the fullest extent their original capability."

Week Twelve

✦ LAW I

Noble purpose creates fruitful lives. —John Marks Templeton

A bird pecks its way out of an egg.
A bud blossoms into a rose.
A star forms out of the condensation of interstellar gas.
Molten minerals cool into a beautiful crystal pattern.

There seems to be a way for things to happen which is intrinsically right *for them; they become what they were meant to be. Aristotle called the end of this process "entelechy"—the full and perfect realization of what was previously in a potential state. Whether it appears in a butterfly flying out of its cocoon, in a ripe fruit falling from a tree, or in the development of an acorn into an oak, this process clearly evidences qualities of harmony and underlying intelligence.*

—Piero Ferrucci, *What We May Be*

DOES HUMAN NATURE also tend to unfold according to such inner designs? Is it a reasonable and useful hypothesis to consider that humans may be like the rest of creation? Are we called upon to achieve a particular life-pattern? How may we discover our individual life-pattern and cooperate with its realization? What steps are needed along the way toward fruitful demonstrations of our life-pattern? Is there something eminently practical and personal about expressing our deepest values, virtues, and noble purposes?

Why is character building and moral development important in your life? Why are some ways of behaving more appropriate than others? Does research on values, virtues, and good character uncover universal spiritual principles? Are values and virtues demonstrated by noble human qualities such as honesty, integrity, kindness, unlimited love, diligence, self-discipline, wisdom, justice, and humility? Worthwhile qualities, such as the ones mentioned, can help us to live in self-respect and happiness and to lead a more fruitful life. Are they positive factors for the entire human community in that they help us live together more harmoniously and productively? Philip Brooks said, "No man or woman of the humblest sort can really be strong, gentle, and good, without the world being better for it, without someone being helped and comforted by the existence of that goodness."

Sean Covey's book, *The Seven Habits of Highly Effective Teens*, refers to natural laws as "principles" and explains that principles rule:

We are all familiar with the effects of gravity. Throw a ball up and it comes down. It's a natural law, or principle. Just as there are principles that rule the physical world, there are principles that rule the human world. Principles aren't religious. They aren't American or Chinese. They aren't mine or yours. They aren't up for discussion. They apply equally to everyone, rich or poor, king or peasant, male or female. They can't be bought or sold. If you live by them, you will excel. If you break them, you will fail. It's that simple.

Having respect for others is an example of a natural moral principle. Think for a moment. What happens if we treat another person disrespectfully? Isn't it likely that he or she can become upset with us? Then, if we fail to make amends, can we damage the relationship? What is the "inner cost" of such action? Can we lose self-respect? How would you feel if someone treated you in a disrespectful manner? Can you see the importance in respecting natural moral laws if you want your life to be fruitful and harmonious?

How is developing character considered a work in progress? What are ways we can learn what is true and appropriate and good? How can we educate our consciences and our conduct to that high standard? In his book *Man's Eternal Quest*, Paramahansa Yogananda stated, "By studying the character of others, one can become alert to ways in which he can improve his own nature . . . Character study is important primarily in this respect: one needs constantly to take note of virtues in others and to implant those good traits in himself."

How about understanding our strengths and weaknesses, recognizing present behavior patterns, and being honest with ourselves? What is the connection between self-esteem and values and moral education? What are some approaches or methods that could teach young people the knowledge,

attitudes, skills, beliefs, and behaviors to be better people?

How do we describe noble purpose? Could it mean having or practicing high moral qualities or ideals or expressing greatness of character in whatever we do? How can we accomplish this? One example could be to forget about our own egos

and to give generously of our talents and abilities in serving the needs of those around us. Being open-minded to knowledge from all wise sources is another. We can always learn more about ourselves, about our Creator, about the universe of which we are members. We can also learn the numerous ways in which each of these virtues relates to the others. What steps can we take to develop the patterns of loving, considerate, and fair behavior until these ways feel natural and normal? How can we develop the ability to control our impulses, to forgo immediate gratification, and to focus on doing what is beneficial in the long run? Can we utilize our creative curiosity for disciplined research and exploratory investigation? How can our actions help, hurt, or affect others? What does our *conscience* tell us? Before making a major decision, would it be helpful to ask the question: "Would the world be a better place if everyone followed this course of action?"

Our choices are important, both for our own futures and for the future of others. It is important that we choose nobly and responsibly, then take responsibility for our choices.

✦ LAW 2

Birds of a feather flock together. —Robert Burton

IN A SCIENCE CLASS, a handful of iron filings were placed on a thin sheet of metal. A certain musical sound was played near the metal sheet. Wondrously, the filings arranged themselves into the form of a snowflake! They were conforming to the vibration sound pattern of the tone that was being played. When another tone was sounded, the filings rearranged their formation. This time the pattern developed a star-like shape! This experiment

He who walks with wise men becomes wise; but the companion of fools will suffer harm.
—*Proverbs 13:20.*

was repeated several times and the results were similar. Every sound had its own pattern, and the visible filings demonstrated the invisible pattern of the sound.

A clear demonstration of the universal *law* or *principle of attraction* is that we attract energies compatible with our thoughts. If we continually think and see goodness and abundance, these elements are drawn into our life. If we dwell upon negativity and pain, that is what we will find. The more we dwell on any thought, the more likely we are to see that thought reflected in our experiences.

We may look at a situation's circumstances and exclaim, "Look what I created!" Another way to express this could be, "Look what I *attracted*!" The word *circumstance* neatly depicts the process. "Circum" means around, and "stance" means stand. Circumstances are the conditions that stand around us, magnetized to us by the central core vibration or "sound" of our thoughts—like the movement of the iron filings placed on the sheet metal. This ability to draw people and conditions to us has tremendous practical implications.

It is natural to enjoy the companionship of oth-

ers whose thoughts, feelings, and beliefs may be compatible with our own. The proverbs "Like attracts like" and "Birds of a feather flock together" address the attraction that can take place between individuals, places, things, and conditions. Our thoughts and beliefs bring to us, by attraction, the people who are a part of our personal world—friends, enemies, relatives, associates, and all others with whom we come in contact. How can we use the message in the law of attraction to help us progress creatively and to live a more fruitful life?

Are the acquaintances in our world supportive? How often has someone's love and friendship invited us to heal our limited perceptions and to see ourselves as beings of greater value? Are those to whom we are attracted helpful to us as we attempt to find and fulfill our life's purpose? Everyone has a special talent and a unique way of expressing it. How do those with whom we affiliate help us enhance and utilize our talents? Often the way we express ourselves arises from observing the people around us. It makes sense to associate with people who display the characteristics we desire.

We inherit our relatives and our features may not escape them; but we can select our clothing and our friends, and let us be careful that both fit us.
—*Volney St. Reamer*

The greatest room in the universe is the "room for improvement." J. Sig Paulson said, "As one becomes conscious of the activity of love in his being, the desire for improvement becomes joyously irresistible." Do those who comprise our circle of friends and those who are an intricate part of various aspects of our life stir us to greater vision and to more noble purpose? Are we inspired to live with greater enthusiasm and fruitfulness?

A faithful friend is
the medicine of life.
—*Ecclesiasticus 6:16*

In choosing a friend,
go up a step.
—*Talmud*

How do those around us assist us on our path to increased self-realization? Are we reciprocal to others in this activity? As we become more deeply aware of the universal creative spirit of love, life, light, and laughter, are we able to rejoice with a healthy, dynamic, creative attitude toward life? Do those around us enhance our soul's commitment to living a passionate life with the inner spirit as the divine architect? What and where are our strongest roots and connections? "The life we want is not merely the one we have chosen and made," the poet Wendell Barry tells us. "It is the one we must be choosing and making." Each life is fluid and ongoing. Just as with a river, one can dam it up or let it flow. You can reroute it. You can swim with it.

Is your life an orderly life? There appears to be sublime order in the universe. An ancient proverb states that "everyone is a house with four rooms: a physical, mental, an emotional, and a spiritual room." It is important to visit each of these rooms daily, even if only to straighten them! Do our associates contribute toward making our "rooms" more effective and livable?

Relationships with other people often form the spiritual web of our lives, with crucial strands being marriage, family, friends, and work associates. Our deepest values may be expressed through these essential bonds. Relationships can also be a training ground. "Being human is an accomplishment like playing an instrument," observed essayist Michael Ignatieff. "It takes practice."

✦ LAW 3

Idle brains are the devil's workshop. —H. G. Bohn

A useless life is an
early death.
—*Goethe*

Minds, like bodies,
will often fall
into a pimpled,
ill-conditioned state
from mere excess
of comfort.
—*Charles Dickens*

DO YOU HAVE a sense of *limitlessness* with regard to your self, your work, your talents, your abilities, your potential, and what you can accomplish with your life? Limitlessness has been described as the sense that there are no boundaries to what we can become or do. Limitlessness is an awareness that fills our minds when we *know* that our evolution is never-ending and that our potential for growth reaches to infinity. Do we start learning the lesson of limitlessness when we begin to transcend boundaries that may exist in our mind, when our minds are enthusiastically seeking and never idle?

Could one of our challenges in life be to uncover the unexpressed, infinite potential within? As Cherie Carter-Scott stated in her book, *If Life Is a Game, These Are the Rules,* "All is within your reach. Know your limits, not so you can honor them, but so that you can smash them to pieces

and reach for magnificence!" Yes! How do we begin to reach for "magnificence"? Do the first steps begin with an active and questing mind, with a mind that is curious, diligent, and purposeful?

The proverb "An idle brain is the devil's workshop" offers considerable food for thought. For example, can excessive entertainment dwarf our life? What is occurring with our thinking processes while we are being entertained? Can six hours of watching television daily be a poisonous narcotic? If your mind isn't directed to some kind of learning or mental challenge, can it become lax and less effective and efficient? Could a person brainwashed by television drama become susceptible to negative or nonproductive thoughts that could lead to painful situations in life? Fear? Anger? Crime?

Let's look at the sports picture as an example.

Stories abound about the meaningful accomplishments of many athletes who participate in various sports. But could excessively *watching* others participate in sports distract the observer from his or her own exercise or accomplishments? Would the mind be more active and responsive in participation than in observation? This does not intend to exclude an appropriate balance between leisure and activity.

Can physical and mental well-being take a downturn when a healthy, productive person is required to retire? In the United States, *some* corporate and government pension plans may encourage or require a productive worker to retire after age sixty-five. Considering the greater longevity of individuals attributed to medical and technological progress, can a person who is put "on the shelf" while in the prime of his or her productive life become a parasite? Would people retain their mental agility longer if they were able to continue working? How many times do we hear of someone retiring and, in a few years, the person dies or becomes ill because life no longer has focus and meaningful purpose? Purpose produces productivity while early retirement can produce unhealthy parasites.

Keep your heart with all diligence;
for from it flow the springs of life.
—Proverbs 4:23

Could meaningful benefits be achieved by allowing all earnings after age sixty-five to become tax-exempt? What incentives can be developed for retirement-age people to contribute in meaningful ways to the community, to the nation, and to humanity as a whole?

The question may arise: What do these thoughts have to do with spiritual principles and lessons from world religions? Well, if divinity is infinite, then everything helps us understand divinity, especially when human lives are involved. Could

The hand of the diligent will rule,
while the slothful will be put to forced labor.
—Proverbs 12: 24

Proverbs 16:4, "The Lord has made everything for its purpose," indicate the importance of all aspects of life? Could consideration along these lines of thought give humans the benefits and joy of more productive and fruitful lives? If the people who wrote the ancient Scriptures were writing them today, would they have a different focus because they would conceive of God as vastly greater than was possible thousands of years ago? Is it wisdom to seek avenues of greater enrichment for everyone, regardless of age? *The Dhammapada* states, "If you see a wise man who steers you away from the wrong path, follow him as you would one who can reveal hidden treasures. Only good can come out of it."

An active mind can view any and all obstacles as lessons, not as indications of failure. When anything appears to be an obstacle, the active mind can search for solutions.

In a film about his boyhood, Albert Einstein describes picking up a compass and watching in fascination as the needle moved when he turned in a different direction. He stated that he became obsessed with understanding the invisible force that moved the compass needle. Where was the force located? Who controlled it? Why did it always work? What was it made of? Were there places where it didn't operate? These are the natural questions of an inquiring genius, not of an idle mind.

◆ LAW 4

You can make the opposition work for you. —Anonymous

ROBERT was an excellent chef who had been terminated from three different restaurants for inappropriate behavior. In each of these instances, he claimed that the management of the restaurant was to blame. He emphasized he either had been victimized by the management, "set up" by his boss, or not given clear guidelines regarding his position. He easily played the role of the victim. Certainly, each release from his position may not have been entirely Robert's fault. It does seem unlikely; however, three different restaurants could have a similar issue with him. There must have been some truth regarding his responsibility to what occurred. How could Robert transform a difficult situation to his advantage?

A certain amount of opposition is a great help to a man; it is what he wants and must have to be good for anything. Hardship and opposition are the native soil of manhood and self-reliance.
—*John Neal*

Sometimes, hindsight or review can help a person recognize that a disastrous experience can be a blessing in disguise. Since three positions were involved, what could be achieved if Robert had been *willing* to look for patterns of unsuitable behavior and to decide to change them? What steps could he take to recognize *his* contribution in creating these circumstances? Once Robert could admit his responsibility in the situation, what could he do to accomplish a different outcome with his next position? Robert definitely has choices concerning how he responds to life.

As an expression of divine intelligence, are we not always greater than any difficulty, condition, experience, or situation? One basic and helpful guideline to remember is that good abides, at some level, in everyone and everything. An important factor is how we *respond* to these adventures! The Christian Bible assures us, "all things work together for good to those who love God"(Romans 8:28). *The Wisdom of Lao Tse* states: "Possibility arises from impossibility, and vice versa. . . . which being the case, the true Sage rejects all distinctions and takes his refuge in Heaven. . . . Hence it is said that there is nothing like using the Light." Every one of us is able to surmount obstacles that may occur in our lives if we are determined, courageous, and willing to work toward greater progress.

As transcendent beings, we have the power to rise above obstacles. We can overcome almost any limiting situation by directing our attention in an appropriate manner. How would we do this? Can we look at ourselves and at the situation before us honestly and openly and review the circumstances that may have caused the murky water? Our strength to remain focused can be developed and enhanced. Rather than concentrating on frustration, disappointment, and whatever obstacle may seem to bar our path, we can remember the great truth, "no one knows what he can do until he tries!" We can more wisely utilize our time. Once we choose to take charge of ourselves and our lives, we can begin creating a more loving, supportive influence in our external world. People respond positively to positive energy!

Is there something we can do to correct a troublesome situation? For example, what would happen if Robert made a phone call and an apology to his three previous employers? Could his willingness to take the first step back into love and harmony make a difference? How fruitful could making a commitment to a lifestyle of honesty and integrity be as a beginning point toward greater usefulness and service? What are some motivators that can assist us in staying centered in an open and clear consciousness? Sincerity? Truthfulness? Diligence? Being respectful to self and others?

First say to yourself
what you would be,
and then do what
you have to do.
—Epictetus

We are responsible for both our condition and our healing. When we have completed a review of a difficult situation and accomplished what we can to heal the experience, perhaps it is time to close the door on the event and move on. There is a universe within us—a unified field of all possibilities—that we can reach. We know there is a divine intelligence that flows through all of us. We can understand and build upon the best within us, which expresses itself as unlimited love, kindness, compassion, diligence, and loving service. When love and noble purpose begin to triumph over the human ego as we make daily decisions in our lives, surely we are making progress on the path of the sacred quest for all of humanity. Then, any seeming opposition will work for us.

Law 5

We are not punished for our anger; we are punished by our anger. —Bhagavad Gita

When anger rises, think of the consequences.
—Confucius

Anger can be a most disruptive, unsettling, nonproductive, and unpleasant feeling. It races through the mind, heart, and body like a raging flame that burns up our self-control and can cause us to say and do things we may later regret.

When a person becomes angry, the response is often to focus on the perceived cause of the anger. Perhaps someone has spoken or acted in a rude, dishonest, discourteous, or even malicious manner. These words or actions may be real, imaginary, or exaggerated. The root of the problem resides in the emotional response of anger itself. And where do we look to find the source? Inside ourselves! Like a firefighter would do, it is important to pour water first on the blaze and not waste valuable time looking for the person who set the house on fire!

If you would cure anger, do not feed it.
—Epictetus

If you refuse to accept anything but the best out of life, you very often get it.
—Somerset Maugham

So often, anger results from a lack of understanding of ourselves and others. Deep-seated as well as immediate experiences could be possible sources. Anger can also stem from fear, pride, ego, agitation, and suspicion. Are these not elements that have their origin within our own minds and hearts? Other people and our environment seem secondary.

Anger is a weed; hate is the tree.
—St. Augustine

What happens when a person becomes angry? Isn't looking for someone or some thing to blame often a first response? Blame may sometimes be used as a convenient excuse for why our lives may not be exactly as we desire. We may blame the world for illness, the stock market for financial conditions, or the bakery down the street for causing overweight. In the world of thought, however, we are responsible for how we have created ourselves. And besides, does blame ever result in a positive experience? When we believe in and live our lives in oneness and unlimited love, doesn't blame literally become impossible? How could we feel anger toward another if we have truly learned to love every person? Wouldn't our life energies be better directed toward finding solutions? Isn't it important to take responsibility for our own roles in the larger drama of life at *all* times? Besides, blaming others or blaming our surroundings is a futile experience, because wherever we go, we carry our anger in our minds!

"We are not punished for our anger; we are punished by our anger" speaks an important truth. How? What happens when someone becomes angry? The entire being is affected. The heartbeat speeds up, palms become moist, breathing accelerates, the face gets red, and eyes flash with indignity! And how long does it take for the body, mind, and spirit to recover from a fit of anger? Why would we ever want to punish ourselves in

Anger is
the foundation
of every evil.
—*Muhammad
Husan Askari*

Unrighteous
anger can never
be excused,
for the weight
of a man's anger
drags him down.
—*Ben Sira*

Your own mind is
a sacred enclosure
into which nothing
harmful can enter
except by your
permission.
—*Arnold Bennett*

such a manner by allowing anger to gain the upper hand? When anger is allowed to reside in our consciousness, we become one more person who is creating additional disharmony in our world—not just in our personal world, but in our planetary home!

So, what do we do? Perhaps the way to begin is to take *total* responsibility for what and who we are in our lives right now. When the disrupting energy of anger rears its ugly head, we can ask the question: What is the lesson for me to learn in this situation? We can re-examine the troublesome events that preceded the situation. If someone speaks or acts unkindly to us, can we seek to better understand that person? Can we perceive that the person who has precipitated our anger may also be pitifully suffering from negative emotions? Other people are going to be exactly the way they are, independent of our opinions of them. Can we allow each person to be as they are and acknowledge that they are on their own path of growth? It is within every person to give birth to something beautiful.

Think about this for a moment. Consciousness can exist on two levels: first as seeds, and then as manifestations of these seeds. Every time a seed has an occasion to manifest itself, it produces new seeds of the same nature. Suppose we experience a seed of anger. When conditions are favorable, that seed may manifest as a zone of energy called anger. If we are angry for five minutes, new seeds of anger are produced and deposited in the soil of our minds. Can you imagine how difficult it is to be joyful when a seed of anger is manifesting?

What would happen if we offered understanding, compassion, and love as our response to every situation rather than anger? Keep in mind that grievances often bring turmoil, while true communication can bring peace and harmony. Can we look for the spiritual solution to every so-called problem we may encounter? The unlimited love we activate for ourselves begins to radiate outward. Soon, there can be love where blame and anger once resided. Hate never overcomes hate, but love soon overcomes hate.

Many spiritual leaders have invited us to fill our selves with love, even toward those who may appear to be enemies. If we can send love where we may have once sent blame, anger becomes an option we no longer elect.

Spotlights ✦ ✦

1. How may we discover our individual life-patterns and their supportive talents and cooperate with their realization?

2. Why is character building and moral development important in a person's life?

3. How is developing our character considered a work in progress?

4. In *your* words, how would you describe the law or principle of attraction?

5. If we desire a role model, why is it important to associate with people who *demonstrate* the characteristics we desire?

6. Why is the greatest room in the universe the "room for improvement"?

7. How does a sense of *limitlessness* represent tremendous opportunity for personal growth?

8. Why is it important to "feed" our brain with meaningful activity and focus of purpose?

9. How could early retirement produce parasites? How would you define "parasite"?

10. We can be greater than any problem, condition, experience, or situation.

11. How are we responsible for both our conditions and our healing?

12. How are we "punished" by our anger?

13. What lessons can we learn from less-than-positive emotions?

Living the Various Spiritual Laws ✦ ✦

I am, O my God, but a tiny seed which Thou hast sown in the soil of Thy Love, and caused to spring forth from the hand of Thy bounty. This seed craveth, therefore, in its inmost being, for the waters of Thy mercy and the living fountain of Thy grace. Send down upon it, from the heaven of Thy loving-kindness, that which will enable it to flourish beneath Thy shadow and within the borders of Thy court. Thou art He Who waterest the hearts of all that have recognized Thee from Thy plenteous stream and the fountain of Thy living waters."

Praise be god, the Lord of the worlds.

—Bahá'u'lláh, Bahá'í prayer

Week Thirteen

✦ Law 1

Life is filled with infinite possibilities. —John Marks Templeton

As human beings, the Creator endows us with highly developed, extremely adaptable minds. Are we created for a purpose, including possibly as helpers in the acceleration of creativity? We are endowed with the mental capacity to search, learn, evaluate, solve problems, improve ourselves and the societies of the world. Can we be helpful in future progress?

Has each person been given a mind capable of creative activity in the maturation of the universe, as well as in the maturation of his or her soul? By following the humble approach to life, we keep our minds as open and receptive as possible because we never know what new opportunities are coming our way. Is it important to keep our minds strongly linked to our souls and our souls linked to the Creator? Why? In this way, can the creative process in which we are engaged flow from the mind of God through our souls to our minds, where creative thinking can produce creative results in the tiny part of ultimate reality that humans have the ability to perceive?

The creative process goes from thoughts to deeds. Our words are our thoughts crystallized. How do the objects we build and the concepts we express emanate from our thoughts and our words? Do our *thoughts* and *words* affirm our openness and receptivity to infinite possibilities? In taking advantage of these opportunities, do our *actions* support our thoughts and words? Perhaps the big question is: Are we *willing* to acknowledge and accept the possibilities? Could a willing attitude be an uppermost important factor for our enthusiasm, diligence, research, creativity, and progress? Is willingness actually a state of mind? Could it be an internal statement that says, "Yes!" to life? Does willingness affirm that we will take appropriate steps to formalize possibilities into actualities? If we are willing to accept life's wonderful possibilities, can obstructions or discouragement enter or remain long in our consciousness? Do willingness and openness go hand in hand, guiding us to an internal harmony that produces greater creativity? Then, does increased creativity invite more infinite possibilities? How can we conceivably know what seemingly insignificant events may be loaded with possibilities to change the course of our lives for the better?

Can many things be mysterious and strange to ordinary human perception? Is it possible we often overlook their strangeness and their mystery because we are so accustomed to them? Do we only dimly understand the true nature of things? And what are "things," anyway? Are they God's love expressed in various manifestations?

In *Abide in Love*, Ernesto Cardenal stated: "God also communicates with us by way of all things. They are messages of love. When I read a book,

God is speaking to me through this book. I raise my eyes and look at the countryside. God created it for me to see. The picture I look at today was inspired by God in the painter, for me to see. Everything I enjoy was given lovingly by God for me to enjoy, and even my pain is God's loving gift."

If divinity is infinite, then wouldn't it follow that nothing can exist separate from divinity? Would matter and energy, space and time, then be understood as aspects of divinity? From this perspective, would each of us, every day, be swimming in an ocean of infinite possibilities? What a powerful thought! By constant reminders such as this, can we avoid the most common pitfall of theology: the attempt by humans to put limits on the Creator?

Does optimism toward infinite possibilities and an attitude of thankfulness go hand in hand? Can you imagine that each person is one cell in the body of humanity? Can we understand that each individual cell or person, functioning from harmony within, can cooperate with the adjacent cells of humanity? Once we have trained ourselves in the process of being appreciative for everything and everyone that comes our way, our lives become increasingly filled with infinite possibili-

ties. In addition, when we have a sense of purpose, we can feel purposeful about all of life. How does it *feel* to be excited and enthusiastic about life? How can we bring this emotion of enthusiasm into every thing we do? What are some assignments we can give ourselves to work on to enhance our abilities to perceive greater possibilities in everything around us?

Consider these words from Patanjali, an author of the *Yoga Sutras*: "When you are inspired by some great purpose, some extraordinary project, all your thoughts break their bonds. Your mind transcends limitations, your consciousness expands in every direction, and you find yourself in a new, great, and wonderful world. Dormant forces, faculties, and talents become alive, and you discover yourself to be a greater person by far than you ever dreamed yourself to be."

✦ LAW 2

Thoughts are things. —Charles Fillmore

BUCKMINSTER FULLER once remarked that 99 percent of who we are is invisible and untouchable. Is it our ability to think and to reach beyond the human form that determines the quality of our lives? Thoughts are things. Thoughts create things. Thoughts shape things. Thoughts become ultimately, tangibly real!

The invisible process taking place in our minds

that we call "thinking" can produce objects as real as the ground upon which we walk or the food that we eat! Almost everything we use and come in contact with on a daily basis had its beginning as a thought. For example, the paper this book is printed on and the machines that made the paper were once thoughts, ideas, theories, or dreams in someone's mind. Similarly, the car we drive, its

There is nothing
either good or bad,
but thinking
makes it so.
—*William Shakespeare*

motor, tires, wheels, and mechanical parts are literally the "products" of someone's visualizations! The material things we take for granted that make living easier or more pleasant, such as radios, television, telephones, schools, libraries, churches, books, newspapers, magazines, medical equipment, and so much more, began as a thought, or an idea.

Always aim at complete harmony of thought and word and deed. Always aim at purifying your thoughts and everything will be well. There is nothing more potent than thought . . . Where the thought is mighty and pure, the result is mighty and pure.
—*Mahatma Gandhi*

While the mind may seem an elusive component of every human being, it is the link between the body and the soul. With the faculty of mind, we can think about the nature of our being, our lives, our bodies, other people, and our spiritual perspectives. Could this be the distinguishing factor between human mental capacity and that of animals? Are animals at a less evolved level than humans precisely because they do not seem to be able to step back mentally and think about themselves? Animals have instincts, some level of primitive thought, and even emotion. They can build environments and communicate with each other and even with humans, to a degree. But as far as we can tell, animals cannot philosophize about anything.

To be conscious
that we are
perceiving or
thinking is to be
conscious of our
own existence.
—*Aristotle*

Since humans experience the gift of self-consciousness, wouldn't it be meaningful to examine our lives from time to time to determine how we may be using our minds and our imaginations? Are we utilizing these magnificent "tools" to build heaven on earth through our expression of unlimited love and selfless service? Do we exert creative control over our thoughts? Why is it so important to stand watch over each thought that sprouts in the mind? If our thinking consists of loving thoughts, we can cultivate more of the same. If our

thoughts are disturbing, we have the ability to transform them. Our thoughts can carry us to places that have no boundaries and no limitations.

We, as the gardeners of our minds, can cultivate whatever thoughts we choose to live in our minds. Wouldn't a good gardener nourish the positive thoughts and weed out the negative ones? By careful thought control, our minds can become gardens of indescribable beauty: "As a man thinketh, so is he" (Proverbs 23:7).

Your body is like a house. So is your mind. It is important to take care of your *house of living,* using your mind to develop your soul. We have received the blessing of our being as a temporary trust. Obviously, to build a house, we begin with thoughts, followed by words, then expressed through deeds. Every object produced by man is created through this process. The proficiency of creative thought provides us with the ability to make virtually any connection to thought we may choose. Nations are formed in this way. So are the sciences, religions, and all the organizations and institutions of human society. As we become more alert to this probability, "coincidences" may no longer be surprising.

Thought is much more than something that you do. It is in fact what you are, and all the rest of us are as well. Thought constitutes our entire being except for the portion of us that is form, or the packaging that carries around our minds.
—*Wayne Dyer*

Even more awesome is the fact that thoughts build not only outwardly, but also inwardly. By the power of our thoughts, we create not only our possessions, but also our personalities and our souls. Through the process of working to control our thoughts, can we make ourselves the kind of people we want to be? How would we begin this process of improvement? Can continual negative thoughts and attitudes help bring about physical

Think before
thou speakest.
—*Miguel de Cervantes*

To him whose
elastic and vigorous
thought keeps
pace with the sun,
the day is a
perpetual morning.
—*Henry David Thoreau*

illness? Do they also negatively influence the rate of healing in our bodies as well in as our minds?

What do you think of the idea that our *casual* words reflect what we truly believe, deep within ourselves? Often, they spontaneously express what our thoughts have focused on over long periods and are unimpeded by deliberation. So, can we say that thoughtless words may reflect true expressions of what is actually in our minds? Are what some people call "slips of the tongue" really the products of minds that have made wrong choices in the use of ideas?

Ramakrishna once said, "It is the mind that makes one wise or ignorant, bound or emancipated. One is holy because of his mind, one is wicked because of his mind, one is a sinner because of his mind, and it is the mind that makes one virtuous. So he whose mind is always fixed on God requires no other practices, devotion, or spiritual exercises."

As helpers in divine creativity, why is it necessary to control our thoughts, directing them toward creativity, benefits, and progress? If our thoughts do not flow in beneficial directions, are we self-indulgent or lazy?

Our thoughts and words carry tremendous power. It is important to discipline and manage them wisely. Our thoughts, words, and deeds can separate us from the rest of creation, or they can connect us more closely to others and to the Creator.

✦ Law 3

As within, so without. —Hermetic principle

The Lord has
made everything
for its purpose.
—*Proverbs 16:4*

A sense of Purpose
can, and must,
be the experience
of those who
belong to God.
—*Daniel H. Osmond*

Is there any mystery of the physical world that does not point to a mystery beyond itself? One great mystery is that we have the mental ability to think about our Creator. Are we ourselves part of the world we seek to explore? Our bodies and brains are mosaics of the same elemental particles that compose the drifting clouds of interstellar space. As an analogy, can anyone yet comprehensively define gravity? But scientists can calculate gravity by its effects! Time, space, and energy seem to extend beyond the limits of human existence and beyond the limits of our present knowledge. Our Creator, of course, is not bound in these ways.

Emanuel Swedenborg wrote that nothing exists separate from God. God, he stated, is all of us, and we are a little part of God. Swedenborg taught that man is not in heaven until heaven is in man. As within, so without! The "within" is generally accepted as the realm of mind, of spirit, while the "without" is the manifest world or world of form. We are citizens of the spiritual world, and we are spirits from the day of our conception. Love, mercy, patience, integrity, loyalty, compassion, and

They (Mankind) are the waves of one sea, the drops of
one river, the stars of one heaven, the rays of one sun,
the trees of one orchard, the flowers of one garden.
—*principles of Bahá'í administration*

truth are more real than tangible objects. Is the Creator seeking to instill these spiritual realities into our lives at this moment through our associations and interactions with others? If everything created by God is a part of God, then should our spirits seek their ultimate expression through our purpose for being? Do we *experience* the love and guidance of the Creator in our life whose Spirit infuses life with purpose, meaning, and hope?

In the book *Evidence of Purpose,* Daniel H. Osmond states: "Purpose has to do with ends, 'that for the sake of which a thing (person) exists.' One can ask about the purpose of the universe, or of the world, of animate beings generally, or of humans specifically. And, in relation to humans, several levels of purpose can be identified, ranging from the basic requirements for physical survival and gratification to the ultimate and most searching intellectual and spiritual issues of life. Sooner or later, thoughtful people ask, 'For what purpose, do I exist?'"

The scope of a person's purpose can range from a primal fight for survival to the highest levels of intellectual and spiritual aspiration and attainment. Can our purpose change with the circumstances of life? Could a person be moving toward a purpose in one direction, only to learn that he or she needs something more satisfying to fulfill his or her life? Is it worth discovering "true purpose" for

Yet I doubt not through the ages one increasing purpose runs, and the thoughts of men are widened with the process of the suns.
—Alfred, Lord Tennyson

the whole of our lives, if such a thing exists? Why? Is "purpose" an ongoing discovery? For example, is the hard work of discovering the full dimensions of our purpose beneficial on a daily basis? Is purpose both the *messenger* and the *message* of greater spiritual awareness? "Light has come into the world . . . for a purpose" (John 3:19).

All thoughts, all passions, all delights, whatever stirs this mortal frame, All are but ministers of Love, and feed his sacred flame.
—Samuel Taylor Coleridge

For everything that lives is holy.
—William Blake

What happens when we become simultaneously aware that we have a physical presence or self and an essential spiritual or invisible presence? Do our

This is our purpose: to make as meaningful as possible this life that has been bestowed upon us; to live in such a way that we may be proud of ourselves; to act in such a way that some part of us lives on.
—Oswald Spengler

priorities shift and the invisible becomes as real, or more real, to us as the visible? Does the invisible power of sacred consciousness become an experiential reality? Is the road to the spirit of integration and wholeness of body and soul paved by the principle of *priority*? We can talk all we want to about our spiritual values and our materialistic goals; however, if our priorities are in the wrong order, can our lives progress, as we desire? As we mature spiritually, are we more influenced by the Spirit's inner leading? Is day-to-day life a profound school of growth where the goal is not only to know and to understand our purpose and the holiness within, but also to become expressions of both?

To live successfully in the outer world, it is important to live successfully in the inner world! Truth teaches us to relate the inner to the outer, to integrate the spiritual with the physical, and to unify our thoughts, feelings, and actions into a harmonious oneness. "As within, so without." The door to a fruitful life opens from within. The friends, associates, opportunities, careers, and life experiences of our outer world are reflections of what is happening within us. It is for each person to discover the wondrous capabilities with which he or she is endowed. With the discovery of this "inner" awareness often comes the power and energy to move forward in "outer" progression and utilize our innate gifts.

✦ Law 4

Thanksgiving, not complaining, attracts people to you. —John Marks Templeton

ONE OBJECTIVE of the various true spiritual activities unfolding through the ages has been that of assisting the sincere individual who is searching for truth to find God within his or her own heart and mind. The guidance has been to look within and not to some far-off vista of blue sky and mythological expression. Adepts from various religions attempt to assist their students, along with other seekers, in finding the inner creative source.

If we study history, we can observe that those wise prophets who bore testimony to the Creator's inspiration always gave thanks. Recognition, gratitude, and devout appreciation flowed from the heart of the sincere seeker as a spirit of thanksgiving for wisdom, for the things of daily need, and for the ever-present awareness of the Creator learned by studying all things.

We presently live in a wonderful age. This is a time of unprecedented discovery and opportunity, a blossoming time for humanity. It is also a time of dramatic improvements—politically, economically, culturally, and spiritually. What will the next twenty or thirty years portend? What will business opportunities be like? What types of materials and services, which currently may not exist, could likely be commonplace within a few years? Will humanity's lifestyles twenty or thirty years from now be as different from our current lives as today's lifestyles are from those of thirty or forty years ago? What is the shape of the future? What will our religious and spiritual future hold? How can we, as a world family, fit successfully into it?

Perhaps a positive, workable avenue lies in adapting the *spiritual principle of thanksgiving*—rather than complaining—as a daily practice! This attitude could be beneficial to individuals, to families, to business associates, to countries, to governments, and, ultimately, to the global community. The spiritual principle of thanksgiving is simple: "To whatever we give our attention and enthusiasm, that becomes our experience!" Why thanksgiving? True thanksgiving has been called the soul's recognition of its relation to God, and there is no limit to our souls' capacities.

The spiritual law of mind action, "As in mind, so in manifestation," increases whatever the mind praises and appreciates. Thanksgiving is a creative force that, if *lived* on a continuous basis, can create wondrous good in a person's life. So, wouldn't

life become more effective and fruitful if we placed our attention on the way we would like to see ourselves and our lives unfold? Cicero once said, "There is no quality I would rather have . . . than gratitude. It is not only the greatest virtue, it is the mother of all the rest." So where does one begin? What are some things we can be grateful for, and how can we put our gratitude into action?

A man once attended a large banquet. As the waiters moved among the tables serving the coffee, they twice passed him by. Other diners were served, but not this man. Finally, the man stopped a waiter and asked for coffee.

"Mister," the waiter said, "If you want coffee, please turn up your cup. We only pour for those who have turned up their cups!"

Some people move through life with their cup of gratitude turned down and wonder why their life is unfulfilled! Rigidity of thought may cause some people to ridicule or complain. Lack of compassion or understanding can prompt attitudes and comments that turn others off. Look at the variety of complaining attitudes about the weather! This represents a prime example of a natural phenomenon over which we have no control! Would positive, appreciative people be attracted to others exhibiting these negative attitudes? What kind of energy do we desire to invite into our daily living? Does becoming increasingly understanding of our position as finite creatures in a vast universe of infinite complexity help release us from prejudices? Then, can unlimited love and thanksgiving further open our minds to the great plan of which we are all a part?

When we consistently live in an awareness of joy and thanksgiving, are we effecting a conscious choice to express and experience God in these ways? When we give thanks for our many blessings, are we participating in a powerful force that is already active in our lives and in the world? Is the law of gratitude and thanksgiving really about combining the expectations of the mind with the power of the heart to bring an increase of good? In other words, is our "cup" upright and ready to receive?

Gratitude and sincerity of purpose flow as sparkling streams from the foundation of unlimited love, bringing greater unity to all. Thanksgiving is a spiritual quality that can be built into the soul with each day's practice. The rewards are rich and satisfying. Not outer conditions, circumstances, or appearances make any difference to the heart of an individual or a nation that is lifted up in thanksgiving. A bird could never leave the ground on folded wings! Thanksgiving is the power that can lift an individual or a country on widespread wings of faith and joy into the life and light of God.

◆ LAW 5

If earth is a school, who are the teachers? —John Marks Templeton

WHAT is the purpose of our life on earth? Philosophers, spiritual leaders, and other individuals often refer to the earth as a school for souls. A lifetime on earth may seem like a slow way to create a soul. And billions of years may seem an even slower way to create the school building! But who is measuring time, anyway? Perhaps the pertinent question is: How much progress can our souls make while in human form?

Various major religions have also referred to earth as a school. Buddhism, teaching that the life of the spirit transcends the life of man on earth, emphasizes that this life of the spirit is the true reality and the purpose of earth living is to grow spiritually through exercising free will, reason, love, prayer, and creativity.

The *Bhagavad Gita* offers something for every kind of spiritual aspirant, of whatever temperament, by whatever path. Various themes of life are presented and the Hindu deity, Krishna, clearly shifts his emphasis as he uses the word: *yogas*—the four main paths of Hindu mysticism. In one place his teachings focus on transcendental knowledge, in another on selfless action, in another on meditation, and in still another, on love.

The Christian faith provides the laws of the Old Testament and the parables of the New Testament as guidelines for spiritual growth. Jesus said, "If your mind and heart are set upon me constantly, you will come to know me." When he said that his kingdom was not of this world, could he have meant that the kingdom of heaven can be within our minds and souls, rather than in outward material surroundings?

Teilhard de Chardin, speaking from long years as a scientist, priest, and poet, said, "It is a law of the universe that in all things there is prior existence. Before every form, there is a prior, but lesser evolved form. Each one of us is evolving towards the God-head." Could this evolving toward God be our primary purpose on earth? Can this search for God take us through our own unconscious into the kingdom of heaven that is at hand? Is the

kingdom of heaven perhaps the state of fruitfulness that lies in embryo within each of us?

How could a soul understand divine joy or be thankful for heaven if it had not previously experienced earth? How could a soul comprehend the joy of surrender to God's will if it had never witnessed the hell on earth brought about by human self-will? What do we learn from human atrocities or from soulless, man-made governments? How are experiences involving adversities, disappointments, and mistakes often great teachers? What

To offer service to the gods, to the good, to the wise, and to your spiritual teacher; purity, honesty, continence, and nonviolence: these are the disciplines of the body. To offer soothing words, to speak truly, kindly, and helpfully, and to study the scriptures: these are the disciplines of speech. Calmness, gentleness, silence, self-restraint, and purity: these are the disciplines of the mind."

—*Bhagavad Gita*

can we learn through deep experiences of faith, hope, love, forgiveness, compassion, and service to others?

Could the earth have been designed as a place of hardship as a definite way to build the human soul? Would you send your child to a school that gave no exams? Is life experience designed to teach spiritual love and joy versus bodily ills and hard times? What is meant by the statement: "Into every life some rain must fall?" It is apparent that sometimes a soul begins developing into a greater soul when a person has gone through some intense tragedy. What can be realized is that the soul is fully capable of moving through these intensities of life! Can we also learn through powerful expressions of friendship, beauty, compassion, enthusiasm, diligence, creativity, and progress? Can we humbly admit that the Creator knows best how to build a soul? If the soul were born perfect, how would it understand or appreciate the absence of pain and sorrow?

St. Paul wrote: "More than this: let us even exult

in our present sufferings, because we know that suffering trains us to endure, and endurance brings proof that we have stood the test, and this proof is the ground of hope. Such a hope is no mockery, because God's love has flooded our inmost heart through the Holy Spirit he has given us" (Romans 5:3-5).

So, how does a soul grow in this school of life? And who are the teachers? Can spiritual growth take place through human reason and divine revelation, by communing with nature and with God, and by diligent use of the talents we are given? Can we increase our learning by making studied and wise choices? Our spiritual growth can also be achieved, in part, through knowledge—by overcoming our ignorance and self-centeredness until we are in tune with the divine. One of the laws of the spirit seems to indicate that self-improvement comes mainly from loving service in helping others to change from takers to givers.

When selfish egos can become "as a little child and enter into the kingdom of heaven," we can be pure like clear windowpanes, allowing the truth and light of God to shine through into our minds, heart, spirits, and souls. Great spiritual truths, which are the truths of real, everyday life, are the same in all ages and in all spiritual pursuits. They can come to any person who paves the way for their emergence in his or her life. God speaks into every listening ear, whether the ear belongs to Jew or Gentile, Hindu or Parsee, American or East Indian, Christian or Muslim.

Consider the Exodus story that tells of forty years of wandering by the children of Israel in the wilderness before reaching the Promised Land. What are some of the similarities to this story experienced by each person between birth and the time when we begin to learn and activate the spiritual laws in our life and reach heaven on earth?

Someone said, "Often it takes forty years for a self-centered little animal to become a God-centered little angel!"

The idea that heaven can only be some distant locality situated on the other side of death holds no meaning for the awakening consciousness. Has the idea that we must be totally in heaven or wholly in hell stunted progress in religion and possibly influenced it to march more slowly than business and science? The wellsprings of eternal life bubble up within each soul. How do we tap these living waters? It is up to each person to situate himself or herself with the appropriate mental condition and to couple it with unlimited love, faith, and expectancy. Sufficient time in study, worship, and prayer also allows us to clearly hear and rightly interpret the still, small voice of divine wisdom.

Spotlights ✦ ✦

1. Each person has a mind capable of creative activity in the maturation of the universe, as well as in the maturation of the soul.

2. How would you describe the creative process—from thoughts to deeds?

3. What are some ways we can learn more about divinity?

4. How would you describe "thoughts as things"?

5. Why is paying attention to our words so important?

6. Could anything exist separate from God? How? How not?

7. Why is the practice of thanksgiving an attracting energy?

8. Who are the happiest people you have ever met? If you wrote down the names of five persons who continually bubble with happiness, what would be the primary energy radiating from them? Love? Enthusiasm? Spiritual joy? Commitment to serving others?

9. How would you describe the purpose of your life on earth?

10. Which attitudes and endeavors can lead to heaven on earth?

11. How are you directing *your* life toward fruitful service and heaven on earth?

Living the Various Spiritual Laws ✦ ✦

In the *Book of Prayers*, Gandhi expressed a way of worship that was inclusive yet simple. Every morning and evening people would assemble in an open field, squatting on grass, or even on dirt, to participate in a truly interfaith experience. Those who came belonged to different faiths and some to no faith. There were Muslims, Hindus, Christians, Sikhs, Jews, agnostics, atheists, and others, because Gandhi's prayers were an attempt to search for the truth. This is one of Gandhi's inclusive prayers:

As long as the secret of the soul is not known,
all practices are useless;
thy life as a human being has passed away
uselessly, like the rains out of season.
What though thou bathest daily and performest
worship and dost service in the temples,
what though thou givest alms staying in thy own house,
what though thou adoptest long hair,
smearest thy body with the sacred ashes.
What though thou hast removed thy hair,
performest austerities and visitest holy places,
what though thou takest the rosary and takest his name;
what though thou markest the sacred mark
on the forehead, and keepest the tulsi leaf,
what though thou drinkest the Ganges water;
what though thou can recite the Vedas
and knowest the grammar and pronouncest correctly,
what though thou knowest the tunes and their effect,
what though thou knowest the six systems
and the permutations and combinations of letters.
All these are devices for finding
the wherewithal for one's support
if thou hast not known the soul of souls.
Narsaiyo says,
Thou hast wasted the priceless human heritage
if thou hast not known the secret of the universe.

Week Fourteen

✦ Law 1

The secret of a productive life can be sought and found. —John Marks Templeton

WHEN HE WAS ASKED which was the right way, that of sorrow or that of joy, the Rabbi of the Berditchev said:

There are two kinds of sorrow and two kinds of joy. When a man broods over the misfortunes that have come upon him, when he cowers in a corner and despairs of help that is a bad kind of sorrow, concerning which it is said: "The Divine Presence does not dwell in a place of dejection." The other kind is the honest grief of a man who knows what he lacks. The same is true of joy. He who is devoid of inner substance and in the midst of his empty pleasures, does not feel it, nor tries to fill his lack, is a fool. But he who is truly joyful is like a man whose house has burned down, who feels his need deep in his soul and begins to build anew. Over every stone that is laid, his heart rejoices.

To live fully and fruitfully, to love in unlimited expression, to grow in purpose and humility, and to find a wise and timeless understanding—these attributes can arise out of our capacity to experience and to know the present. Does the heart of the spiritual life emerge from living in awareness of purpose in the ever-changing reality of the present? Can the secret of a productive life be sought and found? A sign regarding a local contest puts it this way: You must be present to win! The Chasidic story illustrates that the simplicity of our focus in the present is what really matters.

The fruitfulness we seek is not usually found in more sights or sounds or tastes or thoughts. It can be found in the living reality of any moment we touch with our sincerity of purpose to lead a productive life. One element of living a productive life can be described as "*consciously* putting one foot in front of another, one day at a time." We would add, "with purpose, diligence, integrity, and vision!" In *The Hidden Words*, Bahá'u'lláh tells us, "Thou art but one step away from the glorious heights above and from the celestial tree of love." If we touch the experiences of everyday living more intimately, can our hearts open to a deeper level? Can we keep uppermost in our minds that there is a place where "all things are possible to those who love God"? When we set time aside for prayer on a regular basis, we can get to that place; our creativity and productivity can flourish.

Every moment of our lives is unique and, therefore, precious. Could the sunrise or sunset on this day ever be precisely duplicated? Could a special sharing with another, or the exuberant laughter of a child, be felt or repeated in the exact same manner? Could the present moment's vision ever be recaptured, literally, if we let it slip by? So, if we desire a more productive life, isn't the present moment a good place to begin? Let's look at some possibilities.

How about considering simplicity, living the simple life? Now, this does not mean that we withdraw from the world and the meaningful work to be accomplished in order to discover true simplicity of the heart. Nor are dramatic gestures called for. William Blake said, "If one is to do good, good must be done in the minute particulars. General good is the plea of the hypocrite, the flatterer, and the scoundrel." The productive simplicity mentioned here is without pretension. It is like the water that simply runs downhill. In Zen Buddhism, it is called "resuming our true nature."

Every person who has ever lived on the planet unfolds a human story line. It begins with our conception, continues through our childhood, includes all of our personal triumphs and tribulations, and brings us to this present moment in our lives. There is also a divine whisper, paralleling this story line, reminding us that earth is not our ultimate home. We may sense that there is an eternal aspect flowing beneath the surface of our beings. In some respects, we might compare ourselves with Michelangelo and the truth he knew as he sculpted the statue of David. Michelangelo *knew* the statue of David already resided in the block of marble. Part of his artistic life was spent chipping away the excess to reveal the inner creation. Can you perceive the similarities? Can you visualize your inner life in this fashion?

A mystic once said, "Of what avail is the open eye if the heart is blind?" Can wisdom and balance represent two of the "arts" of living a productive life—the wisdom of an inspired intellect merged with the unlimited love of an open heart? True wisdom doesn't eliminate the travails and sorrows of the world. Instead, doesn't it teach us to live with greater integrity and compassion in the midst of all life experiences? Wisdom reveals how to respond to the challenges of this very life with great love and serenity. When wisdom and balance abide, "hand in hand," we neither resist the challenges life may bring, nor do they overwhelm us. When a balanced life becomes realized, do we naturally become more productive?

How do we create and establish our lives as an embodiment of wisdom, serenity, compassion, unlimited love, integrity, and productivity? What are the qualities that enable us to walk in the spirit of freedom and learn our greatest lessons? How could today's educational processes assist in discovering the special gifts or talents inherent within each child? In addition, how can educational processes be helpful in the development of these areas? What do knowledge and achievements matter if we do not understand how to touch the heart of another or to be touched? Does a productive life open the door a little wider to *heaven on earth*?

Can you *imagine* what it might feel like to live a productive life and then *assume* that attitude? How would it feel to do what you are doing so well that life could be amazed at how talented you have grown to be?

✦ LAW 2

Happiness is always a by-product. —John Marks Templeton

MOST OF US know within our hearts that there is a great value in being happy, and we seek to experience this aspect of life. Many people try to find happiness in a variety of ways, few of which produce lasting results. Why do some lives seem filled with turmoil, anxiety, or depression while the ones living these lives are desperately seeking happiness? Some people search for happiness in accumulating wealth. But do riches produce lasting happiness? Some people think they can discover happiness in relationships, and meaningful relationships are wonderful. However, can a person experience a relationship with another and still miss the point of ultimate happiness? We may feel sad because we haven't yet achieved the degree of success we desire. Why is it that many of the ways we may have been taught to "pursue" happiness only reinforce the feelings and activities that result in unhappiness? Why do we continue to seek happiness *outside* ourselves?

Many people may spend years, even lifetimes, in the pursuit of happiness. Someone once asked, "If we humans are so smart, why aren't we happy?" Could it be because we have yet to create the vision, understanding, and purpose to support such a wonderful reality? Why does it seem so many people "seek" happiness and fail to find it? Is the *pursuit* of happiness unsuccessful because happiness is always a by-product? What is meant by "by-product"?

In *What All the World's A'seeking*, written in 1896, Ralph Waldo Trine stated:

A corollary of the great principle already enunciated might be formulated thus: there is no such thing as finding true happiness by searching for it directly. It must come, if it comes at all, indirectly, or by the service, the love, and the happiness we give to others. So there is no such thing as finding true greatness by searching for it directly. It always, without a single exception, has come indirectly in this same way, and it is not at all probable that this great eternal law is going to be changed to suit any particular case or cases. Then recognize it, put your life into harmony with it, and reap the rewards of its observance, or fail to recognize it and pay the penalty accordingly; for the law itself will remain unchanged. Life is not, we may say, for mere passing pleasure, but for

the highest unfoldment that one can attain to, the noblest character that one can grow, and for the greatest service that one can render to all mankind. In this, however, we will find the highest pleasure, for in this the only real pleasure lies.

Our journey through life may sometimes seem like a major challenge when unexpected difficulties arise. Could feelings of unhappiness result

from certain beliefs and judgments that we choose and that we can change? What could happen in our lives if we chose a *daily intention* of "living happy"? Would a happier and more loving embrace of ourselves and those around us produce more harmonious and joyful results? What could happen if we released all judgments of others? How would our lives be affected if words of criticism no longer passed our lips? What if we began to see people and events through increasingly optimistic eyes? Is optimism a forerunner of happiness? Is a happy and loving attitude a tremendous transforming power in facing the big and little challenges of everyday living?

Happiness comes from seeking to give, not get. Happiness is never the completion—the getting. Happiness comes from the work, the endeavor, the pursuit of a goal, the giving! Production, not consumption, is at the core of happiness and success. How does this happen? When we inspire others to be happy, do we also inspire ourselves? How can every situation of every day become an opportunity for expressed happiness? Does each step we take toward more fruitful lives enhance the measure of our happiness?

In his book *Happiness Is a Choice*, Barry Kaufman describes how a Dutch scientist discovered something quite startling. If he took two pendulum clocks, each a different size and made of different materials, and placed them on a wall in close proximity to each other, they would begin to alter their rhythms subtly until they beat in perfect unison. More recently, scientists have found that two heart cells from two different living creatures, when put near each other under the microscope, will synchronize and start beating together despite the space between the cells.

If a diverse group of people, including a newborn infant, occupies a room in which a radio or stereo system plays music with a distinct melody and beat, many in the group, including the infant, will move their feet and fingers to the music. Some might rock their torsos or move their heads. It could be said that these people are "entraining" themselves to the rhythms and motions around them.

Consider the possible impact on a nation by a happy and loving head of state. Could there also be a similar effect on children by happy and loving parents, on patients by happy and loving doctors and nurses, on students by happy and loving teachers, and on relationships by happy and loving

spouses? If being happy means that we become easier, more comfortable with ourselves, more accepting, respectful, excited, and appreciative of what we do and with whom we interface, would we not then become a gift to all we meet? Would we not become a continuously incredible gift to ourselves as well?

Kaufman further asks: "All life forms pulsate, but why the tendency to do it together? Why do

Happiness is not best achieved by those who seek it directly.
—Bertrand Russell

we mimic the tempo of music even at birth? Why do separate heart cells or pendulum clocks, in close proximity, synchronize their beat? Why does one loving and happy person have a similar effect on another? What force determines such a propensity for harmony? What common energy moves all living creatures so strongly toward synergistic interaction? Some call it intelligence; others recognize it as God."

◆ LAW 3

The way to mend the bad world is to create the right world. —Ralph Waldo Emerson

"LET THERE BE peace on earth and let it begin with me" are the opening words to a famous hymn. But what do the words really mean? How can being filled with peace inside yourself lead to peace on earth? The brilliant philosopher, Teilhard de Chardin, refers to the "unimpeachable wholeness of the universe." What does this mean to us? It means that we are a part of the universe; we are a part of the wholeness of creation. We do not walk the path of life alone. The whole universe walks

with us and we, as the human race, are coming to a greater realization that we are all "one" in spirit.

Maybe each one of us is somewhat like a pixel. Just as a hologram is made up of numerous pixels —each one containing all of the information that can be found in the total image—so each person may be a tiny particle of life, containing all the data that is present in the sum total of existence.

Guatama Buddha, whose original name was Prince Siddhartha, grappled with the problems of human existence. Although his words were not written down as he spoke them, his disciples memorized many of his teachings and passed them on to succeeding generations by word of mouth. The principal teachings of the Buddha are called the Four Noble Truths: first, that human life is intrinsically unhappy; second, that the cause of this unhappiness is human selfishness and desire; third, that individual selfishness and desire can be brought to an end; and fourth, that the method of escape from selfishness involves what is called the eight-fold path. The eight-fold path includes: right views, right thought, right speech, right action, right livelihood, right effort, right mindfulness, and right meditation. Certainly, this awareness of "rightness" and the letting go of personal negatives can do a tremendous amount to create a loving, caring, and more beautiful world.

A good way to create a better world is for each of us to be better individuals. There are certain universal laws of life that, when followed, can make life sweeter, more harmonious, prosperous, healthy, and free. When we choose to abide by these laws, we reap the benefits of living in harmony with the universe. When we don't, we risk experiencing sickness, war, economic insecurity, and unemployment. The problems that create turmoil, pain, misery, and suffering in our world can change when each person makes a *conscious* decision to act and think for the good of all. Personal motive is always a good guide. Ask yourself, "Why am I doing the things I do?" and allow the inherent wisdom of spirit to provide the true answer. If your motives are pure, then good shall come of them. The positive ideas we believe in today can constantly expand and grow in our consciousness. This could be termed being "on the beam" with life. Pilots often fly using a radio beam as a guide.

As long as they remain "on the beam," they are safe. If they get off the beam, they are in danger.

Each human person, too, has an inborn "beam"—a conscience. While we are in tune with the way things were designed to be, we are "safe." When we are out of tune, we may show it in the form of greed, fear, sickness, addiction, and jealousy.

By thinking and acting always with good in our hearts; by becoming responsible for ourselves, and by recognizing, as an old Irish saying has it, "If you see a job that needs doing, that means it's yours to do," we can begin to change our wrong world into a right world. It is time to stop saying that "they" need to be changing things around here. When we start saying, "I need to be giving life a helping hand," we begin to benefit life. It has been said, "a journey of a thousand miles begins with the first step." Let each one of us take that step and make it count!

✦ Law 4

It is better to praise than to criticize. —John Marks Templeton

A GROUP of Boy Scouts embarked on a camping trip, pitching their tents in an open field for the night. As the campfire sputtered its last breath in a shower of sparks and the stars began to sparkle in the night sky, the boys settled down to sleep. Some hours later, in the middle of the night, a cry of agony awakened the sleepers. One of the boys had been bitten by a scorpion and was in intense pain. What could be done? There was no doctor, no nurse, no medical facility, near the camping area. The scoutmaster exclaimed, "Oh, what can we do?"

A small voice responded, "We can pray!"

The entire group closed their eyes and prayed, "God, send help! And soon!"

Almost before their eyes were open, the group heard the screeching tires of a car. It stopped on the side of the road, just across from where the scouts were camped. The scoutmaster ran to the car. Imagine his surprise when he discovered the occupant was a doctor! The doctor was returning from a medical meeting in a nearby town when his car developed mechanical trouble and came to a sudden stop. The scoutmaster caught the doctor by the hand and pulled him toward the camp. "We need help," he stated.

The doctor examined the little boy but told the group he couldn't do anything without the appropriate medicine. Once again, the group felt helpless.

Again, the small voice spoke, "The One who sent us the doctor can send the medicine!"

Soon after an ambulance van passed, stopped, and backed up. The doctor and scoutmaster informed the driver of the situation. The required medicine was available. The doctor injected the boy, and the child was immediately relieved.

Again, the small voice piped up, "Praise God, from whom all blessings flow!"

Praise is one of the most useful attitudes for transforming life. It can be used at any time of the day or night. It is especially useful when our lives may not seem to be progressing as well as they could! The spoken word is like a seed. It must grow! We can leave the how, when, and where to God. Our job is to enthusiastically speak what is good and to pour forth blessings, knowing that the moment we give forth praise and gratitude we begin to receive abundant good.

Experiencing praise and gratitude is like overflowing into greater spiritual awakening. It is joyous! It is exciting! Actually, could we ever make anything more holy than it already is? Everything is already completely blessed! What we can do, however, is to see and appreciate the God-infused blessedness in every person and in every thing.

As we express praise and appreciation for someone or for some thing, are we not blessing them in a most powerful way? Isn't this a wonderful way to acknowledge their divine origins? In one sense, we are giving thanks for a gift from God. Have you ever thought of praise as a form of prayer? If you haven't, just start praising everything in your life and watch what happens! When we consciously focus on the good in our lives, do we unite our minds with the power of divine creativity and make ourselves available to receive the greater good that is everywhere present?

On the other hand, can criticism, complaining, or wrestling with life block creative energies and cut us off from possibilities of abundance? Is being ungrateful a sure "door slammer" on fruitfulness and progress? Have you had the experience of railing against a problem, only to find increasing pain? Why do you think this happened? Until we recognize the lesson a situation may be bringing, do we continue to increase our own sense of separation from happiness? Is lack of appreciation simply a matter of limited seeing? Is praise and appreciation another avenue for introducing heaven on earth? When rearing your children, have you found praise to be constructive and criticism to be destructive?

New possibilities can come to us in the most amazing ways! How astounding it can be to look beyond surface appearances until we discover the treasure of the inner person or experience. Thus, we derive a great deal more benefit from praise than from criticism!

✦ LAW 5

Laughter is the best medicine. —Norman Cousins

> Our smile affirms our awareness and determination to live in peace and joy. The source of a true smile is an awakened mind.
> —Thich Nhat Hanh

HAVE YOU EVER noticed how you feel when you laugh? Muscles relax. Breathing becomes deeper and slower. The bloodstream becomes more fully oxygenated. Gloomy thoughts disappear, or at least seem to lessen! The maxim "Laughter is the best medicine" has a basis in reality. Endorphins are the body's natural anesthetics. It has been lately learned that laughter stimulates the secretion of endorphins. So, when we laugh, in one sense we are administering our own pain-killers!

Studies published in a psychology journal claim that if we smile, we feel happy for several reasons. One reason emphasizes that by tightening and loosening the muscles of the face, we activate a network of nerves that send signals to the emotion centers of the brain. A frown turns on the depression center. A smile turns on the elation center. Another reason why smiling can trigger feelings of happiness has to do with blood temperature in the body. Have you ever heard someone referred to as being *boiling* mad? Or, have you ever been accused of being *hot-headed*? Our very way of speaking provides a clue. When we frown, some muscles tighten, diverting more of our blood to the brain, warming it up. Smiling tightens a different set of muscles, decreasing blood flow to the brain. Not enough to impair functioning, but just enough to cool it!

> He deserves paradise who makes his companions laugh.
> —Qu'ran

If we really know how to live, what better way than to start the day with a smile? A smile can help us approach a new day with enthusiasm and understanding. Our smile can also bring happiness to us and to those around us. And this precious gift requires no monetary funds!

> In one Old Testament concordance, there are 57 references to laughter, and countless references to joy, gladness, rejoicing, and happiness. In one New Testament concordance, there are 287 references to joy, gladness, merriment, rejoicing, delighting, laughing, etc.
> —Cal Samra

This story from Thich Nhat Hanh, entitled "Flower Insights," illustrates our point:

There is a story about a flower that is well known in Zen circles. One day the Buddha held up a flower in front of an audience of 1,250 monks and nuns. He did not say anything for quite a long time. The audience was perfectly silent. Everyone seemed to be thinking hard, trying to see the meaning behind the Buddha's gesture. Then, suddenly, the Buddha smiled. He smiled because someone in the audience smiled at him and at the flower. The name of that monk was Mahakashyapa. He was the only person who smiled, and the Buddha smiled back and said, "I have a treasure of insight, and I have transmitted it to Mahakashyapa." That story has been discussed by many generations of Zen students, and people continue to look for its meaning. The meaning is quite simple. When someone holds up a flower and shows it to you, he wants you to see it. If you keep thinking, you miss the flower! The person who was not thinking, who was just himself, was able to encounter the flower in depth, and he smiled.

Some people tend to think that after they become successful, they can afford to be joyous. In the meantime, they grit their teeth and solemnly trudge toward their goals. But laughter and joy are qualities that can be cultivated along the way to help us be more fruitful and successful. A thirst for happiness seems to be a common instinct in humankind. The same glorious energy that pulsates through our hearts and brains also operates our hands and feet and muscles! Learning to utilize this inherent energy can be one of the greatest assets in our life, especially when we smile!

Have you ever watched someone work with a gentle smile on his or her face? Would you conclude that the smiling person is happy with what he or she is doing? The world-famous philosopher and physician Albert Schweitzer commented, "I don't know what your destiny will be, but one thing I know. The only ones among you who will be really happy are those who will have sought and found how to serve." Have you ever paused to consider how joyous you feel when your life is full of purpose? How does it *feel* to forget about yourself and give your energy in service for others? How does it feel to laugh for the sheer joy of being alive?

When the green woods laugh with the voice of joy,
And the dimpling stream runs laughing by;
When the air does laugh with our merry wit,
And the green hill laughs with the noise of it;

When the meadows laugh with lively green,
And the grasshopper laughs in the merry scene,
When Mary and Susan and Emily
With their sweet round mouths sing, "Ha, Ha, He!"

When the painted birds laugh in the shade,
Where our table with cherries and nuts is spread,
Come live and be merry, and join with me,
To sing the sweet chorus of, "Ha, Ha, He!"
—William Butler Yeats, "Laughing Song"

Spotlights ✦ ✦

1. What are some ways a productive life can be sought and found?

2. How can we keep uppermost in our minds that there is a place where "all things are possible to those who love God?"

3. How can living a simple life be advantageous?

4. Why does pursuing happiness often result in futility?

5. How would you describe happiness as an inside job?

6. How would you describe happiness as a "by-product"?

7. How is a noble mind able to see a question from all sides without bias?

8. How would you describe a "noble mind"?

9. How is a noble mind developed?

10. Why is it better to praise than to criticize?

11. Why is criticism so painful—to the one being criticized *and* to the one who is criticizing?

12. How would you explain the saying "Laughter is the best medicine"?

13. How could laughter be considered by some to be a form of prayer?

14. How are those who bring laughter to others also beneficiaries?

Living the Various Spiritual Laws ✦ ✦

If I can throw a single ray of light across the darkened pathway of another; if I can aid some soul to clearer sight of life and duty, and thus bless my brother; if I can wipe from any human cheek a tear, I shall not have lived my life in vain while here.

If I can guide some erring one to truth, inspire within his heart a sense of duty; if I can plant within my soul of rosy youth a sense of right, a love of truth and beauty; if I can teach one man that God and heaven are near, I shall not then have lived in vain while here.

If from my mind I banish doubt and fear, and keep my life attuned to love and kindness; if I can scatter light and hope and cheer, and help remove the curse of mental blindness; if I can make more joy, more hope, less pain, I shall have not lived and loved in vain.

If by life's roadside I can plant a tree, beneath whose shade some wearied lad may rest, though I may never share its beauty, I shall yet be truly blest—though no one knows my name, nor drops a flower upon my grave, I shall not have lived in vain while here.

—Anonymous

Week Fifteen

◆ Law 1

Humility, like darkness, reveals the heavenly light. —Henry David Thoreau

Is HUMILITY often a misunderstood virtue? It can mean serving others, as when Jesus said, "Whoever would be great among you must be your servant, and whoever would be first among you must be your slave" (Matthew 20:26, 27). The word "humility" can also mean awareness that God infinitely exceeds anything anyone has ever said of him and is vastly beyond human comprehension and understanding.

Is humility especially rewarding when its essence is humility toward God? When we can admit to ourselves that no human has ever known more than a tiny bit of the infinity and eternity of God, are we ready to activate our desire to seek and learn? Can a humble approach provide enthusiasm and diligence for varieties of research on invisible realities deemed spiritual?

There seems to be an intrinsic human need in our world for spiritual qualities such as moral values, integrity, compassion, unlimited love, and humility. The development of a searching mind, a responsive heart, or a feeling of closeness with others is not only for people who believe and participate in religious practices. Are not these qualities pertinent for everyone, irrespective of race, religion, or political affiliation? Do these qualities represent invitations for members of the human family to see things in larger terms? Can humility, then, offer an avenue of research that looks forward, not backward, one that expects to grow and learn from its mistakes? A strong structure has to rest on a stable foundation. Is this not an applicable analogy also for spiritual growth? If we wish to grow spiritually, what building blocks are most useful? *Desire, humility, flexibility,* and *love* seem like excellent cornerstones!

Desire, like fuel in a rocket, is the driving force that propels us forward. In order for a buggy to move up a hill, it needs a spirited and powerful

horse pulling it! When friendship with God becomes important enough to us, do we devote increased energy and attention to our spiritual life?

From the spiritual perspective, *humility* is a sign of strength. In his book, *Reaching High: The Psychology of Spiritual Living,* Marvin Gawryn writes, "True humility is rooted in self-respect and faith. The spiritually humble person can look honestly at his weak points because he has faith in his ability to overcome them. Being humble does not mean being passive and retiring. It means seeing ourselves clearly in order to act. Humility is the launching pad for aggressive growth."

Could we ever make progress without, at some point along the way, releasing old ways of living and exploring new and unknown territory? Have you ever watched a young tree bending with the wind? It may seem to bend in half when the strong wind blows. Yet, it rises straight and true when the wind ceases. Its roots and trunk become stronger and it is able to continue growing. If we are afraid to change, can we become inflexible and halt our growth? One aspect of humility is an open and receptive mind. Our agility in learning from the life experiences that come our way can become a tremendous strength.

Of course, the foremost quality of God's nature is all-encompassing, unlimited *love!* To the extent that we give and receive love, can we utilize the central progressive activity of the spiritual life? The love of God and the love of man mightily reinforce each other! Isn't the experience of *loving* as deeply rewarding as the experience of *being loved*—perhaps more so?

Can a humble consciousness help us reduce the stumbling blocks placed in our paths toward experiencing "heaven on earth?" Are the people who have reduced their ego desires more likely to *give* rather than *get?* Our egos can cause us to think that

we are in the center—rather than one small temporary outward manifestation—of a vast universe of being that subsists in the eternal and infinite reality that is God. So, wouldn't life be a part of God, rather than vice versa? Have you heard someone use the words, "the realm of spirit"? Is there any other realm? Is not everything of spirit? How can we experience and express a more humble approach to life?

If we walk outside on a clear, dark night and look up into the sky, it is possible to see thousands of stars. Have you ever considered that if it were not for the darkness of space, the starlight could not be revealed to us on Earth? Could the heavenly light within each of us—our divine purpose and potential—become more illumined from the vast background of the soul? Is the unseen beauty existing within each of us the potential that makes us truly alive?

There was a song by a group called The Band with the chorus, "When you wake up, you will remember everything." Is humanity beginning to awaken? Is the morning light revealing that we are children of a divinity and that heaven on earth is available to us? Why? Isn't it a father's greatest pleasure to share his life with his children?

✦ LAW 2

Which entertainment is beneficial? —John Marks Templeton

DO YOU EVER find yourself watching an awful television program and hesitate to turn it off? The raucous noises, explosions of gunfire, shrieking voices and, often, overall violence of some programs can be upsetting. Yet many people don't get out of their seats and turn off the TV! Isn't it as important to close the door to negative entertainment as it is to close the door to winter cold? Why

do we hesitate to do so?

What happens when we watch a bad TV program? If we are what we feel and perceive, does the program we are watching have an effect on our own characters? If we are angry, can we become angrier? If we are fearful, can we become more afraid? If we are uneasy or upset, can we become even less peaceful? If we are planning and working toward establishing beneficial goals, why do we open our minds, hearts, and emotions to harmful programming? Many of these are often programs made by sensationalist producers in search of easy money. Watching some of the most popular programs can make our hearts pound, our fists clench, and leave us drained and exhausted! In some instances, can excessive entertainment become like a drug? Can we become so caught up with media dramas that we leave almost no room in our schedule for beneficial or creative activities?

Since the early years of television, the entertainment industry has brainwashed many young people to assume that their primary purpose in life is to bring happiness to themselves. But such pursuit usually reduces happiness for themselves and others. Of course, television isn't the only media that offers unprincipled entertainment. For example, consider the effects of some of the products of the movie industry or the publishing industry or some sports programs. It could be interesting to note how many times during a day we may become entranced or scattered by less than helpful entertainment. A day wasted is gone forever, so isn't it logical and beneficial to make the best beneficial use of every hour of every day?

When is television educational and when can it

be harmful? Granted, many educational television programs provide wonderful opportunities to learn. How can we discern which programs can do harm to our nervous systems, minds, and hearts, and which programs can be quite beneficial?

How can we help young people to comprehend

that real happiness flows from within, not from external programming? Could this erroneous pursuit of happiness be a reason why America, the center of the entertainment industry, also has twice as high a percentage of people in jail than most nations? Do the fundamental pragmatics of life

necessitate learning and discernment about the meaning and conduct of life and human development toward excellence in mind and virtue?

"Claiming our power" means believing in ourselves and in our possibilities. Can surrendering to external influences undermine our personal power? Can passive and excessive entertainment reduce the fruitfulness of our lives? By ceasing to utilize our talents, could we change from being benefactors to humanity to being parasites? All the choices we make form building blocks for our lives. We are given the opportunity to mold and shape our world through our consciousness. The way we perceive and respond to the world in which we live results from the choices we make. We have the power of free will to determine what we want in life. Some decisions may be easy; some may be difficult. However, we *do* have choices!

If it is obvious that we are constantly making choices every moment of every day, isn't it important to choose "rightly"? Which possibilities represent the highest good for ourselves and for others? Which entertainment is beneficial? What alternatives do we have? A productive life requires discipline and discernment. Whatever may be offered, we can choose that which is beneficial to our progress.

✦ LAW 3

If you do not know what you want to achieve
in your life, you may not achieve much! —John Marks Templeton

SOME PEOPLE seem to be quite clear about what they *don't* want in their lives, but how many are prepared to do the necessary visioning and planning and exert the effort to achieve what they *do* want? If someone asked for directions on how to get from point "A" to point "B," most likely we would inform the questioner of the appropriate direction and describe the correct turns to make to arrive at the desired destination. Our lives can be run on the same principle. Once we know what we want, we can move into a position to establish desired goals and then work toward achieving those goals.

When we establish goals for what we want in life, are we providing ourselves with the opportunity to develop greater potential? Now, think about this for a moment. Do we have to know *exactly* where we are going in order to get there? Not necessarily! As an instrument of the Creator, aren't we ever in the presence of loving guidance? Isn't this the kind of awareness that encourages us to work a little harder, produce more effectively, and feel more purposeful about what we are doing and where we are going? So, would a plan of action and direction, coupled with an open mind and consciousness, and supported by a strong foundation of prayer, be a workable formula for greater fruitfulness? A minister friend, when planning and setting certain goals, always adds, "This, or something better, God!" This willingness opens the door of his receptivity to a better idea than he may presently have from the divine source.

Life is filled with transition and growth. Every step along the path is both a singular experience and a part of the whole of life. There are no ordinary moments. For example, this one moment that you are alive right now is a totality and not some-

thing separate from your entire life. Keep in mind the old saying, "Life is what happens to you while you are making other plans!" Every part of our day

The source of all creation is pure consciousness . . . pure potentiality seeking expression from the unmanifest to the manifest. And when we realize our true Self is one of pure potentiality, we align with the power that manifests everything in the universe.
—*Deepak Chopra*

is important. Just as we make ourselves resonant with positive qualities by holding our minds focused on particular thoughts, so too we can align our focus with desired goals toward continual progress.

Making a decision of what we want to achieve can be similar to putting a bit into a horse's mouth. The bit is probably the smallest part of the harness of a horse, yet it is the most important. With the bit in place, it is possible to control and guide the movements of the horse. With a gentle tug on the bit, we can direct the horse to move his body in whatever direction we wish it to go. Without guidance, the horse may wander off to munch grass in the pasture! Without a vision or goal to inspire us and invite us to greater expression, we may not achieve the useful and progressive life we desire!

A story is told about a man who sat by his window, watching the March wind chase the dark clouds across the sky. With his head in his hands, he moaned, "How sad and desolate is this landscape before me!" And he got no further. Meanwhile, not far away another man was working in his field. He, too, saw the wind chasing the clouds and deeply inhaled the living breath that flowed all around him. As this man followed his plow, cutting through the rich loam of the field, he sensed life stirring everywhere. He was in tune with a victorious power that cannot be held in restraint. This man understood the message of the March wind, because he was a worker in a fertile field! He knew that new life may be hidden, but the seeds are present! Isn't it easy to understand that the workers in the fertile field of life are aware of the infinite spirit of nature?

Could a sincere self-analysis play an important role in setting meaningful goals? In *Man's Eternal Quest,* Paramahansa Yogananda states: "True self-analysis is the greatest art of progress." Would it be helpful to write down our thoughts and aspirations daily for a period of time? Would this enable us to learn more of what we are, and where we desire to go with our lives? What would happen if we left the confines of ego and wandered in the vast fields of soul progress? Would our desires and goals be different from the present moment?

Would freeing ourselves from the debris of unbeneficial human habits help us start to sow the seeds of the success we desire? We have the ability to alter ourselves and to change the direction of our lives quickly with strong vision and determination. Are we therefore the architects of our own destinies?

What do we want to achieve with our lives? If we ask this question of many people, we may receive many responses. What would be our acme of spiritual and human achievement? How can we benefit from all-around universal principles of living from the religions of the world and the lives of the great people we admire? Where are we going? What is our motive? Where do we wish to be? What is the surest and best way to reach our destination?

◆ Law 4

More is wrought by prayer than this world dreams of. —Alfred, Lord Tennyson

A BUSINESSMAN was working through a tough personal problem and felt he was not making much progress. He decided to seek help from a counselor. During their meeting, the man shrugged and threw up his hands in exasperation and said, "I've tried everything I know to try, so I guess it's time to pray!" How many times have we heard this comment in one form or another? *When all else fails . . . pray!*

What would happen if we made the conscious decision to preface our day and all it may contain with prayer? Would business meetings flow more smoothly and effectively if prayer were the first item on the agenda? If an uncomfortable situation should arise, could a brief moment of prayer set

the stage for understanding and compassion? How can daily prayer affect family life and the way we interact with others? When we allow God to work through us quietly and peacefully, without worry and strain, can we not feel the healing balm of infinite presence? How may prayer be a powerful tool for "practicing the presence of God" in all areas of our life?

In his book *Prayer Is Good Medicine,* Dr. Larry Dossey makes the statement: "In its simplest form, prayer is an attitude of the heart—a matter of being, not doing. Prayer is the desire to contact the Absolute, however it may be conceived. When we experience the need to enact this connection, we are praying, whether or not we use words." *Prayer is communion between God and man.* It is an attitude of the soul that, at times, expresses itself in words. At other times, the expression may be in the silence. Can you imagine the benefits to an individual when prayer becomes a *way of life* rather than a series of isolated acts? There is a mystic power in prayer and it works! Through our times of prayer and this special at-tunement with divinity, we are increasing our own spiritual light. We are building a better way of life in every way and we are attracting what we are building—more spiri-tual light!

A respected and quite effective teacher spoke of prayer in this way. She said, "I often work on the idea of an 'island of prayer' in the middle of a 'sea of chaos,' wherever I may be. Why? Because prayer can lift our attention above the chaos! For example, I may enter my office and the telephone is ringing. Three people are waiting in the recep-tion area to see me, each with an urgent situation. The secretary has several important messages, and a list of a dozen things needing attention waits on my desktop. *Where is the starting point?* I close the door, settle in my chair and, for a few minutes, tune out everything except God and me! I build a mental island of peace, quietude, and accomplish-ment around me by becoming attuned with the presence of God in thought, feeling, and action. I immerse myself in God's presence, and all things cooperate for good—for myself and for all with whom I come in contact . . . and everybody ben-efits! Then I go to work!"

Could part of the beauty of prayer be that it isn't necessary to know precisely how it works in order to benefit from its miraculous effects? Could a key factor in the effectiveness of prayer be the feeling and expression of unlimited love? The power of spirit lies within each of us; the question is how to develop it. What truths may lie behind

You pray in your distress and in your needs;
would that you might pray also in the fullness
of your joy and in your days of abundance.
—Kahlil Gibran

the statement: "More is wrought by prayer than this world dreams of?"

The call to prayer is heard in all languages. Have not various religious and spiritual practices down through the ages, as well as in our current time, asked us to weave the threads of prayer into the fabric of our lives? For what purpose? Could this be one way of bring-ing an expression of "heaven on earth" into daily living? Every culture in the world, every civilization—regardless of how primitive—has some kind of spiritual activity that may be referred to as a "prayer process." Prayer is a natural function and prayer is indigenous to man. The beloved philosopher Kahlil Gibran caught this theme when he said, "For what is prayer but the expansion of one's self into the living ethers."

Why is the simple prayer, "Thy will be done," so powerful? Are we invoking a greater wisdom than our present understanding? Are we perhaps sur-rendering our preferences and demands for a par-ticular outcome in favor of the highest and best for all involved? Even when we may think we are praying for what is best, is our human knowledge possibly limited in the universal scheme of things?

In one of his seminars, Gregg Braden, author of *The Isaiah Effect*, was asked the question, "Why prayer? What good does it really do?" He responded:

Prayer is, to us, as water is to the seed of a plant. . . . The seed of a plant is whole and complete unto itself. Under the right conditions [as with seeds found in some of the ancient tombs], a seed may exist for hundreds of years simply as a seed, a rigid shell protecting a greater possi-bility. Only in the presence of water will the seed realize the greatest expression of its life.

We are like those seeds. We come into this world whole and complete unto ourselves, carrying the seed of some-thing even greater. Our time with one another, in the pres-

ence of life's challenges, awakens within us the greatest possibilities of love and compassion. It is in the presence of prayer that we blossom to fulfill our potential.

Based on some of the recent research programs regarding prayer, could prayer be viewed as a "language" as well as a "philosophy," bridging the worlds of science and spirit? Just as other philosophies may be expressed through unique words and a vocabulary relative to that particular philosophy, does prayer have a vocabulary of its own in the silent language of feelings? For example, cannot the philosophy of peace be expressed through languages as diverse as physics, astronomy, theology, and politics, as well as prayer?

To change the conditions of our outer world, we are invited to actually become a manifestation of our desire from within. Is prayer an effective avenue to achieve this purpose? When we focus in prayer, do we not love the creative principle of life itself, our Creator, with all of our heart, mind, soul, and strength? Can this be the underlying reason why more is wrought by prayer than this world dreams of?

✦ Law 5

Everything and everyone around you is your teacher. —Ken Keyes

WHAT WOULD it be like to study with the greatest teacher in the world? The one who could teach us what we most need to learn at this moment? Each person can be a student of the greatest teacher, and it's easier than we may think! How? Take a look around. Our teachers are everywhere! Look at the people who are in our lives—our family, friends, coworkers, associates, strangers, why, even ourselves! Life is set up to bring the situations and experiences that can be most fulfilling to our growth. How does this happen?

One possibility is that, quite often, what we see in others may be a reflection of something within ourselves. Perhaps the thing we most admire in another may be a quality we possess but have failed to recognize. Could another possibility be that what we most dislike in another may reflect a trait within ourselves that we may be unaware is present? Can this be especially true when we experience strong feelings, either positive or negative, about another person?

Can the way people *respond* to us teach us something about the energy we are projecting? Are we able to learn more about ourselves by observing the characteristics of the people with whom we associate? What are their values? Do they live their lives with integrity? Are they honest, loyal, dependable? What does the way we prioritize our time tell us about ourselves? What can we learn from the kinds of activities we pursue? How do we spend our leisure time? How do we invest and spend our money? What thoughts most often fill our minds? Negative? Positive? Prayerful? Progressive? Goal-setting? What feelings do we most often experience? Joy? Love? Laughter? Compassion? Enthusiasm? A desire to serve?

What would be the meaning of human life on earth if it didn't afford us sufficient opportunities to learn, to grow, to develop our potential, and to be fruitful in what we do? How can the ideals of love for God and service to humanity find full expression in our lives? How can we glean the precious lessons of greater growth from everyone and everything around us? According to spiritual science, the attitude of the mind is the foundation for everything unfolding in our lives. Thoughts are like rivers flowing from the reservoir of spirit. How can we channel these streams of living energy into useful purpose?

In *The Development of Religion as a Science*, Franklin Loehr tells an amusing but insightful story. Before a lecture on a newly published book, Dr. Loehr was having dinner with another minister and his wife when their young daughter burst into the room. She was filled with exciting new knowledge. "Mommy, four plus four equals eight! Did you know that?"

"Yes," replied her mother. "How do *you* know that?"

"Teacher said so!" the child responded.

Upon the authority of a teacher—who may be anyone we accept as a teacher—we learn a great deal of what we "know." This is the first way information was received and dispersed in the human community, and passed from generation to generation. However, the real proof that "four plus four equals eight" does not reside in the fact that "teacher said so!" Doesn't the validity of anything that a teacher or anyone else may present lie in the reality behind the given statement? Is the information presented by any teacher true only insofar as the teacher is correct and reports the facts accurately?

Is much of the knowledge passed from teacher to student or from parent to child often derived from the traditions of a particular culture? For example, the African bushman's concept of God is passed along with inherited hunting skills from father to son. The housekeeping and child-care skills pass from mother to daughter.

As we gather information from many sources,

> Learning is the very essence of humility.
> —J. Krishnamurti

how may we discern what is true and what may be false? How do we determine which information may be pertinent and utilized toward a fruitful life and what may be acknowledged and then released? Human beings possess the quality of individuation and self-consciousness, with the consequent ability to make meaningful choices and personal decisions. Along with this, we also have minds that can speculate, think freely, "brainstorm," and research many things. This is wonderful and can lead toward increased creativity and enthusiasm about the various aspects of life.

Great teachers counsel their students to be diligent, perceptive, humble, focused, and balanced. It is important to perform our duties in this world conscientiously and with unlimited love. It is also important to recognize the divinity of life and the Creator of all there is. Yes, everyone and everything around us may be our teachers. Our lives and the world in which we live often provide "textbooks" and "classrooms" for all levels of education! Ultimately, can each of us become our own greatest teacher?

"Come forth into the light of things, let Nature be your teacher.
—William Wordsworth

Never regard study as a duty, but as the enviable opportunity to learn to know the liberating influence of beauty in the realm of the spirit for your own personal joy and to the profit of the community to which your later work belongs.
—Albert Einstein

Growth is the only evidence of life.
—Cardinal John Henry Newman

The more I learn, the more I realize I don't know.
—Albert Einstein

Spotlights ✦ ✦

1. How is humility often a misunderstood virtue?

2. How can an attitude of humility reveal the heavenly light of the soul?

3. How would you describe humility as a sign of strength?

4. How may we perceive which entertainment is beneficial?

5. When is television educational and when can it be harmful?

6. What are some alternatives to excessive entertainment?

7. How can establishing goals along the journey of life offer opportunities to develop greater potential, leading to greater fruitfulness?

8. How do you equate setting goals with achievement?

9. What do you want to achieve with your life?

10. How is the power to choose aligned with the power to create?

11. How would you describe prayer as communion between God and man?

12. How would you describe prayer as an attitude of the heart?

13. What benefits could occur if we made the conscious decision to preface our day and its activities with prayer?

14. In what way does everyone and everything around us serve as a teacher?

15. How can we become our own greatest teacher?

16. What are some ways we can learn from nature?

Living the Various Spiritual Laws ◆ ◆

PRAYER FOR THE TWENTY-FIRST CENTURY —John Marks Templeton

Creative Divinity, infinite and eternal, as manifest in Jesus and other great teachers, we are overwhelmingly grateful for the millions of blessings and miracles with which you surround each of us every day.

We are especially grateful for prayers answered and also grateful for the challenges that provide opportunities for growth. We are especially grateful for abundant health in mind, body, and soul. We are grateful that you are all of us, and also vastly more, and that we may be tiny parts of Thee.

Help us to become more open-minded and diligent in searching for opportunities to be helpful in the accelera-

tion of divine creativity. Help us to develop further perceptive abilities so, in this century alone, humans may discover over one-hundred-fold more of the infinity of divinity.

Help us to learn more about spiritual realities and principles, so our lives can be more fruitful. Help us to grow in pure unlimited love for every person with never any exception. Help us to radiate to others divine unlimited love and wisdom.

In humility, always, we seek to serve thy mysterious and divine purposes for us. Amen

Week Sixteen

✦ LAW 1

Purpose and praise can increase productivity. —John Marks Templeton

WOODROW WILSON made the statement, "You are not here merely to make a living. You are here in order to enable the world to live more amply, with greater vision, with a finer spirit of hope and achievement. You are here to enrich the world, and you impoverish yourself if you forget the errand." As you allow these words to sink into your consciousness, you may wonder: How can I enrich the world with my presence? How can my efforts enable the world to live more amply, or with greater vision, or with a finer spirit of hope and achievement?

The benefits in terms of our deeper understanding of ourselves and our purpose in the cosmos could be immense. Once we get a glimmer of what we feel is our purpose, how may we then become more productive in our chosen work? Could a defined purpose and an attitude of praise contribute to increased productivity, both for ourselves and for others?

When we recognize that all human beings resemble each other in their desires for happiness and fruitful expression, we may feel an empathy and closeness and desire to be of assistance. Beneficial compassion is not simply an emotional response; it is a firm commitment founded on reason. Purposeful assistance, motivated by compassion and enriched with sincere praise, can ultimately bring beneficial results. How?

Can you think of any person who would not respond favorably to sincere words of praise? How do you feel when someone expresses appreciation for your work? Does a desire arise from deep within you, encouraging you to perform more effectively and efficiently, to accomplish more? Why does this response occur? Ideas, concepts, and opinions about how to do a better job of increasing our productivity may emerge. Does our ticket to greater satisfaction lie in mastering the task at hand? People are energized when they possess a purposeful vision in their work. They often forsake sleep, food, and comfort for the evolution of a project they love.

There seems to be something very holy about a person dedicated to a purpose. Is it the miracle of creation? Might the energy of this miracle enable us to transcend circumstances? Any circumstance can be a good starting point for God! Is it possible that purpose and praise can increase productivity and enable us to work in greater harmony with God's purpose?

To achieve progress, guidelines should be established. Goals and a value system are also necessary ingredients. The value system is important to determine whether things are improving; otherwise, the upward movement that constitutes human purpose and progress may become random, aimless motion. At this point, spiritual progress often joins hands with other kinds of progress and contributes ultimate meaning and direction. How does praise fit into this process?

By careful observation, can the creative and successful person learn from others? What are some guidelines for monitoring the efforts and results of someone's actions? How can we learn from other's mistakes and not repeat them? How can we begin to perceive who is happy and *why* they are happy? Listening intelligently is a key to success because it helps us to observe the wisdom or folly of others and to begin to discern between the two.

The path of purposeful action bears a double blessing for those who walk it: the blessing you offer the world is the blessing that returns to live in your heart. Perhaps the very intention to fill our work with the light of love, praise, and purpose gives us happiness. We are blessed by the positive response our work generates. Through every useful career, you can find a way to discover and express God. The *type* of work we do doesn't matter so much as our desire to accomplish good. In the ultimate analogy, have we all come to this earth to learn the lessons that the earth has to teach, and to bless the world through sharing? Is the drumbeat in our heart our connection to our soul's purpose?

✦ LAW 2

The price of greatness is responsibility. —Winston Churchill

AS WINSTON CHURCHILL's comment indicates, the climb to greatness, as well as the time spent there, often requires accepting various responsibilities and handling them with diligence and skill. In addition, his words can refer not only to future greatness but are applicable toward what can be accomplished in *daily* living. Small things can mean a lot in the journey to greater accomplishments.

For example, if a person fails to act with the positive character traits of care, consideration, and responsibility at home and with friends, can this attitude affect crucial personal and professional relationships later in life? The student who fails to complete homework assignments may not develop the knowledge and ability necessary for successful accomplishments as an adult. The accountant who is lax in record keeping may have a negative effect on the overall success of his business.

Can being watchful of life experiences help us become more mindful of how small actions may lead to larger consequences? We can easily see how routine maintenance on our cars assures that we own a dependable and smoothly operating vehicle. Likewise, regular visits to the dentist, and

> Success on any major scale requires you to
> accept responsibility . . . In the final analysis,
> the one quality that all successful people have . . .
> is the ability to take on responsibility.
> —Michael Korda

practicing good nutrition can make a major difference in our lives. Taken individually, small actions may not seem like much. However, the cumulative effect of their presence or absence can be undeniable. Cultivating healthy habits establishes self-reinforcing positive cycles.

As we become more aware of the patterns in the world around us, can we begin to better understand how the parts relate to the whole? Is our *consciousness* the greatest natural resource of any individual? How does our consciousness play a role in accepting responsibility? What are some ways we can learn from our experiences, look to the larger patterns around us, and discover new solutions for various adversities? How can neglecting vital research and development and concentrating only on short-term gain, in any situation, usually lead to long-term loss? How do these ideas apply to the statement "The price of greatness is responsibility?"

Think for a moment of the people of Japan. Could we consider the greatest natural resource of the Japanese people to be their minds? Japan is an island nation with little landmass, limited agricultural potential, and few minerals. In addition, it was set back by bombings during World War II. Yet, Japan again became a world economic power in a single generation through vision and hard work. Did this happen because allied leadership understood the principles of whole systems and continuous growth and had the insight to take action to revitalize the country's economy?

Is insight a quality we can cultivate? How can we transform what *is* (a situation, circumstance, or activity) into what *might be* by application of courage and insight? What factual evidence is consistent with what we value? How does taking responsibility for our lives nurture self-confidence? What is our definition of "greatness"?

American President Franklin D. Roosevelt's courageous response to the crippling effects of polio can be an excellent example of the inner working of Churchill's statement. Roosevelt revived people's spirits with his fireside chats. His wit and good humor served him well in many contexts. His White House staff and his friends became an extended family with whom he shared meals and witty anecdotes. He used humor to distract people's attention from his disability and to defeat criticism.

Responsibility denotes authorship. When we take responsibility for our thoughts, words, and actions, we admit our accountability. We also acknowledge our roles in whatever circumstances we may find ourselves. We become answerable for our behavior and we accept whatever consequences may be created by our actions. In this manner, we can create a life about which we feel enthusiastic and purposeful. Being responsible means we will do what we say we will do. It also propels us forward and onward towards the greater good.

◆

✦ Law 3

Good words are worth much and cost little. —George Herbert

Is THERE a greater energy in our words than perhaps we can even imagine? Do we literally shape our world with our words because words can have tremendous creative power? Do our words often give form and shape to present and future experiences? Emerson once said, "What you are speaks forth so loudly, I cannot hear what you are saying!" Repeatedly speaking negative words throughout the day can affect our health, effectiveness, happiness, and every aspect of our lives. Speaking positive and constructive words can bless and enrich our lives. Have you ever stopped to

But be doers of
the word, and not
hearers only.
—James 1:22

First learn the mean-
ing of what you say,
and then speak.
—Epictetus

Words have a longer
life than deeds.
—Pindar

consider that a loud yell in a snow-covered mountain area can induce an avalanche? That's powerful!

We probably speak enough words in one day to fill a manuscript of twenty thousand words or more! We also read many words and think many thoughts that we don't express verbally. All of these words contain a concept of some type. How do we feel when we hear someone say, "I'm sick," "I can't," or "I can't stand that . . ."? How do we feel when we hear someone say, "I can do that!" or "I feel terrific!" or "I really like . . ."? Truly, "Good words are worth much and cost little," from a variety of perspectives. What kind of words do we use liberally in our conversations?

Could we determine to start right now, right where we are, and make the "words of my mouth and the meditation of my heart be acceptable in thy sight, O Lord"(Psalms 19:1)? What does this statement mean? Could perhaps one meaning be to keep our ears open to the words we speak, to *listen* to them? In fact, if for one day we were required to really listen to every word that we spoke, would we exert greater effort to govern our thoughts before we verbalized them? Would we become more aware of the tone and inflection of our words?

The old phrase "priming the pump" provides a good analogy for watching our words. A woman tells the story of going to visit her great aunt who lived in the country. Since the house did not have indoor plumbing, the water source was an old-fashioned pump. In the kitchen was what looked like an ordinary sink, but rather than having faucets, it held a small pump. Beside the pump was always a bucket of water. A large ladle lay beside the bucket. Water had to be used to get water. It was necessary to "prime" the pump with water in order for it to work.

Using what we have in order to receive more is a spiritual principle of life. It's like "priming the pump." The priming of our verbal pump can be two-fold; there are inner and outer requirements. As we think in terms of what we wish to accom-

plish, we can fill our thinking with joy and abundance and let that energy flow through our words. What mental and emotional responses do we want from life? What mental and emotional energies are we sending forth through our words? We can "prime" our life by utilizing our present talents and abilities, especially the spoken word.

Manifestation is not magic. It is a process of working with the natural principles and laws in

Your words are the seed, your soul is the farmer, the
world is your field. Let the farmer look to the sowing, that
the soil may abundance yield.
—Nasir-I-Khusraw

order to translate energy from one level of reality to another. For example, an orator has a mental concept. Through enthusiastic speech to his audience, he may be able to fire their emotions in response to that concept. If his concept is free enterprise, for example, he has translated mental energy into emotional energy directed toward free enterprise.

In this electronic age, many people use computers equipped with word processing programs. It is easy to type the words and then review them on the monitor screen to be sure the words we are using say what we really want to express. This is a way of fine-tuning our written words. How can this "word management" process be accomplished in our daily life? Can we control our words by being willing to change our views about life? Could we move from a "judging" perspective to discernment and focus on the tremendous possibilities of life? Can we also change the way we speak by becoming more compassionate and forgiving? What about developing greater understanding? Or becoming a more loving person? If we change the way we think, and feel and perceive the world around us, isn't it logical that our words will reflect our changing consciousness?

What would happen if we began each day with

an idea, a word, or a prayer that is positive, uplifting, and inspiring? What difference would this make to ourselves and to others? If we expressed only positive, productive ideas through good words throughout the day, would the closure of the day find us with feelings of fruitful accomplishment? Doesn't this sound like a good investment in life!

We live in a marvelous time when humankind seems to be awakening on a massive scale to our inner spiritual radiance. Paralleling this inner awakening are great discoveries in all areas of human endeavor—science, religion, physics, psychology, etc. If we learn to respond to all situations and experiences with constructive words and ideas, are we contributing in a profound way to the uplifting of the planet and its people? Words are symbols of our thoughts and feelings. Good words are worth much and cost little. Let's make the commitment to use our energy in constructive ways by speaking the good word, the optimistic thought, and the useful and loving expression.

✦ LAW 4

You can never solve a problem at the same level as the problem. —Emmet Fox

EMMET FOX, a twentieth-century author and problem-solver, wrote that the only way to solve a problem is to "lift your consciousness above the level where you met the problem." Often, a successful problem-solver is one who creates a new context from which to view the problem or situation. In some instances, this can be accomplished by directing the focus of attention *away* from the distracting details of the difficulty. From a detached perspective, we may be able to examine the situation in a new or different light. Then, after exploring the available information and a variety of options, a beneficial course of action may be chosen.

Laying the first Atlantic cable was a huge achievement because of the many difficulties of working underwater. Later on, laying marine cable became a routine business. Then, along came the opportunity to transmit radio signals across the ocean! Once again, seemingly insurmountable problems arose. These difficulties, too, were overcome. In each of these instances, the technicians, engineers, and other workers were required to rise to a higher level of comprehension and intelligence in order to achieve the desired goals. These entrepreneurs utilized an old adage: "Whatever you perceive as a difficulty—capitalize upon it!" To repeat, "You can never solve a problem on the same level as the problem."

Is viewing problems as *challenges* a helpful way

to resolve a variety of situations? From this perspective, a situation no longer presents a negative barrier to progress. Instead, it becomes an opportunity to move forward. Isn't the mental idea the first step in any experience that can excite and prompt fruitful action? Did man discover fire because the idea of warmth provided a response to the challenge of cold? Intelligent minds designed a variety of tools to overcome the practical problems of daily living and assisted in making life easier. Was the "discovery" of music a response to a desire for a higher emotional expression of rhythm and harmony? Do telephones, automobiles, airplanes, sky labs, computers, and space stations represent partial responses to solving today's problems of time and space?

Emmet Fox made another statement regarding problems. He said, "Problems are signposts on the road to God." How can this be? Numerous instances are recorded where problem situations became avenues for spiritually inspired human service to others. Many are familiar with the story of Florence Nightingale and her acceptance of the challenge of upgrading hospital standards, improving patient care, enhancing sanitation, and promoting nursing education. The dedicated efforts of this Englishwoman transformed hospitals to places of hope and healing. Florence Nightingale faced a double challenge. Her own ill-defined illness restricted the activities of her adult life. However, she was deeply committed to meeting the challenge of caring for those who were injured and sick. Her heart was filled with love and compassion for her fellow human beings.

After incredible experiences of saving lives with her contingent of trained nurses, Florence Nightingale returned to her home in England. Although ill herself and restricted to her bed, this brave soul somehow managed, at the age of forty, to establish the Nightingale School and Home for Nurses in London. She created a medical revolution from her bed and continued to mastermind and direct those

efforts until her death at the age of ninety. Florence Nightingale may not have enjoyed the benefits of a typical, "normal" lifestyle, but she was definitely victorious in her lofty challenge. It seems readily apparent that she lifted her thoughts and efforts to a higher level than the situations in her world. As a result of her strength and vision, her efforts eased the pain of many. She brought a little bit of heaven to earth for her patients.

Isn't the wonderful mind within each person a prime catapult to lift us above the present level of any problem? Although we may be unable to control the people or circumstances around us, are we not able to choose the level of consciousness whereby we meet everyone and respond to any situation? Is there ever any reason to remain fearful or anxious? In fact, can we enthusiastically meet these "signposts" along the journey of life and integrate spiritual purpose and directed response and action into each situation?

Isn't our experience at any moment an out-picturing of our consciousness? Is what we believe and understand on an inner level often what we experience in our everyday life? Each day is a new life. In reality, each moment is a new life. Are what we call memories really present thoughts about past events? Are what we call anticipations or inspirations really present thoughts as well? Are what we call problems really present thoughts? So, how do we resolve problem situations? In this moment, can we elevate our thinking processes and open our mind to inspiration and wisdom's guidance? Can we lift our awareness to a higher level of receptivity? Given our desire and developing faculties, do we need to look for opportunities? Doesn't the door of opportunity open automatically for the sincere, searching heart and mind?

Success is to be measured not so much by the position that one has reached in life as by the obstacles which were overcome while trying to succeed.
—Booker T. Washington

✦ LAW 5

What attitudes and endeavors can guide us
toward experiencing "heaven on earth" as a way of life? —John Marks Templeton

THE IDEAS that we, as humans, create our own reality and are responsible for our own experiences are powerful ones. *Where* is the "heaven on earth" so many people desire to experience? *What* is this "heaven on earth," and *what attitudes and endeavors can guide us to experience "heaven on earth" as a way of life?* Is one of our major lessons to learn while on earth the truth that building our heaven is up to us?

Does enthusiasm for seeking new information and improving older concepts open wider avenues toward heaven on earth? Could spiritual studies on the basic invisible realities such as love, purpose, creativity, intellect, thankfulness, prayer, humility, praise, thrift, compassion, invention, truthfulness, worship, and giving provide beneficial knowledge and growth? Can prayer, worship, and service to others help each of us discover more of heaven on earth? Is our desire to be helpfully creative one way to express our worship and thankfulness for all the blessings in our lives? Does pure unlimited love for every person provide a powerful and fruitful foundational energy for prompting heaven on earth?

Are those who achieve a measure of heaven on earth the ones who are most diligent in trying to sow their love and happiness and who encourage others to do the same? Are these actions in themselves a reflection of infinite divinity? Who would deny the reality of unlimited love? Or of intellect? Or of purpose? Or of creativity? Or of complexity? Or of discovery? If additional scientific research is accomplished relating to invisible realities, can such study increase human concepts of divinity? Is the visible only a tiny, temporary manifestation of reality? What evidence indicates that the invisible can be over one hundred times larger and more varied than the visible? How can we be expressions or agents of divinity through unlimited love and creativity? Does this enhance heaven on earth in our lives?

When you find that your soul, your heart, every wisp of inspiration, every speck of the vast blue sky and its shining star-blossoms, the mountains, the earth, the whippoorwill, and the bluebells are all tied together with one cord of rhythm, one cord of joy, one cord of unity, one cord of Spirit, then you shall know that all are but waves in His cosmic sea.
—*Paramahansa Yogananda*

Increasingly, many sciences are showing that visible or tangible materials may be only those aspects of infinite reality which humans, the intellectual species recently thriving on one little planet, have developed abilities to perceive. Increasingly, humans are finding ways to expand their perceptive abilities. Do multiplying discoveries indicate that reality is vastly greater than things tangible or visible? Will accelerating discoveries continue to reveal multitudes of new mysteries? What is the purpose for humans and for human purpose? Is experiencing heaven on earth facilitated by human purpose?

What are some ways to study evidences that God is creative and purposeful, that we may be living on this little planet to be an agent for progress of God's purposes? Mysteriously, we seem able to participate in and even accelerate creativity. Is it possible that humans were created as agents for that purpose? What would happen if we developed such a spirit of humility that we would be eager to learn from each other and focus on what is shared by all great religions, rather than what is divisive? How could research on the benefits of unlimited love, overwhelming thanksgiving, and total forgiveness produce fruitful guidelines for experiencing more "heaven on earth"? Valuable insights and glimpses toward heaven on earth may be found in many religions. Although no one may presently see the entire picture, can each person feel and understand a part needed for the full description?

Spotlights ✦ ✦

1. How does unlimited love empower us to reach higher levels of consciousness and effectiveness?

2. How would you describe the Bible verse, "You shall know them by their fruits" (Matthew 7:16)? What does this say to you?

3. How does accepting responsibility for small things on a daily basis often parallel accomplishing greater things in life?

4. Responsibility denotes authorship. When we take responsibility for our thoughts, words, and actions, we admit our accountability. How does this influence the growth of our characters?

5. How does speaking positive words bless and enrich our lives?

6. How can speaking negative words create problems and challenges in our lives?

7. What would happen if we began each day with an idea, a word, or a prayer that is positive, uplifting, and inspiring?

8. Why is it important to lift our consciousness above the level where we may be experiencing a problem? How may this be accomplished?

9. Is viewing problems as *challenges* a helpful way to resolve a variety of situations?

10. How do you feel about the idea that we may be responsible for more of our own experiences than we realize? Are you willing to explore this more deeply?

11. How would you describe "heaven on earth"?

Living the Various Spiritual Laws ✦ ✦

The beautiful, mystical instruction, "The Goal Is One," comes from *The Teachings of Rumi*. As part of "The Call," this piece is dedicated to the beauties, glories, trials, and demands of the path of Awakening, and to the necessary commitments to prayer and spiritual discipline that can deepen its truth in the seeker's being.

THE GOAL IS ONE

The paths are many, but the goal is one. Don't you see how many roads there are to the Kaaba? For some the road starts from Rome, for others from Syria, from Persia, or China; some come by sea from India and the Yemen. If you are considering the different roads, the variety is immense and the difference infinite. If you consider the goal, however, they are all in harmony and are one. The hearts of each and every one of them are fixed upon the Kaaba. Each heart has one overriding attachment—a passionate love for the Kaaba—and in that there is no room for contradiction.

That attachment to the Kaaba cannot be called either "impiety" or "faith": it is not mingled with the various paths we have mentioned. Once the traveler arrives at the Kaaba, all quarreling and vicious squabbling about the different paths—this person saying to that, "You're wrong! You're a blasphemer!" and the other shouting back in kind—simply vanish. They realize that what they were fighting about was the roads only, and that their goal was one.

Week Seventeen

✦ Law 1

We receive freely when we give freely. —Anonymous

How can I be useful, of what service can I be? There is something inside me, what can it be?
—*Vincent Van Gogh*

THE CREATOR'S abundance is a universal principle that is often misinterpreted. One description of this principle states: "Prosperity is the consciousness of God as the abundant, everywhere present resource, unfailing, ready for all who open themselves to it." For some people, "abundance" or "prosperity" may mean having material things and striving for more of those things. But is *true abundance* really represented by the understanding that our lives, our beings, our eternity, and our universe are filled with endless opportunities for plenty? Could this perspective reflect a different way of seeing that good is everywhere present?

A little "fish story" beautifully represents the meaning of this perspective.

Excuse me," said one ocean fish to another, "you are older and more experienced than I, and will probably be able to help me. Tell me, please: where can I find this thing they call the ocean? I've been searching for it everywhere, and to no avail."

"The ocean," said the older fish, "is what you are swimming in right now."

"Oh, this? But this is only water. What I'm searching for is the *ocean*," said the young fish, feeling quite disappointed.

Regardless of how far that little fish may swim, he will never run out of ocean! Like the questioning fish, we, too, are already immersed in the ocean of total universal abundance. It isn't necessary to continue looking for it. It isn't something available to a select few. God's abundance is present for us to tune into right now. Perhaps we need

Teach us, good Lord, to serve Thee . . . to give and not to count the cost.
—*St. Ignatius Loyola*

to open our spiritual eyes and behold what is before us! Things may come and things may go, but the spiritual idea of abundance endures.

If we desire to demonstrate prosperity and abundance in our lives, do we begin by giving praise and thanks for *every evidence* of mental, physical, and emotional improvement as well as financial improvement? Do we praise and give thanks for the people and relationships in our lives? Do we praise and give thanks for the many opportu-

He who sows sparingly will also reap sparingly; and he who sows bountifully will also reap bountifully.
—*2 Corinthians 9:6*

nities provided by our chosen work to be of service to others?

We have spoken before of how living and giving with a positive mental attitude can create abundance. On the other hand, can living and giving with a fear of deficiencies or a scarcity mentality lead to having less? A scarcity mentality means that we evaluate our lives in terms of what they lack. The truth is that there *is* enough to go around. There *is* enough for everyone to prosper. There *is* an endless universe for us to work in, and everyone *is* part of that endless universe. "Give, and it shall be given unto you; good measure, pressed down, shaken together, running over" (Luke 6:38). If we shift our focus from some distant point in the future to the present moment, are we more able to see fully the riches and gifts we already have?

When we *feel* abundant and rich with the blessings of life, what is our next natural instinct? Could it be the desire to share, to give? Do we give as freely as we receive? Abundance and prosperity need an inflow and an outflow, just like any body of water if it is to remain fresh, clean, and moving. The Dead Sea is an example of stagnation. It has no outflow! It only receives, so the water becomes stagnant and almost nothing grows there! Remember, whatever we focus our thoughts on expands! Where is your focus?

Do we keep the energy of abundance flowing by circulating part of what we have received through giving to others? Then, miracle of miracles, the more we give away, the more we have! We receive freely when we give freely. This is the joy of allowing the energy of the universe to flow uninterrupted through us.

Is one of our most fruitful gifts the opportunity to teach others how to give? How can this be accomplished? Perhaps one way is simply to remember and activate the old adage, "The best way to teach is by demonstration." What are some examples?

If we are in a position of leadership within an organization, do we create options for the individuals who work with us? Do we help our associates achieve a sense of reference or belonging to the whole? Are we attentive to others when they are speaking? Are we willing to view every person who comes into our lives as a teacher? Do we accept every opportunity to send out unlimited love to every person, situation, and experience in our lives? If we have abundant love within, isn't love what we will have to give away? When we send out love and harmony to others, regardless of their behavior, are we living more in a true oneness of spirit? Have we developed a sense of appreciation for all aliveness; do we demonstrate this through the way we speak and act?

A person cannot drink the word "water." The formula for water, H_2O, cannot float a ship. The word "rain" cannot get us wet. When we *experience* water or rain, do we begin to understand more accurately what the words mean? To truly experience the joy of giving and receiving, we must *participate* in the experience of giving and receiving. When we sincerely incorporate the universal laws of life or spiritual principles into daily living, what happens? Is this a way we can move into a transcendent dimension of thought? Are we practicing "freely giving and freely receiving" to the point that abundant good flows through us and onward to others?

✦ Law 2

The truth will make you free. —John 8:32

IN TODAY'S WORLD, a great deal of media advertising claims all manner of things that seem to have nothing to do with reality. We often listen to national and international news reporting that may be distorted and influenced by and for political advantages. We are encouraged to believe that there is not enough money available to assist the poor, sick, and elderly. Yet, wars in far away places may be eagerly financed. The distortions and deceptions created by human ego may be many. So, how can we know what to believe? What is truth? What is the "truth that will make us free?"

There may not be a simple answer to these questions. However, surely diligent personal research into the subjects of "truth" and "freedom," followed by self-discipline in practicing what is learned, may provide workable insights. Does the movement away from the unreal or phony to the authentic begin within the heart and mind and soul of each individual? As Thomas Merton put it, "We must first be true inside ourselves, before we can know a truth that is outside of us." How do we begin to be "true inside ourselves?" How do we recognize truth? We may find words and descriptions of it in a book, but that is not the whole of truth. Is the hallmark of truth its inclusive nature—no one or no thing could ever be excluded from it? Truth is said to be always present, available, and free to those who sincerely love it and yearn to delight in its brilliant splendor. Truth is not secretive; it can find us wherever we are. When we look for the value of truth in all circumstances, do we open the door for it to take up residence in our consciousness? Can truth be as obvious in a rose as in the most technical encyclopedia?

At any point in our lives, can we begin to release egotistical opinions and dare to develop personal spiritual truths that can be unassailable from outside forces? One man simply declared his personal desire to practice truth and honesty in all aspects of his life and be independent of the good opinion of others! And it worked! Everyone may be suggestible to a certain extent. How many of our beliefs result from what others told us or from

what they believe about us? Will we allow ourselves to be in bondage to these beliefs, or will we declare the unconquerable spirit of truth and claim our freedom? The practice of spiritual honesty may require us to look deeply within and to know

ourselves to a greater degree—the moral rewards are fantastic!

Indian spiritual and political leader Mahatma Gandhi spoke of truth in this way. He said, "In the

dictionary of the seeker of truth, there is no such thing as being 'not successful.' He is, or should be, an irrepressible optimist because of his immovable faith in the ultimate victory of Truth, which is God." The Arab philosopher Rasa'il al-Kindi stated, "We should never be ashamed to approve truth or acquire it, no matter what its source might be, even if it might have come from foreign peoples and alien nations far removed from us. To him who seeks truth, no other subject is higher in value. Neither shall truth be under-rated, nor its exponent belittled. For indeed, truth abases none and ennobles all."

A powerful suggestion for embracing the "truth that sets us free" could be to make an inner commitment to establish a *new relationship* with truth. We can decide to perceive situations and people more clearly and more honestly, simply relating the conditions that occur in every situation—no more and no less. Through this exercise, we may find we are consulting a deeper part of our consciousness, one that flourishes in truth, instead of giving in to false ego demands.

How do we respond in a situation where we are unsure of whether to tell the truth because we feel that the truth may be more painful than doing or saying nothing? In this case, is remaining silent more spiritually appropriate? When we feel secure in the knowledge of who and what we are, do we become more inclined to live as the free souls we are created to be? Life often presents us with many lessons and opportunities to learn. Can any of these be useful to us unless we recognize them and remain open to their inherent truth and value? Can we increase truth in our lives by identifying behaviors and rationales that may be hindrances to our greater good? Essentially, is embracing truth a way of coming to know more of God? Is the real "organ" of truth the heart instead of the brain?

Truth has been proclaimed as the whole of our existence. Some say we have no existence outside truth, and neither can truth exist outside of us. When a human being aligns himself with truth, only good can come of such a commitment. Do we *sense* or *feel* truth more than we think it? Do we *know* it more than we understand it? When we try to analyze truth, we can often lose ourselves in the labyrinth of the thinking mind. When we love truth, however, the storehouse of universal wisdom seems to open to us.

How does the truth make us free? Perhaps one response is that when we are truthful and honest

with ourselves and others, we are able to leave the room of constraints of daily awareness. Within that room, we may have learned of limitations and restrictions. Outside that room, we learn that life offers unlimited possibilities. We are freed from anger, hatred, and bitterness. We are free to love, share, and serve more fruitfully. We begin thinking *from* the ideal of truth, instead of thinking *of* the ideal of truth.

In *The Power of Awareness*, Neville states, "What greater gifts could be given you than to be told the Truth that will set you free? The truth that sets you free is that you can experience in imagination what you desire to experience in reality, and by maintaining this experience in imagination, your desire will become an actuality."

Finally, does authentic freedom actually spring from *knowing* that our identity is not located in the physical world alone, but in the eternal, changeless world of God?

✦ Law 3

Is progress, through competition to serve, a basic invisible reality? —John Marks Templeton

THE ABOVE QUOTE may ask two different questions. First, *is progress a basic invisible reality?* Second, is progress, *through competition to serve,* a basic invisible reality?

In *The State of Humanity*, Julian L. Simon said, "Our species is better off in just about every measurable material way. And there is stronger reason than ever to believe that these progressive trends will continue past the year 2000, past the year 2100, and indefinitely." Many more people are better fed, better clothed, better housed, and better educated than at any previous time in history. Leisure time is increasing along with pay levels, bringing countless benefits to the quality of our lives. In most parts of the world, people are enjoy-

ing longer, healthier, more fruitful lives. They are experiencing great strides in living standards helped by increasing political and economic freedoms. The number of inspirational books being published is growing rapidly. Evidence of progress is widespread. Why is this? Does some kind of "invisible motivator" prompt people to work for greater expressions of good in all aspects of life?

The process of our progress on planet Earth seems to seethe with innovations and superb timing that dispel any notion of blind chance. The extraordinarily complex origin of life, the sudden early appearance of multi-cellular animals in great profusion in the Cambrian, and the proliferation of mammals following the sudden extinction of the dinosaurs sixty-five million years ago, argue for a marvelous creativity and connectedness.

Could it be, for reasons unknown, that divinity uses progress and competition as methods to help us be more creative? How can improvements be produced by competition? Is competition one of God's laws of the universe because through it efficiency and invention are increased? God's law of evolution means progress. If we do not have free competition among ideas, even among religious ideas, old and established theories might never be improved. They might survive long after their time of usefulness.

Can the chemistry of cooperation and creativity exist unless we work respectfully together? Could this be called "progress through competition to serve"? How can we view competition as a valuable opportunity to learn? What are the benefits of learning and teaching free competition as a way to enrich the poor as well as to teach ethics?

The wisdom of God is beyond the limits of men's minds. From the spiritual perspective, in what way can free competition of diverse spiritual concepts accelerate progress in religion, ideas, and human welfare? What progressive talents may be built through competition to serve? What are some beneficial examples of competition to serve? Is progress, through competition to serve, a frontier or field that offers scope for research and developmental activity? Since constant creativity increasingly seems to be the character of our universe, is progress a basic invisible reality?

When you are inspired by some great purpose, some extraordinary project, all your thoughts break their bonds. Your mind transcends limitations, your consciousness expands in every direction, and you find yourself in a new, great, and wonderful world. Dormant forces, faculties, and talents become alive, and you discover yourself to be a greater person by far than you ever dreamed yourself to be.

—*Patanjali*

◆ LAW 4

Habit is the best of servants, the worst of masters. —J. Jelinek

HAVE YOU EVER known a person who did not have a habit of some kind? The time and the way each of us gets up in the morning, how we exercise our bodies, how we practice healthy hygiene, the way we do our work, how we sleep at night—these are habits. A habit is an acquired pattern of behavior that has become so automatic it may be difficult to modify or eliminate.

Everyone enjoys being around a person who has developed habits of courtesy and good manners. Habits of politeness such as saying, "hello," "please," "thank you," "you're welcome," and "excuse me," can promote harmony as we communicate with others in our daily routine.

Some consistently practiced habits can enable a person to develop talent and skill in special areas like sports, music, art, and writing. Riding a bicycle is habitual when a person becomes so accustomed to the process of riding that he doesn't have to continually think, "pedal" or "balance." Playing a musical instrument can become habitual from the perspective that, after years of diligent study and practice, the person knows the piece of music so well that sheet music isn't necessary. The habit of doing things in a certain order can sometimes assure completion of a project.

Not all habits are helpful, and bad habits can become detrimental to our well-being. The habit of thinking negatively about ourselves and others and about situations in life may result in destructive behaviors. Procrastination can be an insidious and self-defeating habit that has ruined many opportunities and lives. Blaming other people or circumstances for our own errors or for difficult situations can turn us away from accepting responsibility. This habit certainly doesn't assure harmonious relationships or fruitful completion of our goals.

Good habits, wisely expressed, can provide wonderful assistance to fruitful living. Negative habits can be detrimental to our development and effectiveness as successful individuals.

When we find things happening in our lives that may have their basis in negative habits, what are some ways we can shift away from old thinking habits? How can purifying our thoughts lead to development of positive habits and higher levels of consciousness? For example, if a person is overweight and makes a decision to spend thirty minutes a day walking or gardening rather than sitting and eating, and follows through with action on the decision, he is purifying his thinking and beginning to practice a beneficial habit.

Our capacity to be creatively alive in virtually all life circumstances may largely depend on the kind of attitudes we choose for ourselves. Every person always has options. In every situation, we can choose how we are going to think and feel about it and how we are going to deal with it. Wherever we find ourselves in life, whatever the circumstances, whatever habits may be influencing our decisions, we can transform each situation into a learning and growing experience. We can determine how to be the masters of our habits so that our habits can be useful servants to us.

> Cultivate only the habits that you would have willingly serve you.
> —Ra

> Habit can be your best friend or your worst enemy.
> —Rebecca Clark

> Sow a thought, and you reap an act;
> Sow an act, and you reap a habit;
> Sow a habit, and you reap a character;
> Sow a character, and you reap a destiny.
> —Anonymous

> Habits form a second nature.
> —Jean Baptiste Lamarck

✦ LAW 5

To discover new oceans you need the courage to lose sight of the shore. —Anonymous

> When in doubt, do the courageous thing!
> —Jan Smuts

A MAN who was living in comfortable circumstances felt restless and unfulfilled. Seeking guidance, the man went to see a certain sage who was reputed to have much knowledge and great wisdom. The man said to the sage: "Great Sage, I have no material problems; yet, I feel unsettled. For years I have sought to be happy, to find answers to my inner thoughts, and to come to terms with the world. But something is missing. I have a deep feeling that something important is undiscovered. Tell me, how may I be cured of this malaise?"

The sage considered the man's question for a while, then responded, "My Friend, what is hidden to some is apparent to others. And, what is apparent to some is hidden to others. I have an answer to your ailment, although it is no ordinary med-

Fortune favors the
audacious.
—Erasmus

No one knows what
he can do until he
tries.
—Publilius Syrus

Only those who risk
going too far can
possibly find out
how far one can go.
—T. S. Eliot

One man with
courage makes a
majority.
—Andrew Jackson

ication. You must set out on a journey that will include many travels. Be alert and aware of what is around you at all times. Keep a journal of your travels, and every day, make a note of your most amazing discovery of the day. Do not miss one single day of discovery. When your travels are concluded and you return home, come and visit with me, and I will tell you the rest of the tale.”

The man returned to his home, prepared for an extensive trip, then left on his journey. He traveled from one country to another, meeting extraordinary people, experiencing exciting adventures, and seeing many unusual things. Faithfully, he recorded in his journal the most amazing discovery of each day. His journal began to read like a novel. It was filled with the excitement and enthusiasm of many unusual discoveries. At last, the man returned home. A few days later, he visited the sage. The wise old man smiled when he beheld the light and sparkle in the man’s eyes and the brightness of his countenance.

“So, you had a good journey?” the sage smiled.

“Oh, yes!” the man exclaimed and proceeded to regale the sage with his tales. The sage listened patiently, then asked the man, “What have you learned from this journey?”

The man was thoughtfully quiet for some time. Then, looking the sage in the eyes and reaching out to clasp his hand, the man chuckled and replied, “You cannot discover new oceans until you have the courage to lose sight of the shore!”

As human beings, we may feel complacent about life when everything seems to be going well. However, when our lives no longer seem to provide enough continuing growth experiences, a stimulating change may be needed. The inner voice of consciousness may whisper, “Divine discontent!” Is this a soul urge emanating from our being, encouraging us to launch out into productive ventures? Occasionally, an unpleasant condition or experience may indicate that we need to explore new areas of our potential. We may feel prompted to leave the familiarity of our present situation behind and journey into unknown terri-

tory. As the proverb says, “Your ship cannot come in if you never send it out!” Likewise, “We cannot discover new oceans until we have the courage to lose sight of the shore.”

Like the man in the story, if we look for a new discovery each day, we can enjoy new challenges. We know that everyone has an innate ability not only to survive, but to “be fruitful and prosper” as well. We never have to settle for less than we are capable of experiencing. In order to embrace our role as students of life, do we need to cultivate the

Change and growth take place when a person
has risked himself and dares to become involved
with experimenting with his own life.
—Herbert Otto

ability to move easily from what is known to the unknown?” In other words, when we learn the lesson of being flexible, is it easier to achieve what may be coming next instead of just clinging to the way things presently are?

Getting a big promotion at work may require leaving a comfortable position to accept increased responsibilities. Embarking on a new relationship may present opportunities for trust and compromise. Becoming a parent for the first time can bring the lessons of patience and discipline. Each of these examples may require that we leave the “safety and security” of a comfortable niche to “discover new oceans.”

Have you ever said to yourself, “I would like to do something like this, but . . . I haven’t had the courage, or time, or money, or . . . ?” Take a look at the urge within your being that may be prompting you to step forward. Are you willing to take the step? Are you open for a new adventure? Are you ready and willing to learn the lesson of trust by taking a leap of faith and believing that your inner knowing is guiding you toward greater good?

A young woman named Sharon dreamed of starting a business creating and selling specialty dolls. Sharon had been creating and selling these dolls to customers in the restaurant where she worked for several years. The dolls were very popular and people often ordered them as gifts for a variety of special occasions. Sharon was excited about turning her hobby into a business, but was hesitant to leave the security of her present job. Besides, a certain capital investment was necessary. She had no business experience. And there was no guarantee the dolls would sell well enough to support a business.

Finally, a friend asked Sharon, "Putting aside the practical considerations, if you could do any-thing in the world, what would it be?" Without a moment's hesitation, Sharon responded, "Start a business selling my dolls!" A door of realization and opportunity had opened. Sharon decided to go for it. Assistance and support came from friends and family as well as from unexpected sources. Within a year, Sharon was established in a small and growing business. She was happy and excited about several new prospects for distribution of her dolls. She was on her way. However, she had to "lose sight of the shore" in order to set sail on the ocean of discovery.

Spotlights ✦ ✦

1. How can giving freely, without expectations of return, set into motion an irresistible momentum of goodness?

2. How would you describe "true abundance"?

3. How can we begin to demonstrate prosperity and abundance in our life?

4. How would you describe progress as an "invisible reality"?

5. How can progress be made through competition to serve?

6. What are some beneficial examples of competition to serve?

7. How may good habits provide wonderful assistance to fruitful living?

8. How are negative habits detrimental to our development and success?

9. Why is it important to sometimes "lose sight of the shore" to embrace a new venture?

10. What are some sources you may turn to for courage in beginning a new activity?

Living the Various Spiritual Laws ✦ ✦

THE CLAY LAMP STORY

One of the greatest admirers of the Buddha was King Bimbisara of Magadha. When he heard that the Buddha was approaching his capital, he hung the city with festive decorations and lined the main street with thousand of lamps in ornate holders, kept lit to honor the Buddha when he passed by.

In Bimbisara's capital lived an old woman who loved the Buddha deeply. She longed to take her own clay lamp and join the crowds that would line the road when he passed by. The lamp was broken, but she was too poor to buy a finer one of brass. She made a wick from the edge of her sari, and the corner shopkeeper, knowing she had no money, poured a little oil into her lamp.

A stiff breeze had come up by the time she reached the main street, and the old woman knew there was not enough oil to last long. She did not light her lamp until the radiant figure of the Buddha came into view at the city gates.

The wind rose, and King Bimbisara must have watched in agony as a sudden gust extinguished all his lamps. When the Buddha passed, only one light remained burning: a broken clay lamp that an old woman guarded with both hands.

The Buddha stopped in front of her. As she knelt to receive his blessing, he turned to his disciples, "Take note of this woman! As long as spiritual disciplines are practiced with this kind of love and dedication, the light of the world will never go out."

—from the Introduction, *The Dhammapada*

Week Eighteen

✦ Law 1

No one's education is ever complete. —John Marks Templeton

Learning is not attained by chance, it must be sought for with ardor and attended to with diligence.
—*Abigail Adams*

What one knows is, in youth, of little moment; they know enough who know how to learn.
—*Henry Brooks Adams*

HAVE YOU EVER heard the expression "Life is for learning"? Learning what? There's a lot to learn, so we can explore in many categories! The more we learn, the more we can do. The more we do, the more we can learn! In the early years of life, we learned physical coordination: how to walk, talk, eat, and interact with those around us. When we began school, we learned reading, writing, arithmetic, history, science, geography, and perhaps music, art, and sports. Our learning experience may have continued as we headed for college. When we moved out into the world, did we continue to learn?

Albert Einstein, one of the great geniuses of our time, once commented, "A day without learning is a day wasted. There is so much to learn and so little time to learn it." He followed his own precept by continuing to work and study diligently until his death. Many other examples of great people who continued the learning process throughout their lives offer beneficial inspiration for us.

The cosmic law of creativity continues to propel us forward. We often find new areas of study and expression. We may feel we have exhausted the "known" through knowledge and enjoyment of it; then we turn to the exploration of the "unknown" for new areas of discovery.

The terms "known" and "unknown" may be relative. However, both are links in the chain of life's progression. What was unknown to the young lad may come to be known to the man the boy becomes. What was unknown to the average person a few centuries ago may be common knowledge to the average citizen of today. We can increasingly know more and more because new multitudes of mysteries are visible at every step of our expanding knowledge. No one's education is ever complete.

Learning is a lifetime activity of vast importance. There is a story about a man who, upon graduating from high school, obtained a job and never read another book. He watched television in his spare time, watched movies, watched sports, but made no effort to expand the frontiers of his mind. At age forty, he was no better educated that he had been at age eighteen. That is the sign of a wasted life! Can wasted lives ever be successful lives? How can continuing education improve the direction our lives take? How do we gather the knowledge we need for beneficial living? Is one way to learn through opening our minds with the implicit understanding we may become more attuned with the flow of infinite wisdom?

Once we become involved in our chosen fields of endeavor, how can books, classes, and various programs of continuing education take on even greater importance? How can we test these areas of learning against our increasing maturity and

Learning is but an
adjunct to our self.
—William Shakespeare

Read, mark, learn,
and inwardly digest.
—Book of Common
Prayer

I expect I shall
be a student to
the end of my days.
—Trofimov

knowledge? How may the various aspects of acquired knowledge be absorbed with a more profound and beneficial understanding?

How can setting the goal of learning something new every day enhance our lives, our relationships, and our chosen professions? What could happen if we chose to learn an unfamiliar word each day? Glean a new insight? Experience a fresh taste, thought, or sensation? Use our time wisely for self-improvement, or cultivating creativity and productivity? Or, how about asking meaningful questions? How much can we learn if we are doing all the talking and listen little to others? Do successful people seek advice more often than they give it? What can we learn from the various people we meet throughout the day? How sincere are we in our desire to improve?

As our awareness and knowledge increase, it may become necessary to release old ideas and ways of doing things that are no longer sufficiently productive. When this occurs, we often find that life becomes more exciting and fulfilling through our expanding potential and growth. Thomas Edison said, "If you are doing something the same way you did it twenty years ago, then there must be a better way." Are we willing to pit ourselves

Learning is a
treasure which
accompanies its
owner everywhere.
—Chinese proverb

against past performances, welcome the entrepreneurial spirit within, and strive constantly to become the best-informed and most creative individuals in our fields?

For I bless God in the libraries of the learned
and for all the booksellers in the world.
—Christopher Smart

Beneficial experiences often come through trial and self-discipline. The person who is willing to say "Yes" to greater knowledge and experience may be the person who is equipping himself or herself to discover new frontiers. Success-oriented people believe in themselves and believe in life, because the new frontiers exist inside of them! Spiritual commitment and insights are also beneficial in accepting challenges and new experiences. Through good times and difficult times, expanding knowledge helps us embrace the future with open arms, minds, and hearts! We have the ability to view the future as an exciting and still-unexplored territory and to move toward it with diligence and enthusiasm.

✦ LAW 2

*Cultivating a positive attitude can bring beneficial results
in all areas of life.* —John Marks Templeton

It is our reactions to
occurrences in life
that cause us to be
happy or unhappy.
—May Rowland

THERE IS A POWER within each individual that could lift the world out of its ignorance and misery if we become aware of it and learn to use it. It is a simple aspect of life, but may require some effort to become most effective. What is it? *Effective use of the power of the mind!* Or, using positive words and positive thoughts in everything we say

and think! Cultivating a positive attitude can bring beneficial results in all areas of life.

What happens when we plant within our minds the perfect seed idea of positive thought? Do we begin to desire to manifest only the highest and best of this seed idea—diligence, purpose, vision, enthusiasm, fruitfulness, usefulness, progress, creativity, humility, unlimited love, and greater awareness and knowledge? How can we fill the seemingly blank spaces around us with thoughts of service and infinite good? We can "Accentuate the positive and eliminate the negative," as the Johnny Mercer song invites us to do!

Conditions on earth today are vastly different from those of even twenty-five years ago. Thus, the requirements of the human family are different from those of ages past. We live in a time of tremendous change. We think and feel in expanding progressive capacities as we have evolved through the ox cart, the horse and buggy, the automobile, the airplane, supersonic jets, and into the age of space travel. We progressed from pale tallow candles to lamps, gas, electricity, and quantum advances into the age of electronics. The children of today live with, understand, and use items that even the greatest minds of the past knew nothing about.

As we practice thinking in positive ways, life may seem to become easier and smoother, to exhibit less tension and stress. We begin to manage our thoughts and feelings instead of allowing outer circumstances to become controlling factors. We can begin at any time to shift our thinking and respond positively to life.

One young woman uses a technique that she calls "choosing." Whenever a negative thought moves into her mind, she immediately chooses to replace the negative thought with a positive attitude. The statement she speaks or thinks is simply: "I give thanks for the abundance of good in my life." Two powerful activities are accomplished with this technique. The thinking processes move from positive to negative, and an attitude of gratitude is immediately prevalent! The young woman confessed that it didn't take long for this choosing

technique to become a lifetime habit that has actually brought many blessings into her life.

For a moment, let's consider how our thoughts

may have contributed to our present life experiences. What percentage of our thoughts could be described as negative or positive? Many respected teachers agree that when we control our thoughts, we control our lives. What is the viability of this statement? How important is it to *recognize* areas of mental activity? How can pleasant and more productive days result from cultivating a positive attitude? The potential and possibility are always present!

Remember: we have the *ability to choose*. Our minds are capable of making choices that are more powerful than any unhealthy craving or negative attitude. We can ask our minds to serve the highest good for all, rather than serving the personal ego. By deciding to cultivate a positive attitude toward all of life and everyone and everything in it, can we truly begin living more beneficially and successfully? We can create a life of giving rather than one of lacking.

Could a part of heaven on earth result from how we use our mind in the face of any and all circumstances? How important is it to acknowledge that nothing or no one outside ourselves can make us unhappy without our consent? Or cause us to be depressed? Or hurt our feelings?

Remember, we are always only a thought away from cultivating a positive attitude. How will you choose?

✦ LAW 3

Forgiving uplifts the forgiver. —John Marks Templeton

A BUSINESSMAN told a story of how forgiveness changed his life. His father walked out on the family when the young man was an infant and never bothered to call home again. The father drank excessively, was abusive to his wife and children, and ultimately spent several years in prison. He died at the age of fifty-two with cirrhosis of the liver and was buried in a pauper's grave.

The businessman carried the burden of hatred and resentment into his early forties. Many were the times he cursed his father for the pain and suffering that had been inflicted upon the family. He bore weighty grudges of hostility. His thoughts and feelings were so intense that they had a detrimental effect on the man's health, his relationships, his work, in fact, every area of his life. He said every hurt he had experienced was like being bitten by a snake. A person rarely died from the injury, but once bitten, it became impossible to be unbitten! The mental and emotional damage resulting from the venom that continued to flow through his system was agonizing.

Fortunately, the man realized this venomous attitude could ultimately destroy his life and peace of mind. One day, feeling the heaviness of this position, the businessman made a visit to his father's grave. As he stood looking down at his father's name on the tombstone, he felt a surge of weariness and unexpected compassion. He didn't know or understand why his father acted the way he had, but the man was tired of carrying the burden of anger and resentment. His heart began to open with the movement of forgiveness. He began to let go of encroaching negative thoughts and feelings. With tears streaming down his face, he finally felt spiritually mature enough to whisper to his father's spirit, "I forgive you, and I'm sorry for all the anger and negativity I directed your way."

As the energy of the man's words hung in the air, the weight began to lift from his shoulders. He later said that his health began to improve significantly. His work took a giant leap forward. His relationships shifted from hostility toward more compassionate, considerate, and loving expressions. And, perhaps most important, the venom was no longer pumping through his veins. In his situation, forgiving uplifted the forgiver! When we learn to pardon those we may feel have wronged us, we can rise above all insults, angers, aggravations, and resentments. The act of forgiveness puts an immediate end to all quarrels! The act of forgiving uplifts the forgiver!

In every area of our lives, we can discover the sweet release that comes from the healing balm of forgiveness. We can develop the flexibility to change our minds and behavior patterns to expressions that are more elevated. We can find new venues to greater freedom. True forgiveness has been described as giving up the false or illusionary and

focusing on the truth. And what is the truth? Could it revert to The Golden Rule: "Do unto [and see] others as you would have them do unto [and see] you"? Forgiveness has also been described as the art of erasing an emotional debt. As we move into an attitude of forgiveness, our hearts become more open and we engage in a conscious and intentional release of resentment.

Like the businessman in the story, the moment we correct an error, we align ourselves with the harmony of the truth of being; the law of forgiveness wipes out our transgressions. Forgiving ourselves can be uplifting, but can total forgiveness of others be more uplifting? When the walls of resentment, anger, and fear begin to crumble, are we then free to build healthy structures for more positive and beneficial living? When our minds are free, strong, and healthy, how does the world reflect our strength and wholeness?

Could unlimited love be an essential ingredient in an attitude of forgiveness? In the Sermon on the Mount, Jesus tells us we are told to "love those who hate us." We are told to "turn the other cheek." If we can give and expect nothing in return, if we can learn to love our enemies, if we can be merciful even as our Creator is merciful, are we practicing the principles of love and forgiveness? If we approach others with an attitude of loving kindness, can we be repaid with a glimpse of brotherly humanity? Is a forgiving attitude a benefit of humility? As thanksgiving opens the door to spiritual growth, does forgiveness open the door to progress in knowledge and understanding? How are the spiritual practices of love, compassion, kindness, and forgiveness essential tools for the maintenance of a healthy body, mind,

and spirit? Could the divine idea of forgiveness also be about loving one's self enough to be honest, open-minded, and willing to move forward in life?

Lives that we touch, for good or ill, can affect other lives. One life touches another life, which

Forgiveness is a unification of the soul with God, comparable to the raindrop's reception by the sea.
—Imelda Shanklin

will in turn touch another. Who knows what far-reaching effects what we think, feel, say, and do may have, or in what far places our touch may be felt? To be forgiven, we must first forgive. Forgiveness brings forgiveness. Failure to forgive creates hell for the person who does not forgive. And the one who is not forgiven may never know the difference!

✦ Law 4

The light of understanding dissolves the phantoms of fear. —Ellie Harold

An elderly man called his three children together and said to them. "My life is nearing its completion. I have little in material wealth to leave you. However, I have four rules of life that, other than you, have been my heart's greatest treasures for many years. If you accept these treasures into your heart and mind, you can be among the happiest of people. And true happiness will take you far in life."

In unison, the young people asked, "Tell us, Father. What are the treasures?"

He smiled at each in turn and replied. "First, fill your hearts with unlimited love. When your heart

is filled with love, there is no room for lesser things. There is no room for fear in love. Perfect love banishes fear. Fear brings with it the pains of judgment, and anyone who is afraid has not attained to unlimited love in its perfection. Love your enemies and do good toward all and love will bring its own reward. Most importantly, not only radiate love to everyone you meet, but also help others to become alive with love.

"Second, fill your mind with understanding. When your mind is focused in seeking understanding for every part of God's creation, there is no room for fear. The light of understanding dissolves the phantoms of fear, which are no more than eerie ghosts that haunt the rooms of an inactive mind. Learn to recognize the illusions surrounding fear. Things are *not* always as they appear, nor will you ever lack the resources to handle any situation. Spirit is always present.

"Third, fill your mind and heart with gratitude. Be appreciative of what you have and be thankful for where you are on your path of spiritual growth. You are each blessed with many gifts and gratitude will keep your heart filled with the joyful feeling of appreciation for everything that arises on your path. Spend time offering assistance to those who may be less fortunate. Regardless of how rich or poor a person may be, everyone can give something to another. This can help you gain perspective in many areas of life. If you create a space in your consciousness right now for gratitude, praise, and thanksgiving, there will be no room for fear and you may live more joyously in the present moment.

"Finally, have pride in who you are and what you have accomplished, but balance this with a spirit of deep humility. If you find yourself harboring secret thoughts of arrogance or conceit, remind yourself of the lesson of humility before the universe does it for you! Humility is a gateway to greater understanding. The Creator loves us all equally and unceasingly. His spirit is like a stream of water, and we are like many beautiful fountains fed by this river of waters. Each one of us is such a fountain, and it is our task to keep the channel open so God's spirit can flow freely. Each of us has been given free will and a mind that is, in itself, a creative power. Remember, however, that humans are only tiny, temporary parts of reality, parts of a limitless, timeless Creator whom some call God. God infinitely exceeds any human concept, and is infinitely beyond human comprehension and understanding.

"My beloved children, broad is the carpet God has spread for your lives, and beautiful are the colors he has given to each of you. Laugh as often as you can. Be filled with the radiance of divine love. Let your eyes sparkle with the genius of infinite mind. Shower your world with thoughts, feelings, words, and actions that bespeak a child of the universe!"

With those words, the old man gathered his children in his arms and love wiped away the tears from each one's eyes!

Whenever we stop to look fear in the face, we can gain strength and courage and grow in confidence. Why is this? Could a fearful attitude ever open the door to victory and success in any phase of life? Why not? How can we transform an uncomfortable fearful response into a blessing for

ourselves and others? How can taking responsibility for situations in our lives help eliminate fearful thoughts and feelings? How can a cheerful, positive frame of mind banish fearful thoughts? What part can prayer play in letting go of fear? How can facing even the most difficult situations with equanimity, patience, and understanding remove doubt and fear?

✦ Law 5

Only one thing is more powerful than learning from experience,
and that is not learning from experience. —John Marks Templeton

WHAT HAVE we learned from personal experiences in our lives? What have we learned from observing others? What effect does this knowledge gleaned from experience have on how we make decisions in the present moment? How does the experience of "trial and error" assist in our personal growth? Do we find our sense of life steadily expanding and improving because we are building on experiences and acquired knowledge? If so, perhaps we emerge as a winner in more ways than one! What factor has ethics played in our experiences? Is spiritual growth observable as a result of our experiences? Have our moral standards increased because of what we have learned through various experiences? Is our creativity strengthened because the "voice of experience" has served as an effective guide toward purposeful achievement?

At some point in our growth, we may feel confused by particular situations. We may act like little white mice in the scientist's maze, running around, bumping into walls, searching for the way out. However, if we look at the maze from above, as the scientist can, the way out of the maze quickly becomes apparent. When we are open to growing into greater awareness, running around and bumping into walls can offer an excellent opportunity to confront error and learn from experience. For example, is the person who is willing to listen to another's point of view and to recognize there may be other approaches than the one he or she has chosen the one who can grow in wisdom? If so, his or her reservoir of experience and knowledge can be expanded.

Can we look at experiences in our life as conduits for good? Regardless of what may occur, there exists a potential for good to come out of experience. People today are alert to new discoveries in spiritual and natural phenomena and to

their relationships to their inner lives, their families, and their society. Could this awareness come partly from observation of what is happening around them and from learning through experience?

We can *consciously* decide to adapt—not only to keep our balance, but also to turn what may seem to be "stumbling blocks" into "stepping stones." What is a most important aspect to this process? Could it be the power of choice? We can choose to learn from our experience, or we can ignore the possibilities before us and not learn from the experience.

Positive and confident attitudes have long been acknowledged as a necessary factor for being a winner in the world of sports. If a participant wants to win the game, it is important for him to believe in his abilities and to have the *desire* to win the game. The business world generally accepts as a fact that to succeed in business, a person must believe he can succeed. In other aspects of life as well, can you incorporate your belief in your talents and abilities, your desire to succeed, your visions of success, and the knowledge you have gleaned from past experiences, and transform them into fruitful living?

Progress and growth may elude us if we continue doing things the way we have always done them. Progress means moving forward. It can also mean developing a higher, better, more advanced state of consciousness. Continuing to do things in the same old way keeps us in the same place. Laps around the same track seldom show us something new. Why would we be reluctant to progress? When we have moved through an experience, can we welcome the next one with enthusiasm and excitement because we have gained new knowledge? The higher and more beneficial way of life that eternally beckons us is called growth!

We may deduce that failing to learn from experience and stubbornly holding on to old ways can create conflict within ourselves. Only one thing is more powerful than learning from experience, and that is not learning from experience! We may open our arms to embrace a friend. Can we likewise open our minds and hearts to embrace new ideas or experiences that can bring the delightful benefits and satisfaction of progress and growth?

Spotlights ✦ ✦

1. "A day without learning is a day wasted" (Albert Einstein).

2. Why is learning as a lifetime activity so important?

3. How can setting the goal of learning something new every day enhance our lives, our relationships, our chosen professions, indeed, all areas of our lives?

4. Consistently turn your thoughts toward the spiritual aspects of life and dwell on the infinite good in yourself and in others.

5. Stop wasting energy in negative thinking. As we remove human negativity, our connection with spiritual power grows stronger.

6. "Accentuate the positive and eliminate the negative" (Johnny Mercer).

7. How are our thoughts contributing to our present lives?

8. We are painting our own cosmic canvas of life. How will the picture unfold?

9. Life is constant change. We cannot remain exactly as we are right now. In which direction are you gong?

10. The courage to step forward to obtain a desired goal is one step closer to success.

11. Forgiveness has been described as the art of erasing an emotional poison.

12. Could unlimited love be an essential ingredient in an attitude of forgiveness?

13. How does the light of understanding dissolve the phantoms of fear?

14. What are some of your "phantoms of fear"?

15. What have you learned from personal experiences in your life?

16. How can reviewing an experience serve as a productive yardstick to measure your performance in the experience?

Living the Various Spiritual Laws ✦ ✦

The Nag Hammadi Library is a collection of religious texts found in Upper Egypt in 1945. While they were copied in the early fourth century, they vary widely from the Gospel of Thomas to homilies to pagan sayings to a selection from Plato's *Republic.* "The Sentences of Sextus" from Nag Hammadi is made up of a collection of wisdom sayings and maxims with a strongly ethical and ascetic tone. Offered below is a selection of these wisdom sayings.

Speak when it is not proper to be silent, but speak concerning the things
    you know, only then when it is fitting.

Do not deceive anyone.

Wisdom leads the soul to the place of God.

A wise man is a doer of good works after God.

Where your thought is, there is your goodness.

He who does not harm the soul neither does so to man.

A godly heart produces a blessed life.

You cannot receive understanding except you know first that you possess nothing.

It is better to serve others than to make others serve you.

The love of man is the beginning of godliness.

If you, from your whole heart, give your bread to the hungry, the gift is small,
    but the willingness is great with God.

Week Nineteen

✦ LAW I

Religion opens new doors for science. —Franklin Loehr

ANY NEW FIELD of exploration can be an inviting door for science and may be a useful opening for the diligent and inquiring mind. There is so much to explore and so much to learn. Two exciting and rewarding areas of scientific research are the vast reaches of the frontiers of space and time, and the tiny, strange nucleotides in the DNA chain. There is an incredible amount to be learned about our material universe, with study following study, and discovery leading to further discovery. We are expanding rapidly in the exploration of our potentials. We are advancing into the fundamental nature of human life.

In *The Development of Religion as a Science*, Franklin Loehr suggests,

Religion offers a whole new realm to be scientifically explored. Religion opens doors to a realm as potentially bigger than all physical science to date . . . Religion is the field of the spiritual, and the spiritual dimension holds promise of geometrical, exponential expansion of knowledge. The physical universe, vast as it is, is yet limited. "Matter can be neither created nor destroyed." But enter the spiritual dimension, the non-physical, and who knows what we have?

★ ★ ★

We stand poised on the spiritual frontier, ready for the brilliant seekers of Science to enter these opening doors to discover and explore other dimensions and realms of reality. The possibilities, even the first promises, of what we shall find are dazzling, inestimable treasures of new knowledge. . . . The spiritual realms of being transcend and surmount the entire physical universe, and are opening to us. The Age of MAN is just beginning to beckon us.

What does the idea of "religion opening new doors for science" mean to us as individuals? Do some of our concepts expand or change, just as previous ideas of health, history, the stars, and the size and placement of the earth changed as science gathered information in these fields? What unknown dimensions and what new explosions of inquiry and discovery may await new research projects as humanity becomes increasingly open and receptive to the element of purpose in life? How can we begin to use the superb tool of knowledge, through scientific methods, to discover some of the "whys" or reasons behind creation?

Could scientific discoveries along spiritual lines help us to understand that material things do not necessarily bring happiness and may be of little use in helping men and women become more creative and effective? External things are significant to us only to the extent they affect us internally— through body, mind, and soul. How does increased spiritual knowledge help us to modify that extent? How could human lives be beneficially affected as scientists direct their laboratories to the study of divinity and prayer? As science and spirituality become closer through research, could the world see more beneficial advancement in one generation than the wonders discovered in the previous ten?

While it may be said that all science is necessarily only human perceptions, are not humans continually finding ways to expand their perceptive abilities? So, does science study reality or only human perceptions of reality? Do most sciences serve to enlarge human perceptions of basic reality? How do we as individuals experience beneficial growth through the expansion of our perceptions of the world around us? If we discover that we have a special talent to produce something the world can use, do we not receive remuneration in some way? There are abundant opportunities for the person who elects to make himself or herself useful and necessary to the world. Could this be the working of the *spiritual* principle of giving and receiving? What *scientific* principle would apply in this analogy? With the sheer driving force of advancing technology, it becomes increasingly clear that numerous oppor-

Jesus of Nazareth was the most scientific man that ever trod the globe. He plunged beneath the material surface of things, and found the spiritual cause.
—*Mary Baker Eddy*

tunities are available in many areas for those who feel an inner desire to be of service.

Do we need new branches of science that would research unseen spiritual principles? Could this avenue of scientific research possibly be even more

beneficial to humanity than to all other sciences? Could scientific research show us that the awesome mysteries of magnetism, gravity, light, creativity, intellect, memory, love, thanksgiving, and purpose may be aspects of divinity, and that divinity may be also much more? How would this kind of information inspire our individual lives? Could

Religion is a candle inside a multi-colored lantern. Everyone looks through a particular color, but the candle is always there.
—*Mohammed Naguil, Egyptian soldier*

we use this type of information, perhaps to adapt a living credo of greater humility and purpose?

Can humans increase their concepts of divinity, first by admitting that evidence indicates realities vastly greater than those previously available to human perception, and thereby becoming enthusiastic for research to discover over one hundred-fold more about divinity? What could be some effects on our daily life by increasing our concept of divinity by even a small percentage? Would we become more sensitive to the needs of others, more caring, compassionate, loving? Would the results of our labors be more beneficial to humanity?

The benefits of spiritual principles show up in offices, businesses, careers, homes, and the lives of individuals. Basic spiritual principles can be just as beneficial in careers of invention and science as they have been proven to be for inward spiritual growth. What could happen if we devoted one-tenth of scientific research to new additional spiritual research to supplement the wonderful ancient scriptures? Could the resulting blessing possibly exceed the blessings received from all other scientific research?

✦ Law 2

Happiness comes from spiritual wealth, not material wealth. —John Marks Templeton

YEARS AGO, Olympic champion Charley Paddock was speaking to the young men at a local high school. "If you think you can, you can!" he challenged the youths. "If you believe a thing strongly enough, it can come to pass in your life!"

Afterward, a spindly legged boy said to Mr. Paddock, "Gee, Sir, I'd give anything if I could be an Olympic champion like you!" It was that young man's moment of inspiration. His life changed! In 1936, that young man went to Berlin, Germany, to compete in the Olympics. And *Jesse Owens* came home with four gold medals!

After returning home to the United States, he was being driven through the streets of Cleveland to the cheers of a large crowd. The car stopped and Jesse Owens signed some autographs. A skinny little boy pressed against the car and said, "Gosh, Mr. Owens, I'd give anything to be an Olympic champion like you!" Jesse Owens felt a tug at his heart. He remembered a similar experience from years before. He reached out the car window and put his hand on the boy's arm as he said, "You know, young fellow, I was about your age when I said the same thing. If you will work and train diligently and believe, you can be an Olympic champion!"

In 1948 at Wembly Stadium in London, England, that same little boy was a young man. He crouched waiting for the starter's gun to go off for the finals of the 100-meter dash. *Harrison "Bones" Dillard* won the race and tied Jesse Owens' Olympic record!

Can you imagine for a moment the happiness and joy that ensued for each of the individuals mentioned in this story? Perhaps most of us have been inspired to do something through someone else's example. A word spoken by someone we admire and respect may catch our attention and ignite the fires of enthusiasm and encouragement. Over a period of time, watching how someone lives and responds to life can provide inspiration for our thoughts and actions. We may admire an apparent reservoir of a person's spiritual strength and spiritual wealth. Spiritual wealth provides abundant blessings. It deepens the feeling of unlimited love in our hearts. It nurtures feelings of compassion for others. We may notice the light of praise and gratitude shining in someone's eyes, or the beautiful expressions of commitment and love on their face. Spiritual wealth can enhance discernment and expand wisdom. It can lead us to increasing happiness through guidance into dedi-

cated service to others. Does greater happiness stem from spiritual growth?

Our material wealth may be easily determined, but what guidelines may be used to determine our spiritual wealth? How would we define spiritual wealth? Does it have a direct connection with the extent of our happiness? How happy are we as individuals? We may think that happiness is a result of positive circumstances. This can be true to a point. However, would a more mature view of happiness indicate that it is a by-product of loving service and sharing our good fortune with others? How do we feel when we have honestly given our best efforts to a job well done, shared sincere communication with another, visited someone who is ill, or laughed aloud in joy with a friend?

Yes, material assets bring comfort, but help little toward happiness or usefulness. As we develop

Thus happiness
depends, as Nature
shows, less on exte-
rior things than most
suppose.
—William Cowper

our spiritual wealth, our inner security is present to serve us. Our spiritual wealth can help us recoup and recover from our losses. Does the gratification of material wealth come through its wise application in service to others and to noble causes?

Could spiritual wealth lie at the very center of man's endeavors to find order and organization in the ultimate realities of the cosmos, the place we live and move and have our being?

✦ LAW 3

Religion is good for your health. —Dale Matthews

We need a religious
system with science
at its very core.
—Margaret Mead

[Prayer] has
saved my life.
—Mahatma Gandhi

I feel the capacity
to care is the thing
which gives life its
deepest significance
and meaning.
—Pablo Casals

A VIVACIOUS and vexing lady frequently visited the medical office of Dr. Dale Matthews. She came armed with a beguiling smile, a rapier wit, and intractable pain from arthritis. Each visit brought forth a languorous litany of incurable woe. She had sampled every painkiller in the pharmacopoeia, with scant success.

"Is there anything that does help you?" Dr. Matthew asked her one day.

"Yes. Faith and prayer!" she exclaimed. "And singing in the church choir!"

Faith and prayer and . . . singing? Are these listed in the *Physician's Desk Reference*? Should they be? Is religion or spirituality, like codeine or other opiates, an effective "drug" for pain and other disorders? What is the proper dose? Do side effects occur?

The medical effects of spiritual faith are not only a matter of faith, but are also a matter of science. Mind-body medicine is one of the fastest-growing areas of medical science, as investigators

Accustomed long to contemplating Love and Compassion, I have
forgotten all difference between myself and others.
—Milarepa

throughout the world have turned their attention to the effects of mental stress, emotional disorder,

and social isolation on the human body. More than three hundred scientific studies demonstrate the medical value of spiritual commitment. This includes prayer, Scripture study, worship attendance, and active participation in a spiritual community. These benefits enhanced prevention and

Active religious involvement also improves health by its
effects on health behaviors.
—Harold Koenig

treatment of mental disorders (e.g., depression, suicide, and anxiety), medical and surgical illnesses (e.g., heart disease, cancer, sexually transmitted diseases), and addictions; reduced pain and disability; and prolonged survival. In addition, spiritual treatment such as prayer and religiously based psychotherapy enhanced recovery.

A cohesive, comforting set of spiritual beliefs and values and participation in sacred rituals may endow individuals with a greater sense of meaning, purpose, and hope. Faith can offer a "peace that passes understanding" in times of pain, grief, and disability. Healthy lifestyles that include exercise and proper diet are more common among religious persons. Persons who are spiritually focused usually cope better with stress, have a strong social support, and enjoy a higher quality of life (e.g., well-being, self-esteem, job and marital satisfaction, altruism).

In *God for the 21st Century*, Herbert Benson wrote:

Spiritual beliefs quiet the mind, short-circuiting the unproductive reasoning that often consumes our thoughts. The body is very effective at healing itself but, all too often, this process is hindered by negative thoughts and doubts. Worries and doubts elicit the fight-or-flight response and its attendant stress-related symptoms and disease that can blunt evolutionary honed healing capaci-

ties. . . . But because faith seems to transcend experience, it is supremely good at relieving distress and generating hope and expectancy. With hope and expectancy comes 'remembered wellness'—the cerebral message for healing that mobilizes the body's resources and reactions.

A new willingness to consider alternative healing practices and a growing cooperation between religion and medicine is in the air. Has the time arrived to reunite these long-separated twin traditions of healing, to join hands, not swords?

◆ LAW 4

Progress requires change. —John Marks Templeton

WHEREVER we look, we find beneficial progress in a variety of areas such as health and medicine, science, economics, communications media, transportation, religion, charity, philanthropy, philosophy, psychology, art, music, education, the family, and the environment. There is a strong sense that the rate of progress is speeding up. This acceleration is likely to continue across countless areas of human endeavor.

When the billowing waves of change come rolling into our lives, it may be worthwhile to remember that progress requires change. If we have little understanding of how to welcome change, we may face some difficult experiences along the way. On the other hand, if we are open and receptive to the presence of divinity in every situation and in every change then we may ride the crest of the wave with enthusiasm! If people look for the good in everyone and in everything, they will find it; in countless ways, this can have constructive consequences. Enthusiasm for life, regardless of appearances or seeming circumstances, breeds effort and success.

This is a wonderful time to be alive on planet Earth! Look at what has happened in terms of our nutrition and health, our living standards and working conditions, our political and economic freedoms, our educational facilities and our ability to communicate with one another, our ease of global movement, the quality of our leisure, and most importantly, our ability to get along with one another and with our Creator. So much progress has been made!

If we are dedicated and glad to grow physically, mentally, and spiritually, are we more likely to welcome change? Do we regularly prepare ourselves for unexpected change through the power of prayer? Do we accelerate the assurance that our growing resilience can move us courageously and triumphantly forward?

Do we have faith in the capacity of our soul quality, knowing that we have the fullness of divine love, wisdom, and intelligence to draw upon? Do we recognize that adversity can be a rich and educational gift as well as a milestone in our personal growth? Are we willing to perceive change as an opportunity to become more productive and useful?

How can we *consciously* contribute to progress through change? For example, today, the opportunity to read or see or hear news from around the world is unprecedented. Could we focus on the *positive* points of news, looking for long-term benefits rather than focusing on the negative aspects?

In this way, might we be more likely to take beneficial action? Do we utilize the life experiences

often brought about by change to gain greater mastery over our thoughts, feelings, and emotions? Have our lives become more simple and sincere through change? What are some positive change aspects of serving as helpers in the acceleration of divine creativity?

✦ Law 5

Beneficial experiences often come though trial and self-discipline. —Unknown

FRIEDRICH NIETZSCHE described a three-fold process in the maturation of consciousness. He said that in the first stage, we are like a *camel* bending down to have hoisted upon us the load of social conditioning, habit, and convention. In the second stage, we are like a *lion* roaring against the "thou shalts" of society. Only after we have completed the work of the lion do we become the *child,* which is to say, a fully human being, capable of spontaneously, intuitively, and competently responding to the world.

Learning from life often requires that we examine the conventions, ideals, and programs of society, as well as the habits and routines we may have unconsciously accumulated. *Beneficial experiences often come through trial and self-discipline.* The trial-and-error method is one way to gain knowledge.

However, the measure of our courage is often reflected in the vision of life we choose, through the knowledge we have gained, and what it takes

for us to continue the journey. Can we move beyond the grief or pain of any experience, learn from it, and live for the good of humanity?

Discipline has been termed "enlightened tenacity." Self-discipline is simply a matter of doing what is necessary to do without wasting time or energy complaining or procrastinating. This may sound like harsh; however, it works! The benefit is that we discover that freedom is not the ability to do what we may feel like doing at a particular time, but the ability to *choose* what to do and follow through! How often do we squander vital energy that could be channeled into creative discipline in attempts to protect our egos? If we would but listen, the wisdom of the heart can tell us what is important and what is unnecessary action.

Perseverance is a great element of success and can be a powerful ally in moving through tough experiences. In his book *The Wings of Joy*, Sri Chinmoy tells an interesting story of perseverance and self-discipline:

Once there was a young boy named Bopdeb who was the worst possible student. His parents and teachers scolded him mercilessly, but nothing did any good. Finally, his teachers gave up and threw him out of school. Neither did Bopdeb's parents want him. So, feeling miserable, Bopdeb left his home and went to the nearest village.

Every day Bopdeb went to pray and meditate under a tree near a large pond. From there, he watched the village women carrying empty pitchers to the pond and filling them. Bopdeb noticed that the women would fill the pitchers, place them on the stone steps, and then go and bathe in the pond. After getting refreshed, they returned home with their pitchers of water.

One day, when no one was there, Bopdeb noticed that the part of the step on which the women put their pitchers was no longer level with the rest. He said to himself, "Because the women have placed their pitchers here repeatedly, the stone is wearing down. If even a stone can wear down, then what is wrong with my brain?" From this experience, Bopdeb came to understand patience and perseverance.

He started praying and meditating more seriously, and a few days later, he started reading his old Sanskrit grammar books again. He had been the worst possible student in Sanskrit, but now he was able to remember what he read. He continued his studies and, with perseverance, eventually became the greatest Sanskrit scholar in India.

Reaching a goal may require repeated attempts. Each attempt can bring us closer toward achieving our objective and, in the process, we may accomplish other goals as well. Beneficial experiences provide a tremendous inner wealth. If we look around us with perceptive eyes, we can see the world is definitely evolving and progressing. You have probably heard or read the following selection from Johann Wolfgang von Goethe. The encouragement to act boldly comes from the experiences of a man who was extraordinarily bold.

That moment one definitely commits oneself,
then Providence moves too.
All sorts of things occur to help one
that would never otherwise have occurred.
A whole stream of events issues from the decision,
raising in one's favor
all manner of unforeseen incidents
and meetings and material assistance,
which no man could have dreamed
would have come his way.
Whatever you can do, or dream
you can begin it.
Boldness has genius, power and magic in it.
Begin it now.

When you are inspired by some great purpose, some extraordinary project, all your thoughts break their bounds. Your mind transcends limitations, your consciousness expands in every direction and you find yourself in a new, great and wonderful world. Dormant forces, faculties and talents become alive, and you discover yourself to be a greater person by far than you ever dreamed yourself to be. —Patanjali

Spotlights ✦ ✦

1. How would you perceive spirituality as offering a whole new realm to be scientifically explored?

2. What does the idea of "religion opening new doors for science" mean to you as an individual? Could this information be personally useful?

3. Would a new branch of science to research spiritual principles be universally beneficial?

4. Our material wealth may be easily determined, but what guidelines might be used to determine our spiritual wealth?

5. How may compassion be demonstrated as a quality of conduct in our daily life?

6. Is compassion a form of unlimited love in expression?

7. How is compassion *not* an invitation to non-action or complacency?

8. What is the principle behind the phrase "progress requires change"?

9. How can change enhance our lives and increase our progress?

10. Does resistance to change indicate that we need to look a little more deeply into ourselves?

11. What does the statement "Discipline has been termed 'enlightened tenacity'" represent to you?

12. How does self-discipline assist you in achieving your goals?

13. Why is our most important journey in life the journey within?

Living the Various Spiritual Laws ✦ ✦

How many times in our lives have we experienced moments of deep sadness or despair, for ourselves or for someone close to us? This could have derived from a severe illness, an accident, the breakup of a relationship, a loss of property, or the death of a friend or a loved one. How did we respond?

Many people often sink into sorrow; they either feel a need to tell everyone about what is happening or they seclude themselves in their misery. We grieve. We may read books offering information on how to handle the grieving process. We may attend support groups to help overcome our loss and regain a sense of stability. Grieving is an acceptable response to a loss or a tragic event.

But what might happen if we truly understood the following words from Rumi, the Persian mystical poet:

I saw grief drinking a cup of sorrow and called out,
"It tastes sweet, does it not?"
"You've caught me," grief answered,
"and you've ruined my business.
How can I sell sorrow when you know it's a blessing?"

What changes might occur in our life if we understood that the falls, pains, heartaches, and disappointments of our lives can provide us with the energy to propel ourselves to a higher level of consciousness? This is not to suggest that we should not respect our genuine feelings. But think about this: Could the truth of Rumi's observation offer another way to respond to difficult circumstances? It isn't necessary to *like* a tragedy or a difficult situation, but could we recognize that there is something beneficial to be learned, even in the midst of sorrow?

Week Twenty

◆ ## LAW 1

Are the visible and tangible only timeless manifestations
of the vast timeless and limitless reality?—John Marks Templeton

> There is no great
> cosmic scale in
> antiquity.
> —*Owen Gingerich*

DO WE KNOW very little, probably less that 1 percent of what can be discovered, about God and fundamental spiritual principles? Most people, even highly trained theologians, seem to have various, restricted views of who God is and what divinity's purpose is in creating this amazing universe, including us. Recent research in physics and cosmology reveals that reality is vastly greater and more mysterious than we thought.

> For what purpose did
> our source of being
> grant us the gifts
> that we possess?
> How, then, shall we
> employ these gifts?
> —*Howard J. Van Till*

Is it possible that the Creator may not be describable adequately in human words and concepts and may not be limited by human rationality? Consider the possibility that God is not limited by our five senses or by our human perceptions of three dimensions in space and one dimension in time. Perhaps there was no absolute beginning and there will be no absolute end, but only everlasting change and variety in the unlimited purposes, freedom, and creativity of God.

Maybe God is all of time and space, and much more! The appearance of humankind on this planet may be said to have heralded the coming of a new quality encircling the earth, the sphere of the intellect. As we have used our intellects to investigate this mysterious universe, accumulating knowledge at an ever-increasing rate, there has

come a growing awareness that material things are not what they seem. Perhaps thoughts are more real and lasting than matter and energy.

Perhaps this heralds a new quality, the sphere of the spirit. God may be creating not only the infinitely large, but also the infinitely small. Not only on the outward, but also the inward; not only the

> When we ask the question, How large is God? we are asking
> whether God transcends all our concepts and images. Another way
> to ask the same question is, How small is human understanding?
> —*Freeman J. Dyson*

tangible, but also the intangible. Thoughts, mind, soul, wisdom, love, originality, inspiration, and enthusiasm may be little manifestations of a Creator who is omniscient, omnipotent, eternal, and infinite. The things that we can see, hear, and touch may be only appearances. They may be only manifestations of underlying forces, including spiritual forces that may persist throughout all the transience of physical existence. Perhaps the spiritual world and the benevolent Creator it reflects may be the only reality.

Presumably, the sphere of the spirit may enclose

not only this planet but also the entire universe, so God includes all of nature and is inseparable from it. Perhaps it is mankind's own ego that leads us to think we are at the center of a vast universe of being that subsists in an eternal and infinite reality which some call God. Maybe all of nature that is visible to us is only a transient wave on the ocean of all that God eternally is. Maybe time, space, and energy provide no limit to the being that is God. Likewise, the fundamental parameters of the universe—the speed of light, the force of gravitation, the weak and strong nuclear forces, and electromagnetism—would seem to pose no limits to the being that can be called God.

Think on these things:

+ Maybe nothing can be separate from God.
+ Maybe the great religions that descended from Abraham have unconsciously overemphasized the visible and tangible aspects of fundamental reality.
+ Maybe unconsciously, these religions have overemphasized God as distant and separate from creation.
+ Maybe it is egotistical to think that any human ever understood even 1 percent of God.
+ Maybe humanity is like a wave on the ocean, and God is like the ocean.
+ Maybe it is self-centered for us to think that nowhere in the universe is there other life capable of thought. Even if only one star in a million has a planet in a similar development stage as Earth, then there may be a hundred thousand other similar planets in our own Milky Way, not to mention the other hundred billion galaxies.
+ Maybe it is egotistical to think that progress in religion is not necessary or possible.

+ Maybe it is self-centered to think that we are approaching an omega point, rather than ever-increasing diversity beyond imagination.
+ Maybe God is only just beginning to create the universe and allows each of his children to participate in small ways in this creative evolution.

I am . . . reminded of the humility of those early theologians who knew that when we seek to speak of God, we do so only out of the glimmers of understanding that sparkle amid the vast background of uncomprehended mystery, a mystery that nevertheless shines in nature and in the human spirit with unquenchable light.
—Robert J. Russell

Could our human concepts of God still be tied to a previous century? Could the twenty-first century possibly represent a new renaissance in human knowledge, a new embarkation into new concepts of the future? Persons living now can hardly imagine the small amount of knowledge and the limited concepts of the cosmos that humans possessed when the holy books of the five major religions were written. Is it possible that an expanded interpretation of the old scriptures could pose interesting and different insights for spiritual and scientific research?

While recognizing that a person's relationship with God may be both personal and impersonal, should our names for God be less heavily focused on personalization, since their usage favors human-centered concepts? The Creator seems to be both transcendent and imminently accessible, both by science and by prayer, ready to transform the lives of those who invite him in.

✦ Law 2

To err is human, to forgive is divine. —Alexander Pope

TODAY'S LIVING seems to call for continual adjustments in interacting human relationships. We rub shoulders with a variety of states of consciousness. We daily contact people with diversified interests. We encounter souls at various points on the path of spiritual progression. Many with whom we come in contact may be experiencing problems or difficulties. Thus, it would seem the art of successful interaction and harmonious relationship with one's fellow man could require a lot of balance, focus, understanding, compassion, and forgiveness on our part!

Is there any one of us who has not, at some time in life, made a mistake, experienced an error in discernment, or erred in some other way? Is there any one of us who has not, at some time, felt irritated, misunderstood, falsely accused, or totally misjudged by another? Carl Jung said, "Everything that irritates us about others can lead us to an understanding of ourselves." Could we acknowledge perhaps a glimmer of truth in this statement? How tolerant are we of others? Is it possible that our judgments of others may be reflections of ourselves, as opposed to some objective reality? Are we willing to learn to embrace all parts of other individuals, to allow them to be and express themselves fully as the unique humans that they are? Can we realize the truth of the maxim "what we

To forgive another is to accept him as he is, though not necessarily as he appears to be!
—*Leddy and Randolph Schmelig*

hold on to holds on to us?" Is this part of the admonition "Live and let live"? What does this statement really mean to us? Is forgiveness part of the picture? To obtain a measurable answer, we

have to be honest with ourselves, even though it may hurt a little—or a lot!

Our thoughts and feelings often represent the measuring rod that determines how life responds

Every action in life is a matter of personal choice. Choose to be unique. Choose to be the best you can be.
—*George W. Cummings Sr.*

to us. Scripture tells us, "The measure you give is the measure you receive" (Matthew 7:2). The unique combination of thoughts and feelings we give are the workers that bring back the harvest to us. And the harvest can be weeds, vegetables, or flowers! What is the *measure* we are giving? How often do we remember, and *practice*, "To err is human, to forgive is divine!

Do we have reputations of loving, caring, and forgiveness? Reputation reflects the perception of others, stemming from what they feel or perceive is our character. A good reputation is slowly built upon a firm foundation of humility, integrity, love, and charity. As we respond to various life experiences, do the choices we make become the building blocks that create and construct our characters?

Deep within each person is a unified field of limitless possibilities. Here is where we are said to create prosperity, shift relationships to new levels of spiritual partnership, make powerful decisions, rid ourselves of toxins, cure our ailments, and forgive ourselves and others! Could this be the place of "going within" and discovering that purpose is about loving in an unlimited way, serving others and the Creator, being humble, and making conscious contact with what there is about us that beneficially alters our personal view and worldview dramatically?

The woman sitting in the counselor's office had

experienced a tragedy. Her nineteen-year-old daughter had been killed in a car accident involving a drunken driver six months earlier. The woman's shoulders were hunched and the shimmer of tears glistened in her eyes. The pain, grief, anger, and self-pity the woman felt overshadowed any truth she knew. The woman had come for counseling because she sought the strength to deal with this crisis in her life in a positive manner.

As the mother poured out her pain, the counselor listened intently. When the mother began repeating portions of her story, the counselor lifted his hand and interjected, "All right. This event has happened. Let's gain some understanding from the situation. So, for a moment, I want to sidetrack to something else."

The counselor then reached toward a small cactus plant in a container near the edge of his desk. He picked it up and handed the cactus plant to the mother, placing it in her right hand. The woman was somewhat surprised and puzzled at what had happened.

The counselor asked, "Does it hurt?"

"Hurt? Well, no," the woman responded. "I'm aware that I am holding a cactus, but it is in a container. I can hold the cactus without pain."

"Very good," the counselor said. "Now, I want you to touch the plant with your left hand and give it a squeeze!"

Of course, the woman refused to do this, saying that if she squeezed the cactus, her entire hand would be in agony from the sharp quills!

The point made to the woman was that sometimes, through tough life situations, we are given emotional cacti to hold. The way many people frequently respond to an emotional cactus is to squeeze and squeeze and squeeze! The pain then becomes so intense that it may be difficult to release. At this point, we have a choice.

We can realize that *we* are the one squeezing the cactus or we can hold on for dear life! When we recognize this truth and look closely at the cactus, at the emotional pain, we can set the cactus down or take steps to release the emotional pain. The woman in the story quickly grasped the meaning of counselor's illustration.

"I see my error." She later smiled at the counselor through her tears. "I choose a different direction." The woman and the counselor talked extensively about the power of love and forgiveness.

A true learning experience is more than a matter of input; it is also a matter of output! It is more than a process of assimilating facts, but also a process of realization and expressing what we have learned and know. The source of strength and compassion are part of the spirit within, ready to be expressed at any time and in any situation. To err is human, to forgive is divine.

✦ LAW 3

A good conscience is a continual feast. —Robert Burton

HAVE YOU EVER noticed that when we tell a lie, white or otherwise, take something that isn't ours, fail to support a friend, or act in a totally selfish manner, an inner alarm bell goes off when we realize what we have done? And what happens to our self-esteem when we realize we have failed to live up to our true worth and our own expectations? Someone said, "Never do anything that you'll have to punish yourself for." Could this statement reflect the positive advantage and guidance of having a clear conscience? Is it a kind of moral wake-up call? Can we look at ourselves—at our thoughts, feelings, and actions—at the end of the day and know that we have made every effort to live up to the core of our foremost values? Do we respect ourselves?

In his book *Hope from My Heart*, Rich DeVoss says, "Respect begins with how you feel about yourself, not what others say about you. Respect begins with knowing who you are, loving yourself, and accepting yourself." And respect carries reciprocal energy! People can instinctively understand the attitudes we exhibit, although they may be unable to express this in words. Think of all the people we come into contact with on a regular basis—our family, friends, coworkers, associates, and colleagues. Each person touches our lives in some unique or special way. Do we respond with honesty, integrity, steadfastness, and a sense of responsibility? Can people count on what we say?

> There is no witness so dreadful, no accuser so terrible as the conscience that dwells in the heart of every man.
> —Polybius

What do we do when a feeling of guilt or shame over something we have said or done gets our attention? Even if no one else knows of the situation, is there a way to make amends and lighten our load of "heart-heaviness"? Perhaps through experiencing the emotions and accepting the ramifications of our words or actions, we can begin to examine and change aspects of ourselves. We can admit the truth of the situation. We can forgive ourselves. We can make a commitment to live in integrity. We can pause, if only for a moment but in any situation, and positively adjust our thinking processes. We can express gratitude for our growing awareness.

The wisdom of the conscience is as essential as the air we breathe, and it is just as intangible! It seems to arise from the depths of our being and yet is reflected in every single word we speak and

> Our conscience, which is a great ledger book, wherein are written all our offenses . . . grinds our souls with the remembrance of some precedent sins, makes us reflect upon, accuse, and condemn ourselves.
> —Robert Burton

in every action we take. It is how we measure our moral worth. It serves as a helpful building block for character. Conscience has nothing to do with our IQ nor with the grades we made in school. On the other hand, does it have *everything* to do with the highest level we express of mental, emotional, and spiritual evolution? Is "conscience" where we align our deepest understandings with our everyday actions? Is it where we "feast" on the assurances of our motive and value structures? The rewards of a clear conscience are bountiful. Peace of mind. Increased joy in living. Beholding goodness in everything. Expressing interest and enthusiasm in the gifts of life. Experiencing life fully and fearlessly.

Conscience has been described as "a divine goodness at the root of all existence." It is present *wherever* we look and *whenever* we look. The touch of this wellspring of divine goodness may be brought to light within an individual at any time. It resides in the recesses of every mind and comes forth when least expected. Henry Van Dyke said, "A clean and sensitive conscience, a steady and scrupulous integrity in small things as well as large, is the most valuable of all possessions, to a nation as to an individual."

✦ LAW 4

A good reputation is more valuable than money. —Publilius Syrus

Never for a moment does a noble person quit the way of Goodness.
—*Confucius*

YOUR REPUTATION is mostly the result of how others see you. A good reputation is slowly built on a firm foundation of humility, integrity, love, and charity. Building a good reputation can be similar to building a house. You begin with a basic foundation and build from that point. The finished house is a product of the choices you made during the construction—from plan to completion. If your house is carelessly constructed of thin walls, then the slightest wind may destroy it. If you have chosen your building materials with attention to strength, quality, and durability, your house can withstand the strong winds that may blow.

Reputation is the perception by others of what they feel is your character. Again, building character may be likened to building a house. As you respond to life's experiences, the choices you make become the building blocks that create and construct your character. *What you are at this point in your life is the product of those choices!* The responsibility of making right choices is yours. Advice from others may be helpful, learning from experience can bring greater understanding and wisdom, and studying the laws of life can open new doors for consideration. But you are the one who decides how to use the knowledge you acquire. No one else can act for you.

To dwell upon goodness is to become the recipient of all that is good.
—*Marcus Bach*

Let's look at an example. By the time he was eighteen, John was saddled with a very poor reputation. He often lied. He would make promises to his friends and then fail to keep them, no matter how important these promises were to the other person. He had even been arrested for shoplifting. Because John's father was very well off financially, John thought he had everything. He lived in a fine house, wore the latest fashions, had his own car and plenty of spending money.

But John did not have everything. Far from it!

He did not have a good reputation. One summer, between his high school graduation and the start of college in September, John applied for a summer job in the field of his planned future career. But he didn't get the job. His poor reputation cost him the position. Then, for the first time, he fell in

I am the captain of my ship of good judgment, will, and activity. I will guide my ship of life, ever beholding the polestar of His peace shining in the firmament of my deep meditation.
—*Paramahansa Yogananda*

love. But because of his well-known reputation, the girl refused to date him. Behavior often speaks as plainly as words, and sometimes even more plainly. Many of us listen to words, and many people listen to the sometimes harsher language of behavior. If we do not pay attention to both, we can be blundering in our human relations. Alexander Pope commented, "At every word a reputation dies."

Fortunately, John came to realize that money is not so important in life if it's joined to a poor reputation. Your reputation, not your money, is the most valuable currency of all. John began to make changes in his life, but many years passed before people completely accepted the "new" John.

Again, what you do in your everyday life affects your reputation. It is up to you and to you alone to make appropriate decisions. Friends, parents, coworkers, clergy, and teachers can help you, advise you, stand by you, but they cannot act for you. If you take the time to think about what effects any action can have on your life and make your decisions based upon that awareness, you can earn a good reputation. It doesn't matter if you are rich or poor, a good reputation increases your chances of leading a life rich in meaning and happiness. This doesn't mean you will never make a mistake. Everyone makes mistakes. It is important, however, to admit your mistakes when you make them and to take what steps you can to correct them. This can keep your reputation intact.

When you have a good reputation, you feel an integrity with yourself. And remember, every moment of your life is spent with yourself. If you don't like and respect who you are, it can be extremely difficult for you to like or respect others. Work to build that good reputation. Money cannot buy it, but hard work can earn it.

What would you like to be able to say about yourself and to have others say about you? Create an image in your mind and think about exactly how you would most like to be. Would you like to feel from within yourself that what you say is honest and true? Would you like for your friends and associates to know the integrity of your intent? What level of confidence would you like to exhibit as you interrelate with people in your everyday world? Would you like to be more loving and gentle? Create in your mind a living picture of the kind of personality and attributes that would serve you best. For a moment, know that those inner imaginings can be translated into physical behavior. That is precisely what you have been doing all along, ever since you showed up in your present physical body! Your vision of the way you wish to be and what you wish to express in your life may require giving up old habits and ways of doing things if those ways do not present the image of yourself you desire. Write down the attributes of a good reputation—as you desire it. Then, look at ways you can begin living what you desire.

✦ Law 5

The visible is the ladder up to the invisible;
the temporal is but the scaffolding of the eternal. —Henry Drummond

SOME ASTRONOMERS at work discovering the vast complexities of the macrocosm and nuclear physicists investigating the awesome variety of the microcosm are concluding that the universe bears the hallmarks of intelligent design. The famous physicist Sir James Jeans wrote: "The universe is beginning to look not so much like a great machine, but like a great thought."

In their own ways, many scientists are reaffirming St. Paul's view that "Our eyes are fixed, not on things that are seen, but on the things that are unseen: for what is seen passes away; what is unseen is eternal" (2 Corinthians 4:18). Or, as Henry Drummond wrote in *Natural Law in the Spiritual World*: "The physical properties of spiritual matter form the alphabet which is put into our hands by God, the study of which, if properly conducted, will enable us more perfectly to read that great book which we call the Universe. . . . Law is great not because the phenomenal world is great, but because these vanishing lines are the avenues into the Eternal Order."

In his book *In Tune with the Infinite*, Ralph Waldo Trine wrote, "Everything exists in the unseen before it is manifested or realized in the seen, and in this sense it is true that the unseen things are the real, while the things that are seen are the unreal. The unseen things are cause; the seen things are the effect. The unseen things are the eternal and the seen things are the changing the transient."

What are these great minds, illumined thinkers,

The world is
full of mostly
invisible things.
—Howard Nemerov

and many others telling us about the vast unseen? Is our world and life on planet Earth more incredible than we may have realized? Are all the objects and events that we observe merely the tip of an enormous iceberg of possibilities?

In his highly acclaimed introduction to Einstein, Lincoln Barnett wrote in 1957 in *The Universe and Dr. Einstein*: "In the evolution of scientific thought, one fact has become impressively clear: there is no mystery of the physical world which does not point to a mystery beyond itself. . . . Man's inescapable impasse is that he himself is part of the world he seeks to explore; his body and proud brain are mosaics of the same elemental particles that compose the dark drifting clouds of interstellar space."

Such lofty thoughts can almost seem mind-boggling! Perhaps a simple analogy would be helpful. Within the human body, there are as many unseen activities as there are in the world of a beehive. Hundreds of bees may die and be replaced by other bees, but the beehive lives on. A human body is produced by billions of cells working together harmoniously. Millions of cells die daily and are replaced. This activity may be invisible to the human eye; nevertheless, it is vital to our functioning and well-being.

Have you ever raced across a meadow or stood on a hilltop and felt the wind blowing across your body? Was the reality of the wind lessened because it was invisible? The wind is just as real as flesh

and equally as temporary! Would a caterpillar deny its natural transformation into the magnificent butterfly because it does not see the working process? Do we question the reality of cosmic rays and radio waves, even though they are invisible? Technology has confirmed their actuality.

Einstein's theory of relativity makes it easier to

> For a moment of night we have a glimpse of ourselves
> and of our world islanded in its stream of stars—
> pilgrims of mortality, voyaging between horizons
> across the eternal seas of space and time.
> —Henry Beston

understand that time and space may not be exactly what they appear to be. New discoveries can indicate that "the visible is the ladder up to the invisible, and the temporal is but the scaffolding of the eternal." Is this statement an invitation for us to refrain from judging by appearances and to take the time to "look beyond the initially apparent, or the seen?" Is it important to hold in the forefront of our minds that, although divine principles are spirit and cannot be seen, they are vastly more real than the visible, tangible things? Spiritual principles are even more far-reaching than the principles of mathematics. Can the Creator be revealing himself more and more to human inquiry through the diligent research of modern scientists?

O world invisible,
we view thee,
O world intangible,
we touch thee,
O world unknowable,
we know thee.
—Francis Thompson

Spirit is the real and
eternal; matter is the
unreal and temporal.
—Mary Baker Eddy

God and all the
attributes of God
are eternal.
—Benedict Spinoza

Spotlights ✦ ✦

1. Does increasing evidence indicate that invisible realities may be vastly more basic than visible things?

2. Can research show that the spiritual aspect is the foundation of material life?

3. Maybe God is all of time and space and much more!

4. How does failure to forgive create a greater "hell" for the unforgiver than for the unforgiven?

5. Is a sure sign of spiritual character the willingness and ability to forgive those who have hurt us?

6. How is self-respect a by-product of a good conscience?

7. Our conscience is present wherever and whenever we look!

8. What perspective encourages us to find good qualities in every person and in every situation?

9. How has science taught us the important lesson that things are not always what they seem?

10. What are some ways we can enlarge our view of the cosmos and its Creator?

11. Could this material world serve as an incubator, provided by divinity, in which our spirits can develop and seek their ultimate expression in a realm invisible to us?

Living the Various Spiritual Laws ✦ ✦

Before Heaven and Earth are born,
    there is something formless
    and complete in itself.
Impalpable and everlasting,
    silent and undisturbed,
    standing alone and unchanging,
    it exercises itself gently,
    and generates itself inexhaustively
    in all dimensions.
It may be regarded as the Mother of all things.
Far beyond humankind's relative conception,
    it cannot be referred to by a specific name,
    yet it may be identified
    as the subtle essence of the universe.
In the absence of an accurate word,
    I shall call it "the Great."
Being great, it extends itself without limit.
Extending itself without limit, it is far-reaching.
Being far-reaching, it ultimately reverts to itself,
    returning to its self-sufficient origin.
Indeed, it had never really left itself!
This indefinable subtle energy flow
    is truly the greatest of all.

Expressing its integral nature,
    the universal subtle essence remains
      intangible,
    yielding and uncontrollable:
    the ultimate expression of the cosmos.

As an expression of its unceasing creativeness,
    it manifests as the spaciousness of the sky.
As an expression of its receptiveness,
    it manifests as the great massiveness
    of galaxies, stars, and planets.
As an expression of harmonious reintegration,
    it manifests as human life.

Thus, in the natural flow of energy
    transformation,
    human life becomes one of the four
      great expressions
    of the subtle essence of the universe.
It is the way of universal subtle integration.
Humankind conforms to Earth.
Earth conforms to the sky.
The sky conforms to the Subtle Origin.
The Subtle Origin conforms to its own nature.
—Lao Tzu

Week Twenty-One

✦ Law 1

Our life is shaped by our mind; we become what we think. —*The Dhammapada*

Beyond waking, dreaming, and sleeping, there are infinite realms of consciousness.
—*Deepak Chopra*

You are today where your thoughts have brought you. You will be tomorrow where your thoughts take you.
—*James Allen*

"Our life is shaped by our mind; we become what we think. Joy follows a pure thought like a shadow that never leaves." These simple statements can be both very subtle and very practical! The words are rich and filled with meaning. Basically, they remind us that the thoughts of our mind are the forerunners of our experiences. In sacred scriptures, the original mind or true self of the human being is considered the proper ground of enlightenment.

Although our mind is neither confined to the brain nor is it a product of the brain, nevertheless, it works through the brain as thoughts. In his book *Recovering the Soul*, Dr. Larry Dossey states, "The primary characteristics of minds are content and some level of conscious awareness: the myriad thoughts, emotions, and sensations that flood us daily. Individual minds are highly susceptible to changes in the physical body: moods, emotions, and even thoughts that can be modified by changes in the brain and body." Thought—the act or process of thinking—is often acknowledged as perhaps the greatest power or ability that humans possess. Thought may be considered pivotal. It may be directed in a positive, fruitful expression, or it may be used in a negative, non-beneficial manner. Our individual thoughts provide the tools with which we may carve our life stories on the substance of the universe. So, since thinking has often been referred to as "the master power of the mind,"

wouldn't more understanding and utilization of this powerful process be beneficial to everyone?

In *What Are You*, Imelda Shanklin wrote, "When you rule your mind, you rule your world. When you choose your thoughts, you choose results. The visible part of your life pours out of your mind, shaped and stamped by your thoughts, as surely as

The body is cleansed by water, the internal organ is purified by truthfulness, the individual soul by sacred learning and austerities, the intellect by true knowledge.
—*from Hindu Laws of Manu*

the coins of nations are shaped and stamped by the mechanisms used to convert ores into specie." So, if we become what we think, how can we trace the "unseen" to the "seen?"

A story is told that Einstein once lay on a couch, closed his eyes, and saw a man traveling at the speed of light. Following up on this intriguing image, he began to conduct various *thought experiments*, seemingly mere musings. Within a few years, however, the attitudes of the entire scientific world would be transformed as nature itself confirmed Einstein's transcendent visions. His thought experiments paid great rewards of progress for humanity. What is a thought experiment? It is

And thou,
my mind, aspire
to higher things.
—Sir Philip Sidney

described as a way of leading our minds into new places, of encouraging ourselves to see things differently. What are some thought experiments you might consider? Changing your attitude about a particular person, place, or situation? Researching new areas of interest? Exploring new areas of spiritual studies? Considering how you and your work could provide beneficial service in your community? Developing a special time of spiritual awareness with your family—like a time of prayer?

In the fields
of observation,
chance favors
only the
prepared mind.
—Louis Pasteur

We are changing every day of our lives. Are we growing with the changes? Are we making conscious choices to enhance the state of our minds, bodies, and souls? What is our motivation? Every day is a new opportunity to choose how we will live. Consider the importance of the choices you make. If you are becoming what you think, what are you thinking?

In her book *Breakthrough*, Rebecca Clark writes: "There is always something beautiful to be found if you will look for it. Concentrate your thoughts

Curiosity is one of the permanent and certain
characteristics of a vigorous mind.
—Samuel Johnson

on the good, beautiful, and true things of life rather than the reverse. This positive, loving attitude of mind towards life and people will help you to perceive the presence of God active in your life, helping you to wonderfully utilize your vital life force and put into operation the divine magic that opens all doors."

✦ LAW 2

Once a word is spoken, it cannot be recalled. —Wentworth Roscommon

Words are
of supreme
importance in
that they make
impressions on the
conscious mind,
and on the
subconscious
mind, and these
impressions often
shape the quality
of our thinking
and action.
—Newton Dillaway

HAVE YOU heard the maxim: "The eyes are the windows of the soul?" It means that our inner consciousness sparkles through our eyes. Another thought to consider might be, "Your words are windows to your heart." How are the words we speak representative of the contents of our hearts? Listen to yourself. Listen to others. What do you hear?

For example, what do you *feel* and *see* when a person speaks in anger? Can you feel the energy of hostility? Sadness? Hurt? Pain? Do you see the person's deep emotions reflected on his face, in the stance of the body, in his eyes? How do you respond? In a helpful, soothing manner, or could your response aggravate the situation? What do you *see* and *feel* when a person speaks in love, sincerity, kindness, and compassion? Do you feel the

honesty and earnestness of what is being said? Do you perceive the clarity of intent on the person's face? Do his eyes reflect steadfastness and focus? Do his words fill you with encouragement? Are they beneficial?

A woman doctor who practiced medicine in a small community was greatly loved and respected by her patients and all who knew her. Often comments were made: "She has the voice and heart of an angel . . .The sincerity of what she says instills confidence in what she does . . . I feel she really cares about my health and well-being." This woman was a living example of what she believed in: the presence of spirit in all things and a commitment to be of loving service to all she met. Her caring, compassion, and desire to serve others radiated through her words, her touch, her expression, her actions, the way she carried herself, in fact, through the totality of her being. Her life was an open window to the love, dedication, and sincerity of her heart.

As we grow into an increasing comprehension of our connection with spirit, the words we speak become filled with a greater awareness of the presence of God. We speak with the energy of *authority*. And speaking with authority does not mean speaking in a booming voice. Often, the person who speaks with a loud, insistent voice may be covering up the fact that he or she may not have much to say! The *quality* of our words is the important factor.

Thou shalt decree a thing, and it will be established unto you and light will shine on your ways.

—Job 22:28

Our words, as with our thoughts, may also serve as instruments with which we build our world. Words have molding power; they give form and shape to present and future experiences. It is possible to literally shape our world through the words we speak. Think about this for a moment. What we say may sometimes be overheard or repeated. If we speak in a harsh or critical manner, our words may cause hurt feelings. Negative words and hurt feelings could cost us valuable friendships. We can avoid this kind of situation by following a very simple rule: *Always think before you speak!*

On the other hand, when our words are helpfully and thoughtfully spoken, they can become fascinating and marvelous tools. We learn to control our words by developing our understanding. We learn to see the positive and constructive side to every situation and every action of another individual. We can learn to control our words by being willing to improve our views about life. Instead of judging by appearances, we choose to look for possibilities! We can learn to change the words we use by expressing a more forgiving attitude toward others. Can you see how words of openness and receptivity have the ability to transform an attitude of resentment or impasse? We can begin to operate more often on spiritual principles.

The power of our words is reflected in Proverbs 15:23: "To make an apt answer is a joy to a man, and a word in season, how good it is!" Words are symbols of our thoughts and feelings; they reflect our consciousness. Words are transparent windows to our hearts.

✦ LAW 3

You have the most powerful weapons on earth—love and prayer. —John Marks Templeton

ONE OF THE GREATEST developments in human history has been the increasing possibility for each person to have the freedom to learn, grow, and design his or her own life. Wherever we may be, whatever lifestyle we choose, however we may express our talents and abilities, we have two of the most powerful weapons (or tools) on earth with which to accomplish our goals. They are the attributes of love and the power of prayer.

We can radiate love and happiness as faithfully as the sun radiates light and warmth. As sunlight is a creative, life-giving source, can our love also be a creative source of increased vitality, fruitful ideas, and ever-present blessings? Love is essential to all of our relationships. Without the warmth of love, our relationships would be dead and cold. Love lends transcendent meaning to our existence. To the extent we are able to receive divine love and express it to others, it likewise becomes the cornerstone of our human relationships. In fact, could one of the best indicators of our inner growth be the extent to which we love God and love other people? Are our love for the divine and our love for others actually two sides of the same spiritual coin?

Love is ever active in essence. How could it possibly remain a mere inner ideal, a static possession, a buried treasure hoarded in our souls? Love is like water pouring through the garden hose. The only way the water can continue to flow through the hose is for it to pour from one end as it is received in the other. As we let love pour from our hearts and our souls, we simply create room for more love to be received. Can one of the identifying marks of spiritual love be the fact that it is freely given? It doesn't ask for anything in return; love simply fulfills its nature of giving.

As we continuously practice unlimited loving in our daily lives, how can both the quantity and the quality of our love improve? What is meant by "wisely" loving? For instance, love, wisely expressed, is balanced. It does not swing from one extreme to another. Temporary tensions of daily living do not disturb the underlying stability of love that is wisely expressed. When we love wisely, are we sensitive to others and more tactful in our communication? Is the wise and loving parent one who is continually looking for information and expressions that can help him love his children in more healthy ways? As parents develop the habit of seeking spiritual guidance in building value guidelines, are they manifesting and expressing a

deeper degree of unlimited love? If we encourage our children to develop a personal connection with spirit, are we planting seeds that can mature into ripened fruit? The family can be a beneficial birthplace of lasting love. It can also be a foundation for effective prayer.

Effective expressions of love can manifest through the power of prayer. And prayer can result in strong decision-making abilities and growth. Every individual has his or her personal needs and desires. And most people are looking for workable tools to build a better life. Prayer is especially meaningful when we are dedicated to lovingly act on the insights gained within our times of prayer. Prayer has been described as one of the most reliable and potent stimulators of spiritual growth. If a person is feeling languid, depressed, dejected, sorrowful, or downcast, a good prayer session can lift his spirit and open the door to new possibilities and opportunities. Prayer can generate greater sensitivity to our ideals. Prayer provides us with a potent spiritual tool for overcoming problems. It can increase our human industry and ingenuity. When our prayer requests are wholehearted, they come from deep enough within us to generate lasting self-transformations.

Divinity seems to understand the deeper meaning of our sincere desires and responds accordingly. God loves us all equally and unceasingly. Is this a basic eternal reality? As we open ourselves through prayer to divine wisdom and guidance, do we send forth the invitation for the divine spirit to move into our lives and make them over from within so that all things are seen in a new light? Does love for all become the spontaneous expression of a spirit-filled soul?

In *In My Own Words*, Mother Teresa wrote:

There are some people who, in order not to pray, use as an excuse the fact that life is so hectic that it prevents them from praying. This cannot be. Prayer does not demand

---

The experience of heaven is a by-product of unlimited love.
—*John Marks Templeton*

More things are wrought by prayer than this world dreams of. Wherefore, let thy voice rise like a fountain for me night and day.
—*Alfred, Lord Tennyson*

Love is the subtlest force in the world.
—*Mahatma Gandhi*

Prayer, like radium, is a luminous and self-generating form of energy.
—*Alexis Carrel*

Many waters cannot quench love, neither can the floods drown it.
—*Song of Solomon 8:7*

Prayer makes your heart bigger, until it is capable of containing the gift of God himself.
—*Mother Teresa*

that we interrupt our work, but that we continue working as if it were a prayer. It is not necessary to always be meditating, nor to consciously experience the sensation that we are talking to God, no matter how nice this would be.

What matters is being with him, living in him, in his will. To love with a pure heart, to love everybody, especially to love the poor, is a twenty-four hour prayer.

◆ LAW 4

Can egotism be a stumbling block to our growth? —John Marks Templeton

IT IS EXCITING to be alive and think about all the wonders of discovery that lie ahead for future generations. Where will these discoveries lead us? What will be the benefits for humanity? The universe is vast and possibly eternal, whereas we are small and mortal. How exciting it is to consider that our creativity may be part of a marvelous plan, not yet comprehended!

Pascal wrote: "It is not from space that I must seek my dignity, but from the government of my thought. I shall have no more if I posses worlds. By space the universe encompasses and swallows me up like an atom; by thought I comprehend the world." So, although we may seem insignificant, perhaps our role might be crucial. As human beings, we are endowed with mind and spirit and purpose. We can think, imagine, and dream. Can we also search for future concepts in the rich, expanding diversity of human thought? We seem to be permitted, in some ways, to be created by infinite divinity for an accelerating adventure of creativity.

Is there, however, a possible obstacle called egotism? Egotism, as used here, refers not so much to the personal flaw, but rather to a habit of mind that inhibits the learning process necessary for future progress. We may be more accustomed to thinking we are bodies with souls than realizing we are souls inhabiting bodies. That body idea has been around for a long time and can send us a false message about our true essence and purpose in the overall scheme of things.

What are some ways egotism can be a stumbling block to our growth? Perhaps one stumbling block occurs when we perceive ourselves as being separate or apart from others. If a person grows up experiencing the pain of loneliness, peer criticism, or emotional hurt, the idea of separateness can begin early in life. Another stumbling block may occur when our egos promote the illusions of guilt or fear. Or, the ego may bombard us with the idea that we must continually have more of the material world to experience satisfaction. However, when we become aware of the ego's influence in our lives, a new kind of spiritual awakening becomes possible.

Fear never dares approach a great soul.
—Phia Rilke

Have you ever been at a point in your life when you were more concerned about others and the world around you than you were concerned about yourself? A great freedom occurs when we are not focused on being separate, feeling offended or fearful of what life may bring! Detachment from self-absorption, from the ego, brings authentic freedom. Then, our minds are free to explore as part of a community of inquiry, focused on the process of research. This seems equally true of the exploration of our spiritual future. Can you consider the possibility of a future of progressively

The best gifts are those which expect no return.
—Norwegian proverb

Life given us by nature is short, but the memory of a well-spent life is eternal.
—Cicero

Turn your stumbling blocks into stepping stones.
—Anonymous

Whoever will be free must make himself free. Freedom is no fairy gift to fall into a man's lap. What is freedom? To have the will to be responsible for one's self.
—Max Stirner

unfolding spiritual discoveries revealed by beneficial scientific discoveries? Essential progress can be made by appreciating the ways that sciences have learned to flourish. Being creatively open to discovery seeking and to future-oriented perspectives can also offer boundless possibilities.

Can *humility* be a key to our future progress and a safeguard against egotism? When a person takes a more humble approach, he or she can welcome new ideas about the spirit just as they welcome new scientific and technological ideas about how to cure infections, how to heat or cool their homes, or how to communicate quickly with people who are far away.

How can we cultivate a spirit of humility? Allowing ourselves to be open to the possibility of our existence within a divine reality that dwarfs our personal reality could be a starting point. Could the spirit of humility promote a hunger to explore boundless new possibilities? Also, is it in open-minded humility that we can learn from each other? An attitude of humility can allow us to be open and receptive to new ideas. We can learn to see things from another's point of view and share our perspectives with others freely. Could the ego

feeling of separateness be replaced by this healthy mental attitude?

Giving more of ourselves and asking less in return is another excellent way to tame the ego. For example, toward the end of his life, Leo Tolstoy went from being self-absorbed to becoming a servant of God, learning many of the lessons on the path of the sacred quest. He wrote: "The sole meaning of life is to serve humanity." So simple! So profound! When serving others becomes a priority, we have found an exciting and beneficial doorway to greater spiritual growth. Trying to serve the needs of others also brings material prosperity and recognition.

To eliminate the stumbling block of egotism, can we remind ourselves that God created each person in perfect unlimited love that is changeless and eternal? Noticing the acts of kindness and positive aspects of others and of life can help dissipate fear. Can we let our thoughts stay focused on love and service and direct our actions to stem from this consciousness? Can we purify our thoughts, emotions, and behavior? Can we gracefully move from outward appearances to our place in the infinity of divinity?

✦ Law 5

One of the greatest blessings to human beings is change, and the present acceleration of change in the world is an overflowing of this blessing. —John Marks Templeton

Every period has something new to teach us.
— Joan Chittister

ROBERT HILLIARS has estimated that if the growth of knowledge continues at the present rate, when a baby born today graduates from a university, the quantity of knowledge on earth will be four times as great. By the time such a child is fifty years old, the amount of knowledge will be thirty-two times as great; and 97% of everything known to human beings will have been learned since the day the

child was born! The futurist John Naisbitt is far more bullish on the growth of information. He affirms an estimate that the quantity of information is doubling every thirty months. At such rate of growth, the quantity may be one thousand times as great in only twenty-five years, and a million times as great in only fifty years.

This information is almost overwhelming but

truly, we live in a blossoming time for human creation. Evolution is accelerating. Progress is accelerating. One of God's great blessings to human
beings is change, and the present acceleration of
discovery in the world is an overflowing of this blessing. The fundamental questions—Where can we go
from here? and What are the possibilities?—signify many spheres of
amazing potential for a sophisticated
species called humans, recently inhabiting this planet!

Perhaps each of us could consider our responses
to the following questions. Why am I here? How
can I assist in bringing about creation through
change? Can I act on my desire to be more fruitful
in my efforts by being as quietly effective as possible? Is creativity accelerated by open minds and
by free competition? Does the world urgently need
to study basic spiritual realities? How can I contribute in this research? Should we be enthusiastic
and diligent to discover more about God? Is God
the only reality? How can learning more about the
laws of life and universal principles better equip
all of us to be helpers for positive change?

Consider taking an inventory of your present
beliefs. Include such areas as your attitude toward
spirituality, prayer, egotism, judgment, praise, gratitude, your own life experiences, what happens at
death, and what it would be like to walk in the
other person's shoes.

*At the back of our brains, so to speak, there is a forgotten blaze or burst
of astonishment at our own existence. The object of the artistic and
spiritual life is to dig for this submerged sunrise of wonder.*
—G. K. Chesterton

In *The Wisdom Teachings of the Dalai Lama*, His
Holiness describes compassion as a tool for
change:

*Deep down we must have real affection for each other, a
clear realization or recognition of our shared human status. At the same time, we must openly accept all ideolo-
gies and systems as a means of solving humanity's
problems. One country, one nation, one ideology, one system, is not sufficient. It is helpful to have a variety of
different approaches on the basis of deep feeling of the
basic sameness of humanity. We can then make a joint
effort to solve the problems of the whole of humankind.
The problems human society is facing in terms of economic development.*

Spotlights ◆ ◆

1. The primary characteristics of minds are *intellect* and some level of *conscious awareness*.

2. Thought—the act or process of thinking—is often acknowledged as perhaps the most productive ability that humans possess.

3. "When you rule your mind, you rule your world" (Imelda Shanklin).

4. How are the words we speak representative of the contents of our hearts?

5. How can the words we speak also serve as tools with which to build our world?

6. How are love and prayer two powerful weapons?

7. How can effective expressions of love manifest through the power of prayer?

8. How would you describe egotism as a stumbling block to greater growth?

9. Can *humility* be a key to our future progress and a safeguard against egotism?

10. How would you describe change as a blessing?

Living the Various Spiritual Laws ✦ ✦

We are what we think.
All that we are arises with our thoughts.
With our thoughts we make the world.
Speak or act with an impure mind
And trouble will follow you
As the wheel follows the ox that draws the cart.

We are what we think.
All that we are arises with our thoughts.
With our thoughts we make the world.
Speak or act with a pure mind
And happiness will follow you

As your shadow, unshakable.
How can a troubled mind
Understand the way?

Your worst enemy cannot harm you
As much as your own thoughts, unguarded.

But once mastered,
No one can help you as much,
Not even your father or your mother.
  —from *The Dhammapada*

Week Twenty-Two

♦ ## LAW 1

World progress needs entrepreneurs. —John Marks Templeton

THE FEATS accomplished in the construction of the many ancient wonders around the world can be overwhelming. How could these long-ago people build such massive structures without the benefit of modern machinery? What types of tools were used for these enormous construction projects? What plans or blueprints guided the workers daily progress? What natural resources were available? Whose idea spearheaded the first elaborate construction? Could this person be considered the first *entrepreneur* in history? Surely, that person must have combined every opportunity available with strong foresight and ingenuity to leave such an impressive gift to the world!

In today's world, the definition of "entrepreneur" is a "person who organizes and manages a business undertaking, assuming the risk for the sake of the profit." Could this definition be expanded to include the brilliance of the questing mind and purposeful research in any field of endeavor? Science? Medicine? Religion? Physics? Economy? Electronics? Genetics? Education? And could part of the "profit" be a better way of life for all of humanity?

People on the road to success are often not afraid to take calculated risks. They prepare carefully for their forays into uncharted territory. The ability to take risks and accept challenges is often keenest among those with wide-open minds. In *The State of Humanity*, Julian L. Simon commented:

"Our species is better off in just about every measurable material way. And there is stronger reason than ever to believe that these progressive trends will continue past the year 2000, past the year 2100, and indefinitely." Thus, there are fertile fields of exploration and research waiting for the efforts, talents, and inventive and dynamic consciousness of the entrepreneur. The bright future envisioned by many progressive-thinking individuals seems increasingly probable.

> We have no eternal allies and we have no perpetual
> enemies. Our interests are eternal and perpetual,
> and these interests it is our duty to follow.
> —*Henry John Temple*

Living a beneficial and purposeful life is an important foundation for building the dreams of humanity, individually and collectively. Progress is a necessity and entrepreneurs are needed. Within the creative genius of the mind lies the real "land of opportunity." Within a pioneering person lie a possible insight, purpose, idea, vision, strength, courage, intellect, freedom, and ability to achieve wondrous success. So, what is necessary to become an innovator? Do we first *recognize* that we have the power within to be creative? Are we *willing* to try new experiences and explore new fields of endeavor that may offer fertile areas for developmental activities? Does our receptivity invite new knowledge, vitality, and purpose into our consciousness?

To gain the fruits of our discoveries, we must allow time to educate our spirits as well as our bodies and minds. The spirit of humanity can be nourished in wonderful ways by the pioneers who capture the wonder of our world. Ralph Waldo Trine's *In Tune with the Infinite* and Carl Sagan's *The Dragons of Eden* are two excellent examples of written nourishment for the human soul.

Significant research support for the acquisition of new spiritual information could be a powerful avenue for entrepreneurs. Entrepreneurs in the area of spiritual research? Why not? Here are just a few examples of the thousands of questions that might be addressed.

Human evolution. Studies have shown that late Neanderthals and early Homo sapiens had definite ideas of a hereafter, which was reflected in their burial practices and cave drawings. Further research might establish the fundamental nature of this spiritual understanding.

Genetic basis for well-being. Dr. Herbert Benson has analyzed the nature of some spiritual factors in healing and has proposed that humans are "hardwired" for wellness. Research could be carried out to study wellness as a genetic trait or group of traits.

Brain capacity. Neural science indicates we utilize less that 10 percent of our brain capacity. Research of the bio-chemical basis of genius and creativity, especially with the great mystics and the Nobel laureates, might be revealing and suggest ways to unlock the potential of the brain.

Neuroendocrine relationships. Research into spiritual activities (e.g., prayer, meditation, and especially thanksgiving) to ascertain various hormone-release actions—such as endorphins and other "pleasure" agents—might establish a basis for spiritual experience as an alternative to various psychoactive drugs (e.g., cocaine and heroin) currently ravaging society.

Violence as a social problem. Research into genetic and neurological bases for anti-social behavior is an area of political sensitivity, but scientifically rigorous research might arrive at a much-needed understanding and possible therapies.

Through good times and tough times, entrepreneur-type people will seek new frontiers to explore and to enhance. They will gladly accept risk and challenge, because through risk and challenge we grow both in worldly wisdom and in spiritual strength. If you look to the future as a vast, exciting, and still-unexplored territory, you may be on your way to becoming a beneficial discoverer.

✦ LAW 2

As you are active in blessing others, they learn to bless others also. —John Marks Templeton

ARE THERE so many deeply beneficial ways we can give? Have you ever considered that our contributions to life and to those around us can be accomplished from three levels of our being—*spiritual,*

mental, and *physical?* On the spiritual level, we can give through prayer or the spirit of love that we hold toward others. On the mental level, we can give thoughts, ideas, wisdom, and encouragement.

On the physical level, we can give our time, presence, effort, money, and material goods. As an example, let's follow a smile as it comes from the three levels of our being. Given from the *heart*, a smile carries a spiritual blessing. A smile given through a *mind* attuned with spiritual principle can carry thoughts of unlimited love, which carry through into the *physical* expressions of compassion and caring!

One of the purest forms of ministry is to help others and to seek the welfare of others without the expectation of reward. In *Bhagavad Gita* and paralleled by passages in the Tao Te Ching, the way of selfless service is described as "the fundamental principle by which God creates and sustains the universe. Whenever a person acts selflessly in the service of others, that act is born of God."

When we desire to be a blessing, we find there are many ways in which we can bless many. We can utilize the talents we are given in aid and assistance. We can share our knowledge. When it is appropriate, we can offer the benefit of our experiences in overcoming difficult situations. We can offer ourselves in service to bless someone who is ill. In almost every area of the human experience, opportunities are available to be a blessing to others. It's true. Every act of blessing that flows from us to another can multiply as more receivers learn the joy of becoming givers. And we, too, experience the joy of giving! Service is essential to our growth. It is a universal law that as we give assistance to others, more help comes to us.

In his book *Speaker's Library of Business*, Joe Griffith tells a story about Albert Schweitzer:

Albert Schweitzer is what service is all about. He gave up a prestigious career as a doctor and went to Africa to help build hospitals for the poor natives. Many of his friends, who felt that he was throwing away his talents and training, sent a delegation to Africa to attempt to persuade him to return back to his native land. They asked, "Why should such a gifted man as you give up so much to labor among African natives?"

Schweitzer replied, "Don't talk about sacrifice. What does it matter where one goes provided one can do good work there? Much as I appreciate your kind words, I have made up my mind to stay here and look after my African friends." He remained there until he died in 1965, at the age of 90! He worked until the very end, maintaining his zest for living.

The man of perfect virtue, wishing to be established himself, seeks also to establish others; wishing to be enlarged himself, he seeks also to enlarge others.
—Confucius

Another beautiful story of blessing comes to light through the work of a pioneering nurse named Carol who worked at a large university hospital. Carol wanted to learn how deeply caring nurses remained healthy while maintaining close relationships with the patients they served. She knew that caregivers had been taught and had lived by the premise that they were supposed to care deeply for their clients while not getting too involved because of the real potential of burnout.

In interviewing those nurses who had a reputation for being seasoned experts at care giving, Carol discovered that they did nothing in particular. It was the genuine sense of *presence*, of *being*, rather than of *doing*, which established the deep bond between nurse and patient. By allowing this form of interaction, the nurses found themselves uplifted and nurtured with an expanded ability to tap into energy, love, and wisdom. Not one of the nurses found themselves depleted or burned out by their deep and sincere caring and close relationship with their patients.

Perhaps right now is a good time to pause and give thanks for our many blessings and for the fact that we can *be* blessings! Set an ideal in the spiritual sense, and know that he who would be greatest among men should be the servant of all.

✦ Law 3

Expect the best and your positive outlook opens the door to opportunity.
—John Marks Templeton

HAVE YOU EVER considered that your positive attitude can open doors to opportunities that may otherwise seem tightly closed? A strong, hopeful vision can assert potential in the face of what may seem a limitation. Resourceful, open-minded search can persevere when fear would have you quit! What is the message? Search widely for the best possible outworking in every situation!

A well-known and effective businesswoman begins her day with the greeting, "Good morning, God! What wonderful experiences do you have in store for me today?" She then goes forward into the day's activities, expecting the best! And the best things in life happen *to* her and *for* her! She's often amazed at what unfolds. When asked how she began this habit, the woman responded that she took a most important step to transform her life by deeply searching her soul and then establishing beneficial ideals. Then she worked diligently and persistently to achieve these goals. This can be a transforming process because your ideals set standards for you. They are excellent guides for making choices that can uplift your life.

It is a very great thing to be able to think as you like, but, after all, an important question remains: *what* you think.
—Matthew Arnold

Can setting our ideals in accordance with spiritual principles provide a most positive outlook? If we hold limited ideals, we actually restrict ourselves. In *Your Life . . . Understanding the Universal Laws,* Bruce McArthur lists five important considerations for establishing noble ideals. They are:

1. Your ideals are the standards by which you make your choices. They are like a road map that you use to guide you to your destination.
2. Your ideals set the attitudes by which you live.
3. Your ideals determine the path and the direction in which you are moving in consciousness.

It is interesting to notice how some minds seem almost to create themselves, springing up under every disadvantage and working their solitary, but irresistible way, through a thousand obstacles.
—Washington Irving

4. Your ideals provide the balancing tie among body, mind, and soul. Through them, you coordinate the spirit within, the mind, and your physical aspects.

Clearly, anything that affects you and your life in such vital ways should be well thought out and should be something you have developed carefully and chosen from the highest consciousness you can achieve.

Are you familiar with the expression "possibility thinking"? We have touched, in earlier essays, on the tremendous powers of the mind. A possibility thinker is a person who looks at every idea with an open mind and with receptivity to its possibilities. Possibility thinking actually focuses on the management of ideas. And a primary point is this: *Never underestimate the positive value of an idea!* Every positive idea has within it the potential for beneficial manifestation if it is managed properly. How do we manage ideas so effectively that we are likely to build success? Look for the highest and best expression of your idea. Is it a good idea? How can it be helpful for others? For your community? For our country? For the world? For yourself? How does your idea "fit" with your ideals? What are the most effective ways to implement your idea? Expect the best and your positive outlook opens the door to opportunity.

Even a seemingly "problem situation" can benefit greatly from a positive perspective. Look for the best of what can be possible in every situation and you can experience the opportunity to turn any problem into a lesson for greater good. Give thanks for the spirit that is working *for* you by working *through* you!

✦ LAW 4

Anger and selfish desire are our greatest enemies. —Bhagavad Gita

ONE OF THE FUNDAMENTAL rules of life that has been revered through the ages is "Do unto others as you would have them do unto you." It is otherwise known as The Golden Rule. The great significance of this ancient teaching, honored by all religions, is far-reaching in its application in every phase of human relationships. The Golden Rule is a principle as old as time, as inexorable as gravity, as impersonal as sunlight. It is the opposite of greed, avarice, hatred, anger, and selfish desire. As we practice this teaching in daily living, we will naturally treat others with the same love and respect that we wish to be treated.

The energy we send out in mental, material, and physical relationships is like a cosmic boomerang and will be measured back to us again. One of the fundamental qualities desired in relationships is *caring*. Caring can keep interactions between ourselves and others more positive, loving, and less stressful. Sincere caring can eliminate, regenerate, or heal many of the problems that often occur in daily association with others.

In his book *Self-Empowerment: The Heart Approach to Stress Management*, Doc Lew Childre gives this example of caring. "To operate a car without oil in the pistons is equivalent to a human living a life without care in his or her system. True care is a frequency, or feeling, that radiates from your heart. It flows through your system and lubricates your thought and feeling nature, while decreasing friction and resistance in your life. Care not only acts as a mental and emotional detergent within your system, it also adds quality and texture to your relationship with people and all issues." Anger and selfish desire are definitely not aspects of caring and can certainly prove to be two of our greatest enemies. Angry words and actions do not serve a useful purpose. Instead, they tend to set up a chain of negative responses that often create enemies. Once anger takes over, common sense and reasonableness usually fly out the window! Hurt feelings often ensue and seeds can be planted that sprout into negative consequences that may be hard to turn around. When a person feels the first flush of the emotion of anger, it is beneficial if he or she can examine the situation at hand with an awareness of spiritual principles. Such brief analysis can often channel a person's awareness and energy into a more productive expression.

The light that shines above the heavens and above the world, the light that shines in the highest world, beyond which there are no others—that is the light that shines in the hearts of men.
—from The Upanishads

Selfishness has been described as a characteristic of the personality that can manifest as neglect, disrespect, or disregard of others. Selfishness is often an aspect of an out-of-balance ego personality. When a person is coming from a selfish aspect of consciousness, can you see how the law of giving and receiving can be stymied? True giving is a free and natural response that takes place when we are attuned with our spiritual nature. When our mind is receptive to that part of ourselves, we become channels for the expression of that spiritual presence. It becomes a joyous experience to give. Can you also perceive how the law of giving and receiving results in greater unlimited love flowing through us without thought of reward? We give lovingly and unselfishly; we receive graciously!

So, how can a person change an attitude of selfish desire? What can we do to modify anger? Is unlimited love a key? What kind of love would you like to have others show you? What kind of love are you willing to express? We can transform our consciousness by recognizing and living in accordance with spiritual principles and by basing our thoughts, words, and deeds on our spiritually derived purposes, ideals, and guidance. We can let

our lights shine! We can practice The Golden Rule in every area of our lives.

We have met the enemy, and he is us.
—*Walt Kelly*

What are some results of letting go of these emotional enemies, anger and selfish desire? Does it follow that when we see God everywhere, when we experience God in everything we do, when we acknowledge everyone as part of God, we are in the kingdom of heaven on earth? Heaven on earth has been described as a blessing given by the Creator as we express his higher purpose and power through living the universal laws. Learning to live the universal laws or principles is not too difficult. However, it does require diligence, purpose, and focused action to be all that we can be! Every time we take a step in the direction of a higher response to life, great progress is made.

✦ Law 5

The wise person looks within his heart and finds eternal peace. —Hindu proverb

DOWN THROUGH THE AGES and throughout all parts of the world, people have sought inner peace. Yet for centuries, many people have been at war with themselves and with one another. Around the world, in the home, and on the job many people's lives are filled with stress. Could the roots of discontent be caused by the ways we live our daily lives? When a difficult situation occurs, how do we respond? Do we compare ourselves with others as a measurement of our performance or success? Do we allow ourselves to be caught up in unnecessary worry or concern? Do we add pressure to our lives through setting unrealistic goals or time restric-

tions? Do we feel a sense of pride or accomplishment through the accumulation of more things? Are there times when we retreat from the world, either physically or emotionally, when things do not go the way we wish? Do we tend to feel more at peace when everything is "under control"?

Where do you reside in your search for peace? What have you found? Are you at peace with your life? With yourself? With your family? With your body? In your relationships? How do you feel about your finances or your career? Do you respect yourself? Do you harmonize with nature and with the people in your personal world? Do you view a difficult situation as actually an open door of potential? Can you leave old assumptions and prejudices behind you and go forward toward new discoveries? Do you hunger and thirst for knowledge? Are you focused, creative, and helpful? Do you have a reverence for all of life? Can you accept the gift of each day you are alive and make the best possible use of it? When you sit down to dinner and look at a plate filled with fragrant, nourishing, and appetizing food, do you nourish the awareness of praise, gratitude, and thanksgiving?

Life is a dynamic experience. Like a winding river, it constantly flows with its currents forming new patterns from the interacting elements. Whatever may be happening in our lives, whatever stress, whatever turmoil or conflict, the first step toward inner peace can begin with a shift in our attitudes. Why is this so important? When we begin to shift our attitudes, we begin to see a different picture of what may be happening around us. The particular situation doesn't matter nearly as much as how we *perceive* it! Once we are willing to become more open-minded, we can begin to see the larger pattern of a situation. We can start taking effective action to harmonize with the spiritual principles underlying all existence. A growing awareness can often provide a basis for the spiritual fulfillment that is the promise of the sacred quest.

The explorer Ponce de Leon spent many fruitless years searching for a fountain of youth. Today, are we beginning to discover that the youth-sustaining elixir is not in some faraway exotic geographical location but very close at hand—perhaps even within ourselves! Could an enthusiasm for noble life purposes be a key to physical, mental, emotional, and spiritual health? And this means youthfulness in every aspect of our beings. The health we are considering here means not only being alive but being mentally, productively, joyously alive!

No discord can enter your mind without your consent. An old story from *The Way of Life According to Lao Tzu*, translated by Witter Bynner, says that once Confucius visited Lao Tzu and was mystified by the source of his power. It was not rational, not predictable. Confucius understood the power in the wings of birds, the fins of fish, the legs of animals, which can be overcome with arrows, nets, and traps. But, he said, "Who knows how dragons surmount wind and cloud into heaven? This day I have seen Lao Tzu and he is a dragon."

Two things fill the mind with ever increasing wonder and awe . . .
the starry heavens above me and the moral law within me.
—Immanuel Kant

Much is said about preventing wars. And this seems a high and desirable goal. Although the internal transformation of individuals may be difficult, could this be an effective place to begin? We cannot always control other people, but we can be in control of ourselves. We may not be able to control outer conditions, but we can learn to govern our inward responses to outer conditions. Our calmness can quiet the choppy sea of destructive emotions. Once love, compassion, and altruism, which are fundamental bases for peace, are established within our individual consciousness, then we can create an atmosphere of peace and harmony. This atmosphere can be expanded and extended from the individual to his family. Then it can proceed from the family to the community and eventually to the entire world! Truly, "The wise person looks within his heart and finds eternal peace."

Spotlights ✦ ✦

1. Can sciences help reveal the enormous complexity and vastness of God?

2. How can science and religion join hands in the investigation of spiritual realities?

3. Are there possible new ways to research the spiritual nature of human beings?

4. What are some of the deeply loving ways you can give and be a blessing?

5. Why is selfless service often described as a fundamental spiritual principle?

6. How does possibility thinking open doors to opportunity?

7. What are some ideals you can establish in your life that are in accord with spiritual principles? How can you bring these into your activities?

8. How would you describe anger and selfish desire as enemies to your growth?

9. What are some benefits that can occur in releasing anger and selfish desire?

10. Make a list of thoughts, feelings, actions, and behaviors that can contribute to inner peace.

Living the Various Spiritual Laws ✦ ✦

At the beginning, mankind and the obligation of selfless service were created together. "Through selfless service, you will always be fruitful and find the fulfillment of your desires": this is the promise of the Creator . . .

Every selfless act, Arjuna, is born from the eternal, infinite Godhead. God is present in every act of service. All life turns on this law, O Arjuna. Whoever violates it, indulging his senses for his own pleasure and ignoring the need of others has wasted his life. But those who realize the god within are always satisfied. Having found the source of joy and fulfillment, they no longer seek happiness from the external world. They have nothing to gain or lose by any action; neither people nor things can affect their security.

Strive constantly to serve the welfare of the world; by devotion to selfless work one attains the supreme goal in life. Do your work with the welfare of others always in mind. It was by such work that Janaka attained perfection; others, too, have followed this path.

—Bhagavad Gita

Week Twenty-Three

✦ Law 1

Every discovery is a discovery of God. —John Marks Templeton

We have to come to terms with a mystery that defies our normal categories of thought and our usual ways of organizing information.
—*Russell Stannard*

Our knowledge of the divine does not come from neon signs in the sky, from a message on the Internet magically created out of its static, or from a set of scientific experiments. It must come from human channels, via human thought.
—*Owen Gingerich*

God moves in a mysterious way His wonders to perform.
—*William Cowper*

DOES EVERY DISCOVERY we make, in any area of life, become a discovery of God? As we discover more of God, are we then nurturing all that is true, beautiful, and good?

Can the sincere seeker after truth in one area afford to ignore findings in other fields? The search for reality, though it may seem extremely difficult, is greatly enhanced by realizing the interconnectedness of knowledge.

The amazing fruitfulness of scientific research in a variety of fields has been focused on many questions of "how," but can scientific research also help with the deeper question of "why"? Why is there *something* rather than *nothing*? Is God limited or unlimited? Why would anyone prefer to worship a god who is limited instead of unlimited and timeless? If God is infinite, then can anything be separate? Can God infinitely transcend meager human perceptions?

Could an expansion of human concepts come more quickly if we use the word "divinity" rather than words like *God, Jehovah,* or *Allah,* which may imply limited personhood? What could be some of the advantages of perceiving God to be the ultimate reality? Now that science has demonstrated that reality is vastly more than the visible world, is it egotistical to cling to the idea that *reality* means things that humans can see or touch? If science can study only human perceptions rather than reality, should we begin to use the word "reality"

to mean the total of appearances plus fundamentals? Can present human perceptions of reality be as meager as a clam's perceptions of humans?

In the book *How Large Is God?* Robert J. Russell writes:

When we experience wonder and awe at the immensity and beauty of the universe, we are led to think of God as utterly wondrous, terribly awesome, and the source of ecstatic beauty. When we experience love in our lives; when we are forgiven our iniquities by those we have wronged; when we know the goodness of home, hearth, health, and family; then we speak of God as perfect love, unconditional mercy, the source of all that is good, and our final home. Most important, when we look up from the routine of life and witness the sacred in our midst, as Moses did when he turned aside from tending to his sheep to go to see the burning bush (Exodus 3:1–6), then we confess God as utterly holy.

Thus, we are surrounded with the mystery of God that surpasses all present knowing; yet we know that this God seeks us and would be known by us, and we move ahead in the light of expanding discovery. To do so, we must remember the poverty of human perceptions in light of the surpassing mystery of God. Then we cloak all that we wish to affirm in the spreading folds of our unknowing.

The many technological advances have given meaning to our scientific culture, but there still remains that deep desire for greater meaning, for a cosmic explanation of ourselves. With all our scientific understanding of our world and with all the expansive spiritual teachings, what we are and how we have come to be yet eludes us. The deeper we probe into the nature of things, the more we discover additional mysteries to investigate. I hope you, the reader, will be moved to begin the exploration into a deeper understanding of the ways of God with all of his creatures. The manifold discoveries of the late twentieth century cause the visible and tangible to appear less and less real and point to a greater reality in the ongoing and accelerating creative process within the enormity of the vast unseen.

There is surely a piece of divinity in us, something that was before the elements, and owes no homage unto the sun.
—Sir Thomas Browne

Who can tell how powerful and fruitful future progress can be when men and women return in humility to that first great quest, to "think god's thoughts after him"?

It is the modest, not the presumptuous, inquirer who makes a real and safe progress in the discovery of divine truths.
—Henry St. John, Viscount Bolingbroke

◆ Law 2

Live each day as a new beginning. —John Marks Templeton

WHAT ARE YOUR first thoughts when you open your eyes in the morning? How do you feel about the day unfolding before you? What song of life does your spirit sing as you prepare for the day ahead? Everything visible to us in the universe, including the earth, the sun, the moon, and human beings had a beginning! One of our most important *beginnings* can be the start of each new day! How we begin the day can set the tone for our experiences from that point on.

We can feel the joy of spirit and give thanks. We can listen and open our hearts to unlimited love. The excitement and enthusiasm for the work before us each day can stimulate fruitful productivity. We can cultivate a positive mental perception of life. Appreciation, gratitude, and the sheer joy of living can shine from our eyes and radiate as powerful life energy flowing through us. We can perceive situations, opportunities, and people around us in a new light and in a larger perspective.

Can you imagine how your day could progress when inspired with such a level of awareness and these positive attitudes? Often a person's success or failure, happiness or misery, may be a matter of individual perspective. Does your mind represent a sanctuary of ideas, joy, and opportunity? Do you understand your own physical and spiritual nature as a preparation to work successfully with your mind? Is the light of increasing wisdom and intelligence reflected in your words, your actions, and the love you give forth? When you choose to live each day as a new beginning, do you become excited about what you are going to write in your "book of life" for that day?

We may consider the question: What can I do to make this the most exciting, productive, and beneficial day of my life thus far? Do we seek opportunities? If so, abundant doors to all kinds of opportunities can immediately swing open. Do we take the calculated risks to dream large, to build, and to succeed? Do we set about the tasks at hand with a resolution to do our best? Do we have an established plan or program directing us toward a beneficial vision or goal? Are we excited about the learning possibilities this day may bring? Do we accept the challenges of life and experience the thrill of working in harmony with the divine?

As our eyes open each morning, do we see spread before us a banquet of the greatest treasures life can offer? What do we consider "treasures"? Life itself? Family? Friends? Talent and ability to achieve? The opportunity for useful work? How will we go about expressing thanksgiving for and interacting with these treasures?

Think of it! The same tremendous power that flows like gigantic rivers throughout the cosmos is at our fingertips. The soul of man is often said to be immortal. Our future is the future of growth and unlimited fruitfulness. Life-giving principles abide within each person. Spirit is eternally beneficent and, while it may not be physically seen or heard, may be felt by the person who desires to perceive it.

What would happen if, when we awakened each day, we recognized that we were human souls representing the vital life force of all human life in the divine process of evolution? Think of the beneficial changes we could bring about within our personal sphere of life with such an attitude.

If someone gave you a magnificent birthday present and you tucked it away in a drawer or a closet and never opened it, what good would it bring to you? If someone gave you a beautiful new car, with the stipulation that you must pick up the keys at the factory, dust would billow from your heels as you hastened to claim your gift. No one would neglect to claim the car. Yet, this is what we sometimes do with one of the greatest gifts in the world—*each precious new day*!

Welcome each new day. It represents another glorious opportunity for you. It is a thrilling new experience and a happy adventure in soul growth. You can find the sky suddenly becoming brilliantly blue . . . the trees an *alive* green . . . and every creation of nature radiating an effervescent glow! And no, nothing has really changed—except you! You may be beginning to see the work of the Creator

through new eyes, spiritual eyes, and it is good. It is very good!

To learn more truth about the great cosmic universe, first begin to learn more truth about yourself. Explore your home, your neighborhood, your town, your nation, and let your awareness expand to the entire, wonderful world! Knowledge is like a sparkling, cheerful fire that warms and brightens everything in the room. Knowledge and understanding, living each day as a new beginning, can enhance every aspect and every relationship in your life. There can be pure magic in such insight!

You are divinely designed and perfectly meant for the work of loving service. You are necessary in the overall scheme of life. And life will never abandon you. Put away false ideas of smallness and allow life's greatness to manifest itself. Grow and expand in spirit continually from dawn to dusk, from horizon to horizon. Transmit love and joy wherever you go and remember without ceasing, "This is the day the Lord has made. Let us rejoice and be glad in it!" (Psalms 118:24).

✦ LAW 3

Thanksgiving leads to giving and forgiving, and to spiritual growth. —John Marks Templeton

IS A FOUNDATIONAL part of true education becoming more spiritually aware? Is it through the spirit of divinity that the consciousness learns to govern itself by universal principles? We work daily to understand the majesty and mystery of divinity and our relationship to the whole as well as to the parts. We begin to experience the enthusiasm and excitement of becoming more informed as our desire to learn and to understand universal principles increases.

One of the most powerful and beneficial universal principles is the *law of thanksgiving*, sometimes referred to as the *law of gratitude*. Could our development of thanksgiving and gratitude be considered complete and full responses of the human heart to everything in the universe? Thanksgiving has been described as an act of kindness that frees our mind to focus on the blessings of the moment. Does this attitude represent our acknowledgment and appreciation of divine energy flowing through all things, everywhere? Thanksgiving has also been considered an aspect of unlimited love. Can giving thanks indicate a loving response from ourselves and our personal relationships to the whole of creation?

Every time we inhale a breath and then exhale, we are engaged in a process that is vital to our lives and to our world. With each in-drawn breath, we receive into our body the oxygen that is necessary for us to exist. With every exhaled breath, we return the carbon dioxide that supplies the plants in our world. We can feel the joy of spirit in this simple but vital process of exchange and give thanks. When was the last time you felt gratitude for the simple conveniences of your life? There is

so much in our lives to be grateful for and yet we often fail to recognize simple blessings or even to acknowledge them.

Inner peace can be reached only when we practice forgiveness. Forgiveness is the letting go of the past, and is therefore the means of correcting our misperceptions.
—*Gerald G. Jampolsky*

Thanksgiving leads to giving and forgiving, and to spiritual growth. As we work with the process of thanksgiving, we may also recognize the sweet release of letting go of a burden of nettlesome grievance or of a long-lived grudge. Forgiveness, letting go of past grievances or actions, is another key to spiritual growth. The practice of forgiving ourselves and others can make a beneficial contribution to the healing of our lives and our world. When we cling to old hurts or wounds, we can imprison ourselves in lives ruled by negative emotions. Attitudes of thanksgiving and forgiveness

The measure of a man is not determined by his show of outward strength or the volume of his voice, or the thunder of his action. It is to be seen rather in terms of the strength of his inner self, in terms of the nature and depth of his commitments, the sincerity of his purpose, and his willingness to continue "growing up."
—*Grade E. Poulard*

allow us to move to higher levels of consciousness and to evolve in our spiritual growth. Although forgiveness can be taught by definition, do we understand how important it is to *live* the process of forgiveness? Emotions like hate, envy, jealousy, anger, remorse, suspicion, and even mild dislike can be stumbling blocks to our progress. They can keep us from realizing our full potential over happiness.

The path to real spiritual growth is a choice. The journey commences the moment an individual chooses to become master over the mental and emotional and to follow a higher path, rather than follow the path that the ego wishes. Once the choice is made to move toward spiritual growth, a new way of living emerges. Hope springs forth like the lilies in the spring. When we let go, a lighter, happier feeling begins to fill our minds, hearts, and souls. The heart's capacity for charity is then activated, bringing blessings to ourselves and others.

✦ Law 4

There is no difficulty that enough love will not conquer. —Emmet Fox

In *Power Through Constructive Thinking*, Emmet Fox writes:

There is no difficulty that enough love will not conquer; no disease that enough love will not heal; no door that enough love will not open; no gulf that enough love will not bridge; no wall that enough love will not throw down; no wrong that enough love will not set right; it makes no difference how deeply seated may be the trouble; how helpless the outlook; how muddled the tangle; how great the mistake; a sufficient realization of love will dissolve it all—if only you will love enough, you will be the happiest, most powerful being in the world.

A story is told about a gentleman who was searching for the oldest thing in the world. In his determination to find the oldest thing, he visited many places and talked with people of many races and creeds. Each person with whom he talked told the man a personal version of the oldest thing in the world. In his quest, the man traveled extensively and was often rewarded by beautiful vistas. However, when he heard of a very ancient thing and traveled to see it, someone would tell him of something even older!

After many years of searching, the man returned to his home. He still had not found the oldest thing in the world. One day, as he sat in his garden, the man noticed a little girl walking along the sidewalk. In her arms, she tenderly held an old doll. The man watched as the little girl smoothed the doll's tangled hair, straightened the doll's dress, and cradled the doll in her arms. The little girl spoke to her doll as a mother would speak to her child. "At last," the man sighed, "Here is the oldest thing in the world. It is love!"

Has unlimited love always been present? We have heard the expression, "God is love." If this is true, was all of creation brought forth by divinity expressing itself as love? Divine love never fails, so we have a dependable ally in every tough situation. How would we describe what happens when we fill our hearts with unlimited love by thinking it, feeling it, and *expressing* it? Is loving, kind, nurturing behavior an expression of our *natural* state of consciousness? What could happen if people devoted similar energy to understanding and expressing unlimited love in daily living that we devote to harnessing the forces of nature?

If we looked beneath human conditioning, would we discover that the basic nature of the human brain is a wonderful openness to greater reality, an *aware presence*? We are naturally curious, responsive, and alert to the world around us. Our longing to drink more deeply from the wellspring of life often sets us on a particular pathway of

Love means to love
that which is unlov-
able, or it is no
virtue at all.
—G. K. Chesterton

When love becomes
a vehicle for tuning
in to the great mys-
teries of creation all
around us, it pro-
vides a deeper sense
of purpose and direc-
tion. The personal
and sacred are two
overlapping sides of
one and the same
path.
—John Welwood

experience. Is our innate sensitivity and searching a desire to connect with greater reality? Is this a seed of the wisdom of love that can ripen into fruitful expression within each one of us?

Is unlimited love concerned with conditions? Does it make a difference how long a condition or difficulty has lasted? Constant, unlimited love can communicate itself to the most bitter person or situation. Any time! Any place! It is the one power that can eventually and successfully cut through the obstacles of practically any situation or difficulty. And success often follows the overcoming of difficulties.

How can we increase our own ability to love? Well, although we may need to exert some effort and attention to the process, the nature of unlimited love is really quite simple. Whenever our heart fully opens and responds to another person, place, or situation, *without reservation*, we experience a moment of pure, unlimited love. This quality of love is often glimpsed more vividly in beginnings and endings. At a child's birth, at a loved one's death, or when first falling in love. At times like these, something infinite and spiritual inside us radiates like sunlight.

So, when we truly begin to comprehend the statement, "There is no difficulty that enough love will not conquer," do we begin to discover spiritual realities where old, familiar ways of *being* and *doing*

Peace comes only from loving, from mutual self-sacrifice and self-forgetfulness. Few today have humility or wisdom enough to know the world's deep need of love.
—Horace W. B. Donegan

may simply lay the foundation for an expanding and more beneficial way of life? Can this experience be a state of growing consciousness where new possibilities keep opening up before us? As Paul Tillich put it, "The boundary is the best place for acquiring knowledge." The path of unlimited love can become a mighty force for good in our lives. It can plow through the noisy commotion of inflated egos, break up the coarse and rocky places inside our thoughts and emotions, and enrich the fertile soil of our beings so that the beauty of the spiritual life flourishes in the garden of our souls. This can be a sacred path, connecting us with larger energies and joining heaven with earth in joyous, living expression.

Staggering amounts of manpower and money are devoted each year to discovering, understanding, and harnessing the forces of nature. Almost everyone agrees, however, that one of the greatest forces on earth is love. Should churches finance research into this elemental force? Should schools offer courses for credit, with homework, examinations, and grades? The real wealth of a nation does not come from mineral resources, but from what lies in the minds and hearts of its people . . . This love force can be harnessed if we listen to our hearts and minds, and follow its laws of life that lead to a joyous existence.

—John Marks Templeton

✦ Law 5

Self-control leads to success. —John Marks Templeton

IN THE ADVENTURE of life, we may not always immediately understand what is happening at any given time or in any particular situation. The script may not make sense and a person may feel confused regarding the plot of the story. We may fail to grasp the grand scope of the universal divine drama and our part in it. We may feel very much like the patron who has gone to the theater and found that the play has been in progress for some time. The latecomer has no knowledge of the beginning of the story and no idea of what the outcome may be.

Also, in the adventure of life, if we remain diligent and steadfast in the part of the drama unfolding around us, we may become more aware of the story line. We may encounter problem lessons that challenge our self-control. How do we beneficially handle these opportunities? The meaning of life is different for each individual. The one thing we can count on is that we will be presented with the lessons that we specifically need to learn. Do we seek and strive to learn more about ourselves and life as a whole? As part of this process, what is an effective tool of awareness that can help us to discover our own unique purpose?

We learn the importance of self-control. When we ride the pendulum of emotions, we may swing from one end of the spectrum of feelings to the other. If we allow our emotions to be anchored to whatever may be happening in our lives, are we giving power to the changing tide of circumstances? These out-of-control situations do not bring real happiness or success. There are many

ways to satisfy or nourish our emotions. Art, music, song, dance, poetry, walking in nature, going to the theater, sharing a cup of tea with a friend, and many other activities provide uplifting energy and joy to the soul. These are some ways of directing emotional energy into creative activities.

In the midst of an intense situation, how can we move from possible severity of emotions to creative awareness? How can we change a response from resistance to receptivity? How may we experience and exhibit more self-control? Perhaps the power of *choice* is an appropriate consideration. Choice represents the exploration of a situation, then selecting an appropriate action. Our experience of any moment is a reflection of our mind ideas at that time. What we believe and understand in the inner is what we experience in the outer. Every moment of every day, we are making choices. Are you aware of how even the smallest gesture has a direction? Do your choices move you closer to your desired goal, or farther away from it? How may we ascertain more clearly the direction of our choices?

The ultimate goal of making a shift in perception from being "out-of-control" to "self-control" can lead to greater success in any endeavor. Moving from outer appearances to deeper perception, we can ask ourselves what we are feeling and through what personal lens we are viewing circumstances. When we see life in clear focus, we can find some way to turn every experience into a step toward success. As we achieve greater clarity and self-control, we are less likely to judge ourselves or others. When we move out of judgment,

> To rule self
> and subdue
> our passions
> is the more
> praiseworthy
> because so few
> know how
> to do it.
> —*Francesco Guicciardini*

can we use our experiences as guidelines to greater growth? When we refrain from judging, can we become problem-solvers, not problem-makers? Problem-solving can be a necessary aspect of a successful venture. Successful people see failure as part of a helpful education and overcome obstacles as they proceed. Successful people often find ways to help people. They practice the *law of responsibility.*

To be truly successful, should we seek to build our souls in imitation of the Creator? Would this include appreciation of others and allowing deep humility and unlimited love to enhance our spirits? Are we then better able to accept new challenges and new experiences? People on the road to success and happiness often view the future as an exciting and still unexplored territory and move toward the frontier with enthusiasm.

Spotlights ✦ ✦

1. What does "Every discovery is a discovery of God" mean to you?

2. What is *your* concept of God?

3. Are the visible and tangible only tiny manifestations of the vast and timeless and limitless reality?

4. How may we discover more of divinity?

5. How do *you* begin each day?

6. What are your first thoughts when you open your eyes in the morning?

7. "This is the day the Lord has made. Let us rejoice and be glad in it" (Psalms 118:24).

8. Make a list of things for which you are thankful.

9. How does thanksgiving lead to spiritual growth?

10. How is unlimited love a conquering power over difficulties?

11. How can *you* increase your ability to love?

12. What are some ways you practice self-control?

13. What is your vision of success for your life?

Living the Various Spiritual Laws ✦ ✦

Waking up this morning, I see the blue sky,
I join my hands in thanks for the many wonders of life;
 For having twenty-four brand new hours.
The sun is rising on the forest
 and so is my awareness.

I walk across the field of sunflowers.
Tens of thousands of flowers waving at me;
My awareness is like the sunflower;
My hands are sowing seeds for the next harvest.
My ear is hearing the sound of the rising tide on the
 magnificent sky.

I see clouds approaching with joy from many directions.
I can see the fragrant lotus ponds of my homeland.
I can see coconut trees along the rivers;
I can see rice fields stretch their shoulders
laughing at the sun and the rain.
Mother Earth gives me coriander, basilicum, and celery.
Tomorrow, the hills and mountains of the country will be
 green again.
Tomorrow, the buds of life will grow quickly;
The folk poetry will be as sweet as the songs of the children.
The whole family of humans will sing together with me in
 my work.

 —Thich Nhat Hanh

Week Twenty-Four

♦ ## LAW 1

The tree is known by its fruit. —English proverb

"THE TREE is known by its fruit" is a proverb many of us have probably heard expressed in a variety of ways. Other familiar expressions are: "Judge the tree by its fruit, not by its leaves," and "A tree should be judged by its fruits."

Some close human analogies of this proverb are: "Teach a pure faith, and abuses will disappear," or, "He that would eat the fruit must climb its tree," and, "Never judge a man by his mask."

A young man named John inherited a fertile and productive farm that boasted a large apple orchard at the back of the property. This orchard was long acclaimed throughout the area for producing the best tasting and juiciest apples. In the fall, when apple-picking time arrived, people would arrive at the farm from miles around to pick and purchase the apples. John welcomed everyone who came to buy apples, and there was always an abundance of the fruit.

John had a special connection with the orchard. He remembered when he was a boy, following his father among the apple trees as he cared for them. When he was ten, John planted an apple seed that his father gave him in a pot, grew it into a seedling tree, then planted it in the ground. John watched the awesome miracle of his special tree growing from the tiny seed, eventually becoming a beautiful tree, billowing with blossoms that became delicious fruit. While growing up, John learned a lot about apple trees. He learned how the tree lifted water from its roots up the trunk into its beautiful, fragrant blossoms. He watched the bees swarm around the blossoms, gathering nectar to make honey. As years passed and John grew into adulthood, he watched the apple trees endure storms and below zero hardships to again blossom in the spring and produce more fruit in the fall.

One day, while sitting beneath his special tree, John experienced an awakening. He realized he knew a lot about his apple tree and could easily describe its attributes. But the tree's perceptive abilities were not large enough to comprehend its gardener! There, with the warm sun caressing his shoulders, a gentle wind ruffling his hair, and the tree supporting his back, John realized he knew as little about his own Creator as the apple tree did about him!

Why should we expect to be able to describe God when we know so little about divinity? Would a God we were able to describe be little more than a good, wise human? Probably no human has yet learned even 1% of what humans can learn about divinity. For example, in only two centuries, has science research discovered over one hundred-fold more information, previously invisible and inconceivable, about cosmology, subatomic realities, electronics, and cellular activity? Can even more awesome discoveries be made about such basic invisible spiritual realities as unlimited love, purpose, intellect, creativity, and prayer?

Are you God's apple tree? Evidence indicates that we are created by God's infinite love and truly flourish only if we radiate unlimited, overflowing love for our Creator and love for every human—without exception. Do you suppose an infinite Creator could be so small or self-centered as to demand our worship? Or instead, is our humble worship a creative force that causes us to be fruitful? Is unlimited love a vital element in our growth and productivity? Does our love vanish when bottled up? On the other hand, is love, flowing forth abundantly, miraculously multiplied endlessly?

Do careers flourish when they focus on deriving more productive ways to benefit everyone rather than on selfish pursuits? What can we learn, as life participants, from the parable of the talents (Matthew 25:14–30), or the parable of the fig tree (Matthew 21:19–24)? Do customers flock to the salesperson who is most honest and diligent in serving customers? Is diligent service to customers like a boomerang that returns with blessings to the salesperson? If a person focuses his or her career efforts on doing good, will he or she then do well?

What is the reasoning behind this perspective?

What happens to an apple tree when it no longer produces flowers or fruit? Doesn't it usually die or get cut down? Do people who retire, even with no disability, tend to wither more quickly in body, mind, and self-respect? Do they sometimes become unhappy parasites on those who continue to be productive? Can idleness be termed a form of slow suicide? What are some remedies for overcoming this situation? Why do people who devote their lives to noble purposes automatically become happier individuals?

We are the recipients of so many divine blessings. We always have the opportunity to draw from the reservoir of spirit as much as we may choose to receive and use. When we begin to realize and appreciate the wonders of God's creation, we grow in beneficial ways in all aspects of our lives. We can be like the apple trees in our story: beautiful, fragrant, vital, productive, and beneficial to many. What do the fruits of our efforts say about us? Do we give forth abundantly; do we receive abundantly?

✦ LAW 2

Rid yourself of negative attitudes and beliefs and negative conditions will die of starvation. —Russell W. Lake

IN HER BOOK *What Are You?* Imelda Shanklin writes: "Your thoughts are the tools with which you carve your life story on the substance of the universe. When you choose your thoughts, you choose results. The visible part of your life pours out of your mind, shaped and stamped by your thoughts, as surely as the coins of nations are shaped and stamped by the mechanisms used to convert ores into specie."

Mental habits can make a deeper life impres-sion than facial lines betray. Think about this for a moment. Can *any* negative attitude or belief be resolved into its mental form and erased from your mind? How may this be accomplished? Rid yourself of negative attitudes and beliefs and negative conditions will die of starvation. Refuse to entertain any thought in your mind that you would not wish objectified in your life.

Should our purpose or objective in life be one of the most important considerations in our thought processes? Does your purpose represent what you supremely wish to do? Is it what you most ardently wish to become? Does your purpose or objective represent the ideal you endeavor to achieve within yourself with the utmost passion of your soul? Could there be a fruitful place for us in life if ever we allow our minds to be purposeless? How do our present thoughts contribute to our purpose?

Intentionally or unintentionally, our thoughts are directing how we live our lives, our relationships to ourselves, and our relationships to the world. Does living by *intent* and *choice* make a lot more sense than living by whatever random thoughts may cross our minds? How is being *consciously* aware of our thoughts helpful and effective? What changes might occur in our lives if we *chose* to allow our minds to dwell only on the lessons that can be learned from all situations? What would happen if we chose to remain centered in a positive attitude, regardless of what might seem to be happening around us? What difference would a choice to *respond* rather than to *react* make in any situation? What kind of fruitful benefits could ensue from working with a positive trend of mind?

The superior man, seeing what is good, imitates it; seeing what is bad, he corrects it in himself.
—I Ching

If we could somehow use an instrument that would record our thinking processes for a day, then play back those thoughts, we might be surprised to learn why things go amiss and activities become snarled. We may initially find selfish, critical, judgmental, irrelevant, nonsensical, and fearful thoughts interspersed with thoughts of love, compassion, courage, creativity, and thanksgiving.

The good news is that we can do something beneficial about the way we think.

Our minds respond to our intentions and controls. If a difficult situation arises, think about it gently. Look at the facts and aspects of the situation from all angles. Know that a positive response is already present in the divine mind. Then bless the situation and release it for a time to allow the spirit to blend your mind with the divine mind. You may find that when you take up the matter again, a workable response has become clear to you. Be sensible, modest, confident, and humble! Let the creative mind think through you. The integrity of our efforts in thinking counts! Life pays us in the currency of the realm wherein we operate.

All that we are is the result of what we have thought; it is founded on our thoughts and made up of our thoughts. If a man speak or act with an evil thought, suffering follows him as a wheel follows the hoof of the beast that draws the cart.
—The Dhammapada

How many times have we heard the statement that the worker reveals his trade by the kind of tools that he uses? A mediocre product is often the sign of a mediocre worker, while a superior product is often the sign of a conscientious worker. The superior worker uses all the equipment at his disposal and remains open and receptive to grow in awareness and to increase his abilities. Every thought on any topic and every moment's consideration on any subject may serve as preparations that enable us to progress. Thoughts form the mental equipment that we use each day. What mental tools (thoughts) are we using? While we are awake, our minds appropriate and gather the thoughts we have allowed entry as food for growth. As we sleep, our minds assimilate the food we have given them. Certainly positive thoughts, attitudes, and beliefs provide greater life nourishment. We have all of life in which to achieve, but we have not one precious minute to devote to negative attitudes and beliefs!

✦ Law 3

An hour wasted is never found. —John Marks Templeton

There is no time like
the present.
—English proverb

Time is money.
—English proverb

Do little things
now; so shall big
things come to
thee by and by
asking to be done.
—Persian proverb

THE BUDDHA TAUGHT that the root of humanity's suffering is ignorance, but the root of ignorance itself is our mind's habitual tendency to distraction. Mindfulness, or being aware of how we use every moment of every day, is often considered the gateway to fruitfulness.

We are constantly making decisions as we move throughout our day. Our habits of perception, thought, feeling, and acting can lead us into many varied experiences. In this busy activity of our minds, what can being mindful bring to the enhancement of the day? How does being mindful contribute to using our time wisely and productively?

Time is precious. It is given in equal measure each day to all of us. We have 24 hours in each day. That equals 168 hours in a week. This is our wealth in time. We're going to spend that time doing *something*, and what we do with that time often determines how we live our lives and what we achieve in our lives.

> Dost thou love life? Then do not squander time;
> for that's the stuff life is made of.
> —Benjamin Franklin

Now, let's do a small exercise. Write a desired goal, vision, or purpose at the top of a piece of paper. How many hours do you sleep each night? For example, if you sleep 7 hours a night, multiplied by 7 days, you would contribute 49 hours each week to sleep. Subtract your sleep hours (49) from the number of hours in a week (168), and you will have 119 remaining hours. How much time do you spend in bathing, dressing and cosmetics? Possibly an hour? Multiply that by 7 and subtract from 119. You have 112 hours left. How much time do you spend eating each day? An

hour? More? Less? Hypothetically, let's allow 2 hours for breakfast, lunch, and dinner. That's 14 hours for a week. Subtracted from 112, you have 98 hours left.

> Time is the coin of your life. It is the only coin you have,
> and only you can determine how it will be spent.
> —Carl Sandburg

List other necessary tasks you perform on a consistent basis, like laundry, grocery shopping, working out, transportation time to various activities, medical appointments, traveling to work and back, going to church, and time for prayer. Calculate how much time you spend on these activities and subtract that amount from your total. If time for these activities totals 20 hours, for example, then there are only 78 remaining hours in the week! And we haven't even included time for your work, time for your family, maintenance on your lawn or house or car, for beneficial recreation, or for more education.

You have probably heard the maxim, "There's only so much time to go around." The purpose of this exercise is to help you become more mindful of how you utilize the 24 hours in each day. Are you the master of time and not its slave? What are some ways you can more fruitfully use your energy and time to achieve desired goals? Here are some idea starters. Do you set your watch a few minutes ahead in order to be prompt for appointments? Promptness is a form of politeness and consideration. It's also good business. When you are given an assignment, do you complete it when requested or even ahead of schedule? Promptness with everyone is a prerequisite of success. It tells others that you have regard for them, that you refuse to waste their time. Do you maintain an hourly schedule for the appointments and activities of

Time is flying,
never to return.
—Virgil

each day? Do you prepare an advance list of the next day's engagements? Pre-planning can offer tremendous advantages and is a time-saver as well. Time is a tool we can use sporadically, misuse, or use wisely. The choice is ours. However, *an hour wasted is never found.* Those afflicted with the procrastination habit are never likely to be successful.

There are additional benefits to being mindful and timely. Being mindful or cognizant in our daily lives can help us perceive people and situations more accurately and discriminatingly so we can respond in a more beneficial manner. Being

mindful, or thoughtful and timely, can help defuse negativity. Being mindful or conscientious can help us realize more of the fruitful nature of our being.

Could there be any better way to operate than to do now what needs to be done now? Sir Richard Tangye put time management in a simple statement. He said, "During a very busy life, I have often been asked, 'How did you manage to do it all?' The answer is very simple: It is because I did everything promptly. Tomorrow is never. Yesterday is gone. The only moment is now."

✦ LAW 4

To be upset over what you don't have is to waste what you do have. —Ken Keyes

All the affairs of
the universe come
within the range
of my duty.
My duties include
all the affairs of
the universe.
The universe is
my mind. My mind
is the universe.
—Lu Hsiang-Shan

MANY MEDIA commercials encourage us to believe that if we buy a certain product, we can be physically appealing or popular or successful. According to the commercial message, it may be easy to make friends and influence people if we simply do what we're told to do. It would be wonderful if that were true; unfortunately, life does not seem to work that way. What is inside of us can be much more important and influential than what is outside.

Many people today think that money and the things it can buy are the measures of success. In truth, things we can buy are simply things we can buy—no more, no less. They do not remake the real person in any way. We can change the color of our hair, the style of our clothes, and the car we drive, but these things may not be accurate indicators of the kind of person we are inside.

Before making a change of any sort, think about who you are and what you have now. You may be fine just as you are, even though you may admire someone who is different from you. The difference may be in looks, in abilities, in work, or

in family or love relationships, and the difference can be very attractive to you. You may think how much better it would be to be like them than to be like yourself. But is it?

Choose always the way that seems the best,
however rough it may be. Custom will soon
render it easy and agreeable.
—Pythagoras

Each of us has things we would like to change and problems we might prefer not to have. Consider that the challenging situations in your life may not be as intense as the problems in the life of the person you would like to emulate. Ken Keyes says, "To be upset over the things you don't have is to waste what you do have."

Have you taken a recent inventory of your spiritual and life assets? What are the talents and abilities that have contributed to your present capabilities? Are you presently using these capabilities to your

Tell me, I'll forget.
Show me, I may
remember. But
involve me, and
I'll understand.
—Chinese proverb

best advantage? What steps are you taking to expand and further develop these capabilities? Have you explored your talents carefully, chosen your career with care, and made certain that you love what you do? What are you doing to increase your stockpile of strengths? Is it necessary to reverse any patterns of consciousness that might hinder the attainment of your purpose in life? Do you observe the actions of others so that you can benefit from both their strengths and their mistakes? By studying the behavior of those with whom we come in contact, it can soon become apparent that the most happy and productive among them are the ones who truly care and rejoice in the good fortune of others. Is your work helping you by helping at least one other human being? Are you progressively building and developing your character? Do you fill your mind to

capacity with good and productive thoughts? Do your thoughts and actions build up rather than tear down?

It is not too late to turn your life around or to break patterns of negativity that may have manifested themselves in it. You can bring about change by embracing the attitudes and feelings that you might have if you were experiencing the desired conditions.

◆ LAW 5

Honesty is the best policy. —Miguel de Cervantes

Is HONESTY a way of being in natural harmony with all of life? Can honesty be an important part of conscious oneness with the life process and with our own life purpose? Can honesty take us beyond our limited, linear view and aid us in celebrating growth and perpetual renewal? Can you imagine what might happen if an individual made a personal agreement to practice truth and honesty and to be independent of the opinions of others? What would be the benefits if a person continually turned to the sacred and holy nature and loving presence of divinity for daily guidance?

Being truthful, honest, and sincere is like a mountain of rock that the stormy seas of deceptive, unscrupulous, or untrustworthy energies cannot touch. Sir Thomas More, nobly portrayed in *A Man for All Seasons*, was faced with intense pres-

sures to abandon his code of ethics. His position, his family, and his life were under threat of death. But Sir Thomas was a man who stood strong for his beliefs. While pressuring him to uphold an unscrupulous king and to sign an oath of allegiance, one of his colleagues asked him, "Why don't you just do it for the sake of comradery?" More responded, "When you go to Heaven for following your conscience, and I go to hell for not following mine, will you then join me there, 'for the sake of comradery'?"

We live in a world of multifarious thoughts. We deal not only with our own thoughts, but also with the thoughts of the people around us. Every day we are given perhaps hundreds of little opportunities to choose between clarity or confusion, unlimited love or dissension, peace or turmoil, falsehood or truth, deceit or honesty. When we stay in touch with the center of truth within us, when we walk with honesty and integrity, we walk with God.

Ted Engstrom tells the following story in his book titled *Integrity*:

For Coach Cleveland Stroud and the Bulldogs of Rockdale County High School (in the small town of Conyers, Georgia in the United States) it was their championship season. The team had 21 wins and 5 losses on the way to the Georgia boy's basketball tournament last March, then a dramatic come-from-behind victory in the state finals.

But now the new trophy case outside the high school gymnasium is bare. Earlier this month, the Georgia High School Association deprived Rockdale County of the championship after school officials said that a player who was scholastically ineligible had played 45 seconds in the first of the school's five post-season games.

"We didn't know he was ineligible at the time; we didn't know it until a few weeks ago," Mr. Stroud said. "Some people have said we should have just kept quiet about it, that it was just 45 seconds and the player wasn't an impact player. But you've got to do what's honest and right and what the rules say. I told my team that people forget the scores of basketball games; they don't ever forget what you're made of."

To persistently align ourselves with spiritual principles and to apply what we know of them to our daily life experiences can be fruitful and beneficial. There may be times when it seems that one little lie—what is called a "little, white lie" — might make life easier. "After all, who would know?" can be a rationalization we may use when considering taking the easy way. But deceptions

can become linked to further and more damaging deceptions, which may cause our thoughts and actions to become confused and impure. This sad state of affairs may be clearly expressed in the saying, "Oh, what a tangled web we weave, when first we practice to deceive." Deceit often takes a terrible toll on our sense of integrity and self-worth.

Have you considered writing your own personal honor code? This could prove to be quite insightful. In your own words, describe your intentions to establish truth, honesty, sincerity, integrity, and noble aims as the continuing pathway for your thoughts and actions. List some ways you can accomplish these goals. Could this commitment help eliminate any habit of exaggeration? Could it suspend any need or desire to deceive yourself or others? Could it help shed any veils of distortion around any subject, person, place, or thing in your life? Making the choice and developing greater strength to choose truth and honesty over lies and deceptions can indeed be a powerful tool. Like positive thinking and giving thanks, we must apply ourselves to remembering and acting on the truth. Is this what honesty and integrity is all about?

Spotlights ✦ ✦

1. Are you God's apple tree?

2. Is our perception of God about as large as the apple tree's perception of the gardener?

3. Refuse to entertain any thought in your mind that you would not wish objectified in your life.

4. The integrity of our efforts in thinking is vastly important.

5. Time is precious. Being aware of how we use every moment of every day can move us effectively toward our goals and produce fruitful results.

6. Are you the master of time and not its slave?

7. Consider the value of the people, experiences, and awareness that brought you to this present moment in your life.

8. Think of examples where you have been able to put various virtues into practice.

9. If you are faced with a difficult problem to solve, pray for guidance.

10. Why is honesty *always* the best policy?

Living the Various Spiritual Laws ✦ ✦

THE EIGHTFOLD PATH OF BUDDHISM

Right Belief—that Truth is the guide of man.

Right Resolve—to be calm at all times and not to harm any living creature.

Right Speech—never to lie, never to slander anyone, and never to use coarse or harsh language.

Right Behavior—never to steal, never to kill, and never to do anything one may later regret or be ashamed of.

Right Occupation—never to choose an occupation that is considered bad.

Right Effort—always to strive for that which is good and avoid that which is evil.

Right Contemplation—of the Noble Truths, in calmness and detachment.

Right Concentration—will then follow and lead to the path of perfect peace.

— Joseph Gaer, *What the Great Religions Believe*

Week Twenty-Five

✦ LAW 1

Your prayers can be answered by "yes," but also by "no," and by alternatives. —Ruth Stafford Peale

THE POWER of positive thinking offers avenues for your fruitful progress. Many ministers, philosophers, psychologists, and psychiatrists provide evidence that the power of the mind becomes one of the great tools utilized by men and women to help them gain benefits from challenges. Frequent positive use of this mind-tool can help us become more skillful and productive in daily living. However, with so much emphasis on positive thinking, some people may hold the erroneous idea that saying or hearing "no" can be a negative experience. The truth is that there may be times when "no" is the appropriate response.

Our prayers can also be answered by "yes," or by "no," or by alternatives. Let's look at this possibility from three perspectives.

First, when we become still and quiet and ask for guidance, we may receive a clear and unmistakable "yes" or "no" response to our prayers and no further consideration may seem necessary. Second, when we have contributed whatever we can to a situation and have placed it prayerfully in unlimited love and thanksgiving, we can release the outcome to infinite divinity. Whether the response is "yes" or "no," we can continue with our daily activities with the thought that the manifestation of the desire of our hearts may progress according to universal wisdom. Third, a most significant lesson for us to learn may be to realize that no matter how impossible a situation may seem, regardless of how difficult the circumstances may appear, an opportunity for blessing and growth is present within the prayer experience. The blessing may arrive in a most unexpected manner, and the growth may point us in an entirely new and beneficial direction! Alternative answers to our prayers can offer evidences of divinity through astonishing and eye-opening opportunities.

Yet, sometimes, when our prayers seem to be answered but not in the way we had hoped, we may question whether or nor we are in tune with the timeless, unlimited, universal Creator. However, if God is infinite, can anything ever be separated from God?

Spiritual communion occurs in two directions. We express to God our heartfelt feelings and sincere desires. The Creator's response to us may be realized in multitudinous ways. To humbly open

> Mental prayer is that in which God so occupies the mind that it thinks of nothing else.
> —*Angela of Foligno*

> [The Lord said:] "Do not, therefore, be surprised if you do not see the fruits of your prayers with your bodily eyes, because I dispose of them according to My eternal wisdom."
> —*St. Gertrude the Great*

> Sometimes it seems we have prayed long, and yet we think that we have not our asking. Here we should not be in heaviness. For I am sure our Lord's meaning is that we wait for a better time or more grace or a better gift.
> —*Julian of Norwich*

our little minds to divine inspiration, cultivating the *quality* of our thinking process, is definitely beneficial. We can be wide open-minded, attentive, and listening for new insights. We can also be spontaneous, attentive, and flowing with the insights we receive. The quick and striking benefits that are often obtained can be amazing!

Our spiritually directed thoughts may be likened to a river moving within its banks. The banks keep the water moving in a certain direction. Yet, within those banks the water is free to swirl spontaneously over and around obstacles. We incline our thoughts in a spiritual direction, while leaving them flexible enough to be influenced and guided by the divine infinite intellect that is vastly beyond human intellect. For our prayers to be maximally effective, do we ask not only for wisdom to *understand* the divine guidance but also the strength to take action and *accomplish* the appropriate work?

How may the results of our prayers allow us to observe divinity in our lives? Do we move focused and steadfastly, learning from difficult situations? Are we able to see that divine purpose may be more beneficial for us than the request in our prayers? Do we monitor the thoughts, ideas, and impressions that enter our field of awareness, looking for opportunities to learn? Do we feel the surge of joy empowered by the Spirit filling our endeavors? Are our interactions with others changing for the better as we move through various experiences? Does the process of daily living become more directional, fruitful, and filled with greater purpose? The universe is abundant with meaning and purpose. Our humble prayers and our growth in spiritual life are worthy of our best effort.

Worship can have a tremendous benefit on the human personality. Its transforming impact, in many instances, has been quite beyond description. So, does it really matter whether the answer to our prayer is "yes," "no," or an "alternative," as long as we continue moving forward with the divine purpose for each of us?

✦ LAW 2

Healthy minds tend to cause healthy bodies. —John Marks Templeton

THE LEAD ARTICLES in many of today's books, magazines, and newspapers often focus on rampant, stress-related problems. Worry, fear, envy, anger, pride, frustration, and various emotional stresses are only a few areas that can reduce a person's physical and mental health. Resentments, regrets, or doubts from past activities may sometimes carry over into the present and cause conflicts. People may bring stress into their lives through bad habits and bad attitudes. Visible conditions often depict invisible thinking. How much better off would we be if we understood that "Healthy minds tend to cause healthy bodies," and unhealthy minds tend to cause unhealthy bodies?

What steps can be taken when faced with adversity? There may be no easy answers, but could some simple stress relievers prove helpful? Going for a brisk walk in fresh air, listening to the

I can elect to change all thoughts that hurt.
—Gerald G. Jampolsky

Safeguard the health of both body and soul.
—Cleobulus

sounds of a trickling stream, or feeling the coolness of freshly mowed grass or soft sand, beneath our feet can often serve as a soothing balm for frayed nerves and tense muscles. Would getting up half an hour earlier to start the day make a difference? Laughter and a spirit of joy are also "good medicines." The health benefits of prayer, thanksgiving, and meditation have been tested and recognized by scientists and physicians. These activities are often credited with lowering blood pressure, slowing the aging process, and helping keep the emotions in balance. Doing what we can to improve our relations with others is beneficial. And appropriate exercise can offer benefits to both mind and body.

A healthy body is the guest-chamber of the soul, a sick, its prison.
—Francis Bacon

Another proven method for reducing stress is attributed to owning a pet. Long-range studies with the ill and elderly report that having a dog or cat to stroke and love can increase happiness and extend longevity. Mother Teresa of Calcutta often provided animals as therapy for insane children. Some nursing homes and care facilities now provide pet "mascots" for the mental health of their residents.

A helpful and possibly enlightening exercise is to write down everything in your day that produces stress, checking the aggravations that create the greatest stress. Then, analyze the various ways you might improve these situations.

An old maxim states, "Wherever we are, the sky constantly meets the horizon." In other words, that which is important continues. Is it more helpful to concentrate on the *possibilities* and *opportunities* of whatever circumstances may surround us? Could any person, place, or situation disturb us if we realize we are the masters of our thoughts and may only need to change our minds about a situation? Could *changing* our minds be a major step toward *healing* our minds and bodies?

In *365 Tao*, Deng Ming-Dao tells the story of a wanderer who cared nothing for fame. Although many chances for position were offered to the man, he continued to search for teachers who could help him master five things: the zither, chess, books, painting, and the sword.

The zither gave him music, which expressed the soul. Chess cultivated strategy and a response to the actions of another. Books offered the man academic education. Painting was the exercise of beauty and sensitivity. Sword was a means for health and defense.

One day a little boy asked the wanderer what he would do if he lost his five things. At first, the wanderer was frightened by the thought of this possibility. However, he soon realized that his zither could not play itself. The chess game board and pieces meant nothing without players. The book needed a reader. Brush and ink could not move on their own accord. A sword could not be unsheathed without a hand. The man quickly understood that his cultivation was not merely for the acquisition of skills, it was a path to the innermost part of his being.

How can healthy bodies and healthy minds

Have we found that anxiety about possible consequences increased the clearness of our judgment, made us wiser and braver in meeting the present, and arming ourselves for the future?
—F. D. Maurice

help us attune to the divine part of our beings? Life is really simple. What we give out, we get back. Every thought is a contributor toward creating our present and future experiences. There are many positive ways to approach any situation. Nothing is really worth getting angry about or feeling hurt or bitter. There are plenty of opportunities to set things right again. Think of what a wonderful demonstration can be made from any situation, and valuable lessons may be learned in the process. How does the way we think affect how we feel? We are continuously treating the conditions in life with the thoughts we hold about them. To heal the mind is to heal the body. Healthy minds tend to cause healthy bodies, and vice versa.

✦ LAW 3

Give me beauty in the inward soul; and may the outward and inward man be at one. —Plato

BENEATH ALL THE STORIES of past human experiences, beneath the joys and sorrows of living, we have within us an essential nature that is beautiful and whole and complete. What is this true nature, and how do we find it? Every person has a gift to bring to the table of life, and the family of earth yearns to receive each gift.

Plato spoke truly when he said, "Give me beauty in the inward soul; and may the outward and inward man be at one." If we speak with ten different people, we may receive ten different responses and descriptions of "beauty." Our personal definition of the word "beauty" may lie in our attitude toward others and how we perceive the world around us. Do we look to the heart of any person or situation rather than getting caught up in the outer trappings? Can we see the beckoning beauty in noble goals, virtues, selflessness, and deep compassion? Do we strive to call upon the richness of our minds, the depths of our creativity, the reality of our spiritual identification? Do we hold a high respect for all of life and dare to immerse ourselves in the reality of our spiritual identification? Can we look at the world in which we live and how we live in that world and say frankly that our ways engender happiness for others?

A story is told that one day, a poor young lad was selling goods from door to door to pay his way through school. In the process of accomplishing his work, the boy felt hungry and reached his hand into his pocket. His fingers wrapped around one thin dime! That wasn't enough to buy even a piece of fruit!

The boy decided he would ask for a meal at the next house on his route. He rang the doorbell and immediately lost his nerve when a beautiful young woman opened the door. Instead, the boy asked for a drink of water. The young woman thought the boy looked hungry, so she brought him a large glass of milk. The boy drank the milk slowly, then asked, "How much do I owe you?"

"You don't owe me anything," the young woman replied. "Mother taught us never to accept pay for a kindness."

The boy bowed his head and replied, "Then, I thank you from the bottom of my heart."

As Howard Kelly left that house, he not only felt stronger physically, but his faith in God and man was improved. He had been ready to give up and quit, but the unexpected kindness stirred tremendous encouragement.

Years later, the young woman who had befriended Howard Kelly became critically ill. Local doctors were baffled by her illness. Finally, they sent her to a hospital in a nearby large city. Specialists were called in to study her rare disease. Dr. Howard Kelly was called in for the consultation.

When Dr. Kelly heard the name of the town the woman came from, a strange light filled his eyes. Immediately, he rose from his chair at the nurse's desk and walked down the hospital hall to the woman's room. Dressed in his doctor's coat, he

To have reached
two noble goals,
selflessness and
flawlessness, is the
highest beauty.
—Hsi K'ang

Beauty in all
things exists in
the mind which
contemplates them.
—David Hume

leaned over the woman's bed and immediately recognized her. He returned to the consultation room, determined to do his best to save her life.

From that day forward, he gave special attention to the woman's case. After a long struggle, the battle was finally won. Dr. Kelly requested the hospital's business office to pass the final bill to him for approval. When the bill arrived, Dr. Kelly looked at it, then wrote something at the bottom of the bill. The bill was sent to the woman's room.

The woman hesitated before opening the bill. She was certain it would probably take the rest of her life to pay the costs for the doctors and hospital. Finally, as she opened the bill, tears filled her eyes and she clasped the piece of paper to her heart. At the bottom of the bill she read, "Paid in full with one glass of milk." The bill was signed, "Dr. Howard Kelly."

There is a very practical lesson in this touching story of true beauty and thanksgiving. One of the great spiritual principles is giving and receiving. What is received must be given in an ungrudging outflow of love and generosity and beneficence, not only towards humankind, but to everything that lives. For with the same measure that we give,

it shall be measured to us again. Even such a seemingly simple matter as a kind word or act is repaid with multiplied blessings.

Never lose an opportunity of seeing
anything that is beautiful; for beauty is God's
handwriting—a wayside sacrament. . . .
and thank God for it as a cup of blessing.
—Ralph Waldo Emerson

Yes, we all have a gift to give. Perhaps a portion of our gift is to affirm that we are alive on the earth and are part of all that is happening. We receive and we give. Could there be any greater gift than that of unlimited love? When the innermost part of our being is filled with light, love, praise, humility, and thanksgiving, is the outward person not then a reflection of the inner person? The work we accomplish when we give and receive unlimited love is indeed far-reaching. Our world can become a garden paradise—a heaven on earth—rich with beauty and fruitful expressions.

✦ LAW 4

Happiness has nothing to do with wealth and status, but is a matter of harmony. —Lao Tzu

What does it mean
to be happy?
—Anonymous

A LARGE PART of the makeup of the human personality may derive from the attitudes we reinforce mentally and emotionally. If we worry or become anxious, we may enforce this depleting energy and experience its effect. The same can be said for positive attitudes. If we decide to make a cake, whatever ingredients we put into the mixing bowl will appear in the finished cake. It is easy to realize the truth of this statement in connection with a material object like a cake. Yet, people may fail to see

that the same process applies equally in the realm of the mind. The thoughts and beliefs with which we fill our minds often appear in the "cake" called life experiences. *The way we choose to see the world creates the world we see!* Each one of us has the opportunity to access an amazing attitudinal advantage within ourselves once we come to know that *happiness is a choice and misery is optional!*

Do you believe you can claim happiness at any time? Are you aware this is possible regardless of

All external reward comes about as a result of internal effort.
—Paul D. Cummings

Having great wealth is meaningless unless you use the money for good.
—George W. Cummings Sr.

Happiness is knowing that you do not necessarily require happiness.
—William Saroyan

your personal history or your past experiences? Would you dare to experiment with this idea, recreate yourself in accordance with a greater perspective of happiness, and then live in ways to experience endless opportunities for your own momentous changes? Is now the time to begin *understanding* the happiness you truly want? Are you ready and willing to let happiness become the child of your choices, decisions, and actions?

Often raised in the drama and complexities of daily living, we sometimes fail to see with a simple eye. Yet, the simple things in life can bring great joy—the smell of a wet summer afternoon, the taste of a perfectly ripe piece of fruit, the color of the sky at sunset, the softness of a snowflake melting on our cheek. In moments of greater awareness, these things can vibrate in our hearts with an energy that is deep and true.

A man is rich according to what he is, not according to what he has.
—Anonymous

Happiness is not a matter of events; it depends upon the tides of the mind.
—Alice Meynell

As a matter of experience, we find that true happiness comes in producing beneficial things, in the manifold activities of life, in the healthful outgoing of all human powers. Happiness has nothing to do with wealth and status; it is a matter of harmony. Are the most infectiously joyous men and women those who forget themselves in thinking about others and serving others? How are happiness and success awarded to those who do not seek these attributes as ends in themselves, but make the effort to excel at their tasks?

Have you ever heard someone say, "Oh, if I had fifty thousand dollars (or whatever amount), I'd be really happy?" Yet, these are often the people who would most likely still be unhappy, regardless of the amount of money they may have. Why? Money alone does not bring happiness. Status alone does not bring happiness. Happiness is never

the completion, or the getting. Happiness comes from the work, the endeavor, the pursuit of a goal. The giving brings the joy. Production, not consumption, is at the core of happiness and success. If we see progress in our work, then we can know happiness as part of that progress.

Certain aspects of happiness can derive from certain kinds of positive self-awareness and expectancy. Consider these ideas for a moment. What do you think could happen if you:

+ Chose, as a daily intention, a happier and more loving embrace of yourself and others and viewed every person, circumstance, and situation as an opportunity for growth and learning?
+ Learned how to become more relaxed and in control of your level of stress?
+ Began each day with joy, anticipation, and positive affirmations?
+ Looked for and expected the best in others?
+ Made an effort to do things that offered opportunities for joy, purpose, and a sense of thanksgiving, things that were beneficial to everyone?
+ Made an effort to express unlimited love to everyone you met?
+ Lived up to the aspirations that you regard as personally productive?
+ Established a program for greater educational achievements?

One of the real fallacies is the popular notion that happiness depends on external circumstances and surroundings. There is no question that our internal moods may be colored by external situations. But does the real personal joy come from internal conviction, determined by character that is the direct result of holding high ideals and purpose? High ideals and purpose are reflected in the values one places on life, in lifting up the downtrodden, and in bringing courage to those who may be discouraged. Success often comes to the one who is consistently progressing toward a worthy purpose. The by-product is often the joy of service and personal advancement.

✦ LAW 5

Help yourself by helping others. —John Marks Templeton

Compassion is a mind that savors only mercy and love for all sentient beings.
—*Buddhism, Nagarjuna*

But those immersed in the love of God feel love for all things.
—*Sikhism*

Be ashamed to die until you have won some victory for humanity.
—*Horace Mann*

WHEN AN INDIVIDUAL realizes the power of spiritual principles for fulfilling God's purpose for his life, does he begin to embody unlimited love? Does such a person delight in the well-being of others and selflessly work for the greater good of all? Why is it that giving ourselves in loving service often brings a sense of happiness into our lives that nothing else in our knowledge and techniques for living ever seem to bring? Why do we experience a feeling of personal growth from loving acts of helping someone? How is service to others a creative process that releases powerful energy into our lives?

A man is a true Muslim when no other Muslim has to fear anything from either his tongue or his hand.
—*Hadith of Bukhari*

Have you considered that everything productive and beneficial that you can accomplish in life is a ministry? When people hear the word "ministry," some automatically think of a church or government office. But in truth, every productive person is a minister. The helpful ways we think, feel, speak, and act are ministering, in some way, to others. For example, do we love our work? Are we dedicated to the job at hand? Do we work to "earn a living," or do we work because we love what we do? If our job is making garments to provide warmth, we are performing a ministry. If we make quality shoes that last, we are involved in a ministry. If we are an internist who saves lives, or a novelist who creates beauty, these things, too, are ministries.

The more one works and plants, the more one will harvest. The more good one can do, the more success one can achieve. The divine is infinite and within it abound infinite resources. Have you considered the possibility that the more we utilize the talents and abilities we have, additional gifts may be uncovered? How much understanding can we grasp? How much unlimited love can we express? How much evidence of divinity can we comprehend?

A visit to the ocean introduces practically an unlimited supply of seawater stretching before us. Billions and billions of gallons of water are available. However, if we want to take some of the water home with us, the amount we take depends on the size of container we provide. If we brought a gallon container, we can take a gallon of water from the great ocean. If we brought a small jar, we can take a much smaller amount of water. So it is with divine substance. The only limit is how we limit our capacity to receive. Helping ourselves by helping others is like installing a pipeline from the ocean to our homes!

The value that any experience holds for us is often the significance we place upon it in our thoughts. As we learn to appreciate the spiritual benefits available in all situations, perhaps new avenues of service may be uncovered. Those of us who contemplate our world often encounter a

If we do not lay out ourselves in the service of mankind, whom should we serve?
—*Abigail Adams*

growing sense of wonder. The perfection of the stars, the order of the cycles of nature, the astounding beauty of land and sea, and the invigorating quality of clean air can touch us deeply. In our individual ways, we can invite this sense of wonder and creativity into the things we do, how we live our life, and the ways we communicate with others. We can also encourage a beneficial sense of responsibility and a stately determination to make something worthy of the materials at hand—our light, our love, our creativity, our enthusiasm, our efforts, and our dedication to helping ourselves by helping others.

Spotlights ◆ ◆

1. How do you feel about the various ways your prayers are answered?

2. What are the two avenues in which spiritual communion with divinity occurs?

3. How may the *results* of our prayers allow us to observe the influence of divinity in our lives?

4. How does a healthy mind contribute to a healthy body?

5. How can a healthy body contribute to a healthy mind?

6. What would be a healthy way to handle an adversity in your life?

7. What do you think of the idea of taking God as your partner?

8. How does a "beautiful soul" indicate a "beautiful person"?

9. How would you explain the saying "Beauty is more than skin deep"?

10. How is happiness a matter of creativity rather than of wealth and status?

11. Do you believe you can choose to be happy at any time?

12. From your perspective, why is helping others such an important part of a happy and fruitful life?

Living the Various Spiritual Laws ◆ ◆

How resplendent the luminaries of knowledge that shine in an atom, and how vast the oceans of wisdom that surge within a drop! To a supreme degree is this true of man, who, among all created things, hath been invested with the robe of such gifts, and hath been singled out for the glory of such distinction. For in him are potentially revealed all the attributes and names of God to a degree that no other created being hath excelled or surpassed. All these names and attributes are applicable to him. Even as He hath said: "Man is My mystery, and I am his mystery."

    — Bahá'u'lláh, *The Kitáb-i-íqán*
       (The Book of Certitude)

✦ LAW I

You create your own reality. —Jane Roberts

Circumstances are
so complicated,
thought is so
deeply rooted,
and the conditions
of happiness vary
so vastly with
individuals that
a man's entire
soul-condition
(although it may
be known to
himself) cannot be
judged by another
from the external
aspect of his life.
—*James Allen*

DO YOU BELIEVE that "reality" may be something outside of yourself? We often hear reference made to the "real world out there." To be sure, there can be a world beyond our personal reality—an outer world with appearances and distinctions of its own. However, another world, an inner one, may be much more real! This is a place where our beliefs, thoughts, and feelings reside. This inner world may be less tangible and less solid than the outer world, yet it is truly where we live. Our happiness, peace of mind, and enjoyment of work, friends, and loved ones is often more dependant on this inner world than on the outer one.

Some people might say that the world within can be simply a reflection of the outer world, and that the outer world presents the true reality, whereas personal perceptions, thoughts, and feelings can be the results of outer conditions. After all, when we are unhappy, don't we often try to change the external conditions of our lives first?" Yet, it may be possible that our inner world can quite capably reflect a strength that is independent of outer circumstances.

Two people could have similar *external* circumstances and have very different *internal* experiences. Suppose, for example, two men were given the task of speaking before a large audience. Mr. Smith may enjoy speaking in public, and the experience can be a most pleasant one for him. Mr. Jones, on the other hand, may be extremely fearful of public speaking and find the experience a harrowing test of willpower. Both men share a similar reality, but their internal realities may be far removed from each other. To cite another example, two youngsters may jump into a pool of deep water. While one enjoys a rejuvenating swim, the other may be terrified of drowning. The pool of water is the same, but the experience of the two individuals may be vastly different.

I am seeking, I am striving, I am in it with all my heart.
—*Vincent van Gogh*

A dozen people could carefully study a lovely panoramic view and then draw or paint a picture of it. The results may reveal a dozen pictures with strikingly different details. Each person is observing the scene that appears before him or her with eyes that may have the same basic physical anatomical structure. However, each person expresses a unique preconditioning of consciousness. An unhappy person may see things that tend to justify unhappiness. The pessimist may see discouraging signs wherever he or she looks. The optimist usually seeks to find the good in a situation. And the honest person can discover the truth in the situation at hand and create his or her own reality.

We may have lived many years believing that

experiencing happiness and peace of mind can result from changing our outer world. But happiness is an inside job. Outer changes alone may not bring the happiness we desire.

It may help to remember that we have far more control over our inner world than over our outer world. We may have developed deeply ingrained thinking and feeling patterns or belief systems. Change may not always be easy, but it can be accomplished. Examining our beliefs and attitudes and observing our thoughts and feelings can be a place to begin. Change often occurs when we recognize false beliefs and make an effort to bring them in line with reality; when we recognize negative thoughts and choose not to listen to them;

and when we recognize negative feelings and choose to replace them with constructive plans. We have the power to create our own reality by choosing thoughts and belief systems that are positive and inspiring. So, in truth, we do create our own reality, our inner reality, the only reality in which we truly live.

We are essentially spiritual beings. Our world is essentially a spiritual world, and the underlying controlling forces may be identified as spiritual laws or universal principles. When we establish conscious unity with this spiritual essence, we begin to recognize that this is a good world. We can behold goodness in all people and we can draw goodness from them.

◆

✦ LAW 2

A task takes as long as there is time to do it. —Parkinson's Law

> Men are wise in proportion not to their experience, but in their capacity for experience.
> —George Bernard Shaw

PUT YOUR IMAGINATION to work for a moment. It is the week before school vacation. A lot is happening. It is a very busy time. Moving toward completion of what seems like endless study and writing papers in a small framework of time may bring some feelings of pressure. Yet this deadline, which may seem to threaten certain doom if not met, can have the power to save you from what is often called the worst enemy you can have when it comes to accomplishing great things and seemingly impossible projects—yourself!

> Man is not the creature of circumstances. Circumstances are the creatures of man.
> —Benjamin Disraeli

A deadline has been said "to be to a task what a corral is to a herd of wild horses." Working within a timeline surrounds untamed impressions, thoughts, and feelings with a clear boundary that can allow your ideas to formulate as an attainable goal. As a lifeline, a deadline draws you into alignment with your purpose and allows you to tame your time, talent, and resources, and apply them where they may be most useful.

It is asked, how can the laboring man find time for self-culture? I answer, that an earnest purpose finds time, or makes it. It seizes on spare moments, and turns fragments to golden account. A man who follows his calling with industry and spirit, and uses his earnings economically, will always have some portion of the day at his command. And it is astonishing how fruitful of improvement a short season becomes, when eagerly seized and faithfully used. It has often been observed that those who have the most time at their disposal profit by it the least. A single hour in the day, steadily given to the study of some interesting subject, begins unexpected accumulations of knowledge.
—William Ellery Channing

A deadline also invites you to concentrate your energies on those interests that have greater value to you. Just as a spoonful of honey can sweeten a cup of tea more readily than it would a lake, our

Make it thy business to know thyself, which is the most difficult lesson in the world.
—Miguel de Cervantes

efforts need to be concentrated in the direction of our priorities in order to be more effective. Time-management experts say the best deadlines are the ones you choose for yourself. Setting reasonable time frames to accomplish a goal often results in a more effective use of your time.

As you meet the challenge of doing the best you can with what you have, your vigorous cooperation can reward you with a sense of great vitality and feeling of accomplishment.

What would you like to achieve in your lifetime? How do you visualize making a difference in this world? Whatever large or small ambition you may have, begin today to create goals that suit your purpose, and set deadlines or target dates for those goals. Remember, deadlines can be lifelines that define your success!

All that I have accomplished, or expect to accomplish, has been and will be by that plodding, patient, persevering, process of accretion which builds the ant heap particle by particle, thought by thought, fact by fact.
—Elihu Burritt

Law 3

It is a duty to cultivate kindness. — Sefer Hachinukh *(Medieval text)*

Good works are links that form a chain of love.
—Mother Teresa

The heart benevolent and kind, the most resembles God.
—Robert Burns

THERE IS A SUFI STORY about a man who was so benevolent and humble of spirit that the angels asked God to grant him the gift of miracles. God wisely told the angels to ask the man if he *desired* to receive the gift of miracles. So, the angels visited this good man and offered him three gifts. The first was the gift of healing by hands. The second was the gift of conversion of souls. The third was the gift of virtue. After considering the offer of these gifts, the man decided to refuse them. However, the angels insisted that the man must choose one of the gifts, or they would select one for him.

"Very well," the man replied. "I request that I may do a great deal of good wherever I go without ever knowing about it."

The angels were perplexed. How could this be accomplished? They counseled among themselves and resolved upon the following plan. Every time the man's shadow fell behind him, it would have the power to cure disease, soothe pain, and comfort sorrow. So, as the man walked about in his travels, wherever his shadow fell, arid paths became green, withered plants bloomed, pale children were transformed with radiant good health, and joy uplifted the countenances of the people.

The story concludes that the man went about his daily life, diffusing kindness and noble virtue as the stars diffuse light and the flowers waft their scent. He had no awareness of the powerful path of love left in the wake of his diligence in spiritual commitment. People everywhere responded to the man's presence and respected his humility. They never spoke of the miracles. After a while, they

So many gods, so many creeds, so many paths that wind and wind, when just the art of being kind is all this sad world needs.
—Ella Wheeler Wilcox

even forgot the man's name and simply called him the "Holy Shadow."

Isn't it comforting and exciting to realize that each of us has the ability to be helpful to others in ways we may not even realize? When we look at ourselves reflectively, are our lives enriched with radiant love and enthusiasm that overflows to others? What beneficial attributes are we cultivating in the garden of the soul? Are our intellectual lives kept clean and healthy through the discipline of our thoughts? Do our thoughts, feelings, and actions flow in a constant stream from a fountainhead of unlimited love? Are we kind to every aspect of life? Thought sustains and nourishes consciousness. Is kindness a perpetual quality of our minds and hearts that immediately responds in a beneficial manner to every situation?

In lines of poetry and in common speech, the feelings of unlimited love may be likened to the warming effects of fire. These fine, inward radiant energies are active, cheering, warming, and dynamic. The practice of kindness can be a most effective way to pursue the best interests of others as well as our own. Kindness, by nature, is peaceful and gentle, but it is also very powerful. It often is a true sign of inner strength. Wherever there abides a kind and compassionate person, others will find a pleasant atmosphere.

I believe happiness comes from kindness.
—Dalai Lama

In his book *Love Is Letting Go of Fear,* Gerald Jampolsky writes, "Today there is a rapidly expanding search for a better way of going through life that is producing a new awareness and change of consciousness. It is like a spiritual flood that is about to cleanse the earth. Although there are many pathways that lead to transformation, we find that kindness, wisdom, and compassion represent positive doorways toward helping everyone to build an atmosphere of love and kindness."

Consider carefully before you say a hard word to a man, but never let a chance to say a good one go by.
—George Horace Lorimer

✦ LAW 4

Give credit and help to all who have helped you. —John Marks Templeton

PERHAPS THE END of another day draws near. We may feel relief at this awareness, especially if it was a busy day. We may feel appreciative of the accomplishments we achieved during the day. We may feel grateful for the overall activities of this day. However, being grateful means more than giving thanks or recognition for achieving something beneficial. Being grateful means recognizing and honoring the events and the people who touched our lives and contributed to this day! Many of the good or beneficial effects that come about in the world are often based on an attitude of apprecia-tion for what people have contributed toward our success. Others frequently play a helpful role in our achievements and it is important to acknowledge their contributions.

It is one thing to express gratitude for the many wonderful experiences and people in our life, but do we go one step further and express gratitude directly to the people who help us? We know how we feel and respond when someone expresses appreciation to us. Do we pass this supportive energy along to others? Are we eager to acknowledge and give credit to those who show us love

We should give
as we would
receive, cheerfully,
quickly, and without
hesitation; for there
is no grace in
a benefit that sticks
to the fingers.
—Seneca

Give credit where
credit is due.
—English proverb

What comes from
the heart, goes
to the heart.
—Samuel Taylor
Coleridge

and kindness and who contribute in a variety of ways to our progress and well-being? Is recognition and acknowledgement of the contributions made by others a golden opportunity for spiritual enhancement in our lives and in the lives of others? Can feeling gratitude and failing to express it be like wrapping a present and not giving it to someone?

A beautiful expression of acknowledging the help we receive is contained in the following story. It was the late 1800s and an important member of the British Parliament was hurrying through the rain and fog of the bleak Scottish countryside to deliver a crucial speech. He was still miles from his destination when his carriage was forced off the road, its wheels plunging axle deep in mud. Try as they might, the horse and driver could not move the carriage. The speech to be given to Parliament was so important that even the aristocratic Englishman, dressed in formal attire, got out of the carriage to assist. But it was no use. The carriage would not budge.

As things sometimes happen, a young Scottish farm boy was driving a team of horses past the distraught parliamentarian and volunteered to help pull the carriage loose. After much effort and considerable exertion, the carriage was finally pulled free. When the boy steadfastly refused to accept any money for his help or for his torn and dirty clothes, the Englishman asked the lad what he wanted to be when he grew up.

Constant kindness can accomplish much. As the sun makes ice melt, kindness causes misunderstanding, mistrust and hostility to evaporate.
—Albert Schweitzer

"A doctor, sir. I want to be a doctor," was the reply. The gentleman was so impressed with the boy and so grateful for his kindness that he said, "Well, I want to help." And, sure enough, he kept his word. Through the Englishman's generosity, the young lad was able to attend the university.

More than fifty years later while in Morocco, Winston Churchill became dangerously ill with pneumonia. His life was saved by a new wonder drug called penicillin, which had been discovered a few years earlier by a Scottish-born physician, Sir Alexander Fleming.

Fleming was the farm boy who helped the member of Parliament on that dark and rainy night in Scotland, half a century before! Who was the member of Parliament? None other than Winston Churchill's father, Randolph!

The good you do returns, so give credit and help to all those who help you.

◆ LAW 5

Enthusiasm spells the difference between mediocrity and accomplishment.
—Norman Vincent Peale

WE MAY NOT fully understand what life is, but we know a lot of things about it. Some people seem to radiate *vitally* and a kind of *aliveness* in everything they do. Could part of this vitality be a reflection of how we perceive ourselves and others and how and where we focus our strengths and abilities?

The spirit of man, from its very nature, tends to seek vital, engaging contact with divinity. The writer of *Letters of the Scattered Brotherhood* tells us, "There is within us a power that could lift the world out of its ignorance and misery if we only knew how to use it." Could this statement describe, perhaps in part, the power of enthusiasm? Scientist Louis Pasteur commented, "The Greeks have given us one of the most beautiful words of our language—the word 'enthusiasm'— a God within. The grandeur of the acts of men is measured by the inspiration from which they spring. Happy is he who bears a God within." There is something awesome about people who practice this spiritual quality; they are vibrantly alive!

Ralph Waldo Emerson wrote, "Every great and commanding moment in the annals of the world is a triumph of enthusiasm." That is a powerful statement, and it expresses truth! It is difficult to stifle the ardor or dampen the spirit of someone who really believes in what they are doing. Their excitement shows and they operate on full throttle! Enthusiasm is not a great talent granted to some people and absent in others. Some people choose to acknowledge and utilize this powerful energy, while others may not realize they are carriers of an invisible treasure.

A story is told about three brick masons who were busily at work. A man came along and paused to watch them in their activities. He asked, "What are you building?"

Without looking up from his work, the first brick mason replied, "I am just laying bricks."

The second brick mason said, "I am constructing a sturdy wall."

But the third man enthusiastically responded, "I am building a cathedral!"

From this perspective, the statement "Enthusiasm makes the difference between mediocrity and accomplishment" could be important food for thought. Does the spark of enthusiasm ignite the fire of spirit within? What are some of the results of this emergence of divinity through enthusiasm? We may wish to take a long look at the brief span of time given to us—the span we call our lives—and decide to adopt a more enthusiastic and grateful attitude for all that we are and all that we can be.

The great Greek dramatist Aeschylus once proclaimed, "When a man's willing and eager, God joins in." Authentic enthusiasm is a quality that nourishes success. It can be infectious and contagious! It spreads joy because there is nothing sad or depressing about enthusiasm. Galatians 5:22 tells us "Joy is the fruit of the spirit." Would we deny ourselves that fruit? Have you ever noticed that fear seems to subside when enthusiasm is present?

The spiritual quality of enthusiasm gives added value to everything it touches, and life is filled with opportunities. Enthusiasm is a catalyst for delight and creativity on the job. It can pump zest and added benefits into our every activity. Enthusiastic people continue to pursue and achieve regardless of their circumstances. They have the ability to get excited over the smallest things. They never seem to get bored. They love to laugh. If you give an enthusiastic person a gift, he or she may hug you appreciatively and immediately put

the gift to use. When you are in the presence on an enthusiastic person, his or her sparkling eyes seem to be open in appreciation of everything around them. And it's stimulating to be around enthusiastic people! They are refreshing! They get things accomplished!

How can the seed of enthusiasm in you be encouraged to grow? Begin to look at things around you with fresh eyes and receptivity toward enthusiasm. Whatever you are doing, approach it from the perspective that you may be having this experience for the first time. Live the experience with freshness and newness. Become an active participant in life. Decide that there will be no more standing on the sidelines watching others. Get involved. As Longfellow stated in "The Psalm of Life," "Let us then be up and doing, with a heart for any fate."

People who are enthusiastic about what they desire to achieve and who hold to their vision of the goal seem to manifest what they desire in their lives.

Enthusiasm often spells the difference between mediocrity and fruitful accomplishment.

Spotlights ✦ ✦

1. The "inner" world is the abiding place of our thoughts, feelings, and beliefs.

2. Our individual perspective defines our individual "realities."

3. Change often happens when we recognize false beliefs and make an effort to bring them in line with reality.

4. A goal without some kind of deadline may be a goal unattained.

5. Successful people finish what they begin. Consider carefully what may be involved before you take on a task. But once you start it, complete it with thoroughness, enthusiastic energy, and resolve.

6. Ask yourself: Am I doing or preparing for the things that I am best qualified to do? Do I love what I am doing?

7. What spiritual qualities would you like to cultivate in your life?

8. Is kindness a perpetual quality of your mind and heart and actions?

9. How you feel when you sincerely give honest credit to another person?

10. Do you look for ways to bless and credit others?

11. What are you doing to enhance the seed of enthusiasm within yourself and within others?

12. How would you describe enthusiasm as an "invisible treasure"?

Living the Various Spiritual Laws ✦ ✦

"What is the gist of your teaching?" said Lao Tzu.

"The gist of it," said Confucius, "is benevolence and righteousness."

"May I ask if benevolence and righteousness belong to the inborn nature of man?" asked Lao Tzu.

"Of course," said Confucius. "If the gentleman lacks benevolence, he will get nowhere; if he lacks righteousness, he cannot even stay alive. Benevolence and righteousness are truly the inborn nature of man. What else could they be?"

Lao Tzu said, "May I ask your definition of benevolence and righteousness?"

Confucius said, "To be glad and joyful in mind; to embrace universal love and be without partisanship—this is the true form of benevolence and righteousness."

Lao Tzu said, "Hmm—close—except for the last part. 'Universal love'—that's a rather nebulous ideal, isn't it? And to be without partisanship is already a kind of partisanship. Do you want to keep the world from losing its simplicity? Heaven and earth hold fast to their constant ways, the sun and moon to their brightness, the stars and planets to their ranks, the birds and beasts to their flocks, the trees and shrubs to their strands. You have only to go along with virtue in your actions, to follow the Way in your journey, and already you will be there. Why these flags of benevolence and righteousness so bravely upraised as though you were beating a drum and searching for a lost child? Ah, you will bring confusion to the nature of man."

—Taoism, *Chuang Tzu*

Week
Twenty-Seven

◆ LAW 1

You can build your own heaven or hell on earth. —John Marks Templeton

Sometimes life's
shadows are caused
by our standing in
our own sunshine.
—Ralph Waldo
Emerson

Somewhere down
the path of human
experience we will
all awake to the
realization that we
ourselves are
heaven or hell.
—Ernest Holmes

PEOPLE SOMETIMES comment that following a spiritual pathway is simple, but not necessarily easy. One difficult part may be in learning to overcome a tendency toward inertia with respect to our daily spiritual learning. Ernest Holmes stated, "It is far easier to teach the Truth than it is to practice it." And spirituality, like most worthwhile processes, does require commitment and practice. But the benefits are most desirable! We have an opportunity, through personal choice, to build our own heaven or hell on earth.

Most of the world's spiritual traditions have advocated various inner-directed ways of life. God is described in the Qur'an as "nearer than the jugular vein," knowing all a person's thoughts and desires, and abiding within the human heart. The Sufis interpret the parable of the lamp as expressing the presence of God in the human heart as illuminating the lamp of the body. This realization of divinity as everywhere seems beneficially supportive of the idea of working toward a heaven on earth. Let's consider some possible ways for sustaining regular spiritual growth and activities as a foundation toward creating our personal heaven on earth.

Prayer, of course, is perhaps a most fundamental spiritual practice. The habit of taking some time daily, in a quiet place and in communion with one's Creator, can bring direction to our lives. However, what we think, say, and do when we are not praying also can help the effectiveness of our prayers. Do we live gratefully and joyously between our prayers, or do we sometimes think or speak in an unconscious manner from habitual patterns? The material world can be seductive, and if we do not maintain a conscious awareness of immersion in spirit, we may fail to monitor the effectiveness of our thoughts, feelings, words, and actions between our prayers. If we truly desire a life of "heaven on earth" as our goal, then would choosing to live *each moment* in the spiritual context of ever-present divinity move us more quickly toward this goal?

Our lives are shaped not so much by
our experience as by our expectations.
—George Bernard Shaw

What part does self-awakening to the realization that we are free to reconstruct our attitudes contribute toward creating a heaven on earth experience? At times, regardless of our best intentions and disciplines, the experience of heaven may seem to elude us and the experience of hell may seem to pursue us. This often happens when we begin to compare what we have with others, or compare where we are in consciousness with others, and feel either superior or inferior to them. If we judge only the outer appearances of anything, we can create a private hell that permeates the various areas of our life. Here is where a practice of gratitude and thanksgiving helps us improve.

It is essential to awaken and sustain a consciousness of thanksgiving. Gratitude represents a key to many of the highest, noblest, and most life-enhancing sacred emotions. A grateful heart grows increasingly humble and can become fearless through its recognition of universal divine presence. We begin to develop the sacred ecstasy of service as helpers in infinite creativity. When we begin the personal awareness and discovery of our spiritual paths, our whole lives change. We begin to discover with wonder and delight who we are and why we are here.

Is choosing a way of life of giving, thanksgiving, and helping others an effective pathway toward creating more heaven on earth?

In his book *Promise Ahead: A Vision of Hope and Action for Humanity's Future*, Duane Elgin described some of the priorities that he found characterized a simpler way of living. "Those choosing the simple life tend to place a high priority on the quality and integrity of their relationships with every aspect of life—with themselves, other people, other creatures, the Earth, and the universe."

Each of us is born with the freedom to choose the thoughts that can build our lives. We may choose the path we desire to walk and we may choose the "luggage" we wish to carry along the way. When we get a glimpse of heaven on earth, it is the natural desire to help others grow also. Spiritual awakening takes patience, hard work, and the grace of God. Learning to know what we admire and then to honestly take steps in that direction can be a heavenly achievement.

❖ Law 2

Science without religion is lame; religion without science is blind. —Albert Einstein

On June 1, 1940, an eminent group of seventy-nine scientists, philosophers, and theologians met to "rally intellectual and spiritual forces" to discuss ways to further integrate science, philosophy, and religion in relation to traditional ethical values and the democratic way of life. The aim of the conference was to bring together representatives of various disciplines to meet on a common ground and obtain first-hand knowledge of one another's ideas regarding the totality of the human experience. Their hope was to promote respect and understanding between the three disciplines involved. Philosophy, science, and religion recognize a bond of unity.

Albert Einstein's paper, *Science and Religion*, ensued as part of the work of the above-mentioned conference. His writing seemed to indicate a search for greater understanding and for the words to describe the possible unity of science and religion. To Einstein, science represented "the century-old endeavor to bring together by means of

The health of a culture, like the health of the body, consists in the harmonious functioning of its parts. Science, philosophy, and religion are certainly major parts of . . . culture.
—Mortimer J. Adler

systematic thought the perceptible phenomenon of this world into as thoroughgoing an association as possible." However, when he sought to describe religion, he stated, "I cannot think of the answer so easily. And even after finding an answer which may satisfy me at this particular moment, I still remain convinced that I can never, under any circumstances, bring together, even to a slight extent, all those who have given this question serious consideration." His words and feelings could be applicable for many of us today.

Religion in some form has been part of the human experience from the very beginning. We are also heavily indebted to scientific ways of thinking and in many respects rely upon the technology that science has so richly provided. George Field and Eric Chaisson wrote in their preface to *The Invisible Universe*: "We are in a period of grand technological progress, a time of learning, a time of groping in the darkness—more a time of exploration than of mature science." Questions bring more questions and the mystery deepens! Can empirical science methods be thought of as methods to reveal to us further aspects of God? Or should the word "god" have a more limited meaning than the word "reality"?

In his paper, Einstein also wrote:

Science can only ascertain what is, but not what should be, and outside of its domain value judgments of all kinds remain necessary. Religion, on the other hand, deals only with evaluations of human thought and action; it cannot justifiably speak of facts and relationships between facts. . . . Now, even though the realms of religion and science in themselves are clearly marked off from each other, nevertheless there exist between the two, strong reciprocal relationships and dependencies . . . The situation may be expressed by an image: science without religion is lame, religion without science is blind.

So, the search goes on. Is God the only reality? What are the changing faces of reality? We live in a world of progress, and nowhere does progress seem more pronounced than in the sciences. For example, a textbook not revised for five years is practically useless in most fields, and a laboratory with ten-year-old equipment is mainly a museum! The last few decades of the twentieth century brought accelerating changes to our understanding of the physical reality we approach through science. So, too, has a major upheaval been developing in our understanding of the reality of God that religion provides and theology interprets? If science has multiplied human perceptions over one-hundred-fold in a single century, can perceptions multiply even more rapidly in the next century?

Can various researches in statistics on evidences help human perceptions accelerate many aspects of God? The benefits for individuals and society could be more beneficial than the discoveries in electronics or in medicine.

In *God for the 21st Century*, Joel Primack writes: "In 1992, when astronomer George Smoot announced the discovery of ripples in the heat radiation still arriving from the Big Bang, he said it was 'like seeing the face of God.' A somewhat more modest astrophysicist, whose theory had correctly predicted the discovery, was quoted as calling the ripples 'the handwriting of God.' Can such metaphors help us gain vastly larger concepts of divinity?"

✦ LAW 3

The unknown before us may be a million times greater than we know.
—John Marks Templeton

IN PREVIOUS ESSAYS, we have talked about the infinite Creator as the divinity that seeks to be revealed in our universe through intricate design and purpose. We look at the love and continuity revealed in human freedom and natural law, chance and necessity working together to create a world of infinite variety and beauty, and form set free to dance! We have been struck with the remarkable contrast between ourselves—minute specks in one tiny star system in one of the smaller galaxies of the known universe—and the God who brought all of this into being.

My current spiritual views have largely resulted from a collision in my life between science and religion.
—Larry Dossey

With a new sense of humility, the way is now open to examine scientifically the spiritual nature of human beings. And, *the unknown before us may be a million times greater than what we now know*! So, where do we go from here? Perhaps the future will see research foundations and religious institutions devoting huge resources to spiritual research just as today we provide enormous amounts of funding into physical health. There would be great rewards in terms of increased human peace, harmony, happiness, creativity, and productivity. Evidence accumulates that mankind's spiritual nature is the fundamental aspect of our personhood. Another goal could be to research and learn about ultimate reality by every avenue open to us. Surely, the best and most profound studies in all of history will come when performed humbly with the expectation of more fully comprehending the Creator God and his purposes for his creatures.

For many of us, our spiritual pilgrimage may not have been punctuated by events of high drama. However, the forthcoming decades may offer astounding adventures into the unknown. If discoveries keep pointing our search toward multiplying mysteries, will we begin to comprehend more about creativity? Already some thinkers are pondering the concept that every discovery, in any science, helps humans to enlarge their definition of the word "God." For example, can humans learn something about God from X-ray astronomy, by subatomic physics, or by quantum nonlocality? If the expensive research for extraterrestrial intelligence, SETI, ever finds something, will we enlarge our present theology? Clarifying the meaning of the world's "spiritual information" may be as difficult now as the difficulty in the year 1800 in foreseeing the expansion of medical information or electromagnetic knowledge. Is it self-centered to believe that we stand at the end rather than near the beginning of God's creative process?

Meister Eckhart wrote: "No work is ever so properly begun or so well done, no man is ever so free and so certain in his actions, that he can afford to let his mind relax or go to sleep. But he ought with his twin powers, intellect and will, to be forever hoisting himself up and seizing, at the summit, his very best therein and . . . always making first-rate progress."

And I said to the man who stood at the gate of the year: "Give me a light that I may tread safely into the unknown." And he replied: "Go out into the darkness and put your hand into the hand of God. That shall be to you better than light and safer than a known way."
—Minnie Louise Haskins

We, too, must keep our minds alert and awake and lift ourselves up. The open-minded approach is to look for God in a multitude of ways—in the kind of empirical questioning pursued by natural scientists and by those theologians who recognize that some of tomorrow's spiritual heroes may be among those considered today as heretics! *The Theology of Humility* encourages thinking that is open and receptive to new information, and allows conclusions that are qualified with the tentative word "maybe." The unknown before us may be open to the scientific exploration of spiritual subjects such as love, prayer, purpose, and thanksgiving. This new exploration may reveal that there are spiritual laws, universal principles, possibly more infinite and eternal than those natural laws that operate in the tangible and visible realms.

◆ LAW 4

Worry achieves nothing and wastes valuable time. —John Marks Templeton

A HUSBAND AND WIFE were having a serious discussion about a domestic situation. The husband had spent long hours worrying about how they would meet the month's financial responsibilities. The wife, having listened to the husband's discouraging remarks for several hours, asked him to come and sit with her at the kitchen table.

She laid the bills for the month's expenses on the table and picked up a pencil and piece of paper. She looked at her husband and said, "Now, Jim, give me one good reason how worrying is going to help pay these bills and I'll sit here and worry with you for the rest of the day! Otherwise, let's discuss possible ways we can meet these responsibilities."

The woman was right, of course. Worrying seldom accomplishes positive results. Instead, it can become a familiar behavior that might trick us into believing we are taking active steps to resolve a problem. Worrying can also waste valuable time that could be used for finding ways to remedy a challenging situation creatively.

If we locate the word "worry" in the dictionary, we find its meaning described as to "strangle or choke, to annoy or bother." Think about this for a moment. When we worry, we can strangle the flow of creative ideas that could help us solve the prob-

lem. We can literally choke or block the life current and keep it from flowing freely through us. Worry can certainly cause anxiety, and anxiety is defined as "worry or uneasiness about what may happen." With this description and understanding of worry and its partner, anxiety, it can be easy to determine that worrying is not a desirable way to meet life.

What could be a foundational *cause* of worry? Could it be that we need to lift our vision, our sight? The great Italian painter, sculptor, architect, and poet, Michelangelo, said: "The greatest danger for most of us is not that our aim is too high and we miss it, but that it is too low and we reach it!" When we get caught up in worry, are we possibly concentrating on outer appearances and forgetting to express thanksgiving for blessings and abilities? What happens when we change our focus? Could the size, the majesty, and the spirit that seem to jump right out of Michelangelo's wonderful sculpture *David* be the artist's way of saying to each of us to aim higher?

And speaking of aiming high, consider the ceiling of the Sistine Chapel! Michelangelo worked every day for four years, painting the ceiling by lying on his back! And no word is written that the great artist worried about getting the job done!

If we place our attention on the present moment and the situation at hand, paying bills, for example, we realize that an opportunity for choice is before us. We can decide to release ourselves from worry and choose more productive life options, more creative and inspiring attitudes, and more fruitful states of mind and healthier beliefs.

We may look at options for increasing our income to meet present responsibilities. If necessary, a timely and methodical system of payment can be arranged. Better yet, we can consider ways to eliminate creating unnecessary bills. Worry can serve us like a short curriculum in school. Learn the lesson the problem brings, and graduate!

Remember that our minds are capable of making choices that are more powerful than any present craving! Making beneficial choices can help eliminate self-destructive behaviors. And worry is definitely a self-destructive behavior! Again, it achieves nothing and wastes valuable time and energy!

✦ LAW 5

Failure is an event, not a person. —William D. Brown

AT SOME POINT in our lives, we may have experienced the feeling that we failed in some way. But upon reviewing a situation, we might recognize that, at the time, we gave our best. In retrospect, we may decide that more effort could have been extended, or the situation may have been approached differently. These thoughts can be simply nebulous assertions, or they can be opportunities to review a situation objectively and to learn from the experience. Failure is an event, not a person.

Although we strive to do our best, it is important to remember that the outcome of a particular situation may not always be in our control. Human interactions are often built upon agreements. People may agree on times of meeting, rules of procedure, and appropriate behaviors for many situations. Human beings are not error free. We may forget things, misplace our keys, run over a toy left in the driveway, or back into a telephone pole. How we respond, however, *is* in our control.

The Chinese teacher and philosopher Confucius once said, "Isn't it a great pleasure to learn and

relearn again?" From this statement, it would seem that we have a great deal to learn from life, from the experiences of life, and from our own nature. Learning is a continual process. Wide-open minds and perseverance can be fruitful keys to learning about various processes of the natural world and also to learning about our personal world.

If we are involved in accomplishing a task that can be beneficial, would we let a small disruption, a seeming failure, deter us? This so-called failure could simply be a learning event along the way toward greater success. Thomas Edison said he failed a hundred times before inventing the electric light.

The work needed for accomplishment may not always be immediately visible. For example, the hours of preparation extended to accomplish a job may not be visibly evident on the face of a worker. A seeming failure should not reduce the perseverance and resourcefulness of a committed mind and a dedicated heart toward accomplishing a desired goal! Could you imagine a successful person ever insisting that a thing is impossible to accomplish because he hasn't yet accomplished it? Would a successful person spend valuable time worrying about things that cannot be changed or corrected? Wouldn't he or she choose to work on the most promising opportunities toward accomplishing the desired goal? Wouldn't the successful person put his attention on his life and how to improve it?

Another important thing to remember is "The greatness is not in me; I am in the greatness." We are not the *source* of the powerful divine ideas that call us to accomplishment. We can, however, be the pipelines through which wondrous virtues may be poured upon humanity. As we move throughout the day, our senses are often bombarded with a

There are admirable potentialities in every human being.
—André Gide

variety of stimuli. The successful person often asks, "With what consciousness and purpose do I utilize the ideas and events in my world?"

Keep in mind that there is no such thing as failure; there are simply tasks that have not yet been accomplished! If a man swings a golf club with the intent to hit a golf ball two hundred yards down the fairway and the ball dribbles off to the left, has he failed? No, he simply produced a result, experienced an event. So, what happens? The man can berate himself and call himself a failure, or he can place the golf ball back on the tee and proceed from that point. If we want our visions to become reality, we must be willing to do whatever it takes to accomplish our goals. This often requires commitment, enthusiasm, resourcefulness, and perseverance. What we make of our lives is ultimately up to us. Ignite the child-like sense of wonder and remember the thrill of discovering new worlds! This spark often shows up as bigger and bolder steps toward living our dreams.

◆

Spotlights ◆ ◆

1. Your spiritual life, like anything worthwhile, requires commitment and practice.

2. We have an opportunity, through personal choice and discipline, to build our own heaven or hell on earth.

3. Can empirical science methods be considered as methods to reveal to us further aspects of God?

4. Should the word "god" have a more limited meaning than the word "reality"?

5. Does every discovery in any science help humans to enlarge their definition of the word "god"?

6. How do *you* perceive science and religion working together?

7. In truth, could a legitimate conflict actually exist between religion and science?

8. The unknown before us may be a million times greater than what we presently know.

9. Worry may cause anxiety and strangle the flow of creative ideas.

10. What are some optional attitudes to oust worry?

11. Failure is an event, not a person!

12. There is no such thing as failure; there are simply tasks that have not yet been accomplished!

Living the Various Spiritual Laws ✦ ✦

PLOWING

Early one morning, while on his alms round, the Buddha approached the area being plowed in springtime when Bharadvaja, the Brahmin, was distributing food to his workers. When Bharadvaja saw the Buddha coming for alms he said, "I, O monk, plow and sow, and having plowed and sown, then I eat. Do you likewise plow and sow and, having plowed and sown, eat?"

The Buddha replied, "I, also, Brahmin, plow and sow and, having plowed and sown, eat."

Then Bharadvaja said, "You claim yourself to be a plowman? I see no plow! Tell me, O plowman, what kind of plowing it is you do?"

The Buddha replied, "Trust is the seed and composure the rain. Clarity is my plow and yoke, conscience is my guide-pole, and my mind is the harness. Wakefulness is my plow-blade and my goad. Well-guarded in action and in speech, and moderate in food, I use truth to weed and cultivate release. True effort is my oxen, drawing the plow steadily toward Nirvana, freedom without regret. This is how I plow; it bears the deathless as its fruit. Whoever plows in this way will become free of all sorrow and distress."

Then Bharadvaja exclaimed, "Let the Venerable monk eat! You are indeed a plowman and your plowing bears the fruit of freedom."

—adapted from *Samyutta Nikaya*

Week Twenty-Eight

✦ LAW 1

Laugh, and the world laughs with you; weep and you weep alone. —Ella Wheeler Wilcox

All people smile in the same language.
—Anonymous

The world of laughter has always seemed to me the most civilized music in the universe.
—Peter Ustinov

In laughter there is always a kind of joyousness that is incompatible with contempt or indignation.
—Voltaire

Laugh and be well.
—Matthew Green

IN THE OFTEN-QUOTED poem "Solitude," Ella Wheeler Wilcox seems to be telling us that whatever attitude we choose to adopt is precisely the energy we will attract into our lives. The line "Laugh, and the world laughs with you; weep, and you weep alone" could be reminding us that when we are weepy and sad, we are most likely to be alone, and when we fill our hearts with joy and laughter, we attract lots of company!

An old adage tells us "a smile breeds a smile" Like a bonfire on a crisp autumn evening, a smile has a way of sparking a light that may contagiously ignite into happiness. People with excessively serious minds and heavy hearts may need to exercise caution around smiles and laughter. These delightful energies may consume the sad and somber in their gentle flames, leaving in the glowing embers a sense of joy, enthusiasm, and purpose.

Can you see the importance in maintaining a positive attitude and state of mind? Studies have also shown that it takes far fewer facial muscles to create a smile than it does to make a frown. The choice of attempting to smile during a difficult time may be hard to do, yet a smile can help us "lighten up" and perhaps make important adjustments to our attitudes.

Why do most people prefer to be around others whose positive attitude is displayed through their smile? Could one reason be that a smile is often the expression of a grateful person? Or that a smile can display our willingness to relax and enjoy the moment, to be fully present in the "now," regardless of possible stressful circumstances? A smile can also let others know that we are open and receptive to their thoughts and ideas. A smile can be a warm invitation for others to enter our world and to get to know us better. A smile emphasizes a happy heart that perceives each discovery as a blessing. And a happy heart has the endurance to meet life's situations graciously and productively.

Joy is the most infallible sign of the awareness of the presence of God.
—Teilhard de Chardin

Humor can often show us the ambiguity of situations, sometimes revealing a different and startling awareness. In *The Joyful Christ*, Cal Samra tells the story of Father Tom Walsh, a psychotherapist who taught a popular course called "Humor, Hilarity, Healing, and Happy Hypothalami" at the Franciscan Renewal Center in the Phoenix, Arizona, area. Walsh, who has counseled many depressed persons, observes: "You cannot be depressed, or anxious, or angry when you're laughing. It can't be done." And Walt Disney, the great film producer, is said to have refused to release a film until it expressed a certain kind of lasting quality. After six months of work on the film, *Pinocchio,* Disney suddenly suspended production because he felt the film didn't have "heart." He said: "I don't think anything without heart is good or will last. To me, humor involves both laughter and tears."

Certainly, times may arise in life when our eyes fill with tears and we might feel alone. However, being on our own does not mean being deserted! It does not mean we are without assistance. It does not mean we are truly totally alone. There can be times when being alone, on our own, may be considered to be important to our growth and necessary for our maturity. Alone times, such as times

of prayer, meditation, and contemplation, can also be essential to the expression of greater mental clarity, to developing our spiritual strengths. Loneliness and choosing time to be alone are two different energies. We are ever held within the creative power of the universe. We abide infinitely within the embrace of unlimited love. Having the awareness that we are never totally alone could make the difference between feeling devastated by circumstances, or being filled with strength and confidence in our ability to persevere. This awareness can also make the difference between tears and laughter.

✦ LAW 2

If nothing is ventured, nothing is gained. —Sir John Heywood

THE SPIRIT of adventure is a deeply human trait and one that has helped us develop in many areas over thousands of years of recorded history. It is the potential each of us has to leave the world a better place than we found it. Many of the world's great achievers realize that *a major purpose of life is living a life of purpose.* A vision held clearly in mind and the courage to venture forth pave the way for many a success. If nothing is ventured, nothing is gained. When we choose to leave what may seem to be safe and familiar territory and voyage into the uncharted waters with courage and creativity, we accept an opportunity to become adventurers who dare to go forward into the unknown—pioneers! We choose to become people whose contributions can make a real difference!

George Matthew Adams, author and advertising executive, once said: "We can accomplish almost anything within our ability if we but think that we can. Every great achievement in this world was first carefully thought out. . . . Think—but to a

purpose. Think constructively. Think as you read. Think as you listen. Think as you travel and your eyes reveal new situations. Think as you work daily at your desk, or in the field, or while strolling. Think to raise and improve your place in life. There can be no advancement or success without serious thought."

More than any other single lesson, my experiences have conspired to teach me the value of determined, confident effort.
—Rich DeVoss

One of the great ironies of life is the fact that many people who shoot low are often great shots. But the most powerful forces in the world assist those who dare to aim high and continue working, day after day, until they hit their targets. These people have the determination and will to persevere, regardless of any seeming obstacles. Can we

And so each venture is a new beginning.
—T. S. Eliot

The vitality of thought is in adventure. Ideas won't keep. Something must be done about them.
—Alfred North Whitehead

ever know what we might accomplish until we try? Confidence and the will to succeed are two key ingredients for any endeavor in life. Optimism is another powerful force than can help shape our outlook toward any venture.

In a manner of speaking, all adventure or concerted effort could be considered a voyage into the unknown. If we know precisely where we are going and have complete directions on how to arrive at our destination, then we are most likely not on an adventure! Trust yourself and trust the wisdom that created you! Cultivate a harmony between mind and heart. To the brave of heart and the inquisitive of mind, the venture into an undiscovered and expanded life journey can offer an infinite variety of possibilities and opportunities. From unfolding experiences, we can learn much of significance and benefit. We can experience the excitement of learning and stimulation from the new and the unexpected.

He conquers who endures.
—Italian proverb

Perseverance brings success.
—Dutch proverb

A strong urge to learn is an awesome incentive. Would it be far better to take actions and produce results that we can grow from, rather than to ignore the spirit of discovery and live in mediocrity? *If nothing is ventured, nothing is gained!*

One of the greatest powers in heaven and on earth is pure, unlimited love. Through unlimited love, we can immerse ourselves in the divine source, that unseen intelligence in all things. Is this

the real infinite potential supporting all of creation? And creativity? Is the practice of unlimited love a prerequisite of the manifesting process? What happens when we radiate unlimited love to our family, friends, work associates, community, and every situation around us? From a seemingly bleak, dormant winter can arise the unseen promise of new life, great goodness, and beneficial outcomes. However, "nothing ventured, nothing gained."

Any life truly lived is a risky business, and if one puts up too many fences against the risks, one ends by shutting out life itself.
—Kenneth S. Davis

Today's frontiers may no longer be the uncharted earthly lands that challenged our ancestors, yet the territories of the human mind and heart and soul can be even more awesome in their mystery. The exploration of the power of love may be one of the next great challenges. Priest-scientist Pierre Teilhard de Chardin wrote, "[W]hen we have learned how to harness the energies of love for mankind, we will have discovered fire for the second time in history."

◆ Law 3

Honesty is the first chapter in the book of wisdom —Thomas Jefferson

One should utter the truth.
—The Dhammapada

Thomas Jefferson, former president of the United States, once wrote in a letter to one of his contemporaries: "He who permits himself to tell a lie once, finds it much easier to do it a second and third time, 'til at length it becomes habitual. He tells lies without attending to it and truths without

the world's believing him. This falsehood of the tongue leads to that of the heart, and in time depraves all its good dispositions."

Jefferson was a man who tried to be as farsighted as possible so that a nation of honest men and women would endure. His statement, "Honesty is the first chapter in the book of wisdom," resounds as a great and reliable truth for many people everywhere, in every period of the world's history. A person's commitment to honor truth within and truth without may not always be an easy undertaking to uphold, but could success endure if our efforts were not directed along the lines of honesty and integrity?

Perhaps an important step in the practice of personal honesty is to know ourselves. What does this statement mean? "Know thyself" is an inscription of the early Delphic oracle of ancient Greece. It means to search deeply within our thoughts and feelings and then to enlarge the beneficial traits and discard the harmful ones. Do we look at situations with careful overall observation and analysis and ask if they align with reason and spiritual principles? Will the structure benefit one and all? And is the idea something we desire to live by? Do we follow our own consciences?

> I am honest with those who are honest, and I am also honest with those who are dishonest. Thus honesty is attained.
> —Tao Te Ching

A woman discovered some interesting truths about herself while refinishing an antique chair. Of course, the first step in restoring an old piece of furniture is to strip away the years of grime and the various layers of paint that are piled one on top of the other, down to the original wood. One reason for this stripping process is to get rid of all the junk that accumulated through the years and to determine if the piece of furniture is worth the time necessary to refinish it.

We could use this "stripping" idea as an analogy to better know ourselves. Perhaps every now and then we need to take a closer look at the illusions we may have built up about ourselves, our friends and associates, society, our world, and life in general. Are we carrying around unnecessary excess baggage? Are we living slightly off-center rather than having our feet firmly planted on a strong foundation of principle and integrity?

> Nothing in this world purifies like spiritual wisdom. It is the perfection achieved in time through the path of yoga, the path which leads to the Self within.
> —Bhagavad Gita

Over 2,500 years ago, Lao Tzu wrote: "He who knows others is wise; he who knows himself is enlightened." People everywhere share some of the basic human drives: the need for love, freedom, and respect, and the desire for their lives to have meaning. Desire is a great force-field of energy that can take us far beyond our personal selves. When we are courageous enough to search our own hearts, we may find unrealized reservoirs of spiritual resources, and a greater understanding toward human behavior can be revealed.

Be honest. Be true. Become aware of what is in you. Announce it! Give birth to it in full expression! Love all parts of yourself in this process. Remember that your authentic self is a holy creation. Acknowledge the goodness within you, because it is a foundation for magnificent expression. Claim the aspects of your being that align with the character you desire and release everything else. Our real life journeys are interior; they consist of deepening, growing in wisdom, and perhaps surrendering to the creative action of unlimited love and universal grace.

The world needs our love, energy, and creativity delivered with honesty and integrity. There is a part of us that can be larger than any smallness, stronger than any weakness, wiser than we may think, and braver than any fear. Life is a sacred adventure. Cultivate it!

> Only when we take full responsibility for our actions can we shed the burdens of our mistakes and go forward.
> —Rich DeVoss

> Do not veil the truth with falsehood, nor conceal the truth knowingly.
> —Qur'an

> It is always proper to speak the truth.
> —Mahabharata, Shanti Parva

✦ Law 4

When you judge others, you do not define them; you define yourself. —Wayne Dyer

IN *101 Ways to Transform Your Life,* Wayne Dyer wrote: "Keep in mind that you do not define anyone with your judgment; you only define yourself as someone who needs to judge. Make a daily effort to look upon others without condemnation. Every judgment takes you away from your goal of peace."

Whatever judgment you may make of another person says nothing at all about that person, but the judgment can speak volumes about you. Circumstances may sometimes unfold in such a manner that we may think another person or a particular situation may have prevented us from achieving a goal. Would it be more meaningful and accurate to analyze our own preparation and effort and possibly admit that we could have done better? Such insight can be considerably beneficial.

> My friend, judge not me, Thou seest I judge
> not thee. Betwixt the stirrup and the ground,
> Mercy I asked, and mercy found.
> —*William Camden*

The inclination to judge others can serve as an inhibitor to our personal growth. So, what can we do when we find our thoughts and behaviors leaning toward judgmental terms? Firstly, we can understand that there is no one to blame, not even ourselves. Instead, we can discern that this present situation is an indication of where our concepts may be at the moment. What may be bothering us about someone else might be something we need to look at within our own being. What might we learn if we took a gentle and loving inward look?

Are we willing to take the opportunity to welcome any obstacle—such as judgmental behavior—as an opportunity for growth? Can we set aside any judgment we may be feeling and observe the emotions behind the feelings? Are we upset? If so, what is causing the upset? Are we feeling left out? Then, what can we do to be helpful? Are we feeling misunderstood? How can we better communicate to others? Are we feeling a sense of separateness? How about considering the idea of unity, that we are one in spirit with others? When we develop a sense of appreciation for all of life, we no longer identify with differences. We recognize that differences are only in form.

Basically, we *can* eliminate blame and judgment from our lives. How? By first realizing that blame or judgment do not alter anyone or anything in the universe! When we judge another, we do not define that person; instead, we define ourselves. Judging is one way of describing *our* likes and dislikes! When we can recognize this fact, we can then begin to replace blame and judgment with honoring other people. We may not agree with their expressions or actions; that is our discernment. Discernment means to "make out clearly, to perceive or recognize the difference." Discernment can help us comprehend where another person is on his or her path of growth and eliminate any need to be upset because he or she may come from a different place. Discernment perceives; judgment criticizes.

> You must look into people, as well as at them.
> —*Lord Chesterfield*

Remember the four-minute mile? People had been trying to achieve it since the days of the ancient Greeks. Folklore offers many tales of efforts extended, but nothing worked. People looked for reasons why this feat could not be accomplished. Someone said it could not be done because the human physiology was wrong. Humans didn't have the accommodating bone structure. Wind resistance was blamed. Inadequate lungpower was blamed.

Then one man, one single human being, proved all those who judged and blamed wrong! Roger Bannister broke the four-minute mile! The following year, thirty-seven other runners broke the four-minute mile. What happened the year after that? Three hundred runners broke the four-minute mile. What changed? There were no breakthroughs in training. Human bone structure didn't suddenly improve. However, human attitudes did!

When we use the technique of observing ourselves, we can see that our judgments often come from false ideas we may have. They may be ego-oriented or they may result from fear. Have you ever considered that these petty behaviors could be divine opportunities, providing you with encouragement to choose a different activity? A single act of forgiveness and letting go could open a new doorway of expression!

✦ Law 5

A soul without a high aim is like a ship without a rudder. —Thomas Carlyle

THIS LINE from Thomas Carlyle, "A soul without a high aim is like a ship without a rudder," is an example of practical wisdom, filled with simple but informative insight. A ship with properly trimmed sails can travel in any direction in relation to the wind except directly into it. While the set of the sails determines the most efficient use of the available wind, the rudder enables the ship to travel in a specific heading. Without a guiding rudder, the ship can do little more than be blown aimlessly downwind.

Never rest contented with any circle of ideas, but always be certain that a wider one is still possible.
—Richard Jeffries

What is true of the wind-powered boat may also reflect a truth about people. Some people seem more content to be blown about by the winds of chance than to exert the effort to take charge of their lives. However, being creatively alive involves overcoming inertia and becoming actively engaged in life. After all, isn't inactivity most often a choice? We can meander through life, or we can become inspired by some beneficial purpose that leads us into a new and wonderful field of exploration. We can achieve a heightened level of awareness, liberate ourselves from limitations, and direct our energies toward unlimited possibilities. Extraordinary things can begin to happen for us, particularly in our thinking processes.

Take the story of Ben, for example. Ben was rendered an invalid in World War II. He was confined to bed, but decided he wasn't going to stay there for the rest of his life. He was not into feeling sorry for himself. He had an idea and decided to follow through with it. Ben began his own newspaper-clipping service. He subscribed to twenty newspapers, cut items out of them, and sent the items to the people, companies, etc., mentioned in the stories. His mailing included a request for a small payment if the people wished to keep the clippings. Next, he obtained a group of regular clients for his clipping service; before long, he was conducting a large enterprise. This was accomplished from his bed! Ben became enormously successful by taking a creative approach to overcoming adversity and making his own living. He developed a high aim—went for it—and achieved his goal through an imaginative approach!

What is a determining factor between a life of tough effort and minimum satisfaction and a life of fulfilling joy and success? Often people engage in aimless, undisciplined thinking and nonproductive activity rather than steering themselves in a charted direction. Like rudderless ships, they are blown on the winds of circumstance, wasting precious time and energy, failing to build knowledge and expertise.

On the other hand, high aims and clear purpose can act as rudders, steering the unlimited and unique potential of our minds toward beneficial productivity. If we choose to navigate the course of our lives with care, we can move in unlimited, positive directions. Interesting possibilities may be explored in the quest toward a specific goal, providing valuable knowledge and experience. Then, when we find opportunities in line with our talents and goals, we are prepared to seize the moments of opportunity.

Many of us can identify those times when we feel most "on purpose." We may experience a feeling of connection to the divine when our focus is

on a project that includes service to others. Is this not part of our soul's purpose? These precious moments, often referred to as peak experiences, occur at a level that may be termed "inspirational." Our faculties and talents become alive and we harmonize into a centering in creativity. During these occasions, we often break the bond of old, conditioned ways of thinking and we "seize the moment," allowing it to propel us forward.

Spotlights ◆ ◆

1. A smile has a way of sparking a light that may joyously ignite into happiness.

2. How would you describe the importance of maintaining a positive attitude?

3. A happy heart holds the endurance to meet life's situations graciously and productively.

4. The courage to venture forth in life can pave the way for many a success.

5. Let us ever choose to make the most of wherever we may be.

6. A strong urge to learn is an awesome incentive!

7. Develop the practice of being honest with yourself at all times.

8. What are some steps you can take to better know yourself?

9. The world needs our love, energy, and creativity delivered with honesty and integrity.

10. Make a daily effort to look upon others without judgment.

11. How would *you* describe the difference between "judgment" and "discernment"?

12. Why do you feel it is important to set a direction for your life?

13. How do high aims and clear purpose contribute to a fruitful life?

Living the Various Spiritual Laws ◆ ◆

Since consciousness perceived the unit
of objects as divided, the paths are different. —Patanjali, *Yoga Sutras*

ENLIGHTENMENT

What is the source of different paths? The shattering of consciousness into the illusion of many. It is the consciousness of the knower that determines the experiences of life. If one is straight and clear inside, the path is straight and clear. This is not dependent on the external world, it is entirely dependent on the internal. In the Waking State, it is common to feel that life is happening *to* us, that we are the victims of our environments, of our families, or of a harsh and judgmental God.

Contrast this with any of the stages of enlightenment: we *know* we are the Source of our light. Rather, we know that the Source of our Good is the omnipresent Ascendant Consciousness which we live continually; we also recognize that all that returns to us that is not desirable is the result of our past, unenlightened action. Who is there to blame? No one, for all is our own creation, none others.

The paths we follow through life may seem divided, but the Reality underlying all of them is the same. All objects, all of everything, everywhere, always, have at their root the One Unchanging. Only if we perceive separation in the Primal Unity will we necessarily have to follow separate paths to arrive at our goal.

◆

Week
Twenty-Nine

✦ LAW 1

Joy provides assurance; envy brings loneliness. —John Marks Templeton

GEORGE MATTHEW ADAMS wrote: "It is the spirit of a person that hangs above him like a star in the sky. People identify him at once, and join with him until there is formed a paradise of men and women, thus inspired. No matter where you find this spirit working, whether in a person or an entire organization, you may know that Heaven has dropped a note of joy into the world!"

Joy is such an expressive word! Simply speaking the word "joy" has an ability to lift our spirits and induce optimism! Joy provides assurance. It is a healing agent. Joy helps us overcome obstacles in life. Joy is reciprocal. The joy we express is often felt and shared by others and returns to us in abundance. So, why not "call it all joy?" Envy accomplishes nothing; instead, it often brings loneliness. Trying to measure our success by other's accomplishments simply creates anxiety and unhappiness. Envy can also serve as a warning signal that we need to face our fears or resentments, learn from them, and take charge of our lives.

Whether it be a day, a week, a month, a year, or a lifetime, joy lies within our power to express because no person, condition, circumstance, or outside influence can really separate us from joy or prevent us from sharing it with all whom we meet. Charles F. Lummis said: "I am bigger than anything that can happen to me. All these things—sorrow, misfortune, and suffering—are outside my door. I am in the house and I have the key."

How can our joy be increased? Expressions of unlimited love and gracious service are wonderful joy amplifiers! Appreciating kindness shown to us, honoring our achievements and successes, and

Life is a place of service and in that service one has to suffer a great deal that is hard to bear, but more often to experience a great deal of joy. But that joy can be real only if people look upon their life as a service, and have a definite object in life outside themselves and their personal happiness.
—*Leo Tolstoy*

acknowledging our blessings can enhance feelings of joy. Within each of us resides the possibility of limitless joy. Joy may be difficult to define, but we know it when we experience it and we know it when we lose it! The desire for joy can be one thing that most people have in common. What can constitute a day in joy? Some people find great joy when they are involved in doing things that bring others happiness; when they knowingly live in harmony with the laws of life; when their thoughts, feelings, and actions are honest and honorable; and when their consciences are quiet and peaceful.

The infinite is the source of joy.
—*Chandogya Upanishad*

Envy slays itself by its own arrows.
—*Anonymous*

Joy follows a pure thought like a shadow that never leaves.
—*The Dhammapada*

While reading a magazine article, a woman came across the words: "Until you have joy in your life, you will be neither healthy nor free." The words leaped off the page to the woman, hitting a sensitive area, because she had been moaning and complaining about her unhappiness. She read the words again and angrily objected, saying, "How can I be happy and joyful when I have so much trouble in my life? I'm not like some *others* I know who seem to have everything!" The woman tossed the magazine aside, but the words kept running through her thoughts. So she decided, skeptically at first, to put this challenging idea to the test. Setting aside her problems and envy of others for the moment, she began the enterprise of looking for avenues of greater joy.

No startling developments immediately occurred; nothing much changed. The woman's problems still needed attention. However, time seemed to pass less burdensomely. Gradually, she began to look at herself and recognize the need to improve her own disposition. She became more optimistic and less cynical. Envy and resentment toward others evaporated. She began to take charge of her life. She realized she didn't have to "learn" joy: she began to express it as a natural gift

of the spirit. Friends began to call more often and she spent time in positive pursuits.

"Joy provides assurance; envy brings loneliness" can be an excellent guideline for reviewing our personal feelings and attitudes and examining our value systems. Could envy or discontent stem from feelings of lack within a person's consciousness? Where does our self-esteem relate regarding joy or envy? How we think and feel about ourselves comes from the depths of our being and reflects in every action we take. Does a desire for the advantages another person seems to have form the basis of envy?

Each of us comes into life with a great storehouse of treasures, some of which may lie just beyond our conscious awareness. These gifts came with us from the beginning, and we have the power to bring them into visibility. Joy is one of these gifts. It may be difficult to define, but we *know* it when we experience it. Real joy represents a deep and lasting quality that enables us to transcend difficulties. It enhances our zest for living. We can refuse to allow ourselves to become upset about things that, upon closer examination, are not really a big deal. Life keeps moving forward. There is no better time to be joyful then right now!

◆ # LAW 2

Forgiving builds your spiritual wealth. —Rebekah Alezander

Seek not outside yourself. Heaven is within.
—*Mary Lou Cook*

THE SPIRITUAL PRESENCE of forgiveness builds harmonious community, as do the attributes of love, kindness, gratitude, and prayer. Through forgiveness, beauty, compassion, and human warmth begin to grow in us like flowers on a spring day. What a sweet release it is to let go of the weight of a bothersome grievance or long-held grudge.

How good it is to feel the healing balm of forgiving and of being forgiven! When we forgive, we truly begin to see things and people differently. How is this so? From one perspective, forgiveness helps remove inner barriers that may be blocks to loving ourselves or loving others. Unlimited love is possibly one of our greatest purposes. Unlimited love produces complete forgiveness. Forgiveness releases currents of love to the people we may have judged as wrong, or who we feel may have caused us pain. Forgiveness does not *require* another person to change or apologize. It erases negative associations and provides a practical tool for spiritual triumph. Forgiveness is a way to give love. And when we give love, we cannot help but receive love.

Forgiveness relieves us of the burdens of resentment and past grievances. Forgiveness is another expression of "letting go." Forgiveness extends an invitation to go forward from this moment, with clear mind and conscience. And forgiveness is a most important contribution to the healing of many of the problems of our world. The practice of forgiveness covers every relationship and serves as an indispensable step in the renewal of our lives. If we have ever experienced betrayal or pain or tragedy, the opportunity is ripe to discover forgiveness as the antidote to the cumulative poison of judgment. Every *need* to forgive represents an opportunity for deep personal growth. How can we reach out and grasp the good of today if we are clutching tightly old hurts from yesterday? *Forgive and you will see things differently!* Forgiveness builds our spiritual wealth.

> The real voyage of discovery consists not in seeking new landscapes, but in having new eyes.
> —Marcel Proust

If we desire to practice the laws of the spirit, the universal principles, in our lives, we can call for and encourage expression of the highest and most noble qualities of the human spirit. It is not surprising that forgiveness is sometimes considered an expression of humility, offering spiritual potential far greater than many of us realize. Through humility, we can begin to get a larger perspective of God. As our awareness of divinity increases, we realize that the purpose of life on earth is vastly deeper and much more important than any perceived emotional injury. Forgive—release—and let the unobstructed flow of life work through you.

> No offense is too great. Many may be very challenging, but we can always ask God to help us forgive.
> —James C. Lewis

A Hasidic tale quoted in *Peacemaking Day by Day*, relates the story of an old rabbi who once asked his pupils how they could tell when the night had ended and the day had begun.

"Could it be," asked one of the students, "when you can see an animal in the distance and can tell whether it is a sheep or a dog?"

"No," answered the Rabbi.

Another student asked, "Is it when you can look at a tree in the distance and tell whether it's a fig tree or a peach tree?"

"No," answered the Rabbi.

"Then what is it?" the pupils inquired.

"It is when you can look on the face of any man or woman and see that it is your sister or brother. Because if you cannot see this, it is still night."

Forgiveness can clear the air and remove obstacles between you and another person. As the story describes, we can recognize a bond of unity with others. We begin to see more clearly with "the eyes of spirit." Can we discover that we are able to be more spiritually loving and forgiving in even the most trying of human situations? Truly, this is one way of recognizing when the night of painful experience has ended and the new day of rejoicing has begun!

✦ Law 3

Life is an attitude: have a good one! —Eric L. Lungaard

There isn't a person anywhere who isn't capable of doing more than he thinks he can.
—Henry Ford

HAVE YOU RECENTLY considered that from a vast assortment of options, we choose our responses to whatever situations present themselves? And upon what do we base these responses and choices? Could our attitudes determine the major direction and the quality of our lives? As Henry Ford commented: "Whether you think you can or not, you are right!" Humans are thinking and feeling beings. Through the power of our minds, the positive expression of our thoughts and ideas, we can become better equipped to experience and accomplish our goals and life purpose. So, wouldn't it seem constructive to focus that formative power of the mind on creative and constructive perspectives and attitudes that further our progress in beneficial ways? After all, your attitude in life plays a large part in your living a "good" life.

Life was meant to be lived, and curiosity must be kept alive.
—Eleanor Roosevelt

The secret to success in most areas of human concern is really no secret at all. As we carefully observe how things may be happening in our lives, it becomes obvious that where we focus our attention and the attitudes we express most likely determine the degree and quality of our achievement. If we search out, focus on, and maybe even magnify our "problems," it becomes easier to see unpleasantness.

The actions of men are the best interpreters of their thoughts.
—E. C. McKenzie

On the other hand, if we continue to believe in the basic goodness of humanity, to rely on our inner strengths, and to maintain a positive perspective, most "problems" can be transformed into opportunities for beneficial progress. We must make our choices from an uplifted perspective and with a questing and productive attitude. Life is not all chance; life is mostly choice! As John Milton said: "The mind . . . can make a heaven into a hell, or a hell into a heaven." A story is told that a monkey on a tree hurled a coconut at the head of a devoted Sufi. The man looked up into the tree and smiled. Then he picked up the coconut, opened it, drank the milk, ate the sweet flesh, and made a bowl from the shell! Is this a result of positive, creative thinking?

We live what we know. If we believe the universe and ourselves to be mechanical, we will live mechanically. On the other hand, if we know that we are part of an open universe, and that our minds are a matrix of reality, we will live more creatively and powerfully.
—Marilyn Ferguson

The power of a life that stems from inner spiritual strength is incomparable. As new thoughts and ideas occur, different horizons for achievement may be discovered. How do you feel when the light of a fresh idea dawns in your mind? Are you excited? Do you feel a spontaneity that prompts forward movement? Do you feel a stirring in the atmosphere of the spirit? Do you trust the inner guidance received and proceed accordingly? Think back to an authentic choice you made at some point in your life. Perhaps the idea suggested moving from one avenue of work into a different field. You may have experienced a strong pull to visit another part of the country. Useful insight into a relationship may have developed. How did it feel to act on your choice? Were the results beneficial?

Centuries ago, when a mapmaker would run out of the known world before he ran out of parchment, he would often sketch a dragon at the edge of the scroll. This was intended to be a sign to the explorer that he was entering unknown territory at his own risk. However, many explorers did not perceive the dragon as a mapmaker's warning sign, but rather as a prophecy. They foresaw disaster

The attitude in
which the difficulty
is met makes all
the difference.
—Eric Butterworth

beyond the "known worlds" they traversed. Their fearful attitudes often kept them from pushing on to discover new lands and new people. Other, more adventuresome travelers saw the dragon as a sign of opportunity, the doorway into a new territory worth exploring.

Each of us has a mental "map" that contains the ideas and information that we use for guidance as we explore each new day. Like the maps of long ago, our mental maps may have "edges" to them. For some people, these edges may represent an attitude marked by dragons of fears, disappointments, or difficulties. For the adventurous explorer, those edges can offer perseverance, opportunity, and progress. As Charles F. Kettering believed: "There will always be a frontier where there is an open mind and a willing hand."

The difference between "ordinary" and "extraor-

dinary" can often be a little extra effort . . . a little extra attention . . . a little extra care. A little extra positive attitude may also make the difference between success and failure. And not only that, it can make the difference between good and great! Positive people are much more likely to turn their

We can develop a positive mental attitude through alignment and cooperation with spiritual principles, or the universal laws of life.
—Rebekah Alezander

ideas and life situations into positive behaviors. Positive attitudes *do* change circumstances, nearly always for the better! A magnificent attitude can insure every day of life brings rich adventure. So, "have a good one."

✦ LAW 4

Service is love made manifest. —Maharishi Sadashiva Isham

One who serves and
seeks no recompense finds union
with the Lord.
—Sikhism, Adi Granth,
Gauri Sukhmani

IN AN ARTICLE titled "The Lever That Moves the World," Maharishi Sadashiva Isham wrote:

Service is joy; service is the source and goal of any thinking human's relationship with the rest of humanity. The most evolved humans have always known that true joy comes from giving. They live for others. Their thought is for others. There is nothing they would not do to further the growth of others. They have realized this one truth: there is no true happiness in growth for oneself alone; all true growth is rooted in compassion.

Service is giving back the gift of our life to the Source of our life. Service is a reciprocal relationship between our self and the rest of humanity. True service is love made manifest.

The sacred writings of the various world religions speak about the meaning and importance of love and service. Texts on heartfelt love for others often include general admonitions to kindness, benevolence, gentleness, humility, and service. For example, in the Tao Te Ching, we read: "The sage does not accumulate for himself. The more he uses for others, the more he has himself. The more he gives to others, the more he possesses of his own. The Way of Heaven is to benefit others and not to injure."

Could one of our sacred tasks in life be that of following the spiritual truth of the heart and creating authentic power and spiritual progress through loving service? This seems like a fruitful

Every good
act is charity.
—Islam

The charitable give
out at the door,
and God puts in
at the window.
—John Ray

Thy day of service
is now come.
—Bahá'u'lláh

The whole value
of a benevolent
deed lies in the love
that inspires it.
—Talmud

avenue to follow to discover an inner richness of spirit. Spiritual progress reflects both inner and outer dimensions, promoting personal and social improvement. Our beliefs about what constitutes spiritual progress usually stem from a desire to improve morally and to begin to think and live in harmony with a good universal value system. This inner growth or maturity often motivates a person to do something beneficial that has the potential to improve humankind. True service is also a powerful tool for implementing our own growth. Improvements or constructive endeavors often result from loving service. Some of the immense variety of benefits can be enlargement of vision, better mental functioning, stimulation of creativity, expanded interest in life, tapping of higher energies, increased efficiency, and a joyous sense of interaction with others. It is interesting to note that spiritual progress may include or be combined with, progress in other fields of endeavor. For example, combining scientific insights with an increased understanding of God may constitute a form of spiritual progress. Or, new ways of helping the poor or underprivileged may be a form of much-needed social work and an expression of spiritual progress.

The person who allows unlimited love to flow through him or her into outer expressions of service can represent a living bridge between the inner and outer dimensions mentioned earlier. Selfless giving for others, love of humanity, love of life and nature, active furtherance of universal principles, and communion of divinity are often demonstrated wellsprings of non-diminishing joy.

Devotion to a life of service is an attitude commitment! A commitment of unlimited love! Service

Strive constantly to serve the welfare of the world; by devotion
to selfless work one attains the supreme goal of life.
Do your work with the welfare of others always in mind.
—Bhagavad Gita

is also a path of learning. And could service be truly genuine without humility? We offer our gifts, not in our own names, but in the name of infinite divinity. We can be channels of loving service right where we are. All you need to do is ask, "How may I serve?" and then open your eyes. Opportunities arise daily. We can help weave the tapestry of love around earth and play our part in the great symphony. Step by step. Day by day. One experience at a time.

✦ LAW 5

No man is free who is not a master of himself. —Epictetus

IN THE FIRST CENTURY A.D., the Greek philosopher and slave Epictetus declared this truth, "No man is free who is not master of himself." Epictetus understood that true freedom results from becoming master of one's self, not from escaping a slave master. What is this freedom of which we speak?

Is it the right to do whatever we wish without restraint? Not really. The true freedom we seek is not so much the freedom to *do* as the freedom to *become* all that we can be. It is when we responsibly guide and control our lives that we experience the greatest freedom and mastery.

How is this "mastery of self" attained? The seeds of success lie within us. In a person who is psychologically healthy, the various parts of the personality work together in unified fashion. One of the processes utilized toward self-mastery is the power of our will. We have the opportunity and ability to exercise our faculty of *free will* to reach conscientious conclusions and choose purposeful decisions that guide our actions. If *mind* is the switchboard, then *will* sits at the controls! The vital spark of our will can mobilize us. For example, if you reach out to pick up a pencil from your desk, it is with your will that you decide to take this action. If you develop an intellectual theory from important research, you engage your will. If you express love for a friend or family member, you engage in an act of will. At any point in a situation, you can "rally your will" and take command of your life.

Another step toward self-mastery often begins when we realize that our thoughts, feelings, and actions make our own "prison," and that we ourselves have the key. Have you ever contemplated the awesome mystery and power of your own mind? You cannot see it or touch it. It has no physical substance or boundaries. It has no placement

God did not make us to be eaten up by anxiety, but to walk erect, free, unafraid in a world where there is work to do, truth to seek, love to give.
—*Joseph Fort Newton*

in time or space. Yet, it is ever with you, guiding and directing virtually everything about your life. Our minds inherently tie our thoughts and experiences together. Your mind works like a spider building an intricate web. It can take one thought, connect it with other thoughts, and discover new and beneficial relationships between the thoughts. This is not a random activity. Our thoughts are guided and purposeful as they unify incoming

reality. And what is the directing essence, the power to choose, decide, and act? The human will!

Spiritual consciousness means the use of super wisdom, truth, to do the things that supremely benefit yourself and others.
—*Paramahansa Yogananda*

Perhaps one of the best indicators of our personal level of freedom and self-mastery is the degree of consciousness with which we deal with the variety of life's situations and experiences. Challenges, especially, often represent opportunities for growth. If we wish to continue a path of growth, doesn't it make sense to continually expand our mental and spiritual consciousness? We can make it a habit to monitor our mental-emotional state through self-observation. You might ask, "What is going on inside me at this moment?" Then listen to your soul's response. Observe this energy at both the mental and the emotional levels. What *thoughts* might be creating this situation? Then look at your *emotional* reaction to these thoughts. Are your thoughts and emotions uplifting or degrading? Is this the *soul* you would actually *choose* to develop?

Since we always have a choice, what would happen if we continually chose self-mastery and spiritual freedom? Is it logical thinking that if we get the inside right, the outside will fall into place? If our minds experience thoughts directly on the level of conscious awareness, how can we elevate our consciousness? Through overcoming fear and ignorance? Research? Study? Prayer? Building higher spiritual values? Stretching our minds for greater reality?

Various paths and a diversity of philosophies and practices can lead to self-mastery and freedom. Yet, a common theme runs through them. If we desire our lives to be heaven on earth, it is important to understand that "the kingdom of God" lies within us. Our visit to this Earth is temporary. We are here to learn the necessary lessons of the Earth school and to help those who cross our path. We can experience great joy in allowing the ideal of love for divinity and service to humanity to find full expression in our lives. All great religions teach that when we find divinity everywhere, freedom and self-mastery have begun.

Spotlights ✦ ✦

1. Joy has a tremendous ability to lift our spirits and induce optimism.

2. Joy is a deep and lasting quality that can help us transcend difficulties and restore a zest for life and living.

3. How can *your* joy be increased?

4. How does the activity of forgiveness assist us is seeing things differently?

5. To forgive represents an opportunity for deep personal growth.

6. Our attitude plays a large part in living a "good" life.

7. The power of a life that stems from inner spiritual strength is incomparable.

8. "Service is giving back the gift of our life to the source of our life."

9. Spiritual progress reflects both inner and outer dimensions of our being.

10. Our mind can make a heaven into a hell, or a hell into a heaven.

11. What does becoming "master of yourself" mean to you?

12. What are some ways you can find divinity everywhere?

Living the Various Spiritual Laws ✦ ✦

Having taught the Vedas, the teacher says:
Speak the truth. Do your duty. Neglect not
The scriptures. Give your best to your teacher.
Do not cut off the line of progeny. Swerve not
From the truth. Swerve not from the good.
Protect your spiritual progress always.
Give your best in learning and teaching.
Never fail in respect to the sages.
See the divine in your mother, father,
Teacher, and guest. Never do what is wrong.
Honor those who are worthy of honor.
Give with faith. Give with love. Give with joy.
If you are in doubt about right conduct,
Follow the example of the sages,
Who know what is best for spiritual growth.
This is the instruction of the Vedas;
This is the secret; this is the message.
—*The Upanishads*

Week Thirty

✦ Law 1

It is by forgetting self that one finds self. —St. Francis of Assisi

FINDING THE WAY to spiritual awakening presents many opportunities. In the beginning, we may listen and learn from other people's experiences. Numerous books may be read. We may seek various spiritual paths and become inspired by the rich examples of teachers and sages, past and present. At some point along the way, we often find a common element among those who become wise. Wisdom often includes a forgetting of self and a focusing on service to others. Baal Shem Tov wrote, "There is no room for God in a person who is full of himself."

Is your view of life one of joyous living? Do you consistently practice seeing the good in everything? Do your activities reflect a focus on diligence, purpose, usefulness, creativity, and progress? Are you humble? Does your life reflect pure unlimited love for all people, with never any exceptions? Do you meet the easy experiences with rejoicing and the tough experiences with an enthusiastic and resourceful spirit? It is the nature of man—the dreamer and the builder—to refrain from always accepting things as they may appear, but to utilize the ability to change them into something more beneficial.

Does a part of being wise include the awareness that a closed mind does not grow? Open-minded thinking seems to be necessary for the mind to remain strong and powerful, otherwise it can become stagnant and dormant. There are so many useful things to learn. How do we utilize the many opportunities that invite us to respond to life every day? Are we open and receptive to listen to new ideas that may differ from our present understanding? Since we have the gift of being self-aware, would it be helpful to examine our lives from time to time to determine how we are using our minds, our creativity, and our focus—then put the benefits of what we learn to good purpose in service to others? How we direct our attention is up to us. Can you see the wisdom in St. Francis's statement, "It is in forgetting self that one finds self?" If we open our heart to the people of the world, surely we must also open our minds as well.

When we are giving of ourselves in the creative flow of life, we are receiving immeasurably in return. While our thoughts and feelings are directed in the process of giving in some way to others, we are also expanding the horizons of our own perspectives. In our journeys, our perspectives can move from the personal level to a sense of the bigger picture. And would not the "bigger picture" include all people, all cultures, and all religions on the planet, plus a larger perspective of divinity?

For example, could a larger look at life show us that when we try to describe God in human terms, we might belittle God's infinity?

In the movie *Mr. Holland's Opus*, a high-school music teacher had a dream of writing a symphony. He passionately wanted to create a world-class symphony, and hoped his music would someday earn him a great deal of wealth. However, Mr. Holland did not realize his dream and finally retired from teaching. Feeling dejected and lamenting his

Some people think that supernatural events, such as miracles, are needed to prove God's existence. But natural processes and the laws of nature may be merely methods designed by God for His continuing creative purposes. When new laws are discovered by human scientists, do they not merely discover a little more of God? Each of us every day is swimming in an ocean of unseen miracles. For example, each living cell is a miracle; and the human body is a vast colony of over a hundred billion cells. The miracle of this body includes both our ability to recognize it as well as our inability ever to exhaust the true significance of it.

—*John Marks Templeton*

lost dream, he prepared to leave the building for the last time and walked into the school gymnasium. He stumbled upon a surprise party in his honor, where hundreds of his former students were gathered. The master of ceremonies was a woman who once lacked self-confidence and considered herself a failure. But through the encouragement of her former teacher, she found value in herself and went on to become governor of the state. She spoke before those gathered, saying: "We are your symphony, Mr. Holland. We are the notes of your opus. We are the notes of your life." The great composition of Mr. Holland's life was helping others build their dreams and, in so doing, moment by moment, building himself.

Opportunities are often the most profound and challenging teachers we may ever meet. Opportunities are compassionate teachers and extend no judgment and no censure. They simply mirror life and, in the reflection, we can learn how to see more clearly. They help us realize that we have not yet plumbed the depths and possibilities of our own souls or become receptive to greater learning. We are blessed with the capacity to be more aware. We can connect with and use the inner resources of focus, energy, and unlimited love. We can nurture our capacities for forgiveness and understanding. In this moment, we can forget ourselves and reach out in service to others. Incredibly, in the forgetting of self, we can find the wondrous reality of who we truly are.

✦ LAW 2

Leave no stone unturned. —Euripides

COULD THE SAYING "Leave no stone unturned" represent an expression of going to whatever lengths may be necessary to achieve a worthwhile goal? Could this statement also reflect on the importance of maintaining diligence and perseverance along the path to all levels of our growth and spirituality? As we learn to recognize the subtle, intangible patterns of life, are we better equipped to make wiser decisions? Are we eager to move forward and explore new concepts with confidence?

Does one secret of living a life of alert awareness and sensitivity lie in the willingness to pay attention? Extending loving attention to the details and particulars of a person, place, or situation could be quite helpful. The attention we bring to present endeavors can expand our perception and open our eyes to a freshness of vision. Thus, it seems beneficial to expand ourselves by doing more, giving more.

Diligence is the mother of good fortune, and idleness, its opposite, never brought a man to the goal of any of his best wishes.
—Miguel de Cervantes

Sometimes things come easily in life and sometimes they require more effort. The people who succeed are usually the ones who are willing to hold steadfast to their goals, even in the face of apparent setbacks. Thomas Edison said: "Our greatest weakness lies in giving up. The most certain way to succeed is always to try just one more time." Or perhaps turn over one more stone! Looking at a situation from a larger perspective can make a huge difference. Success often means understanding the "bigger view," devoting ourselves to something, and staying with it. This sounds a great deal like "commitment." We push on every day toward our goal.

Marie Curie spent her entire adult life conducting scientific experiments. Her diligence in the laboratory resulted in the discovery of the elements of radium and polonium and laid the groundwork for nuclear physics and theories of radioactivity. In her case, one stone overturned became a stepping-stone to the next discovery. She became the first person to receive the Nobel Prize twice!

Every individual should have a purpose in life which is worthy of intense effort—and constantly work toward the definite goal ahead.
—Roderick Stevens

We often learn the most when we are the most challenged, coming up with strengths we may not have realized. Removing obstacles often requires stamina. When our strength is severely tested, we may feel temporarily discouraged. This could be a good time to remember 2 Timothy 1:7: "God did not give us a spirit of timidity, but a spirit of power and self-control," as well as the words of Euripides, "Leave no stone unturned." Be courageous! Courage is finding the mental strength necessary to accomplish the task ahead. It can be the spark that ignites the next step. How can you see around the corner unless you take the steps to get there? Engrained deep within the souls of those who succeed are spirit, the confidence to persevere, and the flexibility to surmount all obstacles to achievement.

Be like the bamboo. For centuries, Chinese calligraphers have painted bamboo as a spiritual exercise. The bamboo is graceful, upright, and strong on the outside. On the inside, it is open, receptive, and humble. The bamboo's roots are firmly planted in the ground and freely intertwined with others for mutual strength and support. The stalk moves gently, bending in the wind, but does not break. We, too, can be flexible, resourceful, and open to new possibilities. When life presents changes, we can take stock of our lives, adjust, and continue to learn. We can be ingenious and inventive. We can watch the changing patterns of growth, and turn over another stone!

◆ LAW 3

What you focus on expands. —Arnold Patent

A person who feels good emotions, and thinks good thoughts, and sees only good in nature and people, will remember only good.
—*Paramahansa Yogananda*

Each person chooses for himself the individual patterns within which he will create this personal reality.
—*Jane Roberts*

Our thoughts define our universe.
—*Piero Ferrucci*

IT HAS BEEN ESTIMATED that the average human being has approximately 50,000 thoughts per day! That is a lot of thoughts! Some of these thoughts are going to be positive and productive, and some of them may be negative and possibly poisonous. Thoughts act upon us in profound ways. When we focus on a particular thought, our minds often immediately respond by calling up similar thoughts. Positive and loving thoughts and feelings spark a wide range of similar uplifting thoughts and feelings. On the other hand, negative thoughts and fearful emotions may give rise to unpleasant experiences. So, we have an opportunity to choose where we wish to place our focus, for *what we focus on expands.*

How can our thoughts affect our actual performance? In a very powerful way! One example could be this scenario. Suppose you are asked to perform a complicated task. If your focus rests on the difficulty of the situation, what is the probability of success? On the other hand, if you look at the same task with interest and enthusiasm and see an opportunity waiting to be explored, what is the probability of success? If we dwell upon limitations, then we will meet them. If we think positively of possibilities, this will be the structure of our experience. Practice shows that we can create, vitalize, and strengthen an idea by thinking about it.

An important mental dynamic is to acknowl-

edge and understand the close relationship between our thinking and the way we feel. It is important to realize that we are constantly thinking, and our thinking will return to us as a feeling. Spiritual teachers have often commented, "As you think, so you are." There is a point-to-point relationship between thinking and feeling. In order to experience a feeling, we must first have a thought about that feeling. For example, can you feel happy without having happy thoughts? Or feel sad without sad thoughts? Or feel stressed without stressful thoughts? Or feel relaxed without peaceful thoughts? Try an experiment. The next time you are feeling upset, notice your thoughts. They will most likely be negative! Why? Because there is nothing to hold negative feelings in place except negative thoughts! Then, remind yourself that it is your thinking that is negative, not your life. Then, change your focus!

What you think means more than anything else in your life. More than what you earn, more than where you live, more than your social position, and more than what anyone else may think about you.
—*George Matthew Adams*

One of the basic spiritual principles in many philosophies is to open our hearts to "what is." If we have preconceived ideas about the way things "should be," we may interfere with golden opportunities to enjoy or learn from new concepts and observations. Doesn't it seem logical that the more we learn, the more easily we can walk forward with greater confidence and an increased capacity and ability to accomplish the tasks before us? It often takes practice, patience, and diligence to do anything well, so developing a strong base of knowledge can assist us in making wiser choices.

Our thoughts and feelings can serve as a powerful guidance system, acting as a barometer to navigate us through life. This system can let us know when we may be getting off-track and headed toward conflict or unhappiness. If your life is other than harmonious and productive, can you make a mental adjustment? This guidance system can also remind us when we are on-track and headed toward beneficial accomplishment and joy. In this case, can you give thanks for your blessings and hold your focus on an attitude of gratitude, remembering that: "What we focus on expands?"

In the course of his earth ministry, Jesus said, "By their fruits you shall know them." He went on

to say, "Are grapes gathered from thorns, or figs from thistles?" (Matthew 7:15, 16). He was revealing a very important law of life: "As you think, so you are." The variety of conditions we may find in life could be like the fruit of which Jesus spoke. If we don't like the fruit we are harvesting—poor health, financial struggles, unhappiness with our work, inharmonious relationships, or whatever—it may be essential to harvest from another tree. A positive one!

✦ LAW 4

Change and improvement come from the inside out. —Anonymous

IN *The Tao of Personal Leadership*, Diane Dreher writes: "To succeed in any field, we must look to those skills that make us fully human: the ability to learn continuously throughout life, to communicate with others, to come up with creative new solutions, and to deepen our understanding, looking to the larger patterns within and around us." And the basis for this success is often the change and improvement that comes from the inside out!

Much has been written in recent years about achieving successful leadership. And "leadership"

can encompass many areas, ranging from operating a business to experiencing the personal, day-by-day challenges of expanding our vision and stretching to fulfill our highest human and spiritual potential. In our fast-paced, modern world, the most helpful life lessons are, ironically, often some of the oldest. Drawing on universal principles as old as creation, an individual can bring the wisdom of spiritual teachings into daily life. And, although today's leaders, entrepreneurs, and individuals may be standing on the advancing edge of previous knowledge and ability, can they face the unknown with integrity and enthusiasm?

Universal principles are like compasses; they always point the way. Such spiritual principles are self-evident, self-validating natural laws, which have proved beneficial in all societies. These principles are often expressed as ideas, values, and teachings that uplift, ennoble, inspire, and empower people. For example, the principles of *oneness* and *dynamic growth* often flow from humanly directed skills of *unity* and *expansion*. Through practicing the principles, we begin to see more clearly how everything and everyone is connected, evolving, and blending into various forms of creation.

What are some of "those skills that make us fully human?" Perhaps we could begin with *courage* and *resourcefulness*. These tools are used by individuals who enhance their ability to create new and beneficial opportunities from their life experiences. These people are often the ones who embrace opportunities with enthusiasm and then apply the deepest principles of existence. They respond to uncertainty by joyously seeking a creative balance in dynamic interaction with the challenges of life. Do you remember the old adage, "Is the glass half full or half empty? The difference is not in the glass, but in the attitude of the observer. And to a great degree, our attitudes determine how we utilize opportunities. Developing a positive attitude is a skill everyone can learn.

Learning how to cultivate space for prayer, contemplation, and meditation to enrich the sacred moments in our lives enhances both the spiritual and the human aspects of our being. Prayer often brings a vital shift in our frame of reference and helps us perceive people and situations from a higher perspective. Through this activity, we can develop greater respect for ourselves and others and become better equipped to handle life's experiences.

Successful people usually perceive life as a journey of continuing education. They seek further training in a chosen field. They take useful classes, listen courteously to others, are insatiably curious, and ask meaningful questions. They learn through both their ears and their eyes! They expand their competence, their ability to do things. They develop new skills and new interests. External challenges become opportunities for self-realization and for creative new solutions. Perhaps most importantly, they discover that the more they know, the more they realize they do not know!

One of the "skills" that enables us to evolve into more fully useful persons is to see life as filled with purpose. And one of life's primary purposes can be dedication to living a life of loving service. Working with universal principles helps us develop a sense of spiritual responsibility, of contribution to the betterment of all of God's creations. We seek to become peacemakers and harmonious individuals through our optimistic, positive attitudes.

◆ LAW 5

You choose the path you want to walk down. —John Marks Templeton

KNOWLEDGE of our world has changed dramatically in the last century. The pace of accumulation of new data has quickened expansively. An increasing investment in scientific research should

be targeted for more spiritual knowledge. Theology is experiencing a healthy reassessment of the nature of theological reality. The benefits that scientific research is having on human health show promise of intensifying. The sheer driving force of advancing technology has shown us with increasing clarity that our society is moving from

He who would arrive at the appointed end must follow
a single road and not wander through many ways.
—Seneca

a material-based one to more of an information-oriented and knowledge-intensive base. The great universities of the world are serving a larger concentration of international students. We live in a period of prosperity never before seen in world history. It really is not difficult to envision our future in positive terms—of total human development, hope for all of God's people, and peace with justice. And, it is easy to recognize that opportunities abound for the individual to choose the path he or she wants to walk down.

With a growing awareness of the unlimited good ahead, we can move forward with a sense of expectancy and hope. As the poet said: "Every day that is born into the world comes like a burst of music, and rings the whole day through and you will make of it a dance, a dirge, or a life march, as you will!" Although the winds of circumstance may blow—and not always in the direction you may wish—you *can* always choose the path you want.

Consider the possibility that as *spiritual* beings we have divine built-in attributes of unlimited love, purpose, and creativity. As *human* beings, we can choose the path of loving service, knowing that our efforts help others. Joyfully, we seem to be increasingly aware of our responsibilities to each other as members of the human family. For example, only among human beings can anything be found like the story of a prominent English physician who left his practice on a moment's notice to travel halfway around the world, at his own expense, to come to the aid of survivors of a Russian nuclear accident.

What are some primary factors behind this progress? Do these humanitarian and beneficial impulses spring from our connection to the divine nature of God? Are more and more people coming to believe that a power greater than themselves is in charge? How is this reflected in everyday individual life? When we take charge of our thoughts and "rule" our minds in a positive way, we are choosing the path we want to walk down. We are no longer driven by outer conditions or misled by ego. Instead, each of us can become the master helmsman for our own "ship of state," creating a life filled with fruitful endeavors and noble purpose.

Ella Wheeler Wilcox sat by the East River in New York City years ago, reflecting on the fact that people coming from the same home environment may turn out so differently. Inspired by some sailing vessels pulling up the river to their docks, she wrote:

One ship drives east, and another drives west,
With the self-same winds that blow.
'Tis the set of the sails and not the gales,
Which tells us the way to go.

It seems the main barrier to our full flowering as spiritual beings could be our mindsets and our human egotism. Do our attitudes color how we respond to life? While we may not be able to change the facts of circumstances, we certainly have a choice in how we think and respond. An old Oriental axiom says: "You may not be able to keep the birds from flying over your head, but you can keep them from building nests in your hair!"

Shine by the side of every path we tread with such
a luster, he that runs may read.
—William Cowper

Regarding egotism, we sometimes assume far more knowledge than we actually possess. However, a scientific approach to religion has helped us become more aware of how infinitesimal we may be in the cosmic scheme of things. We are learning that perhaps the essential ingredient for success lies in a humble approach to every aspect of life. So, with an increasing awareness of the unlimited good ahead, we can choose the path we want to walk down and plan the future with a sense of expectancy and hope.

Spotlights ◆ ◆

1. High ideals often include a forgetting of self and a focusing on service to others.

2. Our quest for awakening is a personal and "inside" activity.

3. The present moment is often the most profound and challenging teacher you may ever meet.

4. One stone overturned can become a "stepping-stone" to the next discovery.

5. The people who succeed are usually the ones who are willing to hold steadfast to their dreams, even in the face of apparent setbacks.

6. Whatever we choose to focus upon, our mind can expand.

7. There is a point-to-point relationship between thinking and feeling.

8. Our thoughts and feelings can serve as a powerful guidance system, acting as a barometer to navigate us through life.

9. Universal principles are like compasses; they always point the way.

10. Choose to do what you can, where you are, and with what you have.

Living the Various Spiritual Laws ◆ ◆

Potter at the wheel.
From centering to finished pot,
Form increases as options decrease;
Softness goes to hardness.

When a potter begins to throw a pot, she picks up a lump of clay, shapes it into a rough sphere, and throws it onto the spinning potter's wheel. It may land off-center, and she must carefully begin to shape it until it is a smooth cylinder. Then she works that clay, stretching and compressing it as it turns. First it is a tower, then it is a squat mushroom. Only after bringing it up and down several times does she slowly squeeze the revolving clay until its walls rise from the wheel. She cannot go on too long, for the clay will begin to "tire" and then sag. She gives it the form she imagines, then sets it aside. The next day, the clay will be leather hard, and she can turn it over to shape the foot. Some decoration may be scratched into the surface. Eventually, the bowl will be fired, and then the only options are the colors applied to it; its shape cannot be changed.

This is how we shape all the situations in our lives. We must give them rough shape and then throw them down into the center of our lives. We must stretch and compress, testing the nature of things. As we shape the situation, we must be aware of what form we want things to take. The closer something comes to completion, the harder and more definite it becomes. Our options become fewer, until the full impact of our creation is all that there is. Beauty or ugliness, utility or failure, comes from the process of shaping.

—Deng Ming-Dao, *365 Tao: Daily Meditations*

Week Thirty-One

+ ## LAW I

Destructive language tends to produce destructive results. —John Marks Templeton

MAKING CHOICES has often been considered a means of human evolution. Each choice we make stems from our perspectives or intentions and from the quality of consciousness that we bring to our thoughts, feelings, and actions. Conscious evolution, through making responsible and positive choices, can be a beneficial path. What does making choices have to do with language? Positive choices governing the manner in which we speak or communicate with others helps produce positive and fruitful results, while *destructive language tends to produce destructive results.*

> Clarity is the ability to see the soul in action in the physical world. It results from choosing to learn through wisdom instead of through fear and doubt.
>
> —*Gary Zukav*

Any of us may experience stressful times and situations at home, at school, or in our work. When things are not going well, it can be tempting to complain, blame, or criticize others. We may get caught up in the *illusion* that finding fault with someone else can help us feel better about ourselves. But this false perspective or judgment prevents us from seeing the good that lies beyond appearances. What could happen if we met this challenge by living by the directives of our spiritual selves? We would still "chop wood and carry water," as the ancient Zen proverb tells us. However, our level of awareness could help us see beyond the immediate problems to insights that may have heretofore been hidden.

Belittling or hurting others seldom provides an avenue of resolution to problems. Instead, these attitudes often deepen the chasm. On the other hand, kind, considerate, and understanding words lend support. We can listen with compassion, then speak with consideration—from a position of humility, unlimited love, and enlarged perspective.

In his book *When Bad Things Happen to Good People*, Rabbi Harold Kushner wrote about perspective. He said:

God has created a world in which many more good things than bad things happen. We find life's disasters upsetting not only because they are painful, but because they are exceptional. Most people wake up on most days feeling good. Most illnesses are curable. Most airplanes take off and land safely . . . The accident, the robbery, the inoperable tumor are life-shattering exceptions, but they are very rare exceptions. When you have been hurt by life, it may seem hard to keep that in mind. When you are standing very close to a large object, all you can see is the object. Only by stepping back from it can you also see the rest of the setting around it. When we are stunned by some tragedy, we can only see and feel the tragedy. Only with time and distance can we see the tragedy in the context of a whole life and a whole world.

I have often
regretted my speech,
never my silence.
—Publilius Syrus

If we could keep this perspective in mind when situations appear disruptive or disturbing until the "bigger picture" becomes more apparent, perhaps a lot of destructive language could be avoided. The time-honored proverb: "If you can't say something good, then don't say anything at all," can be a benchmark for the words we speak throughout the day.

It is important to acknowledge emotional upsets. If we are not intimate with our thoughts and emotions, we may fail to perceive the dynamics that lie behind them and associate the *effect* of sadness, grief, disappointment, or anger with the underlying *cause*. How can we understand the sufferings or joys of others if we cannot experience our own?

Douglas was a middle-class, college-educated businessman from the Southwest United States. His childhood years were emotionally difficult; he grew up in a dysfunctional home with an alcoholic father and chronically ill mother. As an adult, Douglas was angry, bitter, manipulative, and seemed incapable of forming lasting and quality relationships. His quarrelsome nature and abusive language kept most people at a distance. The final straw came when Douglas's explosive temper and disagreeable disposition resulted in his wife's leaving him and filing for divorce.

Douglas fell into deep despair, but this latest event prompted intense soul-searching. He began to recognize long-standing negative patterns and determined to confront both these patterns and his underlying pain. While he searched within himself for the deepest causes of his painful life, he arranged to live alone and to attend rehabilitation sessions with a qualified counselor.

When Douglas emerged from his period of rehabilitation a few months later, his perceptions of himself and life, along with his system of values, had changed considerably. During the ensuing year, he developed a more sensitive and considerate way of being with people. His anger melted away and he became less cynical as his self-esteem rose to healthier levels. These changes did not come easily for Douglas. His transition from an angry, arrogant, and manipulative individual to a more caring and considerate person was a journey through personal pain that required a lot of courage. But he did it! By committing himself to that journey of inner exploration, Douglas changed his life.

Be careful not to lash out at others when you may be having a bad day. Be sensitive. The difficult moments will pass, and when they do, there may be no unnecessary wounds to heal!

✦ LAW 2

Success feeds on itself and creates more success. —John Marks Templeton

SUCCESS, whether of a professional or personal nature, is something that nearly every individual seeks. How many people have asked the question, "How can I become more successful?" Perhaps a succinct response would be to *research, plan, analyze,* and *activate the necessary steps* to achieve what you want. Knowing the available resources can

certainly help guide a person's decision-making process. Being *fully successful* includes achievement on a variety of levels, and not simply making a lot of money.

Past performance is often a good indication of a person's future potential. While it is true that success takes "practice," successful people usually start practicing when they are young! It is never too early to clarify our objectives. In so doing, we will be naturally drawn to people whose qualities we admire. In the process, we can learn from one another in a mutually beneficial way. Do our friends and associates mirror the virtues and values we wish to express? Do their lifestyles reflect the positive attributes we desire for ourselves?

Ethics and spiritual principles should be the absolute basis of everything we do in life. All that we say. All that we think. In fact, if everything we did was structured from a foundation of ethics and spiritual principles, how could we not be successful? We would certainly be practicing The Golden Rule: "Do unto others as you would have them do unto you." Let's look at these two ideas for a moment. Having ethics or a system of moral standards or values means not only doing the *right* thing, it also means doing the *smart* thing. Spiritual principles, as mentioned in earlier essays, are the foundation laws of the universe and will always provide a strong framework for any endeavor.

The only place where success comes before work is a dictionary.
—*Vidal Sassoon*

By accepting that obstacles may arise as we pursue our goals, we become better prepared to manage difficulties. Experiencing a setback does not need to break the momentum of a project. When we accept that mistakes may come with any attempt to achieve something, we can acknowledge the experience as an opportunity to go forward, to invent, to create, and to try new things. We can research the origin of each problem and incorporate its lesson as a part of our future choices, decisions, and actions. Nothing worth doing comes easily. Would humanity have achieved all that it has in the last century without trial and error? Aim to be beneficial, which attracts others to you. Absolutely! Allow no setbacks to deter you from your goals!

Another guideline for success is to pave the road of achievement with humanitarian service. Giving is more important than getting, and those who give freely frequently experience a return on their generosity. Giving to worthwhile causes is an investment that pays off on many levels. When we consider the potential impact of what we do, we make certain that the results can be beneficial and far-reaching.

The man who gets ahead is the man who does more
than is necessary, and keeps on doing it.
—*E. C. McKenzie*

Learning discernment is a valuable step in becoming more responsible in your personal being and in your outlook toward life. To do this, take a panoramic view of the whole situation—whether it is a job, a relationship, a business decision, or a spiritual path. Discernment with thoughtful perspective is the foundation of honesty, responsibility, and wise choices. All of these are stepping stones toward greater success.

Life is constantly changing and producing new challenges and new opportunities. If you think we know all the answers, you may be in a very sad state. Being humble is the first step to attaining wisdom. And gaining wisdom is a giant step toward greater success. When we learn to keep our minds open to new perceptions, ideas, and people, with the confidence that those of value will have a positive influence, the negative influences can then fall away. Optimism born of spiritual truths or principles is the power behind growth and progress. Try to temper your hopefulness with a sense of reality; but *know* that the light of your optimism can help improve situations. This optimism might serve as an inspiration for others. Aiming high can lift us up. In the meantime, success feeds on itself and creates more success.

✦ Law 3

Never put off until tomorrow what you can do today. —Lord Chesterfield

It is good to remember that although a tea kettle may be up to its neck in hot water, it continues to sing!
—*American proverb*

Do not delay; the golden moments fly.
—*Henry Wadsworth Longfellow*

HAVE YOU EVER experienced a situation so difficult and complex you were unsure how to solve it? Have you ever faced an examination that involved so much material you didn't know where to begin to study for it? Have you ever said, "Mañana, I will do it tomorrow." Most people have found themselves in such situations and often felt overwhelmed. An initial response to situations of this type may be to set the whole thing aside until another day. But wisdom tells us, "Never put off until tomorrow what you can do today." Tomorrow will brings its own challenges and opportunities and we want to be fresh to face them. This can be difficult if we are carrying the weight of yesterday's "leftovers" into today!

If you were conscious, that is to say totally present in the Now, all negativity would dissolve almost instantly. It could not survive in your presence.
—*Eckhart Tolle*

Procrastination is the thief of time.
—*Edward Young*

And do not say, regarding anything, "I am going to do that tomorrow," but only, "if God will."
—*Qur'an*

Many reasons can be cited regarding why it is important to not delay necessary actions. Problems can grow more serious or complex when they are not addressed promptly. Minor difficulties treated in a timely, positive manner generally do not balloon into major issues. A simple example is that a minor cut, quickly and properly treated, can heal fast. However, if left untreated and exposed to adverse conditions, that cut could become infected and require serious medical attention.

Doing the things today that can make life better can translate into a more orderly and productive tomorrow. One avenue for accomplishment is to assess in detail the overall project, then determine an orderly flow of tasks to achieve successful completion. Steady effort is more productive than sudden, frenzied activity. Orderly progression

can reduce unnecessary stress and enable us to be more productive. Why transform a situation that simply needs to be dealt with into a possible later problem?

Perhaps one of the most important reasons for not putting off until tomorrow what can be done today is to enhance the practice of living in the *now* moment. Whether we realize it or not, every moment is a miracle we should want to savor and enjoy. The eternal present is the space within which our lives unfold. It is the one factor that remains constant. There is clearly an intelligence at work that is far greater than the human mind.

Sometimes people put off doing something today that they want to do because they may think they do not know enough or can not perform the task well enough. The fact is, there is no "magic moment" at which excellence emerges or quality surfaces. Seize the day! Utilize the "now" moments of your life. The moment once past cannot return, and the moment anticipated may never arrive. Can any activity, attempted with an open mind, become a wonderful learning process?

Cultivating a "do it now" attitude can help you progress! As Lord Chesterfield stated: "It is an undoubted truth that the less one has to do the less time one finds to do it in. One yawns, one procrastinates, one can do it when one will, and therefore, one seldom does it at all; whereas those who have a great deal of business must (to use a vulgar expression) buckle to it; and then they always find time enough to do it in."

Don't be afraid of pressure. Remember that pressure is what turns a lump of coal into a diamond.
—*Anonymous*

An old spiritual legend says that God first created birds without wings. Sometime later, God made wings and said to the birds, "Come, take up these burdens and bear them." The birds hesitated at first, but soon obeyed. They tried picking up the wings in their beaks, but found the wings too heavy. They tried picking them up with their claws, but found them too large. Finally, one of the birds managed to get the wings hoisted onto its shoulders where it was finally possible to carry them.

To the amazement of the birds, before long the wings began to grow and soon had attached themselves to their bodies. One of the birds began to flap its wings and others followed. Before long, one of the birds took off and began to soar in the air above. What had once seemed to be a heavy burden now became the very thing that enabled the birds to go where they could never go before and, at the same time, to truly fulfill the destiny of their creation.

✦ Law 4

Invest yourself in your work. —John Marks Templeton

Two people can wake up in the same neighborhood, on the same day, to the same conditions, and yet have a vastly different day—based upon their attitudes. One person may awaken in the morning filled with enthusiasm and anticipation of the positive promise of the day. Another may awaken with thoughts clothed in pessimistic shadows. Perspective is often a key ingredient in experiencing a broad, generous, and friendly world and the wonderful souls who people it! However, nothing is interesting if we are not interested.

How is life unfolding for you? Is it moving forward in positive progression? How do you view the variety of experiences that life gives to you each day? Are you excited about your tremendous potential for creating greater good for yourself, for your family, for your friends, and for the world? Are you deeply interested in the multi-faceted aspects of living? How are you investing your time and talents in your work? In beneficial recreation? In life as a whole? As a matter of fact, have you considered the manner in which you move through each day as *an investment in a progressive life,* an investment for maximum *real* return?

Author Grenville Kleiser believed that "There is honor in labor. Work is the medicine of the soul. It is more: It is your very life, without which you would amount to little." Inasmuch as a large portion of most people's day, is involved with some kind of vocation, it would seem purposeful to perform each daily task the best we can. It is what we *do*, not merely what we say we believe, that determines our success in life. Are we investing our lives

with a spirit of unlimited love, diligence, purpose, enthusiasm, creativity, usefulness, humility, good ethical practices, patience, and thanksgiving? Are we paving the way to both personal and financial success with a solid foundation of spiritual and humanitarian principles?

Growth is usually a product of activity. How can anything be developed, physically or intellectually, without dedicated effort? And effort usually indicates some kind of work. We can begin by asking ourselves: What can I give (or invest) of my talents and abilities that will serve beneficially for others? Then, we can carefully choose a kind of work or industry with which we feel a strong kinship. If we try to be fruitful, we proceed with a positive, success-oriented frame of mind.

A farmer was known in a certain rural area for the excellence of his crops. It seemed they always took first place at the local fair. He also had a reputation for generosity and for sharing his best corn seed with all the other farmers in the area. When asked why he contributed so much to others, the farmer replied, "Well, it is really a matter of self-interest in a way. The wind picks up the pollen from the corn and distributes it from field to field. Cross-pollination is an important factor in a good corn crop. So, if my neighbors plant seed that is inferior, then the quality of all our crops is lessened. Since I want all of us to prosper and raise good crops, it is a joy and a benefit to share the best seed with them."

If you are curious as to what your future may hold, you can look into a mirror. What is reflecting back? Does a sparkle in your eyes indicate excitement about new adventures and opportunities? Does a smile on your lips portray an inner happiness and abundant good will toward others?

Do your words speak blessings, appreciation, and thanksgiving? Does the essence of your being radiate impressions of an alert, active, positive mind and an overall excitement about life? How can we bring more creativity to our work? How can we use each day to be creative? It is good to remember that the more sincere interest we express in life, the more joy and achievement we will find.

✦ Law 5

What good will this do? —John Marks Templeton

Do you want your life to be successful, productive, and happy? Do you desire to live your life in such a beneficial way that your activities can help improve the world for future generations? If so, what better method of introspection, analysis, or guidance can you find than to take a few seconds, several times throughout the day, to ask yourself a powerful and worthwhile question: *What good will this do?* This question can apply to your thoughts, your feelings, your words, or your actions with regard to any person, situation, or activity.

What might occur if, before you begin *any* activity, you asked: What good will this do? Could that moment of contemplation open a door for new or additional creative ideas. If you asked the question "What good will this do?" before talking to or about anybody, could your conversation perhaps be experienced on a deeper and more effective level? What are some benefits that could accrue if you asked "What good will this do?" when planning your day, your week, or your career?

When you decide to watch TV and take the remote control in your hand to select a channel, if you asked, "Will this program be educational, inspirational, healthy, or positively entertaining?" would you still select the program? Would asking, "Will this be beneficial?" before putting food or drink in your mouth make it a difference in you choices? Before choosing an investment, quickly ask yourself, "Are the products and services of this business helpful or harmful?" From half a century of helping people select investments, I have noticed that better investment results come from a portfolio of shares of companies that do good. Is it part of Gods' plan that those who do good will do well?

The Hippocratic Oath taken by all doctors is "Do no harm." If you apply that criterion to each step you take and to each choice you make in your life's work, your life can not only be successful, it can be joyous and happy as well. More and more people will feel that positive energy and want to be your customer or join your team. Happiness eludes those who seek it, but it flows abundantly to those who try to give it to others. One of the most precious and lasting joys in life is to feel that you are helping others.

You may notice that people who help others often have an abundance of friends. Why do you think this happens? One possibility could be that the person who helps others asks the question: How can I help? Problems or difficult situations often occur in the school of life. They may be God's way of providing us with opportunities to grow spiritually and productively. After all, would you choose a school that never gave your child the challenge of exams?

However, if you dwell on a problem or complaint, it can intensify and diffuse your thoughts with negativity. Asking the question "How can I help?" directs the thinking process to possible ways to resolve the problem. If you train yourself to be a problem-solver rather than a complainer, you will have more friends and admirers. Practicing such self-control becomes easier until it results in an almost effortless way or life.

A day wasted is a day forever lost. God designs human lives to include almost daily choices and challenges. Welcoming challenges provides opportunities for mental growth. Resenting challenges only hinders progress. Are you alert for avenues of expression where your particular talents and abilities may be used constructively? A whisper of inspiration and keen awareness can provide ready assets to your life's purpose and progress! If you focus on doing good, you will feel better about yourself. And your achievements can be admirable.

In Confucianism, a master virtue or principle call *Jen* refers to the belief that there is pure good-

ness in the center of our being, where the self or spirit can be found. The master said to the students: "Is goodness indeed so far away? If we really wanted goodness, we should find that it was at our very side. One who really cares for goodness would never let any other consideration come first."

Asking the question "What good will this do?" can tap into that inner wellspring and help you to transcend circumstances, rise above seeming limitations, behold greater good in yourself and in others, and create a life of positive self-esteem, greater success, and continuing joy.

Spotlights ✦ ✦

1. We can make positive choices governing the manner in which we speak or communicate with others.

2. Belittling or hurting others seldom provides an avenue of resolution to problems.

3. Kind and understanding words can provide powerful support.

4. Success may not be a one-time event; an accumulated series of events can create a successful life.

5. Past performance can be an indication of a person's future potential.

6. Ethics and spiritual principles should be the absolute basis of everything we do in life.

7. Pave the road of achievement with humanitarian service.

8. Refuse to carry the weight of yesterday's "leftovers" into today!

9. The eternal present is the space within which our lives unfold.

10. Growth is usually a product of activity. Invest yourself in your work.

11. Our relationships with others can build new patterns of harmony and good will.

12. Inner peace is a precious nourishing of unlimited love in each moment!

Living the Various Spiritual Laws ✦ ✦

The Buddhist *Tripitaka* contains a collection of proverbs called *The Way of the Doctrine* (*The Dhammapada*), which covers some of the basic beliefs of Buddhism presented in an easy-to-understand-and-remember manner.

+ All that we are is the result of what we have thought: it is founded on our thoughts and is made up of our thoughts.

+ If a man speaks or acts with an evil thought, pain follows him, as the wheel follows the foot of the ox that draws the cart; if a man speaks or acts with a pure thought, happiness follows him, as the shadow that never leaves him.

+ By thoughtfulness, by restraint and self-control, the wise man may make for himself an island which no flood can overwhelm.

+ Though a man go out to battle a thousand times against a thousand men, if he conquers himself, he is the greater conqueror.

+ Let a man overcome anger by love, let him overcome evil by good, let him overcome greed with liberality and lies with the truth.

+ Good people shine from afar, like the peaks of the Himalayas.

—Joseph Gaer, *What the Great Religions Believe*

Week Thirty-Two

✦ LAW I

We can become bitter or better as a result of our experiences. —Eric Butterworth

ON A BOOKPLATE dated 1940 are these words by C. Henry Cook:

*This world is just what we make it; 'Tis our **thoughts**
   tell how it shall be.*
*And if our **mind** is so small and narrow that we see
   only just what we see,*
*We'll lack the fine sense of knowing, and the cohesive
   co-efficiency of **Love**.*
*We'll know not the unceasing motive, the love of
   harmony defining our goal,*
*That is forever conveying a message for expanding
   the **light** in our **soul**.*

Every great journey, whether it is an attempt to scale the tallest mountain or to discover more about God, involves the attributes of decision, courage, and steadfastness. To experience the realization of a significant quest or opportunity, do we need to develop creativity, diligence, enthusiasm, and purpose? Few great journeys are completed without an occasional diversion or detour. There may be times when we feel we have lost our way. We may feel we have made mistakes, or wonder what it is really all about. Part of the progression of life's journey is learning how to accept difficulties with graciousness and love. What happens to us as we travel the journey of life is not nearly as important as *how we handle what happens*. Life sometimes takes unexpected twists and turns that can temporarily throw us off course. However, we can learn from these varied experiences and continue from there. We can become bitter or better as a result of our experiences.

A young man came to an old priest and said, "Father, a variety of negative, unacceptable thoughts are coming into my mind and I feel at loss regarding how to deal with them."

The old priest said to the young man, "Come with me, son." and he led the young man outside into a garden.

"Now," said the priest, "open your arms and catch the wind."

Surprised, the young man looked at the old priest. "Father, I cannot grasp the wind!"

The priest smiled and said, "Neither can you prevent thoughts from entering your mind. But what you can do is stand firm against them. Keep the ones that are helpful. Dismiss those unworthy of your attention."

As human beings, we often look for greater understanding in the midst of difficult times. Do we realize that the place to find light and discoveries can be right in the midst of what is happen-

Our joys as winged
dreams do fly;
Why then should
sorrows last?
Since grief but
aggravates thy loss,
Grieve not for
what is past.
—*Anonymous*

ing? Is there an art to learning how to flow with challenges and difficulties? How do we heal ourselves or others when we are hurting?

Perhaps one of the most difficult situations we can experience is that of grief. For most of us, grieving is how we respond to a deeply felt loss or a tragic event. We, or someone close to us, may have experienced an illness, a serious accident, the breakup of a relationship, a financial disaster, a loss of property, or a death. Grieving seems to be a natural way to respond to tragedy. This is often a time when both great love and discipline are helpful. Can difficult times be precious opportunities to bring forth that deep inner strength and to grow in spiritual wealth? The Kabbalah, a mystical text of Judaism, provides us with some words of comfort: "The falls of our life provide us with the energy to propel ourselves to a higher level." Our responses are important. Do we sink into sorrow, or do we open to the gift, the blessing, that grows from the sorrow?

The commitment of giving our best at all times, in all circumstances and under all conditions, can enable us to find value in, and lend value to, every experience. Whatever may have unfolded, if we are aware and open, we can realize that there is always much to be learned. Can we take today's

> Your living is determined not so much by what life brings to you as by the attitude you bring to life; not so much what happens to you as by the way your mind looks at what happens. Circumstances and situations do color life, but you have been given the mind to choose what the color shall be.
> —John Homer Miller

experiences and use them to develop our blessings and talents? And we always have a choice. We can become bitter or we can choose to become bigger and better people. When we learn to recognize that every experience can bring a blessing of some kind, our upset is softened. We gain the energy to soar to a higher level of consciousness in all areas of our lives. We connect with and benefit from the opportunity to discover new depths of wisdom and love in the opportunities that life presents.

I see on an immense
scale, and as clearly
as a demonstration
in a laboratory . . .
that we are made
strong by what
we overcome.
—*John Burroughs*

♦ ## LAW 2

Joy is not in things, but is in you. —John Marks Templeton

The fullness of joy is
to behold God in
everything.
—*Julian of Norwich*

JOY IS AN EXPERIENCE that perhaps every person desires, and a question often asked is: Where can I find joy? *Joy is not in things, but within each of us.* Joy is an inside job! It cannot be found "out there." Some people spend years looking outside themselves—in things, people, places, or situations—to find joy. You may have heard comments like: "If I drove that Mercedes, I would be happy." "If I lived in the big house on the hill, I would be happy." "If I could travel the world, I would be happy." If! Long-lasting and true joy arises from the spiritual

dimension. Joy can spring from releasing our creative abilities to accomplish significant goals or to further useful purposes.

The writer of Proverbs 17:22 tells us, "A cheerful heart is a good medicine, but a downcast spirit dries up the bones." Even some of our medical researchers today are coming to the conclusion that our ability to laugh and be joyful is a valid indication of our state of health. People with a sense of humor and an ability to laugh at themselves can often see the "light" side of life. Did you

The Holy Spirit rests
only on him who has
a joyous heart.
—Talmud

Let us live in
growing joy.
—The Dhammapada

From joy are born
all creatures, by joy
they grow, and to
joy they return.
—The Upanishads

know that joy and laughter can stimulate our internal organs and help reduce blood pressure? Joy can also promote relaxation and, therefore, relieve pain. Some of our muscles are activated through laughter; when we stop laughing, the muscles are relaxed. A cheerful heart is good medicine because positive emotions like joy, good humor, and laughter not only influence our immune systems, they leave us with a feeling that all is right with our world.

Norman Cousins, author of *Anatomy of an Illness*, was told that he suffered from a deterioration of the spinal cord, a disease that was virtually incurable. Knowing the value of laughter and joy, Norman decided to watch as many hilarious films as his family could find and bring to his hospital room. *Anatomy of an Illness* describes how he was cured of his terminal illness through the medicine of laughter. Sounds of joy bring not only healing to the body, but also healing to the spirit.

To "trigger" joy from within, find something purposeful to do. Many avenues are available for providing beneficial service in much-needed areas such as volunteering to help at a local hospital, becoming a "big brother" or "big sister" for children who could be greatly assisted through caring and sharing, or reading to an elderly person in a nursing home. Oh, there are so many possibilities for giving and receiving joy!

The miracle of all that is joy often rests in the divine idea of unlimited love. Not in being loved, but in loving, because when we exude love, we are automatically loved! Remember the prayer of St. Francis of Assisi when he said: "Oh Divine Master, grant that I may not so much seek to be consoled as to console. To be understood as to understand, to be loved as to love. For it is in giving that we receive. And it is in pardoning that we are pardoned." What beautiful truths are represented in his words.

A businessman was speaking to a group of school children about the joy he felt in his work. Looking for an example that the children could

identify with, he told them about an experience from his childhood. As a boy, he loved to climb trees, especially the giant oak tree growing just outside the kitchen window of the family home. Whenever he would feel pressure from school or from his brothers and sisters, he would climb up into a certain crook in the tree and snuggle against the trunk. When the wind blew, he imagined that he and the tree were partnering in a slow, graceful dance with the wind. The tree seemed to welcome his presence. It never questioned him. And the gray squirrel that lived higher in the tree would often come and sit nearby.

The greatest joy of a thinking man is to have searched the explored
and to quietly revere the unexplored.
—Goethe

The man told the students that treetops were also great for praying. Time seemed to stand still. Close to the sky and the movement of the clouds, he realized he was connected to something much greater than himself. Perhaps best of all, from this high perch he could survey the whole horizon and get a squirrel's eye view of things! The man felt like he was held in the embrace of the tree and, by extension, the natural world. He always felt good after a visit to his sacred spot in the tree. Whenever he felt tired, felt the need for comfort or an uplifting of his spirit, he remembered the feeling of joy that always came from those precious moments with the tree.

Universal intelligence—life energy or divinity—is not static. Life itself reminds us that creativity is ever active, ever-flowing. When we allow the universal energy to flow through us, are we projecting ourselves into the ever-moving, harmonious wholeness of spirit? It moves through us. It expresses itself through our minds and our actions. The result is often a feeling of connection with all of life. As we let the power of divine love flow through us, the path of the unfolding soul becomes a joyous one.

✦ Law 3

Retirement can begin a beneficial career. —John Marks Templeton

By the work one knows the workman.
—*Jean de la Fontaine*

All work . . . is noble; work is alone noble . . . A life of ease is not for any man nor for any god.
—*Thomas Carlyle*

MOST PEOPLE achieve greater happiness by remaining productive throughout the years of their lives. Some may express concern about the thought of retirement, while others look forward to the opportunity to do something very beneficial. *Retirement is not an end to life!* A greatly loved and admired teacher, upon nearing retirement age in her chosen profession, exclaimed her excitement: "I can hardly wait to re-tire!" She analogized her retirement from many years of teaching with getting a new set of tires for her car. She was getting "a new set of tires" to continue with her work. The woman planned to tutor special students in mathematics as part of her special "retirement package." A small group of students was eagerly waiting to receive her love and to be nourished by her knowledge. A man, working for a large corporation and nearing mandatory retirement age, said he was simply "changing seasons" in his life's work! Retirement should not be the end of the world or the end of life, any more than getting a first job was the beginning of the world or the beginning of life.

Retirement works best when people plan for it. It is all right to complete one career, providing fruitful activities are planned to fill the empty spaces. It is good to set new and realistic goals for the occasion when we may have more time to accomplish some of the productive things we may have been too busy to do. Often, if we think the future out in detail, our work after retirement can be more rewarding than the work we did for a number of years for a salary!

In an article titled "Never an End," Martha Smock wrote: "Age is a matter of consciousness, and the truth about your age is that in Spirit, you are neither old nor young. You are a spiritual creation, and you are on a continuing journey of life. You have much behind you, but you have much

I pray every single second of my life— not on my knees but with my work. Work and worship are one with me.
—*Susan B. Anthony*

before you . . . Retirement from a job does not absolve you of participation in life. It does not take away anything from your true purpose and place in life.

If a person has no plans, then retirement, especially early retirement, can be a form of suicide. This is not a time to sit back and do nothing. It is not healthy, nor is it wise. What has been put on the shelf insofar as a particular work is concerned is simply one phase of a person's productivity.

Mrs. Talbot was a wealthy woman who lived in Dayton, Ohio. She played no role in the business

Man, unlike any other thing organic or inorganic in the universe, grows beyond his work, walks up the stairs of his concepts, emerges ahead of his accomplishments.
—*John Steinbeck*

from which she drew a large income and could have simply done nothing. Instead, she used her time to help her children, grandchildren, and friends by seeking out inspirational articles. Once a year she would compose a calendar of 365 passages, one for each day of the year. Those people to whom she gave the calendar were frequently uplifted by that day's inspiration. They, in turn, often passed the message on to others who, in turn, benefited from one woman's work! Mrs. Talbot wisely used her precious moments of time on a helpful and happy activity.

There is a reward far greater than any money or accolades that we might receive. This is the feeling that we have accomplished our work and given our service in the very best way possible. This is the feeling of happiness and satisfaction that comes from real giving and helping others to gain the joy of becoming givers as well.

A real estate broker who had been working on

O my people!
Work according
to your power.
—Qur'an

a commission for several years said to one of his friends, "You know, it would be difficult to go back to a salaried position. I give my customers good service, and on a commission basis I am rewarded accordingly." He went on to explain that when he rendered a service to a person, he did so with no idea of receiving his reward from that particular person. He served to the best of his ability and left the rest to God!

As we go forward with a feeling of confidence to meet the new way of life that may open after retirement, the days and years ahead can certainly be happy and fruitful days. If a work is essential to the welfare of all members of the human race, it is ennobling to perform it. Every day, we need only to look for opportunities to be of loving service and recognize the truth that God's good never comes to an end!

✦ LAW 4

Happiness pursued eludes; happiness given returns. —John Marks Templeton

An effort made for the happiness of others lifts us above ourselves.
—Lydia M. Child

HAPPINESS SHINES as a true spiritual quality. It is akin to unlimited love, wisdom, praise, thanksgiving, and all the other divine ideas from the heart of divinity. Happiness is a state of mind that helps everyone. Happiness is an intangible value that helps establish the kingdom of heaven on earth. Mistakenly, we may search for "things" instead of seeking to give happiness to everyone. We may indulge ourselves in the "pursuit of happiness" rather than in giving happiness to others. And what are the results?

Those who are not looking for happiness are the most likely to find it, because those who are searching forget that the surest way to be happy is to seek happiness for others.
—Martin Luther King Jr.

The quote from Helen Keller, "Many persons have a wrong idea of what constitutes real happiness. It is not obtained through self-gratification, but through fidelity to a worthy purpose," speaks a wonderful truth. And Robert J. McCracken wrote: "The most infectiously joyous men and women are those who forget themselves in thinking about others and serving others. Happiness

comes not by deliberately courting and wooing it, but by giving oneself in self-effacing surrender to great values." It is true: *Happiness pursued eludes; happiness given returns.* We carry the mechanism for happiness with us, wherever we are, wherever we go.

So, what *is* happiness? Could it result from finding joy in productive work, and in doing that work with praise and thanksgiving? Is happiness realized in experiencing each new day as a priceless coin, newly minted from the hand of God, and spending it wisely and thoughtfully? Does happiness result from finding joy and thankfulness for what we have and for what we are yet forever reaching forward to achieve greater purpose? Is happiness a by-product of being honest and true to our best selves by living in integrity and noble purpose? Is happiness the peace of mind that comes from forgiving ourselves and others, regardless of the situation? Does happiness expand from experiencing enough difficulty to make us strong and enough adversity to make us wise?

Ask yourself: What is the likelihood that divine purpose is the pursuit of happiness for one of myriad species of creatures living for less than one thousandth of the history of one planet out of billions of planets? Is it more likely that humans were

Anyone who starts out to chase happiness will find it running away from him.
—Harry Emerson Fosdick

Cheerfulness keeps up a kind of daylight in the mind, and fills it with a steady and perpetual serenity.
—Joseph Addison

created to help accelerate divine creativity?

One way to experience happiness is to do something not directly aimed at giving us pleasure. For example, if we develop our talents and become excellent in a particular line of work, we can realize happiness as well as success. One way to better understand happiness is to study happy people. Think of those you know or see who radiate happiness. What is the source of their joy? What lessons can you learn from them? Are you beginning to perceive that happiness, lasting happiness, is not

found by receiving? Rather, it is a result of giving our whole being in response to God's unlimited love flowing through us.

It is so important that we grasp more fully, that we understand in a responsible way, our purpose as human beings, and our own close, continuing relationship with God's life. When we do, we may find that life lives itself through us and expresses itself through the gifts of our hearts, our heads, and our hands to others. And our happiness will overflow to affect all we meet.

✦ LAW 5

Thoughts of doubt and fear are pathways to failure. —Brian Adams

The thing we fear we bring to pass.
—Elbert Hubbard

IN HIS BOOK *The Positive Principle Today*, Norman Vincent Peale wrote:

There is a deep tendency in human nature to become precisely what we imagine or picture ourselves to be. We tend to equate with our own self-appraisal of either depreciation or appreciation. We ourselves determine either self-limitation or unlimited growth potential.

The negative thinker engages ultimately in a self-destroying process. As he constantly sends out negative thoughts, he activates the world around him negatively . . . The negative thinker, projecting negative thoughts, tends thereby to draw back to himself negative results. This is a definite and immutable law of mind. The positive thinker, on the contrary, constantly sends out positive thoughts, together with vital mental images of hope, optimism, and creativity. He therefore activates the world around him positively and strongly tends to draw back to himself positive results. This, too, is a basic law of mind action.

Mastering the principle of thinking positively and developing the ability to utilize positive energy in every situation can be basic to successful per-

formance. This means we let go of gloomy, restricting thoughts. And the twin monster thoughts of doubt and fear are definitely gloomy, restricting thoughts and providing pathways to failure. When allowed to remain in a person's mind, these two negative forces can multiply and overrun a person's ability to develop the positive strategies that can help overcome temporary difficulties.

Attempt the end, and never stand to doubt
nothing is so hard but search will find it out.
—Robert Herrick

How do we take command of the situation? How are we able to arrive at the place in consciousness where we can be positive, enthusiastic, and truly conscious of the working of the spirit? We take command of a situation when we reach the awareness that we have the power to be master over our thoughts and feelings. We rise up out of worry and concern, doubt and fear, when we learn that we can develop remedies and fresh opportunities, and that we are in control of the situation at hand. We were not born to fail; we were

Doubts and jeal-
ousies often beget
the fact they fear.
—*Thomas Jefferson*

Fear and love do not
walk together.
—*Lithuanian proverb*

A person without
self-control is like
a boat without
a rudder.
—*Philippine proverb*

born to succeed. One of the secrets to success is to drop the negatives and the excuses. Instead, adopt a lifestyle of giving. Believe that hard work and persistence pays off.

Thoughts are pathways and positive thoughts are upward pathways. When our minds are clogged by fear and doubt, our thoughts are often of failure and defeat. When the pathways of our thoughts are well chosen, positive, and enthusiastic, outstanding achievements may be accomplished.

Emmet Fox used an expression, "the mental equivalent," that has come to have deep meaning. For example, a person may have an uplifting thought about health and his "mental equivalent" of life will be a positive one that can help him meet and overcome physical disease. Or a person may have a "mental equivalent" of inner peace and harmony so that his life moves along smoothly and easily. Our "mental equivalents" become master designs around which our lives will be built. Although there may be areas in your life where you desire change, undoubtedly the first, and most important area to examine is your mental attitude.

Two friends were having lunch together and thoroughly enjoying each other's company. A lull in the conversation brought a moment of quiet, then one of the women said to the other, "You seem to have such a carefree and untroubled life. Don't you ever have any problems? What is your secret?"

The second woman smiled at her friend and replied, "Oh, yes. I have to deal with the everyday problems of life like everyone else, but I have learned not to worry about them. When a problem pops into my life, I sit down and carefully review the situation. If it is a situation I can do something about, I get busy and take the helpful action. If it seems too big for me to handle, I become still and quiet, and I pray for guidance. Then I listen. Eventually an idea for a solution comes and I act upon it. I could describe a number of seemingly impossible situations that have worked out because I know the source of my good!"

We can make up our minds to not be disturbed or distressed over things happening around us. As we learn to control our emotions, we become centers of helpfulness, thanksgiving, and greater strength. When we know the source of our good and pause daily to connect with that source, there is no opportunity for thoughts of doubt and fear to become active in our lives.

Spotlights ◆ ◆

1. Every great journey involves the attributes of decision, courage, and resourcefulness.

2. It is important to handle every experience to the best of your *current* ability.

3. The commitment of giving your best at all times, in all circumstances, and under all conditions, can enable you to find value in, and lend value to, every experience.

4. Joy is an intrinsic quality. Joy is not in things, but within each of us.

5. The miracle of all that is joy often rests in the divine idea of unlimited love.

6. Retirement works best when people plan how to continue productivity.

7. Your true purpose and place in life continue beyond retirement age.

8. One way to experience happiness is to do something for someone else.

9. Cheerfulness is a state of mind that attracts many blessings.

10. We can change our lives by changing our thoughts.

11. Mastering the principle of thinking positively and developing the ability to utilize positive energy in every situation can be basic to successful performance.

12. Doubt and fear can have no place in our lives unless we allow it.

Living the Various Spiritual Laws ✦ ✦

Whatever is in the heavens and whatever is on the earth is a direct evidence of the revelation within it of the attributes and names of God, inasmuch as within every atom are enshrined the signs that bear eloquent testimony to the revelation of that most great Light. Methinks, but for the potency of that revelation, no being could ever exist. How resplendent the luminaries of knowledge that shine in an atom, and how vast the oceans of wisdom that surge within a drop! To a supreme degree is this true of man, who, among all created things, hath been invested with the robe of such gifts, and hath been singled out for the glory of such distinction. For in him are potentiality revealed all the attributes and names of God to a degree that no other created being hath excelled or surpassed. All these names and attributes are applicable to him. Even as He hath said: "Man is My mystery, and I am his mystery."

—*The Kitáb-i-íqán* (The Book of Certitude)

Week Thirty-Three

◆ LAW I

You will know them by their fruits. —Matthew 7:16

The gentle mind
by gentle deeds
is known.
—Edmund Spenser

DIVINITY CAN TOUCH and move our lives in a variety of ways. One way is through the mystery of purpose, our sense of direction, or how we orient ourselves in life and in work. In his book *The Power of Purpose*, Richard J. Leider, describes "purpose" as: "the recognition of the presence of the sacred within us and the choice of work that is consistent with that presence. Purpose defines our contribution to life. It may find expression through family, community, relationship, work, and spiritual activities. We receive from life what we give, and in the process we understand more of what it means to discover our purpose." The fruits of spiritual living are qualities through which we can bring divine unlimited love, purpose, and beauty into every personal relationship and into every thing we do.

So our lives in acts
exemplary, not only
win ourselves good
names, but doth to
others give matter
for virtuous deeds,
by which we live.
—George Chapman

During his ministry, Jesus told those who were near, "You will know them by their fruits." Later, the Apostle Paul describes what the "good fruits" are: "The fruit of the Spirit is love, joy, peace, patience, kindness, goodness, faithfulness, gentleness, self-control; against these there is no law" (Galatians 5:22–23).

What is meant by the statement, "against these there is no law?" Does it mean that no law is needed? Can you imagine the passing of laws to keep citizens from being loving, joyous, peaceable, patient, kind, good, faithful, gentle, and self-controlled? The wonderful and good possibilities of

the "fruits of the spirit" are part of the divine ideal for every person. Just as within every apple seed is the possibility for a tree bearing delicious, fully ripened fruit, so within each person are realities of potential that have been freely given to us! Our job now is to cultivate these precious seeds and nurture them into abundant harvest.

The great things you intend to do sometime must have a beginning if they are ever to be done, so begin to do something worthwhile today.
—Grenville Kleiser

We may be standing on the threshold of an opening new door. Our uplifted consciousness could take us through the door into an expanded universe of good, giving us an opportunity to truly experience the "kingdom of heaven" on earth.

Let's take a closer look at the shining treasures of the "fruits." One of the great spiritual recommendations is to "Love one another." Could these words be divine sparks that can set our hearts (emotions and feelings), souls (our spiritual capacity), and minds (thoughts, mental ability) aflame with creativity and abundant life? So much has been written about *love*. Love has been called the "unifying, harmonizing substance of the universe." Unlimited love is an inner quality that beholds good everywhere and in everyone. It is often through the process of unfolding love that our capacity to become more useful human beings can be developed. Utilizing the power of unlimited love can help dissolve any disharmony.

What is *joy?* We may think that joy is the result of happy circumstances. And it may be at times. Could a more mature view of joy be that it is a by-product of sharing the good we have and serving others? Joy is a *cause*, not a *result*. Joy is a spiritual principle, available for our use at all times. There are many ways we can express joy and be a positive influence through pleasant words, a sincere smile, and even a sense of humor. Spiritual joy is never out of place, because joy is the deep, abiding serenity and poise we experience when we are centered in the causative power for good. One of the paradoxes of truth is that a happy heart draws to itself all it needs for abiding happiness. We can keep our hearts happy by drawing on the joyous fruitfulness of our spiritual natures.

Could there be any person who, on some deep inner level of being, did not desire the gift of *peace?* Peace is much more than freedom from strife. The kingdom of peace is within us and we have the power to determine how we feel. Peace often comes from knowing that there is no place where we can be that divinity is not, so we live our lives based on universal principles, a sense of purpose, and a commitment to loving service.

How many of us have, at times, longed for more *patience,* especially while in the process of overcoming upsetting circumstances!? Yet, when we know that spirit gives us strength to continue until we work through whatever may be before us, we can be more patient. When we think of patience as a spiritual principle, do we realize that patience is dynamic, not passive? With spiritual patience, we no longer waste precious time or energy resisting a situation. We look for a solution.

Kindness is a beautiful and gentle expression of unlimited love. Kindness can open the way for infinite good to come to us, which can then go forth from us to bless all of life. Kindness releases a flow of divine joy and love within our souls. Everyone benefits from kindness. Can you imagine how our lives could change if we replaced fear and guilt with love, forgiveness, and kindness? Where do we want to focus our attention?

> Man is man because he is free to operate within the framework of his destiny. He is free to deliberate, to make decisions, and to choose between alternatives. He is distinguished from animals by his freedom to do evil or to do good and to walk the high road of beauty, or tread the low road of ugly degeneracy.
> —*Martin Luther King Jr.*

Lowell Fillmore said, "*Goodness* is more than simply refraining from doing evil. It is a definite positive awareness of God's unfailing perfection." In Confucianism, a principle called Jen maintains that there is pure goodness at the center of the human being where the spirit can be found. The pure or good in heart are often distinguished by their thoughts and behaviors. We have an inner spiritual strength that is capable of sustaining us when we need it; it can help us unfold and expand the goodness of our true natures.

Faithfulness means always being reliable. If you are what some people call "a faithful person," you are dependable. You keep your promises. You are honest, and you inspire confidence. You seek to live your life with integrity in all things. You are true to what you believe. Being faithful is not a momentary feeling, but rather a grounding and steadfastness in the universal principles that can guide our lives.

Gentleness can be a tremendous help to someone seeking to develop greater understanding. Those who wish to be wise pray for an understanding heart. An understanding heart is filled with love and wisdom, compassion, vision, and the ability to manifest the vision. Gentleness can pave the way for quietude and humility. Gentleness can often accomplish a worthwhile endeavor when force may fail. Gentle meekness in a person can indicate that universal laws or principles are strong guiding forces in his or her life. Gentleness can also bring a beneficial experience of peace and freedom, success and fulfillment.

Self-control is truly the starting point of all control. There may be times when we do not like the way we are thinking or feeling or acting. When this occurs, we can pause and invite a positive thought or feeling to replace those we do not like. If we are uncomfortable with our actions, we can change our behavior. We are provided with the necessary spiritual "tools" to express ourselves in the highest, most noble way possible. We can claim the ability to take charge of our life, and we begin with self-control.

How could we be truly happy with any life plan that failed to produce the harvest of the good fruits of the spirit? Let's make the choices that reflect our divine self. Let's invite the flow of universal energy to flood our beings, expanding the essence of who and what we are.

✦ LAW 2

Optimism has its roots in abiding goodness. —Anonymous

> There is no greatness where there is no simplicity, goodness, and truth.
> —Leo Tolstoy

> Keep your face in the sunshine and you will never see the shadows.
> —E. C. McKenzie

YOGANANDA SAID, "It is almost impossible to describe in human language the cosmic adventure of God's creation and its subtle intertwining with the individual life-adventures of countless human beings." Life is often considered one of the greatest adventures imaginable. Perhaps in a number of different ways, each of us can sense a deep mystery in being alive. When an infant is born or when the death of a loved one brushes close to us, the mystery of life becomes more personal and tangible. We can behold the glory of divinity in a radiant sunset, in the sweet warmth of spring rain, and in the flowering seasons of our days. We can behold the glory of divinity in our daily lives.

How do we live our daily lives? Not theoretically, not philosophically or idealistically, but how do we actually *live?* Are the things we say and do beneficially productive? Is the world a better place because we are part of it? One woman planted flowers wherever she lived because she wanted to make her little spot on the Earth more beautiful! Every person who passed by enjoyed the beauty of her gardens! Can we live in such a way that every day is all-important? How would we do this? Have you ever realized that you are immersed in a realm of infinite spiritual power and that you can learn to tap into it? How?

> The optimist may not understand, or if he understands he may not agree with prevailing ideas; but he believes, yes, knows, that in the long run and in due course there will prevail whatever is right and best.
> —Thomas A. Buckner

For many people, there seems to be a growing desire toward being more fully and expressively alive. Are we beginning to realize that we are here for a purpose? Does something seem to be drawing us on a spiritual journey? We can become seekers of greater knowledge: a hundred doors can open to the questing spirit!

What is it that draws a person toward spiritual

progress? We may not consciously readily know the reasons that propel us. But is "something" awakening within us? Could this awakening be a growing enthusiasm toward the many opportunities beckoning us to stretch our minds and expand our perspectives? Could the "stirring within" be hopefulness that our goals may be realized? Is there a brightness to living that draws us onward in pursuit of increased usefulness? Could it be that "optimism has its roots in abiding goodness," and we feel the call of positive beliefs? Can thoughts of oneness and unity build confidence and encourage us to learn new ways of thinking, including alternatives to solving our disputes through aggression? Are these things part of the abiding goodness of humanity?

As we discover our souls' capacities to find good in any situation—joyful or sorrowful—can we awaken to greater freedom, greater expression, and greater fruitfulness? Can we become explorers and discoverers of the blessings of spirit? Can we see everything around us with a renewed sense of thanksgiving? Can we demonstrate our enthusiasm for life, allowing our enthusiasm to spill over into everything we do until it affects everyone around us? Could this powerful energy represent what is called "being in touch with the infinity of divinity"?

An optimistic person interprets life in the most favorable ways and confidently works for remedies. Have you noticed that things work out well for the people who *expect* good things to happen?

Being optimistic does not mean that you will not face challenges along the way. However, an optimistic attitude carries the awareness that any situation holds the potential for a positive outcome and greater good. The intent of the optimist is to discover that good! When confronted by difficulty, an optimistic person searches for solutions. He or

> Goodness is always an asset. A man who is straight, friendly, and useful may never be famous, but he is respected and liked by all who know him. He has laid a sound foundation for success and he will have a worthwhile life.
> —Herbert N. Casson

she is open-minded and honest, looking on the bright side for the most beneficial and noble outcome. Optimism spreads joy!

Emerson writes fervently and eloquently about optimism; he did so in the years following the ill health and deaths of his first wife, his two brothers, and his adored six-year old son. The intensity of such tragedies could cause some people to become bitter and cynical. Although Emerson experienced deep grief, his confidence in the goodness of life upheld his love for beneficial ideas.

Each of us can also know and express what Emerson called the "Infallible trust and . . . the vision to see that the best is the true. In that attitude, one may dismiss all uncertainties and fears, and trust that time will reveal the answers to any private puzzlement."

✦ LAW 3

If you think you know it all, you are less likely to learn more. —John Marks Templeton

HUMAN PERSONALITY and development are often considered in the light of realizing some material goal, such as increasing personal, business, or

social opportunities. In dealing with your own fundamental worth as a person, is it important to remind yourself that, by definition, self-worth must come from ourselves? The essence of this magnificent self-worth is often derived from applying our personal talents, abilities, and resources in creative and beneficial ways. This awareness of self-worth is very different from inflated egos and useless pride.

> To think of learning as a preparation for something beyond learning is a defeat of the process. The most important attitude that can be formed is that of the desire to go on learning.
> —Daniel Bell

He who comes up with his own idea of greatness must always have had a very low opinion of it in his mind.
—William Hazlitt

Have you had the experience of being around someone who seems to be caught up in an ego trap, feeling and thinking that he or she knows everything already, has all the answers, and has decided not to listen to what others have to offer? How did *you* feel? It likely was an uncomfortable situation for you because the conversation was one-sided, with the other person extolling his or her perceived accomplishments and knowledge.

There are many interpretations of the word "ego." Some people view the ego as the unconscious part of ourselves that often seeks to control our daily lives. Others describe ego as the exclusive physical aspect of our reality as opposed to the spiritual part that we define as our soul. However, could a more practical and possibly correct definition simply be "the way we perceive ourselves and how we express our perceptions of superiority"?

The modern mind is slowly opening to different visions of reality.
—Sogyal Rinpoche

In *The Tibetan Book of Living and Dying,* Sogyal Rinpoche wrote a helpful description of the ego:

Two people have been living in you all of your life. One is the ego, garrulous, demanding, hysterical, calculating; the other is the hidden spiritual being, whose still voice of wisdom you have only rarely heard or attended to. As you listen more and more to the teachings, contemplate them, and integrate them into your life, your inner voice, your innate wisdom of discernment . . . is awakened and strengthened, and you start to begin to distinguish between

its guidance and the various clamorous and enthralling voices of the ego.

An effective way to gain freedom from the ego is through listening and learning, reflection and discernment. If we think we know it all, we are less likely to learn. And to *really listen* and *learn,* it is helpful to put aside prejudices and preconceived ideas and concepts and *hear with an open mind* what someone else is saying. Open-mindedness is a key for growth, and willingness turns it on. We do not have to accept everyone's beliefs or ideas, but we can thoughtfully examine them. We have the option to retain useful information and to release the unessential. How can we hear the guidance of the whisperings of spirit if we are busy talking about perhaps unessential things? When you become open to another person's point of view, can you discover many new and exciting ways to look at any subject?

> If a man has come to that point where he is so content that he says, "I do not want to know any more, or do any more, or be any more," he is in a state in which he ought to be changed into a mummy.
> —Henry Ward Beecher

The art of listening can be a humbling experience. For example, if you examine a single leaf that has fallen from a giant tree, you literally can discover a number of ways to observe the leaf. The artist or poet may see form, color, and beauty from a completely different perspective. The musician may hear an unsung symphony. The biologist may see evidence of purpose in the simple expressions of nature. The atomic scientist may see trillions of atoms amazingly organized. A groundskeeper may see the leaf as littering his garden path. The caterpillar may see food for metamorphosis into a glorious butterfly. The wonders of God's creation abound, even in a simple leaf!

Those taking the humble approach to life admit

The emptiest man
in all the world is
the man who is full
of himself.
—E. C. McKenzie

God still speaks to
those who take the
time to listen.
—Anonymous

that the whole universe and all the creatures in it—visible and invisible— may come from the limitless and timeless Creator. We know so little. The gift of learning is one of the greatest gifts we can give ourselves! By learning humility, we find that the purpose of life on earth is vastly deeper than any human mind can grasp. Diligently, each child of God should seek to find and obey God's purpose, but not be so egotistical as to think that he or she comprehends the infinite mind of God. Humility is in tune with God and God's purposes,

whereas pride is out of harmony with spiritual principles.

Thinking we know it all is limiting and confining. By nourishing openness, willingness, enthusiasm, breadth of vision, and reverence for all of life, can we change the whole atmosphere of our minds? Then, the divine spirit can move in our life, dissipating the human ego, and filling that created vacuum with unlimited love that prompts us to listen and learn.

Opportunities are often missed because we are broadcasting when we should be listening. —E. C. McKenzie

---

✦ LAW 4

No person was ever honored for what he received.
Honor has been the reward for what he gave. —Calvin Coolidge

We must not judge
a man's merits by
his qualities, but
by the use he
makes of them.
—François, Duc de La
Rochefoucauld

IN THE GOSPEL according to Luke, Jesus said, "Give and it will be given to you; good measure, pressed down, shaken together, running over, will be put into your lap. For the measure you give will be the measure you get back" (6:38). Here, Jesus states a fundamental law of life that has been recognized by most great spiritual leaders as well as by many truly successful men and women.

If you love the work you do, you are going to put all of yourself into it, giving freely of your energy and of your talents. When you give of yourself, you work for the joy of achievement. When you share your abilities with others, the gift of appreciation, tangible or intangible, becomes part of your daily life. Tangible appreciation could be a monetary return or a gift from someone for work you have accomplished. Intangible appreciation could be gratitude from others for what you have done as well as a good reputation. The big reward comes from your own joy at being useful.

On the other hand, if you are working for the paycheck, willing only to do what you believe you are being paid to do and no more, chances are that you will grow to dislike your job.

A man is already of consequence in the world
when it is known that we can implicitly rely upon him.
Often I have known a man to be preferred in stations
of honor and profit because he had this reputation:
when he said he knew a thing, he knew it, and when
he said he would do a thing, he did it.
—Edward Bulwer-Lytton

Bob was such a man. For eight hours a day, five days a week, year after year, he pulled down a salary while putting forth as little effort as possible. Bob always seemed to be tired and discontented, and he blamed his job for many of his problems.

One thing Bob enjoyed doing, however, was

watching his daughter play softball. When he was offered the opportunity to coach her team, he eagerly accepted. Although coaching the girls' team took a great deal of time and commitment, Bob did not mind. He said the hours he spent with the team were energizing. The softball season ended with the girls taking a first-place trophy, and Bob received an outpouring of praise from the parents who were amazed by the energy of his commitment.

Fortunately, the story doesn't end there. At the prompting of his concerned wife, Bob decided to seek spiritual counseling about the problem in his professional life. The counselor suggested that Bob begin to embrace his job with the same enthusiasm that he was pouring into coaching the girl's softball team. Reluctantly, Bob agreed to give the suggestion a try.

To his surprise, Bob began noticing things to do at work that made each day more interesting. He started taking an interest in the lives of his fellow employees. He challenged himself to find ways to improve how he did his job. He worked as if he was the actual owner of the plant instead of just being "another cog in the machine." Bob began making suggestions to his superiors on how his department could operate efficiently. And, to his great surprise, he even found himself thinking about ways to improve his work after hours! Bob now awakens each day with a sense of enthusiasm instead of dull despair. He learned the valuable les-

son of honestly and sincerely giving of yourself in whatever you do.

It isn't likely that you will become competent at something you ignore. And it may not be easy to release inner turmoil until you, as a unique human being, develop a feeling of being active in your own life purpose. Finding and focusing on your purpose can help direct your activities into beneficial arenas where you are able to give so much more to life. Giving can be similar to financial investing. If you invest carelessly and without effort or research, you are likely to fail in the long run. On the other hand, when you wisely invest your energies, interests, and abilities, you are more likely to succeed.

Remember that merely putting time into something does not mean you are giving yourself to it. There are various levels or degrees of giving. Dedicate your attention, your interest, your love, your imagination, and your creativity to the task at hand. In this way, an undesirable condition can be transformed into something that returns benefits in "good measure, pressed down, shaken together, running over. For the measure you give will be the measure you get back." This is a law of life that can work for you in the same way it worked for Bob and has worked for millions of other people who have discovered it. Think less about what you can get and think more about what you can give. Then, you may find that your life takes on a luster you haven't yet dreamed possible.

✦ Law 5

The shadow of ignorance is fear. —J. Jelinek

FEAR IS OFTEN considered one of the greatest challenges we face today, as individuals and as a society. From a less desirable perspective, fear holds us

back from fully expressing ourselves. Fear of rejection may prevent us from working on the communication and friendship a normal life needs. Fear of failure may prevent us from making fruitful commitments. A thought pattern of fear can induce an egocentric lifestyle. Fearing nonconformity, we may relinquish part of our individuality. Fear can result in insensitivity and disrespect. The fear of not having enough may prevent us from seeing the universal principle of abundance that is operative in our lives. Fear can also create a blockage, preventing us from loving ourselves and others. Unreasonable and irrational fear can restrict us in an invisible prison.

Yet, a self-preservation type of fear can serve a useful purpose. An instinctive awareness of danger can alert us to potential harm and help us mobilize the resources needed to keep ourselves from injury.

As advancing communication technology now brings world events quickly into many homes, we learn about other cultures, and the shadow of ignorance can be dissipated along with fear of the unknown. Resistance is often a basic part of the fear of changing. The work necessary in this instance is to use our thoughts on positive images of the goals we seek. The Dutch philosopher Spinoza said, "I saw that all things I feared and which feared me, had nothing good or bad in them save insofar as the mind was affected by them."

Causing fear has long resulted from our human egos. How is this so? When we do not yet understand that we are a part of God's divine design, our ego can cause us to transmit fear energy instead of love energy. Learning to experience unlimited love is a powerful way of banishing fear and transforming our lives. Also, using the technique of observing ourselves can help us release false self-judgments.

In his message to Congress on January 6, 1941, Franklin Delano Roosevelt wrote these immortal words: "We look forward to a world founded upon four essential human freedoms. The first is freedom of speech and expression . . . everywhere in the world. The second is the freedom of every person to worship God in his own way . . . everywhere in the world. The third is freedom from want . . . everywhere in the world. The fourth is freedom from fear . . . anywhere in the world."

Releasing the shadow of ignorance and its companion, fear, often requires a new agreement with reality. The things we most commonly fear can often be explained away by investigative research. Vivekenanda said, "The blossom vanishes of itself as the fruit grows." When we *know* that the loving presence of divinity is always with us, the notion of fear vanishes. As we rid ourselves of fear, a purposeful confidence starts to develop that reflects our increasing awareness. Fear often dissipates when doubt is dismissed.

Any kind of fear, real or imagined, can only impede our progress. Courage and enterprise are among the greatest energies for overcoming fear. They are the sparks that can ignite positive steps toward beneficial growth. Since "the shadow of ignorance is fear," what fears stand in your way in your quest for a better life? Bring your fears to light so that their shadows can be destroyed and their hold over you can be loosened and released. Take a deep breath and banish these fears. Allow the confusion caused by fear and ignorance to be eliminated. Learn the lessons of courage and resourcefulness to create the fruitful life you desire.

Spotlights ✦ ✦

1. Review the "fruits of the spirit" essay. How well are you harvesting this crop in your daily life?

2. The fruits of the spirit are available for your use, all the time, in every circumstance or situation.

3. An optimist interprets life in the most favorable way possible and, with confidence, expects that whatever is best can happen.

4. A pessimist fears misfortunes and, therefore, can attract them!

5. An effective way to discover freedom from the ego is through listening and learning, reflection and discernment.

6. The art of listening can be a humbling experience.

7. Thinking that we already know everything is both limiting and confining.

8. When you give of yourself, you work for the joy of achievement; when you share your bounty with others, the gift of appreciation, tangible or intangible, becomes part of your daily life.

9. There is great value in honestly and sincerely giving of yourself.

10. Learning to experience unlimited love is a powerful way of banishing fear and transforming our lives.

11. The things we most commonly fear can often be explained away by investigative research.

12. Any kind of fear, real or imagined, can impede our progress.

Living the Various Spiritual Laws ✦ ✦

THAT YE ALL MAY BE ONE
—Hilda Kellis

I looked to the East
and saw turban'd and mantled Believers
kneeling toward Mecca.
God/Allah radiated from each heart.
In that moment
I knew the meaning of Oneness.

    I looked to the West,
    my own land and people, then farther still
    to the far West. I saw
    each, in God's own way radiating His Light.

In churches, in temples, and
not in churches or temples;
at picnics, in parks,
at desks in high places—
Light and Love expressed
as they understood it.
In that moment
I knew the meaning of Oneness.

I looked to the South and saw gloriously
    radiant, shining faces
singing of His Love. In tabernacles,
on hillsides, in valleys, in cities.
Little children, tall children—
all expressing the Love of God.
In individual, creative uniqueness.
In that moment, I knew the meaning of Oneness.

Once again my inner gaze swung,
this time to the North.
Friends, families, in rugged mountains
snow-capped and majestic,
around hearth fires, on dogsleds,
cold wind whispering mysterious sounds
on all sides. I saw
in each entity a firm and solid picture
of the Love of God expressed.
And in that moment
I knew the meaning of Oneness.

It's not in our differences,
nor even the sameness of our world religions
that we find the Kingdom, but
in our constant, expanding
expression of Oneness.
I'm grateful for the Power and the Love
that opens our hearts,
"That we all may be one."

✦ LAW I

Man must discipline himself by good thoughts, good words, good deeds.
—Zoroastrian scripture

THE JOURNEY TOWARD wholeness is a common motif in some definitions of spirituality. Psychotherapist Molly Young Brown writes: "When we expand our awareness, strengthen our center, clarify our purpose, transform our inner demons, develop our will, and make conscious choices, we are moving toward deeper connection with our spiritual self." Self-discipline goes a long way toward helping to build a foundation for happy and successful living. Many definitions for living a more productive life suggest that spirituality can be an everyday adventure touching practically every area of our lives. And there are as many expressions of spirituality as there are individuals with different interests, values, beliefs, and traditions.

What image does the word "discipline" bring to your mind? For some people, discipline takes on the appearance of regimen, control, or punishment. For others it can mean a field of study, a branch of knowledge, education, preparation, conduct, or self-mastery. In this essay, let's research "discipline" from the perspective of education. The field of study could be personal growth, whereby we seek to spiritually educate ourselves toward positive conduct, resulting in greater self-mastery. An excellent way of accomplishing this goal can be through *good thoughts, good words,* and *good deeds.* A life of beneficial accomplishment and purpose lies within the grasp of every person, if he or she

will reach for it. The mental, emotional, and physical aspects of our beings can be useful instruments of expression. When we recognize that we have the capacity to choose what we will think, feel, and, to a large degree, experience, we begin making progress toward greater self-mastery.

The actual living process takes place day to day in the profound school called life. In this setting, our goal is not only to *know* and *understand* spirituality, but also to encompass it in all our endeavors. Each person looking for ultimate answers sets out on a unique, searching adventure. Human nature often seems to be looking for the perfect or most helpful pattern by which to guide growth. How can we become more spiritually mature? How can we further develop spiritual habits such as prayer, meditation, and positive attitudes and practices in today's busy world?

Could spiritual growth necessitate a personal discipline that is different from yet includes physical, emotional, and mental disciplines? When we are guided or "disciplined" by our spiritual nature

—which includes wisdom, love, understanding, joy, and compassion—and by life itself, can we change in both beneficial and creative ways?

To quote an old adage, "Before we can start the day, we must first get out of bed!" To enter an advanced class in trigonometry, we must first study courses in basic mathematics. If we wish to grow spiritually, it is important to discipline our self by *good thoughts, good words,* and *good deeds.* Our hunger for developing a higher consciousness must become poignant enough to pierce the humdrum pace of everyday living. Sincere desire, positive attitude, and extended effort largely determine the success of our adventure.

The process of living is definitely not an aimless activity. Every new day presents us with the background, the visible reality, the passing experiences, the opportunities, and the challenging new stretch of road to travel in pursuit of our goals. Could it be that every person has a spiritual reason for being,

and that our world is incomplete until that reason, or purpose, is discovered? When we choose to uplift our everyday activities with spiritual inspi-

Realization of Truth is higher than all else;
higher still is truthful living.
—Sikhism

ration, our way of life can improve dramatically.

In order to do practically anything, the appropriate groundwork is usually necessary. Good *thoughts* require an awareness that what we predominantly think about determines what we experience. Good *words* are symbols for good thoughts. Our words carry power because they are the audible or written expression of thought. So, let's use our words with care and speak the words we sincerely mean. Then, let's follow our good thought and good words with positive *actions,* with good *deeds,* that agree with our words.

✦ Law 2

You are either part of the problem, or part of the solution. —Eldridge Cleaver

It has been said that there are two kinds of people in the world. There are those who see a problem, define and describe the problem, complain about the problem, and finally become part of the problem. And there are those who look at a problem and immediately begin to search for a solution. For the person who focuses on the problem, life can seem like a difficult and uphill struggle. However, for those who are the solution-seekers, life presents many opportunities for growth. The choice of response to any life situation is up to the individual. The result? "You are either part of the problem, or part of the solution."

Being part of the problem can be easy, because focusing on a number of conflicting facts and pos-

sible scenarios can offer many different reasons why something cannot be accomplished. More effort may be necessary to discipline our minds to discover the ways the problem can be solved. Yet, what may seem to be an insurmountable obstacle for people who focus on the problem often becomes an excellent opportunity for discovery and growth for solution-seekers.

A story is told about two men who were walking along a forest path late one night. It was quite dark and the men had difficulty seeing the path. Suddenly, both men fell into a large pit, loosely covered with brush and leaves. Escape seemed impossible without outside help. Lamenting their terrible situation, one man sat down, buried his

Adversity is the
school of heroism,
endurance the
majesty of man, and
hope the torch of
high aspiration.
—Albert A. Whitman

face in his hands, and did nothing but complain about their misfortune. The other man immediately began to search for a way of escape from the pit. He walked around the pit, running his hands along the side. While groping in the dark, his hand touched a long tree root hanging from the side of the wall. Using the tree root for leverage, he quickly pulled himself out of the pit and then reached down to assist his complaining friend.

Regardless of the intensity of the challenges that may arise, the decisions we make about handling the situations can be crucial in terms of success or failure, now and in the future. An excellent help in any situation is a loving, caring, and positive outlook. The loving person can feel the human emotions of hurt, anger, or frustration, but the loving person does not allow negative emotions to become dominant. A person living from an attitude of unlimited love is quick to forgive. He or she may often be the first one to open the door to necessary communication, or to offer a handshake or a hug in reconciliation. A loving person lives in a loving world, regardless of disappointments, sorrows, varying degrees of stress, or problems.

Whether people act beautiful and friendly or unattractive and disruptive, ultimately they are human beings, just like we are. Like us, they pre-

I do not want ever to be indifferent
to the joys and beauties of life.
For through these, as through pain,
we are enabled to see purpose in
randomness, patterns in chaos.
We do not have to understand that
in order to believe that behind
the mystery and the fascination is love.
—Madeleine L'Engle

fer happiness instead of suffering. Because we all share an identical need for love, it becomes easy to understand that the people we meet, in whatever circumstances, are fellow travelers on Earth. Thus, it seems foolish to dwell on external differences or problems, because our basic natures are the same. Look for the *best* elements of a situation. Then be creative!

Mao Zedong of China had this to say about solving problems: "You can't solve a problem? Well, get down and investigate the present facts and the problem's past history! When you have investigated the problem thoroughly, you will know how to solve it." These are wonderful words of encouragement to become more observant and knowledgeable about the facts in any situation.

It seems that most problems can be divided into two main categories: mental and physical. Of the two, the mind exerts the greatest influence on most of us. Unless we are gravely ill or deprived of necessities, the physical aspects of life usually play a secondary role. The mind registers every event. So, wouldn't it seem appropriate that a positive, thought-provoking attitude, coupled with unlimited love, can open wide new avenues of possibilities?

Make a conscious effort to be a solution-seeker. Remember, it does not take great courage, genius, or effort to be a problem person. On the other hand, becoming a solution-seeker helps us feel good about ourselves and often results in feeling more confident about our capabilities.

✦

✦ Law 3

The borrower is a servant to the lender. —Proverbs 22:7

THE WORDS of Shakespeare tell us, "Neither a borrower nor a lender be." How would you express the wisdom contained in this statement? One con-

sideration could be that a person who borrows money possibly lives with the continuing stress of knowing there is a debt that must be repaid. A borrower may find his joy diminished because he is concerned about how he will repay the loan. After all, what caused the shortfall in the first place? And how can you enjoy spending money when it really belongs to someone else? A borrower may feel nervous or uneasy in the presence of the lender if the debt has not yet been repaid. Where is the spirit of personal freedom in this situation?

Abraham Lincoln stated, "You cannot keep out of trouble by spending more than you earn. You cannot establish security on borrowed money." A debt can be like emotional quicksand, pulling one downward into feelings of fear, insecurity, and indignity. Can an increasing number of small debts become a disturbing factor, demanding more and more of a person's time, thought, and energy? Large debts can become overwhelming. When this occurs, a person may find it difficult to think about other important issues of daily living, thus further increasing the level of stress in his or her life.

In their book *Owe No Man*, Ann Ree Colton and Jonathan Murro wrote of the spiritual principles of good stewardship and divine providence: "Travel light: 'Owe no man' (Romans 13:8); hasten to leave your offering, your spiritual promises on the Altar; go forth and work diligently to pay off the debt carelessly made in time of blind motive."

One young man became aware of the danger of debt at an early age, and by the time he was a teenager he decided that the biggest threat to many families' personal finances was excessive borrowing. So he made a vow, then and there, to be a lender if necessary, but *never* a borrower. And until age forty, he never owned a credit card or a store charge account.

A young woman unexpectedly became a widow with two small children to support. The amount of debt left by her husband may have seemed small to many people, but to her, the debt seemed gigantic. She had to immediately find a job and go to work to support herself and her family. Having grown up with parents who taught the importance of "owing no one," the young woman sat down

and worked out a plan of paying off the debts. Fortunately, she quickly found a job. She then visited each person to whom she was indebted and made arrangements to handle each responsibility in a timely manner. Then, working with a longer-range goal, she began part-time studies at a nearby college to gain more education so she could ultimately get a better job. She found a responsible person to care for the children while she worked and attended classes. Through commitment, diligence, and hard work, this young woman succeeded in reaching her goals and earned tremendous respect from her family, friends, coworkers, and employers.

While it may be a fact of life that for many people certain bills seem inevitable, like utility bills, mortgage payment, medical bills, or unexpected necessities that may arise, we can agree with Buckminster Fuller: "I consider it essential to pay all my bills in the swiftest manner possible."

A person continuing to increase his debts by making unnecessary purchases, or perhaps to enjoy a particular overexpanded lifestyle, is experiencing a false sense of prosperity. He is also confining himself to a restricted range of thoughts, actions, and opportunities. A time of reckoning will surely arrive. Certainly, one person would not like to be servant to another from the perspective of indebtedness. However, modern conveniences such as credit cards, home equity loans, revolving charge accounts, and time payments offer seductive enticements to spend money.

Several key ingredients relate to living successfully and profitably. A natural inclination toward independence and self-reliance, along with ambition, hard work, creativity, and resourcefulness, can lay the foundation for living a relatively good life. Being a rational and responsible risk-taker can indicate a bit of the successful entrepreneur. A sense of stewardship is important. Money represents something of more value than mere worldly riches. It can entail the privilege of wisely managing assets that we have earned. One man buys the clothing he needs when the stores have their semi-annual or annual sales. A woman takes advantage of sale items in her local supermarket, especially foods that can be kept in her freezer, and stretches the family food budget.

Perhaps one of the most powerful tools for living within our means and deciding *not* to borrow is *thought control*. This is where we impose a discipline on the direction of our thoughts and emotions. We discern the activities that are beneficial to our well-being and make our choices wisely. We nurture and develop those essential personal qualities that result a resourceful life.

✦ Law 4

Whatever you have, you must use it or lose it. —Henry Ford

A YOUNG ARTIST, struggling to achieve his dream of drawing cartoons for a living, was turned away from every newspaper he approached for a job. The editors would look at his work, shrug their shoulders, and tell him, "Forget it. You have no talent. Find yourself another career." Rejection followed rejection.

One day, the young artist found himself in an old, dilapidated, mice-infested garage, with no money, and not much hope for success. With plenty of time on his hands, he began to sketch the garage and its resident mice. As he watched the mice and drew their antics on paper, he became fascinated with the little creatures. He began to develop a curious and friendly relationship with the mice, especially one little fellow.

Little did the man realize just how important this relationship would become. The man's name was Walt Disney. The little mouse that Walt modeled so many of his drawings after was named Mickey. Well, Walt and Mickey went on to become two of the most successful entertainers in the world. Walt's creativity and the mouse's antics brought joy and laughter to countless numbers of children—of all ages!

What would have happened if Walt Disney had given up when the various editors rejected his art offerings? What if he had taken an "ordinary" job? Would his dream of being an artist have faded into memory? But Walt Disney had faith in himself and in his artistic talent. He did not give up. He continued to draw and, in so doing, he discovered a

It is not enough to have a good mind.
The main thing is to use it well.
—René Descartes

powerful truth: *God's infinite possibilities are everywhere!* And success can be realized, even when a person comes to what seems to be the end of the road! Walt Disney used his talents and achieved what he wanted.

Keep your chin up and your vision high! Every moment of life is precious. Use your time wisely. The people who most often succeed are the ones who adapt, adjust, and make the best use of what they are given to work with. Regardless of disappointments that may have occurred in the past, there is always an opportunity to turn seemingly futile circumstances into a starting point for creativity. Like Walt Disney, your original "intent" may not be exactly what happens, but when sincere effort is extended, something must occur! Use what you have! Like muscles that atrophy when they are not exercised, talent can fade if it is not expressed.

What *are* your talents? In what avenues of expression do you seem to have a natural ability? To date, what activity has been most instrumental in your success? Does this activity or work bring you joy? Does it provide an avenue for service? Would a slight shift in your present perspective

> Each golden sunrise ushers in new opportunities for those who retain faith in themselves, and keep their chins up. No one has ever seen a cock crow with its head down. Courage to start and willingness to keep everlastingly at it are the requisites for success. Meet the sunrise with confidence. Fill every golden minute with right thinking and worthwhile endeavor. Do this and there will be joy for you in each golden sunset.
>
> —*Alonzo Newton Benn*

help you see a greater wholeness in your present training or in your natural talents? Can you bring an understanding of your talents into greater clarity or marketability? You cannot see the purpose of your gifts from the perspective of limitation. How can you refine your understanding of what you have? Exercise good judgment and let the decisions you make today be wise ones.

Accept and express thanks for the talents and abilities you are given. Recognize their preciousness and serve the world through them. Put into practice the maxim: "What you are is God's gift to you; what you make of yourself is your gift to God!"

◆ LAW 5

It is nice to be important, but it is more important to be nice. —John Marks Templeton

WHEN THE PATTERN of our lives is woven from a philosophy of "It is nice to be important, but it is more important to be nice," we set in motion a powerful, beneficial, creative energy. The way we respond and what we do for others certainly returns to us. When we are kind, loving, generous, open, honest, and sincere, other people will often respond in like manner. Our importance to others usually depends on demonstrating, through the things we say and the actions we take, that we sincerely care about them and about what is happening in their lives.

As members of the human family, it is only natural that we enjoy being appreciated and respected. It gives us a warm feeling when someone recognizes our accomplishments or sees potential in our abilities that we may not have recognized. Yet, lasting self-esteem is built on how we measure our own worth and on our ability to meet life's challenges. We know we can have a more fruitful life as long as we approach every experience or situation with a loving and appropriate positive attitude. When we understand the core of our essential value, we know that "being nice" is simply one expression of a lifelong process of personal development to be explored and cultivated.

Our lives develop from the patterns of our thoughts, beliefs, and values. If we believe that "truth will always win," then there is no room for lies or deceit in our consciousness. If we place more importance on consideration for others than on selfish pursuits, then the fabric of our lives can be woven from unlimited love, humility, and service. When we live The Golden Rule, "Do unto others as you would have them do unto you," we express our sincerity and desire for noble purpose

Naked a man comes into the world, and naked he leaves it; after all his toil, he carries away nothing, except the deeds he leaves behind.
—Adapted from Rashi

and our respect for each person's inherent spiritual worth.

Henry David Thoreau said, "Only that day dawns to which we are awake." How awake are we to the process of becoming more fully conscious? How can we become more conscious of ourselves and of the roots of our behaviors? How can we become more conscious of the needs, goals, and visions of others? In what ways can we cultivate greater awareness in the various areas of life? Certainly conscious expansion could greatly assist us in being "nicer" people. Are we aiming to be the best that we can be?

In *Precious Seed*, a lovely poem by Russell A. Kemp, we find some guidelines for being nice along with a description for creating heaven on earth:

In what we live, in what we read,
In what we share with another's need,
In how we grow, to what aspire,
In lifting our vision ever higher;
In deeds of kindness and words of praise,
In quiet hours and busy days,
In little things that are great indeed,
We sow the kingdom's precious seed.

What kind of seeds are we sowing? The seeds of our lives can emerge in beautiful and often inspiring acts of loving kindness to others. Through our connection with divinity, many beneficial things can be accomplished. Are we radiating the sacredness of our beings outward for the collective good of all? Are we free from the egotistical snare of exalted self-importance? We know that a universal divine intelligence flows through all of us. So, if we build our activities around spiritual principles, we begin to think about ourselves in relationship to others who share the planet.

Our world is comprised of a collection of individuals who play various roles in our lives. The love and harmony we feel can make a difference with others. We do not surrender the importance of our unique individuality; rather, we direct our influence and assistance in helping to bring about a higher, better, and healthier set of conditions. When we appeal to divinity, and our lives are governed by principle, we are not unduly influenced. Instead, we operate with focus and the beautiful simplicity that is at once the charm and the power of a growing soul. We discern the meaning of the statement, "It is nice to be important, but it is more important to be nice."

Spotlights ✦ ✦

1. Self-discipline goes a long way toward helping to build a foundation for happy and successful living.

2. What part do good thoughts, good words, and good deeds play in gaining self-mastery?

3. The process of living is definitely not an aimless activity.

4. How often do you ask yourself, "Am I part of the problem, or part of the solution?"

5. What are some things you do to help create a loving world?

6. How do you perceive "owe no man" as a spiritual principle?

7. What are your perceptions of the value of being debt-free?

8. How does wisely using your talents and abilities open the door to greater opportunities?

9. God's infinite possibilities are everywhere!

10. How is being nice one aspect of a lifelong process of personal development?

Living the Various Spiritual Laws ✦ ✦

A SACRED PLACE *(A Jewish Prayer)*

How wonderful, O Lord, are the works of your hands!
The heavens declare Your glory,
the arch of sky displays Your handiwork.
In Your love You have given us the power
to behold the beauty of Your world
robed in all its splendor.
The sun and the stars, the valleys and hills,
the rivers and lakes all disclose Your presence.
The roaring breakers of the sea tell of Your awesome might;
The beasts of the field and the birds of the air
bespeak Your wondrous will.
In Your goodness You have made us able to hear
the music of the world. The voices of loved ones
reveal to us that You are in our midst.
A divine voice sings through all creation.

Week Thirty-Five

◆ LAW 1

Those who seldom make mistakes, seldom make discoveries. —John Marks Templeton

HAVE YOU EVER missed out on an opportunity because you were fearful of making a mistake? How many times have you placed limitations upon yourself because you may have been concerned about appearing "foolish" before your family, friends, or peers? This experience has happened to most of us at some time or other. The more quickly we learn to cope constructively with such fears or concerns, the more fruitful our lives can become. "Those who seldom make mistakes, seldom make discoveries."

Although making a mistake can cause some stress or pain, the experience can also provide an excellent resource for growth and learning. Sometimes we often learn more from making a mistake than from formal instruction. "Trial and error" are often great teachers that allow us to measure our misguided actions. Trial and error make it possible to achieve a better awareness of procedure and of what works and what does not work.

We can always look for the best, most workable solution and then move onward. Think confidently. Worry or undue concern over what may be perceived as a mistake accomplishes nothing. Understanding is usually a process that does not develop all at once. Combine a positive attitude with possibility ideas. Take courage and guidance from a quote from *Guideposts* magazine: "Sorrow looks back, worry looks around, faith looks up!"

Life can be as interesting and stimulating as the discoveries we allow ourselves to make. Staying within known parameters of thought and action may prevent some mistakes, but this reluctance can also prevent us from having richer experiences. Exploring new frontiers of thought, feeling, and action may occasionally necessitate putting ourselves in different surroundings or circumstances. It might be easy to make mistakes in unknown territory. But if we are afraid of making mistakes, we may be making the biggest mistake of all! This does not mean that we cast aside wisdom, discernment, and good judgment. When we are committed to growth, we can use the tools of research, listening to others whom we respect, and prayerfully asking for guidance.

Literature is replete with stories of people who made mistakes, learned from their mistakes, and forged ahead. Albert Einstein did poorly in elementary school, and failed his first college entrance exam at Zurich Polytechnic. Yet, Einstein surmounted these obstacles and became one of the greatest scientists in history. Henry Ford forgot to put reverse gear in the first car he manufactured. Then, in 1957, he bragged about the car of the decade. It was the Edsel, renowned for doors that wouldn't close, a hood that would not open, paint that peeled, a horn that stuck, and a reputation that made it impossible to resell. However, Ford's future track record was excellent. Paul Ehrlich, a German bacteriologist, did not perform well at school and had difficulty with examinations. But he had a flair for microscope-staining work and this ability carried him through his education. Ehrlich eventually used his talent with the microscope to develop the field of chemotherapy, and he was awarded the Nobel Prize in medicine in 1908.

How do we respond when someone makes a mistake that affects us? For example, how do you feel when a cashier overcharges you, the post office misplaces a package, or a mechanic fails to completely repair the problem with your car? Do you become upset and critical, or do you learn to treat the mistakes of others with patience and understanding? Can we respond to mistakes made by other people in the manner we would wish them to respond to our mistakes? Is it important to know that the *effort* is what counts? The error of

Give me a fruitful error any time, full of seeds,
bursting with its own corrections.
—Vilfredo Pareto

the past is often the success of the future. A mistake is evidence that someone tried to do something! We can choose to berate ourselves for our errors, or we can use the mistake as a stepping-stone to a new idea that we may not otherwise have discovered.

◆ LAW 2

The measure of a man's real character is what he would do if he would never be found out. —Thomas Macaulay

HOW DO YOU UTILIZE the many opportunities that daily invite you to respond to various situations? Are you an honorable guardian of your thoughts, feelings, and actions, and do you reach for their highest expression? Are you steadfast in support of your values? Are you totally honest and aboveboard with others? Could you be persuaded to ever cheat or steal? If you found something of value, like a wallet stuffed with money or a piece of expensive jewelry, would you try to locate the owner and return the valuable item? If something done in secret would stay a secret, how would you respond?

Are you self-directed enough to maintain your sense of balance and integrity, regardless of what others may think? Do you make your decisions in life based on an awareness of noble purpose and spiritual growth? Can you suspend judgment of others that may be based on appearances, acquisitions, and outer achievements and lift your vision to see the unfolding spirit in every individual? Can you recognize and act from your own maturity in the variety of experiences life offers? When others recognize and praise your attributes and achievements, can you say "thank you" with a humbleness of spirit that acknowledges your gifts and gives thanks to the source of those gifts? By what standards do you live?

Thomas Macaulay said, "The measure of a man's real character is what he would do if he would never be found out." Much wisdom is found in this statement. Each of us has a subtle measuring stick for honesty and integrity—our *conscience.* The quiet voice within nudges us when we contemplate doing something unethical. And the *voice of conscience* can be our lifetime friend and guide.

If the measure of a person's real character is determined by what he or she would do if they were never found out, the only person capable of judging these actions is the individual. Although a person may seem to "get away" with something in the outer world, the inner being knows the truth of the action. Any time you put a dent in your character, you diminish the virtue of your being, and your self-esteem suffers. A highly respected, elderly gentleman would often say to his children and grandchildren, "If I can look myself in the mirror each day, and face my Creator in prayer with an open heart and peace of mind, then I can comfortably sleep at night."

You alone live with your motives, and only you can set the standards of your personal integrity. You have the power within you to attract a truly fruitful and beneficial life. The universe provides us with many opportunities to learn and grow in wisdom and in character. When temptations to abandon our high standards arise, and they do in most lives, the voice of *conscience* is often the universe's way of saying, "Hey! Wake up! Pay attention to what is happening! There is a strong possibility this situation may be harmful!" If we fail to listen, then those messages often get louder and the pain can become more profound, whether that pain is physical, mental, emotional, or spiritual—or all four! Since we become what we choose for ourselves, why not choose integrity and nobility of purpose? A noble mind enters not into the temptation of false appearances.

If you remain true to your ethical principles, your personal integrity becomes a strong magnet for success at every level of life. It is important to understand your own inner motivations. Are you moving toward a momentary pleasure, or are you moving toward a beneficial and lasting joy? Recognizing that responsibility creates *the ability to respond* to whatever situation may be happening is beneficial.

Being honest with ourselves and with all of life puts us on the right spiritual path. Can you look back over your life to this point and feel satisfied that you are giving your best? Does every room in your house of living reflect the light of sincerity of purpose, honesty, and a commitment to ever-unfolding growth?

A mother was helping her son with his spelling assignment. They came to the words *conscious* and *conscience*. She asked her son, "Do you know the difference between these two words?"

The boy immediately replied, "Sure, Mom. *Conscious* is when you are aware of something. And, *conscience* is when you wish you weren't." But really, *conscience* is an inward knowing that you are facing a situation in which you must make a choice between a beneficial or a harmful response.

◆ # LAW 3

Change your mind to change your life. —John Marks Templeton

WHAT DOES YOUR MIND have to do with your life? Everything! Thinking is a creative process that is constantly at work in humanity and its creation. Thinking is the starting point of every thought, feeling, and act. That magnetic atmosphere of thought travels with you and is a part of you. When we affirm our unity with all of the life, substance, and intelligence of the Creator, we share these spiritual qualities. For example, our mind is like a movie projector, our attitudes are the film, and our experience is the movie projected upon the screen. If the reflected pattern of our thoughts is of positive motives and constructive relationships, we most likely have a creative outlook on life and a healthy respect for ourselves and for others. Conversely, if we believe ourselves to be unworthy, we may attract situations that disappoint, frustrate, and can be painful.

Charles Fillmore said, "The mind is the seat of perception of the things we see, hear, and feel. It is through the mind that we see the beauties of the earth and sky, of music, of art, in fact, of everything. That silent shuttle of thought working in and out through cell and nerve weaves into one harmonious whole the myriad moods of mind, and we call it life." Thoughts are things, and they are just as important as actions. Negative thinking is just as powerful as positive thinking. The way we think forms the foundation of what we are and thereby profoundly affects the world around us.

If you desire to change your life to a more positive living experience, examine your thinking processes. During the course of a day, an average person may fluctuate between confidence and

All wrong-doing arises because of mind.
If mind is transformed, can wrong-doing remain?
—Buddha

uncertainty, decision and indecision, cheerfulness and sadness, peaceful calm and frustration. This type of thinking is like a pendulum, swinging back and forth. But it is unnecessary to accept this vacillation. Most problems have a solution. Every situation has some positive perspective. If you wish to live a more fruitful and beneficial life, you can! Simply *choose* to do so!

Thinking is the movement of ideas in your

mind, or your intellect in action. From these ideas, mental pictures or images are formed, based on

The strongest principle of growth lies in human choice.
—George Eliot

your acquired understanding, which are then brought forth as desires and actions. Thus, the thinking process is a creative force that is continually at work. In the book *Macro-Mind Power*, Rebecca Clark emphasizes: "Begin now to school your impulses and feelings into desired areas. Your dreams and ideals are the parents of your impulses and feelings. What you think about people, places, situations, and things can take shape in your life. Refuse to entertain a thought about someone else that you would not have objectified in yourself. You are the assemblage of your thoughts!"

Science is constantly discovering more mysteries of creation. Each discovery invites humankind on to ever deeper and expanding areas of research. The penetration of each mystery opens for man more profound situations that challenge his intellectual capacity. As we follow the path of investigation, like pilgrims climbing rugged mountains, new vistas of knowledge and understanding unfold. As each mountain peak is crested, another peak, loftier still, appears on the horizon.

Opportunities are everywhere and opportunities carry no limitations! How you use the creative power of your mind and the way you respond to people, things, and events, influence your choices. The seed source for living a fruitful life lies in the direction of your thoughts. How alive, alert, awake, and enthusiastic are you about life? When your thoughts are focused on the life, love, wisdom, and intelligence of divinity, you are training yourself to meet demands as they come.

◆ Law 4

*All aspects of creation are in an evolutionary process
of progress and growth.* —Rebekah Alezander

CHANGE IS BOTH NECESSARY and good. Human evolution on the planet depends upon change. The Center for Islam and Science has launched a new project that promises to transform the discourse on Islam and science by providing hundreds of bio/bibliographical resources on Islam and science. New research is underway on the benefits of forgiveness as well as on finding help for those who wish to forgive but do not seem to know how. An intensive clinical study on healing shows how prayer stimulated an overall decrease in the amount of pain experienced by patients with rheumatoid arthritis. Dialogues between scientists and theologians are opening much needed two-way communications. It seems that wherever we look, science, religion, industry, education, psychology, and other fields of endeavor are exploring broader questions. New ways to create progress and growth are emerging around the planet.

our present positions. Something within us struggles for greater freedom, to break the bonds of stagnation or limitation, and to soar into new dimensions of growth and progress. We can sense the excitement of coming changes whose implications are so enormous we may not presently fathom how we will emerge on the other side. In fact, we may have no inkling of what "the other side" of change may look like. Nevertheless, in this twenty-first century, we seem to be on the threshold of a major renaissance of both inner and outer space! There is so much more going on than meets the eyes. As soon as we become willing to open our minds and experience the seemingly incredible, we begin taking the first steps toward our own progress and growth discoveries.

Are we poised on the verge of experiencing a greater reality? What is this greater reality? In his book, *Exploring Inner and Outer Space*, Astronaut Brian O'Leary describes greater reality in this way:

> Innovation is more than a new method. It is a new view of the universe, as one of risk rather than of chance or certainty. It is a new view of man's role in the universe; he creates order by taking risks. And this means that innovation, rather than being an assertion of human power, is an acceptance of human responsibility.
> —*Peter Drucker*

By forging ahead and looking for new and better ways of living and perhaps discovering unseen or heretofore-unknown resources, we can bring about progress and growth for ourselves and for others. As we consciously choose to see life in a progressive light, as we expand our minds to learn new things, as we become increasingly willing to change, growth can certainly occur.

Like the butterfly going through its metamorphosis, we may find we can no longer remain in

It basically expands our framework for inquiry. It views the mind as more than a brain compiling information like a mere computer. It views human consciousness as part of a greater reality in (and perhaps beyond) time and space, not as the epiphenomenon of an organism with a limited time span in a physical body. It seeks to integrate the subjective with the objective, the right brain and the left brain. It strives toward the unity of all things rather than the reduction of all things into physical components.

The new reality presumes an interconnectedness, a higher order in the universe that cannot be explained simply by known physical laws. It observes the power of the mind. It weighs hypotheses that dare to challenge existing theories or assumptions. It investigates a variety of approaches to the search for extraterrestrial intelligence . . . It considers dimensions beyond time and space, concepts beyond matter and energy as currently understood, and realms beyond the physical.

The moment a man
ceases to progress,
to grow higher,
wider, and deeper,
then his life becomes
stagnant.
—Orison Swett
Marden

In dreams begins
responsibility.
—William Butler Yeats

Unity in variety is the
plan of the universe.
—Vivekananda

At one time in Earth's history, there were no living creatures of any kind on our planet. Oh, there may have been globs of biologically interesting molecules around that were not yet organized into living systems. But now, there are millions of living things walking, crawling, swimming, and flying around. How did that astounding change come about? Is Earth life an indication that *all aspects of creation are in an evolutionary process of progress and growth*? The process of evolution has shaped our world and our own species. It has also definitively shaped the way we *comprehend* our world. What can we, as individuals, do to beneficially assist in this progress and growth? How can we recognize the common journey of life everywhere?

Unlimited love is a principal quality that opens our hearts and minds to a new reality. Moreover, open hearts and minds can be passports into evolving consciousness, individual and collective. Spiritual progress reflects growth in the conception and expression of spiritual ideas. We continue to reach for the good, the beautiful, the true, taking responsibility as an aspect of personal morality and self-control.

Put your heart, mind, intellect, and soul even to your
smallest acts. This is the secret of success.
—Sivananda Sarasvati

Looking to the future is intriguing. Is it possible that God wants human minds, hearts, hands, and voices to carry out the divine plan for the world?

♦ LAW 5

It is more blessed to give than to receive. —Acts 20:35

Years do not
diminish but rather
increase the wage of
love and gratitude
bestowed upon
those who work
beneficently.
—Imelda Shanklin

MANY OF THE MOST successful and influential people in the world have proven the wisdom of the statement: "If you want to get more out of life, you have to give more to life." These people understand the *law of life* that giving leads to more giving and to greater personal rewards. When we give to one another freely and generously and without conditions, sharing our blessings with others, the giving multiplies and we receive far more than what was given. Even when there is no immediate prospect of return, the *joy* of giving bestows gracious gifts to our spirits. On the other hand, giving only in order to receive or giving with strings attached is not likely to attract blessings or friendships!

"As you give, so do you receive" is considered one of the universal laws of love. Can you see why? There are many wonderful, productive ways in which we can give, and the *purpose* for which we give is vital. When we give with no strings attached, we are giving from a heart of unlimited love. When we focus on loving and serving others, we are helping to build heaven on earth. Unselfish giving tends to inspire others to manifest the best that is within themselves.

An additional benefit gained by giving is often increased understanding. How is this so? When the spirit is our base of operations, there is always some kind of increase. When we approach life from the perspective of unlimited love, one form of the increase often occurs in understanding. As a good meal provides nutrients and energy for a physically active life, likewise, divinity is a boundless source of spiritual sustenance. If you talk with a dedicated volunteer, you will likely hear about the many personal satisfactions that accrue from his or her service.

I don't know what your destiny will be, but one thing I do know: the only ones among you who will be really happy are those who have sought and found how to serve.
—Albert Schweitzer

"It is more blessed to give than to receive," Scripture tells us. Why would this statement be true? Every experience of living a universal law or spiritual principle brings us closer to abiding joy and fruitful expression. It becomes our privilege to understand a truth intellectually as well as to *become* the truth experientially. There is an important difference in hearing a beautiful song and in singing it ourselves. If we desire to be happier, then do we bring joy to others? If we want to be successful, do we try to help others to succeed? If we want to have more love in our lives, are we striving to be more loving? The formula is simple: *what you give forth returns, multiplied many-fold!*

Have you considered the law of giving and receiving to be one possible definition of freedom? A well-known businessman's definition of freedom

Be grateful for the joy of life. Be glad for the privilege of work. Be thankful for the opportunity to give and serve. Good works is the great character-builder, the sweetener of life, the maker of destiny.
—Grenville Kleiser

is "living without thinking about yourself." Can you imagine living one complete day, focusing on others instead of on yourself? Would you then be

likely to reach out in service to more people around you and to remain unconcerned about the returns? You simply live, and you are free!

In *There Is a Season*, Sr. Joan Chittister writes:

The Hasidic masters tell the story of the rabbi who disappeared every Shabat eve "to commune with God in the forest," his congregation thought. So one Sabbath night they deputed [sic] one of their cantors to follow the rabbi and observe the holy encounter. Deeper and deeper into the woods the rabbi went until he came to the small cottage of an old Gentile woman, sick to death and crippled into a painful posture. Once there, the rabbi cooked for her and carried her firewood and swept her floor. Then, when the chores were finished, he returned immediately to his little house next to the synagogue.

Back in the village, the people asked of the one they sent to follow the rabbi, "Did our rabbi go up to heaven as we thought?"

"Oh, no," the cantor answered after a thoughtful pause, "our rabbi went much, much higher than that."

He is the wisest and happiest who, by constant attention of thought discovers the greatest opportunity of doing good, and breaks through every opposition that he may improve these opportunities.
—Philip Doddridge

The call to give loving service is a yearning from the heart to live and move beyond ourselves. As we continue to make spiritual choices and decisions over a period of time, the momentum for experiencing and expressing these powerful truths often results in a stronger and more balanced personality. We begin to transform our outer world in the direction of our inner ideas and values. If our human progress is noted by improvement of consciousness, we can learn how to make our lives a richer experience and our rewards can far exceed our efforts. Giving is an excellent place to begin.

Spotlights ✦ ✦

1. Life can be as interesting and beneficial as the discoveries we make.

2. Making a mistake can provide an excellent source for growth and learning.

3. How do you respond when someone makes a mistake that affects you?

4. By what standards do you live?

5. The *voice of conscience* can be a lifetime friend and guide.

6. Only you can set the standards of your personal integrity.

7. One purpose of life's journey is to contribute to the whole.

8. Thinking is a creative process. The process can be guided and directed.

9. Every problem has some solution. Every situation has some positive perspective.

10. Change is both necessary and good.

11. "If you want to get more out of life, you have to give more to life."

12. Divinity is a boundless source of spiritual sustenance.

Living the Various Spiritual Laws ✦ ✦

In Judaism, the third category of the *Tanakh* contains a wide variety of literary works from different periods of early Jewish history. Below is a selection from Psalms.

O LORD, You have examined me and know me.
When I sit down or stand up, You know it;
    You discern my thoughts from afar.
You observe my walking and reclining,
    and are familiar with all my ways.
There is not a word on my tongue
    but that You, O LORD, know it well.
. . . It is beyond my knowledge;
    it is a mystery; I cannot fathom it,
Where can I escape from Your spirit?
Where can I flee from Your presence?
If I ascend to heaven, You are there;
    if I descend to Sheol, You are there too.

If I take wing with the dawn
    to come to rest on the western horizon,
    even there Your hand will find me,
    Your right hand will be holding me fast.
If I say, "Surely darkness will conceal me,
    night will provide me with cover,"
    darkness is not dark for You;
    night is as light as day;
    darkness and light are the same.
It was You who created my conscience,
    You fashioned me in my mother's womb.
I praise You,
for I am awesomely, wondrously made.

Week Thirty-Six

✦ LAW I

Purpose is the quality we choose to shape our lives around. —Richard J. Leider

THE JOURNEY OF LIFE sometimes seems filled with questions. How many times have you asked, "What is my life really all about?" or, "Why am I here?" or, "What should I do with my life?" or, "How can I find meaning and direction?" Have you heard others ask the same or similar questions? Most people want to know that there is a real meaning and purpose to life. We like to feel that our being present on Earth matters. How can we answer these deeply meaningful questions? Does spirit touch and move our lives through the mystery of *purpose*?

Could the purpose of our lives serve as the foundation or essence of our deepest dimension— where we have a profound sense of who we are, where we came from, and where we are going? In his book *The Power of Purpose*, Richard J. Leider offers an interesting definition of purpose. He writes: "Purpose is not a thing. It's never a static condition we can preserve. Purpose is a continuous activity, questions we ask over and over again. It's a process we live every day. It's a process for listening and shaping our life stories."

Leider also presents workable and beneficial ideas for creating meaning and perhaps for finding fruitful purpose in our lives and in our work. He writes,

The key to acting on purpose is to bring together the needs of the world with our unique gifts in a vocation . . . Work-ing on purpose gives us a sense of direction. Without purpose, we eventually lose our way. We live without the true joy in life and work. Until we make peace with our purpose, we will never discover fulfillment in our work or contentment with what we have.

Purpose is a way of life—a discipline to be practiced day in and day out. It requires a steady commitment to face each new workday with the question, "Why do I get up in the morning?" The wisdom to ask and the courage to answer this simple question is the essence of working on purpose.

Harmony and strength express themselves fruitfully in our lives when our outer selves align with our deepest and purest yearnings and with the goals we pursue in life. Does *purpose* mean more than being outwardly faithful in fulfilling our duties? Does *purpose* mean being diligent in everything we accomplish here on earth? Can "living with purpose" indicate that we are maturing in the awareness that one of life's most precious gifts is to live for truth and goodness and for the benefit of others? Is one of the by-products of purpose, then, greater overall happiness?

How can difficult situations help you fulfill your purpose? Perhaps the basic significance of life's difficulties is that they can reorient us from activities taking place externally to the spiritual side of things. When a crisis occurs, like a severe illness or a career setback, we can choose how to handle the

We are all on a
spiral path. No
growth takes
place in a straight
line. There will be
setbacks along the
way . . . There will
be shadows, but
they will be
balanced by patches
of light . . .
Awareness of the
pattern is all you
need to sustain you
along the way.
—Kristin Zambucka

I have a dream.
—Martin Luther King Jr

experience. However, some people will likely ask a barrage of questions: "Why did this happen?" and "What am I going to do?" These events can be like nature's contours of mountains and hills that divert the adjacent river from flowing in a straight course, causing the river to twist and turn, yet always leading it in the right direction. The benefit of a crisis or difficulty is that we are usually so focused on what is before us that we release petty concerns and the need to control. However, we can pause and assess our values and priorities at any time. Any time is a good time to express our highest calling, to fulfill our deepest purpose.

Albert Schweitzer inspired millions by his revelation of how rich a human life can be. For many years, he searched for the key ethic in the modern world. He found it in Africa. One afternoon in September 1915, Dr. Schweitzer was sitting on the deck of a small steamboat making its way up the Ogooue River to Lambarene in Central Africa. He was bringing medical supplies to the local population. As the boat moved slowly through a herd of hippopotamuses in the river, Schweitzer watched the ship's captain maneuver to avoid hitting the animals. He came to a profound realization. The captain represented the highest purpose: reverence for life. Dr. Schweitzer stated: "Just as

the water of the streams we see is small in amount compared to that which flows underground, so the idealism which becomes visible in small amounts compared with what men and women bear locked in their hearts, unreleased or scarcely released. To unbind what is bound, to bring the underground waters to the surface: mankind is waiting and longing for such as can do that."

So, how can we go about "unbinding that which is bound"? Possibly a good place to start is with a regular practice of prayer, followed by some good "listening time." Ask for guidance to discover your gifts and creative and beneficial ways to express them. Begin to realize and understand how *you* can make a difference, right where you are. Time-management and organizational ability can often provide the opportunity for releasing what is irrelevant and focusing on your talents and potential. Direct your activities in areas that have significant meaning for you.

Do you truly live the way you want to live? Henry David Thoreau said, "If a man advances confidently in the direction of his dreams to live the life he has imagined, he will meet with a success unexpected in common hours." Purpose is the quality we choose to shape our lives around. Can you define your purpose?

◆ LAW 2

*The seven deadly sins are: pride, lust, sloth,
envy, anger, covetousness, and gluttony.* —St. Gregory

HUMAN NATURE is an arena where the desires of a dualistic nature can be in protracted conflict. One possible reason for this condition is that people may be living their life in ignorance of God, universal laws, and spiritual purpose. When blinded

by illusion or caught up in false values of materialism and egotism, people sometimes strive in the opposite direction for achieving a life of beneficial purpose. People caught up in materialistic affairs may not recognize the conflict within themselves until some life situation catches their attention. A person who is out of step with life's truest and highest aims may fail to see life's infinite potential for good.

The world's religions conceptualize this conflict in various ways. Although theologians differ in their definition of "sin," most would agree that the nature of sin seems to distort the gift of life as it has been given to us to live. When someone "misses the mark" with an error in thinking or behavior, that individual's relationship to life often changes. A sin can, therefore, be deadly, because it often diminishes the sinner's potential of living a life of peace, joy, creativity, and usefulness.

The "seven deadly sins" are seven common ways many people may deaden themselves to life's goodness. Pride, lust, laziness, envy, anger, covetousness, and excess are often efforts to gain satisfaction and fulfillment in areas where they cannot be found. Let's take a closer look at these "sins."

A person sins when he succumbs to the inclination to contravene the divine will by pursuing inordinate desires.
—*Sekai Kyusei Kyo*

An inordinate perception of one's own self, often called *pride* or egotism, can blind a person to recognizing transcendent reality or restrict an accurate measure of one's self. If we attempt to set ourselves up as special or more important than other people, we may fall into the sin or trap of arrogance. To have a certain amount of pride in ourselves and healthy self-esteem, however, can be useful for success.

Lust is an excessive desire, directed toward selfish purposes, which can lead to "useless, unnecessary pain and suffering" and even to destruction. It can be a source of bondage, poisoning the heart, and deluding the mind. The AIDS epidemic, unwanted teenage pregnancies, and drug and alcohol addictions are some of the present-day conse-

quences of indulging lustful passions. Sexuality is a wonderful part of life and how we choose to express that sexuality says a great deal about our personal integrity.

Selfishness may be sweet only for oneself, but no harmony of the whole can come from it.
—*Tenrikyo Osashizu*

Although the term *sloth* is no longer in current usage, it is synonymous with laziness. While everyone needs occasional times to slow down and relax from the business of daily living, sloth or laziness is a different situation. An English proverb says, "Laziness travels so slowly that poverty soon overtakes him." Laziness is one of the habits or attitudes that can prevent or hinder us from discovering greater meaning in our lives. It can limit life by giving license to inertia. Laziness also acts as to block fruitful creativity and productivity.

One definition of *envy* is "a feeling of discontent and ill will because of another's advantages, possessions, etc." That we see a quality of personality in someone else or success in another's life that we would like to embody is not a deadly sin. We often admire talents and abilities in others. The problem or "sin" arises when we allow envy to fill our lives with such discontent and resentment that we cannot enjoy the other aspects of life. Time and energy spent comparing ourselves with others could be better used mobilizing our own inner resources.

Anger is a crippling emotion that can destroy communications, break apart loving relationships, and close the door on happiness and good feelings. The sin of anger is that it frequently leads to destructive behaviors. Our bodies often respond to anger with clenched fists, frowns, tears, blushing, gnashed teeth, changes in blood pressure, increased heart rate, and the like. Why would we ever do something to create these disturbances within ourselves? What could it ever beneficially accomplish? Instead of denying our feelings, what would happen if we identified the source of the anger and transformed the temptation to anger into some constructive action?

Covetousness or avarice means *greed*. Greed also can be deadly in its opposition to the natural, abundant flow of life. Every major religion recognizes that suffering and evil are caused by excessive desires directed toward selfish purposes. And covetousness or greed forms the basis of much of humanity's distress. The greedy person is the one who tries to build a dam across the stream and selfishly keep all the water. He has not yet learned that blessings come from the flow of water. As old King Midas learned the hard way, a self-centered life based on greed is really no kind of life at all!

Gluttony refers to anything we do in life to excess. Gluttony is frequently aligned with physical addictions. When a person concentrates much of his energy on one thing—such as eating, drinking, drugs, or sex—addictions can occur. Like greed, these addictions can become so self-absorbing that other important aspects of life may be ignored. The sin of gluttony reflects in the damage it does to our physical bodies, our relationships, our careers, and our spiritual awareness. An antidote to gluttony can be to seek to live a balanced life by doing things in moderation.

A universal divine intelligence flows through all of us. We each have a unique connection with that invisible part of ourselves. Desires themselves may be beneficial when expressed in their rightful place within the individual, the family, and society. Our thoughts and choices can carry us to boundless places. As higher expressions of self begin to triumph over "the seven deadly sins" in the daily decision-making of life, we begin to make progress on the path of the sacred quest for purpose.

◆ LAW 3

Appearances are often deceiving. —Aesop

There is a logical reason for everything that is happening in this world and beyond—and it all makes perfect sense. One day you will understand the divine purpose of God's plan.
—*Lois Pearl*

ONE OF THE better-known statements from Aesop's fables could be the one that describes persons, places, situations, or things as being different from what they may seem: "Appearances are often deceiving." Quite possibly, we may have experienced situations in our personal lives where we felt disappointment, discouragement, or disillusionment because the outer appearance did not meet our expectations. These could be good times to remember that appearances do not always speak the truth of a situation.

Epictetus wrote: "Appearances to the mind are of four kinds. Things are either what they appear to be; or they neither are, nor appear to be; or they are, and do not appear to be; or they are not, and yet appear to be. Rightly to aim in all these cases

is the wise man's task." The Gospel according to John gives much simpler counsel: "Judge not according to appearance" (7:24).

The essence of this law of life is that it is important and beneficial to look more deeply into any manifestation. We may be pleasantly surprised if we respond to situations by seeking greater clarity. Whatever *judgment* we make based on appearances might be simply a fragile tool for upgrading our opinion of ourselves by comparison with another. However, when our *discernment* is based on increased awareness and spiritual understanding, we can improve any situation with kind thoughts of love and compassion. One benefit of looking at things more closely is that we may perceive quite useful information in making progress toward our goals. After all, could *experience* simply be another word for growing awareness?

If you *experience* your body, are you becoming more aware of your body? If you *experience* your mind, are you becoming more aware of the thoughts and ideas floating before your mind's inward eye? Experiencing your mind can be quite important because, by bringing awareness to the mind, you begin to transcend its limitations and will no longer be *deceived by appearances*!

In *One Taste*, Ken Wilber writes: "[B]ody, mind, and soul are not mutually exclusive. The desires of the flesh, the ideas of the mind, and the luminosities of the soul—all are perfect expressions of the radiant Spirit that alone inhabits the universe, sublime gestures of that Great Perfection that alone outshines the world. There is only One Taste in the entire Kosmos, and that taste is Divine, whether it appears in the flesh, in the mind, in the soul."

How can we cultivate greater expressions of divinity in our lives that can help us transcend appearances? Perhaps at the top of the list could be exercising the unlimited love that helps us recognize the sacred presence of spirit in everyone and everything. When we look for the loving presence in others, we often find it! Taking a few moments to become still and focused can help us release attachments to the importance of outer impressions. When we remove the "labels" we often attach to our lives—such as age, sex, possessions, accomplishments, heritage, etc.—we can move beyond the senses and attune with the invisible part of ourselves. Practicing thanksgiving and generosity can lift us into a space that is attracted to serving and sharing. Keeping our awareness in the present moment instead of meandering into "what

ifs" is another way of focusing on reality instead of on appearances.

A group of friends, taking a day of vacation from work, drove to an area park in the mountains for a picnic. The day was absolutely perfect—sunny and beautiful, comfortable temperature, beautiful scenery along the way. Arriving in the park, they selected a picnic site near a large reservoir that dominated one section of the park. The friends paused to watch the water spill over the dam and cascade into the river, continuing its journey far below. The water, falling by its own weight, obeying gravitational force, created a natural energy that the generators converted into usable power for electrical customers. As the friends talked among themselves about the vista before them, one man said, "Isn't it interesting that, from one perspective, appearances here can be deceiving." As the others looked at him questioningly, he continued. "The generators do not *create* electricity; they simply *generate*. They take the natural energy and transmute it into a form of power that is then distributed over power lines to the valley below. The power can then be used to drive machinery to do specific things."

How can we discover more of the nature of the reality behind the shadows? Instead of placing our focus on outer appearances, what would happen if we chose *spiritual integrity* as the foundation for our lives? Would life situations and experiences then be viewed from a more factual and realistic perspective rather than from illusionary possibilities? Would the motivation of discovery enable us to bring greater clarity of vision to whatever is before us to help us make more positive and wiser decisions?

✦ LAW 4

Zeal is the inward fire of your soul that urges you onward toward your goal. —Charles Fillmore

EACH TIME an opportunity comes your way that allows you to express your talent, welcome that opportunity with open arms! Feel the stirrings of zeal and enthusiasm move within you, providing the impetus to transform the opportunity into a fruitful realization of good.

Zeal has been described as "the inward fire of the soul that urges man onward." Zeal can generate motivation, resulting in powerful progressive movement. When Charles Fillmore was ninety-four, he remarked: "I fairly sizzle with zeal and enthusiasm and spring forth to do that which should be done by me." What a tremendous positive attitude! Most of us have far greater capacities for achievement than we may have realized. If we accept this truth about ourselves and believe in ideals and principles as realities, we often gain greater mastery over the outer affairs of our lives. Zeal offers the ability to gain distinction through concentrated effort directed toward our goals. Zeal stimulates us to be interested and passionate about life. In fact, zeal is like a *grand passion*—an inner desire that blazes with the fervor of the hot sun on desert sands until the object of its focus sizzles into manifestation. Zeal helps the task at hand to be completed with greater ease.

The Greeks have given us one of the most beautiful words of our language, the word "enthusiasm" —a God within. The grandeur of the acts of men are measured by the inspiration from which they spring. Happy is he who bears a God within.
—Louis Pasteur

Scripture tells us: "For God did not give us a spirit of timidity, but a spirit of power" (2 Timothy 1:7). This source of power with which to accomplish whatever may be before us is an inner energy just waiting to be released and directed. By the

time Rachmaninoff was twenty-five, he was making great strides toward a bright and successful musical career. His musical compositions were well received by both critics and audiences. Then, Rachmaninoff wrote a symphony that flopped. He became discouraged and filled with self-pity. He lost confidence in his musical career and moped around. One day, one of his friends took Rachmaninoff to see a Nicholas Dahl. One of the things Dr. Dahl told the budding musician that stuck with him was, "Great things lie dormant in you, waiting to be given to the world." Rachmaninoff repeated this statement over and over until his confidence returned. Within a year, he composed a concerto that he dedicated to Dr. Dahl. It was his famous *Concerto No. 2 in C Minor.* At the concerto's performance in Moscow, the audience nearly raised the roof of Nobility Hall with enthusiastic shouting. The power of zeal, flamed by encouraging words, urged the great composer onward toward his goal.

We can make our lives what we want them to be. However, it takes effort to use the spiritual qualities, talents, abilities, and power we have been given. Let's explore beyond the boundaries of our limited personal minds and keep asking ourselves, "What if . . . ?" What would happen if we injected more zeal and enthusiasm into the projects at hand? How would family, personal, and work relationships benefit from an injection of zeal and enthusiasm? Think of the many possibilities in various situations that could be enhanced by these powerful energies. What would happen if we *demonstrated* our enthusiasm for life in such a manner that it radiated outward into everything we did. Our enthusiasm could infect all those around us!

A woman who worked for a large manufacturing company had such a positive and enthusiastic outlook on life that her supervisor laughingly told her, "You are contagious!" And she was! Her joyous spirit and caring nature touched every other

Zeal, courage, and earnestness give luster and color to the soul, just as the sparkle of the diamond gives it beauty.
—Cora Fillmore

person who worked with her. Authentic zeal and enthusiasm are not energies granted to some and absent in others. Every one of us can draw from the universal wellspring of divine energy. To be joyous and enthusiastic is a decision we can make at any

time to become a more active participant in life.

"Enthusiasm" is derived from root words that indicate being inspired by the divine and "one with the energy of God." There is something pretty awesome about people who are vibrant with this spiritual quality. Zeal and enthusiasm give added value to everything they touch. Let's send forth the call for our souls to be radiantly alive and expressive in the things that are before us to do. The poet Philip Doddridge expressed this enthusiasm when he wrote: "Awake, my soul! Stretch every nerve, and press with vigor on; A heavenly race demands thy zeal, and an immortal crown."

✦ Law 5

Minds are like parachutes—they only function when they are open. —Dick Sutphen

Education is not the filling of a pail, but the lighting of a fire.
—William Butler Yeats

You are intelligent to the degree in which you give the Mind of God action in you.
—Imelda Shanklin

HAVE YOU WATCHED a parachutist jump from a plane? The aircraft circles overhead, a silhouette against the blue sky. Suddenly, a small, dark speck appears, floating near the plane. The plane flies away and the dark speck seems to fall. You watch breathlessly. Then, a billowing cloud of color begins to unfold as the mushroom shape of the parachute fills with air. Ah, the jumper floats safely and easily down to the ground.

The parachute that is used by a person when jumping from an airplane is constructed with a small pilot chute that is released first to activate the larger chute that is tightly packed within its protective cover. A handle is attached to a "rip cord" that must be forcefully pulled to release the pilot chute, which then fills with air. This air provides the initial power to pull the tightly packed main chute from its container. As you can see, an orderly arrangement of factors is necessary for a successful parachute jump.

Our minds are like parachutes. To be fully oper-

ative, our minds must be open and receptive to incoming ideas. To achieve the greatest benefit from these ideas, an orderly process of observation and evaluation is helpful. Yes, as it takes courage for a parachutist to jump from a plane flying several hundred feet above the ground, it often takes courage to open the "parachute" of your mind to what may appear to be the mysterious unknown. However, when you are receptive to new thoughts and ideas, additional possibilities may appear.

Your mind is your creative center, filled with possibilities of untapped potential. Have we forgotten that the kingdom of heaven on earth, the ingredients of infinity, and the elements of the unlimited self lie within the reach of our thoughts and experiences? Perhaps it is time to get excited about this self-potential. What action will you take to draw it forth into your daily life?

Inspirational ideas may arrive in strange ways. A young woman was sitting at her desk, preparing a school thesis. Suddenly, there were popping sounds coming from the corner of the desk. In the next moment, the woman was being showered with an explosion of tiny projectiles! When she investigated what was happening, to her surprise she discovered that the miniature rockets were, in fact, seeds from exploding seedpods launched from a flower arrangement in a vase on her desk.

The young woman began to laugh, for she realized she had just witnessed a small miracle. The little flower seedpods had actually erupted to send their tiny, ripened passengers on a journey designed to regenerate themselves. Thus, they could sustain their continued existence. As she gathered up the scattered seeds to plant in her garden later, the young woman realized that her mind was equally ripe with divine ideas. How would she plant these *seed ideas* so they could germinate usefully and creatively?

History abounds with stories of great minds that have gifted humanity with wonderful discoveries and inventions. Each discovery or invention began as a "seed idea" in an open and receptive mind. Zeal and enthusiasm surrounded the idea with fertile nourishment for growth. The irresistible power of enthusiasm was the driving force enabling Cyrus W. Field to bring to fruition the idea of successfully laying a cable across the

Atlantic Ocean. Josef Haydn produced over eight hundred musical compositions before he gave the world the matchless oratorio, *The Creation,* at age sixty-six. It took Canadian physician Sir Frederick Banting, working with three other people, about eight months in the early 1920s to develop insulin.

Whether your mind is open or closed can have a profound effect on your future. A narrow and

closed mind quickly becomes the straightest avenue to a narrow life. An open and receptive mind understands the importance of continuing to learn and grow mentally. Living passionately for today and purposefully for tomorrow—with an open mind—can help shape and define your personal achievements. One man compared his open-mindedness to a kitchen colander used to drain water from vegetables. He said that he carefully reviewed the thoughts and ideas that presented themselves, then allowed everything except the best to drain away easily and quickly!

Spotlights ✦ ✦

1. Your life purpose is a continuous activity, a process you live every day.

2. Working with purpose can provide you with a clearer sense of direction.

3. When someone "misses the mark" with an error in thinking or behavior, that individual's relationship to life often changes.

4. Our thoughts and choices can carry us to boundless, elevated places.

5. Educate and train yourself to look beyond appearances.

6. Respond to situations by seeking greater clarity.

7. Cultivate greater expressions of divinity in your life that can help you transcend appearances.

8. Welcome opportunities with open arms!

9. Zeal is an inward fire of the soul that urges man onward.

10. Zeal and enthusiasm can give added value to everything they touch.

11. To be fully operative, our minds must be open, receptive, and discerning to incoming ideas.

12. Whether your mind is open or closed can have a profound effect on your future.

Living the Various Spiritual Laws ✦ ✦

If you pursue honor, it will elude you. But if you flee from honor, it will pursue you.
　—Talmud

Everyone likes to be honored. When our passion and dedication are recognized, we feel good. However, we must learn to pause and examine our motivations. Do we contribute to our communities because we truly care about the issue at hand, or because we feel our work will bring us honor? Some people actively pursue honor and are disappointed when their efforts are not adequately noticed. Their motivations are self-serving from the start. Others work tirelessly because they are passionately committed to their work. They never think about whether they will receive honor or status from their efforts. Their motivations are pure. These are the individuals we should look to honor.
　—Rabbi Lori Forman, *Sacred Intentions*

✦ LAW I

Out of the fullness of the heart, the mouth speaks. —English proverb

As a flower that is lovely, beautiful, and scent-laden, even so fruitful is the well-spoken word of one who practices it.
—*The Dhammapada*

A gentleman is ashamed to let his words outrun his deeds.
—*Confucius*

There is always time to add a word, but none in which to take one back.
—*Baltasar Gracian*

EACH OF US carries who and what we are within us. This reality is often reflected in our eyes, our facial expressions, our mannerisms, our actions, and the words we speak. We may not know what life experiences have shaped another person's outlook. However, we may glimpse a person's perspective on life from the words they speak and from how those words are spoken. The spoken word has weight, sound, and appearance. Words spoken from the heart enfold us in a loving, caring, sincere energy, while words that are negative, hard, and impersonal may be painful or even harmful to the listener.

"You are defined by what comes out of your mouth more than by what goes in" is one way of saying that words are meaningful sounds that symbolize thoughts and represent ideas. Words carry power because they are the predominant audible or written expression of thought, and we can be either creative or destructive through the power of our words. How we listen as well as how we speak is also meaningful. When we listen with the spirit as well as with the ear, we can often perceive the subtle sound of the deeper meaning and content of what someone says. The words chosen, the tone of voice used, and the story line moving through the words, provide a setting for increased understanding and awareness. The voice of the spirit can be heard in numerous ways!

Sacred scriptures speak of the power of our words. The Bible tells us: "Hear and understand: not what goes into the mouth defiles a man, but what comes out of the mouth, this defiles a man" (Matthew 15:10, 11). The sacred Hindu *Kaushitaki Upanishad* expresses the wisdom of looking beyond the spoken word in the statement: "Speech is not what one should desire to understand. One should know the speaker." In Psalms 16:33 we read: "Let the words of my mouth, and the meditation of my heart, be acceptable in thy sight, O Lord, my strength and my redeemer."

Words must be weighed, not counted.
—*Polish proverb*

Our words can be fruitful instruments with which we build and shape our world. Good words are like pure sunlight streaming down upon us. They can bring radiance so bright that we may not discern precise details or hues from the source. When sunlight strikes the gossamer wings of a dragonfly or shines through misty rain, it becomes polarized into millions of tiny rainbows. When we are in touch with our spiritual natures, our words can be like the voice of spirit, bringing blessings to those to whom we speak.

Once a word is spoken, it cannot be recalled. Exercising care in the presentation of our thoughts, especially in the selection and formation

Language exerts hidden power, like the moon on the tides.
—Rita Mae Brown

of our words and speech, can eliminate feelings of regret. Avoiding gossip, falsehood, and careless and unnecessary talk can prevent later concerns of, "Oh, I wish I had not said that!" Since our words can affect others, would it not be more beneficial to speak in a cheerful, tactful, harmonious, and caring manner? And would not this kind of speech flow easily from a heart filled with unlimited love?

Our deeper identities and true characters lie in the subjective nature of our minds. It is to our personal and collective advantage to use all the events of our daily lives as opportunities to clarify and elevate our thoughts and behavior. The more we care about how we express ourselves to others, the greater our own sense of well-being. A genuine sense of responsibility is based on people helping one another. Cultivating a close, warm-hearted awareness of communication can put our minds at ease and eliminate harmful fears and insecurities. Who knows what effect our words may have upon others? Let us choose them well!

◆ LAW 2

The journey of a thousand miles must begin with a single step. —Lao Tzu

Seize this very minute! What you can do or think you can do, begin it.
—*Goethe*

Good work that leaves the world softer and fuller and better than ever before is the stuff of which human satisfaction and spiritual value are made.
—*Joan Chittister*

OUR ADVANCING position in the great universal scheme of life often occurs through personal growth and development. Possibly, one of the most important and meaningful journeys we can make to find the place where we can make a beneficial contribution to life. Although many steps may be taken along the way, every journey or activity begins with that initial step toward discovery.

The first step into a well-rounded and fruitful life could be your outlook. How do you perceive life? How do you respond to the experiences in life? How can you expand the perimeters of your personal world? Will you encourage the wings of your soul to lift in exultation and enthusiastic anticipation? Are you filled with the high vision of the most wonderful journey on earth—living joyfully and fruitfully every day? How can you move beyond the threshold of opportunity and experience the success of the endeavor? How will you discover more about yourself through the act of living?

Expanding our minds or uplifting our consciousness is a thought-by-thought, step-by-step process. Everything is a matter of development. Difficult times may occur when we wonder how we are going to get through tough situations. We may falter in the belief that all things really do

If you have a great ambition, take as big a step as possible in the direction of fulfilling it, but if the step is only a tiny one, don't worry if it is the largest one now possible.
—*Mildred MacAfee*

work together for good. Yet, we should continue taking one step at a time. With commitment and perseverance, we can move through difficult times with a more positive attitude and greater ease than we may have thought possible. Truly, we can follow a pathway leading toward heaven on earth.

The value of a questioning mind and service to others is not something necessarily taught; it is something that is *lived*. Our personal *action* is what is important—our desire to look beyond our present position, to investigate, to discover, and to experience. Perhaps another "first step" could be to comprehend the difference between an intellectual understanding and the *living action* of an experience. This is part of the learning process. We can also embark on a process of discovery by asking questions about everything from the most obvious to the most hidden in our consciousness. A shift in personal consciousness is a shift in human consciousness. Are we willing to experience this transformation and assume the greater responsibility to humanity? If so, we arc surely ready to take the next step on that "journey of a thousand miles."

Focus, commitment, and effort provide major steps of progress. A story is told of an old man who would frequently plant fig trees in a field at the edge of a small village. Over a period of several years, the young plants grew into fruit-producing trees. Still, the old man planted more fig trees. Occasionally, people from the village would ask the man, "Why do you plant so many fig trees? Surely, you cannot eat all the fruit they produce." The old man would smile and respond, "For many years I spent happy hours sitting beneath the shade of fig trees that were planted by other people. I have also enjoyed the fruit of these trees. I want to make sure there will be fig trees to be enjoyed by others." The spirit of love, kindness, and gratitude can build progress and community, one step at a time.

Each fresh morning of the dawning day can be the "first step" into a new lease on life. Something of immense value can be waiting for us. Our lives can be our masterpieces. How will we seize this very minute and experience a clear concept of the beauty, joy, opportunity, and abundance that life spreads before us? How will we acknowledge the immense mystery of divinity? Will we express our gratitude and thanksgiving by planting more fig trees? How will we positively stimulate our latent talents and enhance the talents already expressing? Practice is essential for mastering something new.

Many things are possible. First, we must begin. What steps can be taken to expand the mind, awaken the intuition, and pave the way to greater illumination? What is your vision of wholeness? How will you assemble and use what you have been given in an appropriate way?

✦ LAW 3

It is always darkest just before the day dawns. —Thomas Fuller

A WOMAN SAT in a hospital emergency room in the wee, small hours of the morning, waiting for information from the doctor regarding her husband. The husband had not been feeling well, his condition worsened, and an ambulance transported him to the nearest hospital. Tests and X-rays were being conducted; all the woman could do was wait and pray. She felt completely alone in the midst of a difficult situation. Then she remembered the words: "It is always darkest just before the dawn." As the sun began to lift above the horizon, the doctor entered the waiting room to talk with the woman. Her husband's condition was serious. An operation was needed, but his recovery would be a matter of time and process. She breathed a sigh of relief, knowing that the dark of night was not the end of the world.

Many of us have experienced times when our

world seemed to be crumbling underneath our feet. Perhaps we searched for solid support in the form of guidance, a friend, our family, or some kind of positive and workable response to a difficult situation. Although in its duration a crisis may seem endless, the good news is that these events "come to pass." Life continues. We overcome. Upon reflection, we may realize that difficult times provide valuable opportunities for us to learn important lessons. We grow in many ways.

In *Make Your Life Worthwhile*, Emmet Fox compares the experiences of life with the ebb and flow of the ocean tides. He writes:

ation. The subconscious mind can accept the new thought and mobilize other, similar ideas. So, empty your mind of unhealthy thoughts and replace them with wholesome, creative concepts.

We do not make our spiritual unfoldment in a steady straight line. Human nature does not work in that way. No one moves upward in a path of unbroken progress to the attainment of perfection. What happens is that—if we are working rightly—we move upward, but with a series of "downs" as well as "ups." We move steadily forward for a while, and then we have a little setback. Then we move forward again, and presently we have another little setback of some kind.

These setbacks are not important as long as the general movement of our lives is upward. If each year finds us with a definite advance in consciousness, the temporary setbacks in between are unimportant; and if we worry too much about them they can be a real hindrance. The tide flows in and out . . . This mode of progression seem to be general throughout nature—an advance, a minor retreat, and then a greater advance.

One way of working with these "dark nights" is to substitute distressing thoughts with comforting ones. This exercise may not be as easy as it sounds, but it can be done. Refuse to rehearse the difficulty. Turn your attention to a different subject. There is a place for analysis, but do not dissect things too much. To enable the mind to become creative again, the tension can be released by relax-

A woman who has progressed through some difficult situations uses what she calls her "key for successful overcoming." Rather than dwelling on the difficulty at hand, she praises God for her life—and everything in it. When asked about her successful "technique," she laughingly exclaimed: "Praise and terror cannot abide at the same time in the mind!" A businessman often meets challenging experiences with the statement: "This comes to bless me!" He looks for—and finds—the blessing! What you think upon intensifies. This is a simple law of life or spiritual principle.

The spiritual part of us knows that a beneficial solution to a problem may arise. There are few insoluble problems—there are only circumstances for which we may not presently have appropriate resolutions. The divine forces that created and sustain the universe are available to assist us at any time. The Psalms give us this guidance: "Be still and know that I am God" (46:10). Prayer can help us become more mentally and physically capable in times of distress. Divine wisdom can open a way.

After the darkest night, a new day dawns and the sun does shine. Tough experiences may be but a cloud hiding the luminosity of the sun.

✦ Law 4

Love conquers all things. —Virgil

ONE DAY a father and his ten-year-old daughter climbed to the top of a high point of land overlooking the ocean on one side and a picturesque valley on the opposite side.

The father said, "Look up," and the child gazed into the vast expanse of the sky above.

"Look down," the father spoke softly to his daughter, and the little girl looked down and saw the reflection of white clouds and blue sky in the calm sea below.

"Look out," the father suggested, and his daughter looked and beheld the gentle waves of water rolling over an infinite horizon.

"Now turn around and look over the green valley," he instructed.

As she contemplated the broad, beautiful landscape below, the little girl's father continued:

"My child, so high, so deep, and so wide is the Love of God for His children!"

With an insight characteristic of the childlike heart, the child softly whispered, "Daddy, if God's Love is so high, so wide, and so deep, then we are living right in the middle of it!"

Isn't this a beautiful reality: that *we are living in the middle of universal love!* If we take even one step toward acquiring a greater degree of unlimited love, the universe responds to that one step. Each time we give or receive unlimited love, we begin an experiment that results in an experience that can transform every facet of our life.

Perhaps one of the most tremendous discoveries in the long and checkered history of humanity is revealed in three simple words: "God is love." As we realize and accept the truth these words contain, we can become new creatures, opening our minds, ourselves, in fact, our *entire lives*, to a dynamic and fruitful process of creativity and expression. If the most important element in anything you do is your own attitude toward it, why not take the time to establish the joyous attitude of unlimited love in one of the greatest assignments life has for us—loving one another!

When our hearts are truly open to others, could there ever be conflicts? Could unlimited love reduce the influence of habitual, limited patterns of perception? Love does not parallel the emotions of anger, fear, or resentment; rather, it is a transmuting force for greater good. For example: love sees through a telescope while envy peers through a microscope! It is impossible to express love with a clenched fist. If the greatest room in the universe is the "room for improvement," could unlimited

> Put away all hindrances. Let your mind full of love pervade one quarter of the world, and so too the second quarter, and so the third, and so the fourth. And thus the whole wide world, above, below, around and everywhere, altogether continue to pervade with love-filled thought, abounding, sublime, beyond measure, free from hatred and ill-will.
> —Buddha

love be the central progressive activity of the spiritual life? If so, how?

Love washes away all conflicts because unlimited love keeps no records of mistakes and shortcomings. In the consciousness of love, one is able to rise above adversity, insults, loss, and seeming injustice. There is no condition, circumstance, or situation that unlimited love cannot meet and handle triumphantly. Unlimited love is eternally enduring and, surely, it extends far beyond any present knowledge we may think we have. Unlimited love is too pure to hold onto any negativity; love can wipe out any guilt-edged state of mind. Unlimited love moves immediately to eliminate impatience, unkindness, envy, jealousy, possessiveness, conceit, fear, boastfulness, rudeness, and other elements of self-concern.

As unlimited love continues to do its perfect work within us, we may find that it leads to deep and soul-searching questions: "Am I willing to give up thoughts and feelings of impatience, egotism, excuses?" "Am I *really* willing and ready to live up to my potential?" "Am I ready to be as forgiving and as freeing as love itself?" "Do I deeply desire to relinquish old states of negation and limitation?" Love acts immediately to heal, rejuvenate, and resurrect the person who desires to live in love. As the quality of our love improves, we learn not only to love more, but we learn to love more wisely.

God has woven a marvelous tapestry for the eyes of his creatures to behold. However, in a sense, we may have lost a certain level of perception, a dimension of seeing, a sense of presence in the providential design of all that is. It is important to move beyond a narrow, restrictive point of view, to look beyond numbers, formulas, and models to behold the greater objective—the process, the phenomenon of the miracle of life, as part of a larger, more marvelous, and mysterious whole. Unlimited love delights in the truth of our infinite potential. Is unlimited love a powerful tool to assist us in learning to be helpers in God's purposes? Take the time to exercise your growing ability to love. Let a new envelope of unlimited love consciousness wash away all conflicts.

✦ Law 5

Count your blessings, name them one by one. —Early hymn

WHEN YOU READ or hear the statement: "Count your blessings, name them one by one," what is your first thought? Gratitude? Appreciation? Abundance? Thanksgiving? Each of these words is appropriate. One definition for the word "bless" is to praise or glorify. Some definitions for the word "blessing" are: "an act of prayer," "good wishes," and "thanksgiving."

Any of these words can identify the wonderful feeling we have when we recognize the abundance manifested in our lives. Expressing gratitude to everything and everyone around us becomes a spiritual exercise. We can show our gratitude for the music that uplifts our soul. We can say "thank you" for the sturdy shoes that keep our feet warm and dry in the cold and damp of winter. We can smile our thanks for well-written books that bring tears to our eyes. And what about blessing a precious child who gathers a spring bouquet of daisies? Saying "thank you" to the great Creator is only one part of a life of gratitude. The other part of a life of gratitude is being so aware of our blessings that our consciousness abides in an attitude of gratitude.

Thank You, God, for all my good is a seven-word statement that can propel us forward in fruitful and beneficial ways. A sense of gratitude and appreciation forms an important wellspring for living life more abundantly and more joyfully. Counting our blessings can be an antidote to the illusion of egotism. Thanksgiving lifts us into a higher state of consciousness where we *know* that life is good and that our blessings are abundant. Most of us have experienced times in our lives that were so special and splendid, we didn't want to release the exalted feeling of the moment. If this has happened to you, what was your response to that moment? Was it heartfelt joy and gratitude? So, if you were to begin to "count your blessings, and name them one by one," where would you begin?

How about beginning with the gift of *life*? What would happen if you put a song of praise

To love is to know Me, My innermost nature, the truth that I am.
—Bhagavad Gita

Thou dost show me the path of my life; in thy presence there is fullness of joy.
—Psalms 16:11

As bread is the staff of life, the simple sustenance of the body, so appreciation is the food of the soul.
—Priscilla Wayne

on your lips at the beginning of each day? Would this attitude of praise and thanksgiving help put everyone and everything into a more definitive, positive place and perspective? How about saying "thank you" for the breath of life that fills your lungs to mobilize your unique body? You are a living, breathing, thinking, feeling, human, and spiritual being. How do you consider life from the point of view of the intrinsic nature of, for example, *yourself?* How do you find identity, meaning, and fulfillment in the various activities of your daily living? What immediate blessings come to mind when you consider each of these sacred aspects of yourself?

> Thou that has given so much to me, give one more thing, a grateful heart. Not thankful when it pleaseth me, as if thy blessings had spare days; but such a heart, whose pulse may be thy praise.
> —George Herbert

Are you blessed with good health and a physical and mental ability that allow you to pursue your goals? How are your daily needs of food, clothing, and shelter provided? We often take these "ordinary" aspects of living for granted, but what would your life be without them? What unexpected blessings of joy and happiness shower upon you? Does your chosen profession allow you the opportunity for creativity and personal expression? Do you have the loving support of family and friends? What if you endorsed British writer

G. K. Chesterton's advice: "taking things with gratitude and not taking things for granted"? How would your life change?

The little girl was overflowing with the joy and excitement of her ninth birthday party. It had been a tremendous success. Every invitation had been accepted and, for a while, the house rang with the laughter of children. Now, the party was over and the children were gone. Opened birthday presents were stacked at one end of the dining room table and remnants of birthday cake and fruit punch occupied the other end.

As the child's mother entered the room and began to clear the table, she noticed her daughter sitting in a chair with her eyes closed. The little girl was softly speaking the name of each of her friends who had attended the party. When all the names were spoken and the child opened her eyes, the mother asked, "Honey, what were you doing?"

The little girl smiled and said, "Oh, Mother! I was just *speaking true!*"

"Speaking true?" the mother said. "I don't understand."

"Well," the child responded, "the presents were very nice. And thank you, Mother, for the party. It was great! But the best gift of all was my friends who came to celebrate with me. *Speaking true* was bringing each one close to my heart again."

Speaking true. Seeing true. Counting our blessings is one way of *being* true to who and what we are, of honoring all of the gifts of spirit, and to living life more abundantly.

Spotlights ◆ ◆

1. The realities of *who* and *what* we are abide within us.

2. Our words can be fruitful instruments with which we build and shape our world.

3. Once a word is spoken, it cannot be recalled.

4. Every journey or activity begins with an initial step toward discovery.

5. Focus, commitment, and effort provide major steps toward progress.

6. The spirit within you is larger than any difficulty!

7. The darkest night but paves the way for a new and glorious day.

8. When your heart is truly open to others, could there ever be conflicts?

9. Love washes away all conflicts because love keeps no records of mistakes and shortcomings.

10. Gratitude and appreciation form a wellspring for living life more joyfully and abundantly.

11. Whatever may be happening, remember: "This comes to bless me!"

12. Make a list of your many blessings that come to mind. Add to the list every day.

Living the Various Spiritual Laws ✦ ✦

LOVE

Though I speak with the tongues of men and of angels, but have not love, I am a noisy gong or a clanging cymbal. And if I have prophetic powers, and understand all mysteries and all knowledge; and if I have all faith, so as to remove mountains, but have not love, I am nothing. If I give away all I have, and if I deliver my body to be burned, but have not love, I gain nothing.

Love is patient and kind; love is not jealous or boastful; it is not arrogant or rude. Love does not insist on its own way; it is not irritable or resentful; it does not rejoice at wrong, but rejoices in the right. Love bears all things, believes all things, hopes all things, endures all things.

Love never ends. As for prophecies, they will pass away. As for tongues, they will cease. As for knowledge, *it will pass away. For our knowledge is imperfect and our prophecy is imperfect; but when the perfect comes, the imperfect will pass away.*

When I was a child, I spoke like a child, I thought like a child, I reasoned like a child. When I became a man, I gave up childish ways. For now we see in a mirror dimly, but then face to face. Now I know in part; then I shall understand fully, even as I have been fully understood. So faith, hope, love abide, these three; but the greatest of these is love.

—1 Corinthians 13

✦ LAW I

A merry heart makes a cheerful countenance. — English proverb

> Believe in life! Always human beings will live and progress to greater, broader, and fuller life.
> —W. E. B. Du Bois

> The love of praise, howe'er conceal'd by art, reigns more or less, and glows in ev'ry heart.
> —Edward Young

HAVE YOU EVER met a person in whose very essence and presence you felt good? A person whose eyes sparkled and whose smile held the warmth of a sunny day? Most likely, this person also expressed a positive outlook on life and spread the joy of good will wherever he or she went. If you had the opportunity to get to know the person, you probably found that, not only did "a merry heart make a cheerful countenance," but a strong spiritual belief system, based on unlimited love and integrity, may also have been evidenced. These joyful, precious souls are the ones who shine in our world and in our memories. The loving heart is a joyful heart.

A man was speaking on a radio program. He said, "To live is good. To live joyfully is better. To live joyfully and lovingly is best!" How wonderful it is to hear someone voice the truth that life is for living, and it is good. Each of us can approach life excitedly, hopefully, and enthusiastically. We can walk in the shimmering sunshine and smell the subtle or intense fragrance of a flower. We can let the wind ruffle our hair, watch the golden caprices of a sunset, or laugh with a cheerful heart. How could we ever be depressed or agitated when we savor God's world around us and seek to bring the joy we find to others?

How important is it for us to learn to identify with the beautiful and the joyous aspects of life? How do we associate beauty and joy with our present idea of God? Does the real beauty of life lie in the worth of the individual and the glory of our potential? Does a heart purified with unlimited love and uplifting enthusiasm open the spirit of the individual to a greater influence of divinity?

Could the person of cheerful countenance and loving heart be "a courier of courage?" How often do you find comfort and solace in the love of a family member or a friend? How often do you give of yourself to others for the pure joy of giving? The facts in our lives constantly change. In the normal order of our affairs, questions usually come before answers. Asking the right question, inquiring beyond our present understanding, can create a magnetic affinity with new discoveries. This often includes seeking and knocking on the door that opens on the inner chambers of the mind and the heart. The adventures of life do not need to be experienced through toil, trouble, and suffering. There are better and more joyous ways.

As far as we presently know, man is God's highest intelligent creation. At least on this level of consciousness, we seem to be at a pinnacle of human evolution. Of course, we would be very shortsighted if we did not realize that there could be levels of consciousness and life beyond our human awareness and development. However, this is where we are and, until we can discover or comprehend new dimensions, new forms, new beings, and new life, this is the life we must live. So, does it not make sense to live with a *merry heart and a cheerful countenance?*

Could the ultimate awareness of unlimited love be that which discerns our spiritual nature? When we realize that the human aspect is but one expression of the divine reality, then it would seem that joy would become a powerful extension of spirit in our lives. We always have the opportunity to decide what we want, make up our minds, and start moving toward our goals. We can look within ourselves for guidance about the areas we need or desire to develop, and we must be honest. How far can we see? Each horizon is but a springboard for new goals. Let's broaden our viewpoint and extend the range of our vision. Let's allow the magnificent beauty of wondrous life to fill us with overflowing joy! Let that joy be unrestrained.

We are the keepers of the citadels of our lives. Sing praises from the rooftops! It is *great* to be alive! Exultantly proclaim the good news! Invite the vital surge of divine energy to take up perma-

nent residence in your heart. Enjoy doing what you are doing. Let your laughter ring out. Bubble! Sparkle! Scintillate! Allow your excitement, inter-

est, and enthusiasm to add color and depth to everything you do. Infect others with your joyousness so they will know you are alive in spirit!

Positive thinking, rightly understood, is an affirmative way to meet life by aligning ourselves in consciousness with what is eternally true in spirit. The power of positive thinking is based on a strong universal law or principle. This is the law of attraction. Through love and joy, the ordinary can be transmuted into the extraordinary. Live, love, laugh, and be of good cheer!

✦ LAW 2

Everyone should keep in reserve an alternate plan for livelihood. —John Marks Templeton

MAJOR CHANGES often occur when we least expect them and can result in conditions beyond our present level of imagination. Usually, after the initial shock of such an unexpected event is lessened and some objectivity is gained, we begin to look for alternatives. As the well-known Boy Scout motto encourages us to "Be prepared," so, too, "Everyone should keep in reserve an alternate plan for livelihood." It is beneficial to explore various areas of interest. Many receptive thinkers have turned these interests into lucrative livelihoods when life's circumstances necessitated change. It is never too early to begin to think creatively.

Have you ever invested your time, energy,

enthusiasm, and perhaps finances in an activity, only to have the fruits of your labors seemingly slip through your fingers? Something may have changed unexpectedly and your good seemed to be blocked. But could your good ever be *completely* blocked? Have you heard the old adage, "Where there is a will, there is a way"? Or, "When one door closes, another door opens"? Both of these statements speak of unlimited possibilities. We simply need faith to continue the journey.

And "faith" does not imply a closed, but an open mind. Faith does not mean going forward blindly or unknowingly. Faith means "having respect for," or "standing in awe of." Faith appreciates the vast spiritual realities that may be overlooked by materialist "getting" trapped in the purely physical. "Faith gives substance to our hopes and makes us certain of realities we do not see" (Hebrews 11:1).

Another well-known maxim states, "It is difficult to solve a problem from the same level of consciousness that created the situation in the first place." Moving into a higher level of awareness becomes imperative. We may need to look outside our present arena for an authoritarian guide to provide new direction. It may be necessary as well as beneficial to review and possibly reconsider the initial motivation behind our goal. Sometimes, redirecting our attention to an alternative plan helps us to "keep on keeping on."

In the wide sweep of evolution, we see movement from the simple toward richer complexity and variety. As individuals, we represent a wide range of human thought, ingenuity, and creativity. We are *agents* of creation, and humanity can use every fertile idea that can enlarge the global vision of mankind. This is the type of innovative, advancing spirit that puts no limits on the quest for greater discoveries or on utilization of our abundant talents.

Certainly, the great moments of life include those crisis situations in which fresh, imaginative responses are needed. New discoveries come mainly from progressive minds. And possibly one of the attributes of God is *change*! How do you handle change? Do you give up and stop trying? Or do you continue to research more deeply within and continue to experiment with the meaning of life? Since we have the gift of self-consciousness, are we prepared for difficult situations by having alternative plans? The mind makes one

wise or ignorant, bound or emancipated, floundering or prepared. We need to work at controlling our minds and channeling our thoughts in beneficial and productive avenues.

Creative people can find inspiration from the most mundane things. Architect Eero Saarinen, for instance, was commissioned in 1956 to design a building for Trans-World Airlines at what is now New York's Kennedy Airport. Being discontented with his first model, Saarinen continued to work at new designs. Then, one morning at breakfast, he found himself staring at the curved shell of a grapefruit. He turned the shell over, began carving

There are very few human beings who receive the truth, complete and staggering, by instant illumination. Most of them acquire it fragment by fragment, on a small scale, by successive developments, cellularly, like a laborious mosaic.
—*Anaïs Nin*

arches in it, and carried the finished product off to work, adding it to other models involved in the final design. When the airport terminal was completed, an architectural magazine described it as "a totality of fluid form curving and circling within itself, suggesting the flight of a great bird."

A closing thought: in order to reach our greatest potential, do we also need a time to come apart from the busyness of the day? A "retreat" time, if you will, to withdraw from the world and contemplate the workings of spirit. This quiet time could help us strike a balance between our work and non-pressured reflection. By allowing our minds to roam freely and creatively, we can provide fertile soil for new and developing ideas. Hard work and practical spiritual preparation can provide a springboard from which we can leap into the realm of creative insight.

✦ Law 3

If you are facing in the right direction, all you need to do is keep walking. —Buddhist proverb

I might have been born in a hovel, but I determined to travel with the wind and the stars.
—*Jacqueline Cochran*

First to know, then to act, then to really know.
—*Bishr al Hafifi*

Action, to be effective, must be directed to clearly conceived ends.
—*Jawaharlal Nehru*

AN ENDING is simply a new beginning. Nothing ever ends without something else beginning, or begins without something else ending. What we make of these endings and beginnings is, of course, up to us. We have all the tools and resources we need. The question may be: How shall I go forward? And then, we have a choice of direction. Which direction is aligned with our path of purpose? If the ending you have reached is progressive and you are facing in the right direction toward your goals, then *all you need to do is keep on walking!*

Where does the real nature of your power lie? Do you sometimes become attached to status quo situations, or have you made a commitment to the creativity of your talents? While attachment has its source in the personality, in what the Buddhists refer to as the "desire nature," real commitment springs from the depths of our souls.

> That which we persist in doing becomes easier for us to do. Not that the nature of the thing has changed, but that our power to do it has increased.
>
> —*Hever J. Grant*

Purity of life is the highest and truest art.
—*Mahatma Gandhi*

The truth is that the beginning of anything and its end are alike touching."
—*Yoshida Kenko*

Gary Zukav writes in *The Seat of the Soul*: "Power is energy that is formed by the intentions of the soul. It is Light shaped by the intentions of love and compassion guided by wisdom. It is energy that is focused and directed toward the fulfillment of the tasks of the soul upon the earth, and the development of the personality as a physical instrument of the soul that is appropriate to those tasks." If what we seek is the joy of creatively giving without reservation, we will know the power

> In order to find reality, each must search for his own universe, look for the details that contribute to this reality that one feels under the surface of things.
>
> —*Akira Kurosawa*

of a humble spirit. And this is definitely walking in the right direction!

If you plan to go from point "A" to point "B" in your life journey and you prepare yourself for the journey by studying and planning the route you wish to take, bringing a compass along as a guide, you can ultimately reach your destination. We take action, and we move forward. Oliver Wendell Holmes indicated this when he said: "I find the great thing in this world is not so much where we stand, as in what direction we are moving. To reach the port of heaven, we must sail sometimes with the wind and sometimes against it—but we must sail, and not drift, nor lie at anchor."

When we open our minds to light and truth, there need never be a time when we are at a loss for ideas, inspiration, or guidance. Look at how you yourself have grown through the variety of experiences in your life. Consider the insight and increased awareness each situation has brought. Do new ideas stimulate your thinking processes? Have you learned how to perceive things with greater clarity and wisdom? Can you see beyond the activities of the personality to the greater spiritual force of the immortal soul? Do you comprehend the role of responsible choice and choose accordingly in whatever you may be doing? Are you increasingly aware of your soul's purpose for embodiment? These are simple guidelines for growth. *If you are facing in the right direction, all you need to do is keep walking!*

✦ Law 4

The unknown is not unknowable and is vastly greater than the known. —John Marks Templeton

We especially need imagination in science. It is not all mathematics, nor all logic, but it is somewhat beauty and poetry.
—*Maria Mitchell*

Of all kinds of knowledge that we can ever obtain, the knowledge of God and the knowledge of ourselves are the most important.
—*Jonathan Edwards*

A great discovery is a fact whose appearance in science gives rise to shining ideas, whose light dispels many obscurities and shows us new paths.
—*Claude Bernard*

AN ANCIENT PROVERB states: "We learn what we look for." If we take an open and exploratory look around us, we can see signals of transcendence and pointers to the infinite that are coming to us, not only from mystics, but also through many recent findings of science. The evolution of human knowledge seems to be accelerating quickly and we are reaping the fruits of generations of scientific thought. Many fields of exploration are finding "what is looked for" and more!

In *The God Who Would Be Known*, examples are given that suggest that the unknown is not unknowable, that it is vastly greater than the known. The authors comment:

We find an exciting world in dynamic flux, an unexpected universe whose mechanisms are ever more baffling and staggering in their beauty and complexity. It is a place where predictability is uncertain instead of deterministic, where matter and energy are interchangeable, and where evolutionary change occurs by leaps and bounds that defy mechanistically simple explanation. And ourselves; what has become of us? The physicists tell us that we are particularly situated midway between the immense parameters of the cosmos and the infinitude of the smallest particles of matter and energy. Our arrival on this planet seems remarkable, whether looked at in terms of the requirement for a special relationship among the forces controlling elementary particles, or in terms of the mechanisms of biological evolution. What is becoming increasingly obvious is that the evolutionary process that has resulted in humankind is a unique and undirectional one. And the steps peculiar to Homo sapiens are remarkable in both their timing and their developmental aspects. We are a once-for-all happening, and, most wonderful of all, our journey has just begun!

Could this expanding awareness be an invitation to plan a noble purpose for our lives, both on an individual and on an international level? Are multitudinous opportunities being presented for us to bring forth our special purpose and to direct our talents to action in a chosen career? When we make a commitment and take the first steps to surge ahead, the universe responds and works with us.

Gaining knowledge is like working a quarry. As we chip out bits of information, the mining face gets larger and larger. The more knowledge we gain, the more we can see the extent of the unknown. As we grow in knowledge, we grow in humility. This may be just as true in studying the soul as in the investigations pursued by natural sciences.
—*John Marks Templeton*

The quantity of knowledge that has been discovered within the latest century may be even greater than all the knowledge discovered since the beginning of humanity. Much of this recorded knowledge occurred in the physical sciences and these discoveries continue to accelerate exponentially. The science of physics now reveals a vast variety of previously unknown particles, and particles within particles. Chemistry has revealed the presence of hundreds of previously undreamed-of processes going on within matter. The science of biology has evolved from merely naming and classifying living matter to understanding how a seed germinates and analyzing the genetic code of a living plant. But even now, humans have discovered only a tiny part of ultimate reality.

In some instances, it seems that the creative spirit of the universe may be spreading and energizing new dimensions of research and information for present and future humankind. In the majestic language of the New Testament, we read: "In the beginning was the Word and the Word was with God and the Word was God. All things were made through Him, and without Him was not anything made that was made . . . In Him was life, and the life was the light of men" (John 1:1, 3–4). "Word" in Greek is "logos," "a thought" or " a concept." Logos has also been referred to as "the divine archetype idea that contains all ideas." With this understanding, and based on the language of modern science, the verses above might be translated as: "God is the substance and the Creator of the universe and all therein—and much more. Creation proceeds from idea, to word, to material manifestation." Thus, we obtain a vague idea of the concept of cocreation.

What would happen if research foundations and religious institutions around the world began to devote additional resources and increased manpower to scientific studies in the spiritual realm? Could this provide an unprecedented opportunity for greater progress in spiritual information through science?

Every person's concept of God is too small. Would *humility* be a workable avenue through

> A great discovery is a fact whose appearance in science gives rise to shining ideas, whose light dispels many obscurities and shows us new paths.
> —Claude Bernard

which we could begin to arrive at a true perspective of the infinite mind of God? Through humility, we can learn from one another. Humility also encourages us to be open to others, and ready and willing to study things from another's point of view. In turn, we can freely share our perspectives.

I have called this new kind of humility, this new awareness of the unlimited, all-pervasive, all-encompassing creative spirit, humility theology. Perhaps this guiding principle can help as we begin a new phase of evolution, a spiritual exploration, using the tools of science that have been so productive in the study of the physical universe.

◆ LAW 5

Humility opens the door to progress. —John Marks Templeton

> Always be humble, but not by bowing your head which is external humility. Real humility is internal and has its origin in wisdom.
> —Rabbi Nahman of Bratslav

HUMILITY IS an effective gateway to greater understanding. As thanksgiving opens the door to spiritual growth, so does humility open the door to progress in knowledge and open-mindedness. It is difficult for a person to learn more if he is certain he knows everything already. The close-minded attitude of those who think they know it all inhibits future progress. However, when we begin to comprehend just how little we know, then we become ready to seek, research, and learn.

In the previous essay, we considered the rapid

rate of increasing knowledge; yet, in the coming century over one-hundred-fold more knowledge may be discovered. The acceleration of learning through science has become breathtaking. Could a great opportunity lie before us through the humble approach for mutual learning? Could a partnership between science and religion provide an opportunity for creating spiritual wealth? A new kind of humility has begun to express itself as we recognize the vastness of God's creation and our very small place in the cosmic scheme of things.

Multiplying spiritual wealth is an approach for all of us who are not satisfied to let things drift and who want to channel our creative restlessness toward helping to build heaven on earth.

The potential benefits, from the viewpoint of better understanding God and his vast creation, are irresistible for some of us. Through humility, we can begin to place the infinity of God into a truer perspective. This is the humble approach. Are we ready to begin the formulation of a humble theology that can never become obsolete? This would be a theology really centered upon God, and not upon man-made rituals.

Humility theology means enthusiasm for new spiritual information. To aid in this search for over one-hundred-fold more spiritual discovery, the Templeton Foundation has expanded in scope with the formation of a research center, the Humility Theology Information Center. Major goals include sponsoring various research projects and helping form societies of respected scientists and theologians who are interested in progress.

Humility theology recognizes that there are multiplying mysteries. We may never comprehend more than a small part of reality; maybe we are not the only spiritual beings in the visible and invisible cosmos! After all, is the visible only a tiny, temporary manifestation of reality? Do we think humans are the end-products of creation?

Humility theology applauds the opportunities for new spiritual information through scientific

studies of both the physical and the spiritual spheres. Some questions to ponder are:

Can I be an expression or agent of God in love and creativity?

Are there some laws from the great religions that help produce a happy and fruitful life that can be tested by scientific methods?

How can we learn to be helpers in achieving God's purposes?

Is it possible that research in genetics or other sciences can accelerate progress in human intelligence?

Every passing day brings additional scientific discoveries of the wonders of the universe—in both the microcosm and the macrocosm. Many people stand in awe of the tremendous complex-

There is considerable common ground between science and religion. Part of that common ground lies in their shared emphasis on humility.
—David G. Myers

ity, the diversity, and the exquisite organization of the universe, and experience a sense of humility as such magnificence is increasingly discovered. Thankfully, many of scientists are also aware that their humility toward research can open new doors to progress, even in areas seemingly unrelated to their particular area of science.

Spotlights ✦ ✦

1. The loving heart is a joyful heart.

2. How do you associate beauty and joy with your present idea of God?

3. Sometimes redirecting our attention to an alternative plan helps us to "keep on keeping on."

4. We can be *agents* of creation, and humanity can use every fertile idea that can enlarge the global vision of mankind.

5. An ending is simply a new beginning.

6. When we open our minds to light and truth, there never need be a time when we are at a loss for ideas, inspiration, or guidance.

7. Could egotism be perhaps one of the largest stumbling-blocks to progress?

8. Humility is an effective gateway to greater understanding.

9. Humility theology means enthusiasm for new spiritual information and additional concepts.

10. Progress is definitely speeding up!

Living the Various Spiritual Laws ✦ ✦

HUMILITY

Be humble, be harmless,
Have no pretension,
Be upright, forbearing;
Serve your teacher in true obedience,
Keeping the mind and body in cleanness,
Tranquil, steadfast, master of ego,
Standing apart from the things of the senses,
Free from self
Aware of the weakness in mortal nature.
   —*Bhagavad Gita*

Subdue pride by modesty, overcome hypocrisy by simplicity, and dissolve greed by contentment.
   —*Jainism*

To know when one does not know is best. To think one knows when one does not know is a dire disease.
   —*Tao Te Ching*

Blessed are the meek,
For they shall inherit the earth.
   —*Matthew 5:5*

Week Thirty-Nine

+ ## LAW 1

Forgiveness benefits both the giver and the receiver. —John Marks Templeton

As long as our minds
are captive to the
memory of having
been wronged, they
are not free to wish
for reconciliation
with the one who
wronged us.
—*Lewis Smedes*

FORGIVENESS is powerful evidence of spiritual strength. When we witness an act of forgiveness, we may marvel at its resulting power to heal and to break a seemingly unending cycle of pain. In the overall perspective of life, *forgiveness benefits both the giver and the receiver.* The person who can pour forgiveness from his mind and heart may be expressing pure unlimited love for all people, including even harmful people. The recipient of this life-changing energy experiences the opportunity to move into a clean, fresh world. Old fears, grudges, and feelings of injustice can be eliminated. Heavy burdens of guilt or negative energies are often erased. The technique for achieving forgiveness is simple: *release; let go!* Whatever aspect of any burden we cast off each day means there is less burden we carry forward to the next day. Forgiveness provides an excellent opportunity to merge our humanity with our divinity. The possibility for compassion can exist in even the most extreme of circumstances.

A forgiving spirit
is a unifying force.
—*William L. Fischer*

Advantages from forgiveness come in many ways. Recent research studies show a number of physical and psychological health benefits resulting from forgiveness. Blood pressure can be lowered. Problems with anger, anxiety, and stress can be eliminated. Bouts of depression can be reduced. Peace of mind is enhanced. Communication and relationships are often improved.

What does forgiveness really mean? Does it mean forgetting the hurtful or hateful action taken in a difficult situation? Does forgiveness mean working through our personal grudges? On the one hand, forgiveness is something we do for ourselves—for our personal health, for our sanity, and for our freedom. On the other hand, can forgiveness be a directive from unlimited love to contribute to the overall betterment of humanity? The extraordinary importance of forgiveness, now being studied and validated through scientific research, has long been recognized by the world's religious traditions.

Confucius, for example, said, "to be wronged is nothing unless you continue to remember it." The Qur'an states: "A kind speech and forgiveness is better than alms followed by injury." The Dalai Lama argues, "learning to forgive is much more useful than merely picking up a stone and throwing it at the object of one's anger." And healing and forgiveness were often coupled at the center of Jesus' ministry. "To err is human, to forgive divine," wrote the eighteenth century English poet Alexander Pope. Thus, it isn't surprising that people often link their ability to forgive with their spirituality. An active life of prayer, the importance of faith, and a feeling of closeness with divinity often provide a springboard for forgiveness and unlimited love. Our true spiritual nature is something that cannot be lost to us, even in moments of disillusionment, because it is of the substance of divinity.

How did it happen that the various forms of religion seem to have arrived at the conclusion that forgiveness is vitally important? Is it possible that forgiveness became prominent within religions through the simple empirical observation that people who forgive seem to prosper, whereas those who are unable to forgive tend to wither? How *are* forgiveness and healthier and more prosperous living coupled? What is the connecting link between forgiveness and greater happiness?

Do we feel less vulnerable when we are able to forgive? What help could be given to the people who have experienced such tragic situations that they may feel the price of forgiveness is too high? In these situations, memory seems to bring the most pain. How can these wounded states be healed? Replacing a negative memory with a positive one can bring about a healing, but through what other effective ways can we build roads to reconciliation? The tightly clenched fist must become an open hand in order to receive. The ability to forgive may not come quickly or easily, and it may be necessary to forgive "seventy-times-seven" to achieve the desired results.

Forgiveness plays such a vital role in our lives. It may take varying lengths of time for some to realize that holding tightly to hurts only results in grief to all parties. But if the road to forgiveness is traveled, it can bring peace of mind and true connection with others. When we can forgive, everyone benefits. George Herbert said, "He who cannot forgive breaks the bridge over which he himself must pass."

✦ LAW 2

Your dreams can come true when you activate them. —John Marks Templeton

DREAMS or magnificent inspired ideas have played a major part in many discoveries, and discoveries fulfill many dreams! Visions, dreams, or ideas, by whatever name they may be called, usually exhibit an important factor. In every instance, the successful dreamer *took some kind of action* to bring the dream into manifestation. This fact can serve as encouragement for each of us that *our dreams can come true when we activate them!* And *activate* is the key word. Futuristic vision often lies seeded in the rich soil of adventurous souls and minds. Their vision is uninhibited by what some may call "facts." The "dreamers" can peer beyond the veils and mists of doubt, fear, and uncertainty to perceive unlimited possibilities. After all, according to sacred literature, does not divinity often speak in the language of dreams and visions? "I will pour out my spirit on all flesh; your sons and daughters shall prophesy, your old men shall dream dreams and your young men shall see visions" (Joel 2:28).

"Vision," according to the English writer Jonathan Swift, "is the art of seeing things invisible." This gift or talent belongs to those progressive dreamers who can see possibilities that may be hidden in seeming setbacks or that may be waiting for discovery in the shadows of the unknown. American philosopher Ralph Waldo Emerson wrote: "The high, contemplative, all-consuming

There will always be a frontier where there is an open mind and a willing hand.
—*Charles F. Kettering*

The frontiers are not east or west, north or south, but wherever a man fronts a fact.
—*Henry David Thoreau*

vision, the sense of right and wrong, is alike in all. Its attributes are self-existence, eternity, intuition, and command. It is the mind of the mind."

So, if vision is "the mind of the mind," can it also contribute to our value systems? Can noble purpose be a formative part of our personal blueprint for what is important in life? Could inspired vision put us on a path of creativity and self-discovery that might also take us deeper inside ourselves? Certainly visioning or creative thinking contains elements of beauty, awareness, performance, and transformation. If the world is a work in progress and we are helpers with God in its ongoing creation, can every person be a contributor through creative activities? Our own trials, errors, successes, and triumphs often reflect our personal vision for the world and our place in it.

Dreaming and creativity are pathways to things sacred. Desmond Tutu was quoted in *The NPR Interviews* (1994) as saying, "We were made to enjoy music, to enjoy beautiful sunsets, to enjoy looking at the billows of the sea and to be thrilled with a rose that is bedecked with dew . . . Human beings are actually created for the transcendent,

for the sublime, for the beautiful, for the truthful . . . and all of us are given the task of trying to make this world a little more hospitable to these beautiful things." If the spiritual is our true nature, then perhaps the most important thing we can ever know is the extent and the meaning of our spiritual selves and our relationship to the Creator God of the universe.

What are *your* dreams and visions for the future? What are your plans to activate these possibilities toward successful achievement? How will you tap into the realm of infinite power that is present everywhere? What avenues are you following and what steps are you taking toward making your life more worthwhile?

The law of being provides us with an independence to build our lives in the way we choose, in accordance with our own ideas and ideals. We can plan our futures along the lines that we desire. Progress and happiness are the natural conditions of humankind. Working in harmony with universal principle can help us demonstrate these blessings.

✦ LAW 3

Work is love made visible. —Kahlil Gibran

The way to be effective and find joy and meaning through our work is to discover what is needed and wanted, and then produce it— right where we are!
—*Richard J. Leider*

THE TRANSITION from adolescence to adulthood often points us in the direction of what we wish to do with our lives with regard to work or a chosen vocation. On the one hand, work can be described as a job that sustains your interest while you make enough money to support yourself in a comfortable lifestyle. On the other hand, work can become a vocation or an inner calling to enhance and use our special talents and abilities for a specific and worthwhile purpose. A careful choice of a career

can contribute to humanity as well as provide personal growth and fulfillment. In fact, every useful work can be a ministry of service in the field of your choosing.

Kahlil Gibran wrote in *The Prophet*: "work is love made visible." Our work, what we do and how we do it, is a personal statement. If we look at the work we do from a spiritual perspective, every job has meaning and purpose in the overall scheme of things. Do the work you love and love what you do! A vocation entails much more than putting in hours to earn an income. When you love what you do, you have a chosen outlet through which creativity can be expressed.

Joan Chittister wrote in *There Is a Season*:

A spirituality of work is based on a heightened sense of sacramentality, of the idea that everything that is, is holy and that our hands consecrate it to the service of God. When we grow radishes in a small container in a city apartment, we participate in creation. We sustain the globe. When we sweep the street in front of a house in the dirtiest city in the country, we bring new order to the universe. We tidy the Garden of Eden. We make God's world new again. When we repair what has been broken, or paint what is old, or give away what we have earned that is above and beyond our own sustenance, we swoop down and scoop up the earth and breathe into it new life again, as God did one morning in time only to watch it unfold and unfold and unfold through the ages. When we wrap garbage and recycle cans, when we clean a room and put coasters under glasses, when we care for everything we touch and touch it reverently, we become the creators of a new universe . . . Work enables us to put our personal stamp of approval, our own watermark, the autograph of our souls on the development of the world. In fact, to do less is to do nothing at all.

Every person has a psychological need to find joy in his or her work. When we are pursuing a worthwhile vocation for which we feel a natural passion, a joyful inner purpose seems to be activated. We desire substance in our work. And most

people want to expand their talents and be creatively challenged. As we work with purpose and enthusiasm, success becomes a natural by-product. It is important to feel that the work we do makes a difference. And the time we take to identify elements of purposeful work is time well invested. Yes, our work is often related to income. However, our chosen vocation provides a path also to use our gifts to do something we believe needs doing in the world.

There is a positive and persuasive energy about holding something that we have created in our hands or in seeing that our work has made a difference in someone's life. In a way, accomplishing something visible can serve to further our purpose.

◆ LAW 4

For every effect, there is a cause. —Hermetic principle

HAVE YOU EVER paused to think that a reason exists for whatever may have happened in your life? If you experienced an illness, had a wonderful day, made a new friend, were involved in an accident, accepted a new work position, got married, or started a business, somewhere and on some level a reason existed for each of these experiences. And the reason most likely involved one of the great universal laws by which our lives seem to be shaped—the law of cause and effect.

For example, consider the simple law of nature: "As you sow, so shall you reap." Sowing seeds of any kind is the *cause* that sets the law in operation. The initiated creative forces will inevitably bring about the *effect*, which is the harvest from the seeds. Sow corn; harvest corn. Plant apple trees; gather apples when the trees mature. In each instance, we are the cause—the "planters," so to speak.

> By self do you censure yourself. By self do you examine yourself. Self-guarded and mindful . . . you will live happily. Control, therefore, your own self as a merchant controls a noble steed.
> —The Dhammapada

This same analogy holds true in the various aspects of our lives. The seeds you plant—your consciousness, your attitudes, your actions, how you treat others—insure, unequivocally, that *you* are the instigating cause of the return harvest. However, our thinking processes may offer a dozen reasons why we are *not* the causes for events

> Every cause has its effect; every effect has its cause. Everything happens according to Law.
> — Yogi Ramacharaka

in our lives. But responsibility seems to be a central consideration for what it means to be human. And individual responsibility requires an attitude of self-awareness. What are your strong points? In what areas do you need to grow and expand your abilities? Are you forgiving, or do you get caught up in judgment and blame? Rather than blaming other people or situations for your difficulties, do you consider what probable cause could have emerged from within yourself? If you want to experience an abundant and joyful life, you need to let go of your misperceptions. The creative energies of the universe simply work out what we have

directed, although we may not be *consciously* aware that we initially sent forth the causative energy.

Think about the law of cause and effect for a moment. Life is a learning process rather than a judgment process. If we are responsible for what happens to us, do we not also have vast and unlimited opportunities to be positively creative? This idea can be tremendously exciting. The law of cause and effect is not "positive" or "negative," it simply is. We are the ones who qualify the energy through our ability to choose.

In The *Psyche and Psychism*, Torkom Saraydarian writes:

The Inner Presence and the presence in nature may be called the Law of Cause and Effect. This law is an energy field extending throughout the cosmic planes, and any action upon this energy field creates a corresponding reaction relative to the level and intensity of the action. Thus, a wish, a desire, an aspiration, a thought can be an act of prayer, a form of action which creates the corresponding reaction from the energy field, from the Law of Cause and Effect.

But what about this thing called "chance"? Many people believe that chance, luck, or "accidental" happenings contribute, for better or worse, to our lives. Webster's dictionary defines "chance" as: a "supposed agent or mode of activity other than a force, law, or purpose." How could there be "something" acting in the universe outside of or independent of the infinity of divinity? Does careful examination show that what we call "chance" could

> Nothing that happens in our world or to us personally ever happens by itself or without cause. In the earth plane, cause and effect is the natural law; it is the way the world works.
> —Bruce McArthur

simply be an expression relating to obscure causes that we may not perceive or understand? There is much food for thought in these considerations.

Understanding the workings of universal laws or principles can open a powerful doorway to personal freedom. Just as rules of the road are required to insure safety when we drive a car, laws of the spirit can help us travel safely to a beneficial destination. One way or another, most of the world religions emphasize individual responsibility in the varying matters of life.

✦ LAW 5

Those who do good do well. —John Marks Templeton

IN THE PREVIOUS ESSAY, we considered the universal law of cause and effect. In this process, we are working with a creative principle, providing an avenue whereby we literally create experiences in our lives. It is essential to be aware that each of us is a coworker with the universe through our thoughts, intents, purposes, and desires. Since this creative process is impartial, we can create chaos as well as the beautiful and the good. It is helpful to recognize that our thoughts, intents, purposes, and desires probably derive from basic beliefs. Our belief systems most likely formed from basic thoughts about ourselves, others, our lives, our experiences, and whatever programming we hold in our subconscious minds.

Interestingly, the law of giving and receiving is part of the law of cause and effect. Giving (the cause) prompts circulation (the effect). The law of giving and receiving is also considered part of the law of universal, unlimited love. What are our beliefs about giving and receiving? The purpose for which we give is vital. To give with a secret hope of reward is in direct opposition to the law of love. Sincere giving from the mind and heart, with no strings attached, carries thoughts of unlimited love. Giving in this manner has far-reaching effects, often bringing abundant good to both the giver and the receiver. *Those who do good, do well!*

Giving and receiving touch every area of life, not just tangible or material goods. And there are so many ways we can give. We can give away a portion of what we have through acts of charity for the benefit of others. We can volunteer our time and energy to charitable causes. Local communities offer many opportunities to serve. People express their love through charitable works in order to both alleviate suffering and to elevate the recipients of their love. Feeding the hungry, caring for the sick, clothing the naked are necessary in the short term; however, the long-range goal, the real charity, is to help those in need learn the spiritual traits that lead to prosperity, dignity, and happiness. Possibly the greatest charity is to help a person change from being a receiver to being a giver.

Life is short; within this span, each person must seek to reap the richest possible harvest of discovery and realization. All that is necessary is for each of us to make a daily effort to *practice the presence of God*. The opportunities for service that are before us are unprecedented on both a personal as

well as on a global level. What is it that your heart begs you to do? By what measure are you giving? The person who thinks good thoughts and feels good emotions, and sees only the good in life and in people will remember only good and express only good. The moment we recognize that we are one with the spirit of infinite love, we can become so filled with love that we behold only the good in all. Every new impulse given to the love of truth and goodness brings us a little closer to heaven on earth.

In *After the Ecstasy, the Laundry,* Jack Kornfield

wrote: "Service is the expression of the awakened heart. But whom are we serving? When someone asked Gandhi how he could so continually sacrifice himself for India, he replied, 'I do this for myself alone.' When we serve others, we serve ourselves. The Upanishads call this 'God feeding God.'"

Spotlights ✦ ✦

1. Forgiveness is powerful evidence of spiritual strength.

2. The technique for achieving forgiveness is simple: *release and let go!*

3. Inspired vision can be a path to creativity.

4. What are *your* dreams and visions for the future?

5. Our work makes a personal statement about our lives.

6. Do what you love and love what you do!

7. The law of cause and effect is not "positive" or "negative," it simply is.

8. Life is a learning process rather than a judgment process.

9. Each of us is a coworker with the universe through our thought, intents, purposes, and desires.

10. Giving and receiving touches every area of our lives, not just tangible or material goods.

Living the Various Spiritual Laws ✦ ✦

Listen to the essence of religion
and assimilate it through the heart:
one should never do to others
which one would not wish done to oneself.

That which has been said in countless books
I shall say in half a verse:
Service of others is virtue, injury to others is sin.
—Mahatma Gandhi

Week Forty

✦ LAW 1

Focus on where you want to go instead of where you have been. —John Marks Templeton

The difference between transformation by accident and transformation by a system is like the difference between lightning and a lamp. Both give illumination, but one is dangerous and unreliable, while the other is directed, available.
—*Marilyn Ferguson*

MANY OF THE GREATEST achievements in life are often accomplished by people who have a singular desire that becomes the foundational building block for all they do. For example, when Bob Feller was a child, he loved to throw a ball. By the age of five, he spent hours every day pitching a ball through a hole in the barn wall. At age ten, his father bought him all the necessary equipment and provided him with a playing field on the family farm. At age thirteen, Bob pitched for a local baseball team and averaged twenty strikeouts a game. At seventeen he began playing for the American Cleveland Indians baseball team. As a major league player, Bob had 6 seasons as a 20-game winner, 3 no-hit games, 11 one-hit games, 266 wins, and he set a record of 348 strikeouts in one season. Bob Feller became a member of the Baseball Hall of Fame because he had one burning desire—to play baseball! He kept his eye on the vision he held and continually worked toward his goal.

A businessman employed by a small furniture manufacturing firm held a vision of eventually having his own company. He worked diligently and creatively and learned the mechanics of the business from the inside out. Both office and factory personnel respected his growing ability and appreciated his sincerity and congeniality. A few years passed and the man was offered a top man-

agement position with a much larger manufacturing company. He considered the offer, talking the possibilities over with his family. During the intervening years, the man had planned for the startup of his own company and saved for the appropriate time and opportunity. He and his family felt the time was *now*, so he made the decision and stepped forward. Having established an honorable reputation in his field of endeavor, the man's fledging company began to flourish. Here is another success story. The key element is to *focus on what you want to achieve.*

Other stories are told of people who dream of achievement and certainly have marketable talents and abilities. However, they seem to get "bogged down" in the process. Instead of formulating a workable plan and following the plan through to successful manifestation, they often run around in circles like rudderless ships, gaining speed and momentum but making little progress toward their goals. In some instances, these people may get caught up in looking back and rehashing the events and situations that previously transpired in their lives. With no focus or definite direction, or with too much looking backward, how can their present goals be achieved? One man occasionally spoke of an old maxim that often guided him: "It is all right to look backward for reflection, but don't stare!"

Webster's dictionary defines "focus" as: "*an adjustment to make a clear image.*" One example given is: "to concentrate, as in focusing one's attention." Fine-tuning the vision for our goals can be like focusing or adjusting a camera lens to achieve sharp, crisp, and clear photographs.

Can you imagine where we, as the human race, might be in our present progression if those creative, fine minds that made so many unprecedented discoveries dwelled in the past instead of looking forward? Today's world is stepping boldly into a new golden age of opportunities—technologically, medically, scientifically, culturally, economically, and spiritually. What will the next forty or fifty years portend? How can we focus *today* to perceive the *future* more clearly? From a business perspective, what types of products will we be buying and selling? What careers will be beneficial and productive? What will the job market be like? How will these opportunities be affected by the "electronic age" of computers? In fact, how will our lifestyles be affected by advancing electronic technology? With the power of the information society shifting toward those who excel at analyzing data, how will our workforce successfully access information, analyze it, and draw valid conclusions from that analysis? Will our lifestyles be as different as our current lifestyles are from those of a century ago? What advances will the field of medicine have made? How will international trade be conducted? What scientific advances will be beneficial? What will world religions become like in a more scientific age? How might advancing scientific and theological perspectives on God, the universe, the cosmos, and creativity improve our lives?

Can these questions inspire us in the present

moment? Where do we want to go? How do we desire and plan to go forward? What are we doing to prepare for our desires and goals? What new horizons enchant our hearts and rivet our gaze? Almost unfathomable amounts of information are evolving rapidly. How will we use the new information? Will there be increased understanding, better global communications, and improved dialogue between individuals, religions, and countries?

To enjoy the fruits of our discoveries, we must allow time to educate our bodies, minds, and spirits. An important avenue through which this may be accomplished is to focus on where we want to go and how we wish to go there, instead of on where we have been.

So, as we look into the future, each of us should be overwhelmingly grateful for the multitudes of blessings that surround us and for the prospect of even more wonderful blessings for our children and grandchildren. We should also be overwhelmingly grateful to be living in the most glorious period of God's ongoing and accelerating creative progress. Let's keep our aim high and our focus concentrated on greater good.

✦ Law 2

Each of us can learn to be helpers in achieving God's purpose. —John Marks Templeton

OPPORTUNITIES ABOUND for new spiritual information through scientific studies of both the physical and the spiritual spheres. We anticipate a great influx of new ideas and concepts to supplement the wonderful ancient scriptures. Are we possibly on the brink of a new conception of theology in which truth is approached in an experimental, hypothetical mode, as is done in the sciences? A major expansion in knowledge about divinity certainly seems possible. What is humanity's role in these possible discoveries? In actuality, every one of us can be an expression or agent of God through unlimited love and expanding creativity.

How can we learn to be helpers in achieving God's purpose? Perhaps one of the first steps is to humbly admit that as humans, we know so little of God and the accelerating creativity and purposes for life on earth. The next step could stem from our openness to learn.

Learning is a lifetime activity of vast importance. To learn that each of us might help in the acceleration of creating offers a glorious opportunity. The divine idea of order seems to be the idea of flow and adjustment, and as this idea becomes established in our thought, can all aspects of our lives—minds, ideas, and expressions—be in harmony with the universal creative love?

The genius of the universe created us and instilled a spark of that genius within each of us. When we dare to reach beyond our comfort zones in life and declare that a great dream may be being dreamed through us, do we allow the genius aspect of the great Creator to do its creative work? It is one thing to embrace greater possibilities and quite another to take the steps needed to bring them into fruition.

Are we not spiritual beings in visible form? Is our world essentially a spiritual world? Might the underlying controlling forces or energies be identified as *spiritual principles*? When we recognize our unity with this spiritual essence, do we perhaps

begin to "see with the eyes of spirit?" Do wondrous things then begin to happen in our lives?

Let's encourage creative thinking within ourselves and others. Let's overcome feelings of timidity and throw our talents enthusiastically into a variety of experiences and personal encounters. Let's *believe in ourselves and in others*—for the kingdom of heaven does not come with large signs to be observed! The kingdom of heaven—the realm of expanding consciousness, creativity, progress, and divine opportunity—is already in the midst of us. Is this a new frontier for the further exploration of our own inner beings and our own innate divinity? Has forgetting our divinity or turning away from it created a sense of separation from the great Creator? As we remember our oneness with the supreme source, can we move into the energy flow of creativity?

To a large extent, the future lies before us like a vast wilderness of unexplored reality. The One who created and sustained this evolving universe through eons of progress has not placed us in this present moment at the tag end of the creative process. We *are* at the point of a new beginning. We *are* present for the future! Everyone has something of value to contribute. Each of us has a mind capable of creative activity. Can we be helpers in achieving God's purpose in the ongoing expansion of the cosmos, which includes the expansion of our own souls? This creative process moves through our thoughts, words, and deeds to become manifest in our lives. Why are we the recipients of such powerful spiritual gifts? What shall we do with ourselves and with this power? Possibly, we are created to become helpers in the Creator's accelerating activity.

✦ Law 3

Every useful life is a ministry. —John Marks Templeton

Be useful where thou livest.
— *George Herbert*

He who wishes to expand the field of happiness, let him lay the foundation of it on the bottom of his heart.
—*Taoism*

THOSE WHO CONSIDER their work as a kind of ministry realize that the manner in which they treat others is of great importance. They understand that spirit is truly part of everything we do, and they seek to incorporate universal principles into every segment of their life. The spirituality of work is beautifully described in comments made by Maxine F. Dennis in *Of Human Hands*. She said:

Cashiering in a super market may not seem like a very rewarding position to most. But to me it is. You see, I feel that my job consists of a lot more than ringing up orders, taking people's money, and bagging their groceries. The most important part of my job is not the obvious. Rather, it's the manner in which I present myself to others that will determine whether my customers will leave the store feeling better or worse because of their brief encounter with me. For by doing my job well, I know I have a chance to do God's work too. Because of this, I try to make each of my customers feel special. While I'm serving them, they become the most important people in my life.

Many times, when people hear the word "ministry," they think of a church or perhaps of some kind of government office. In truth, however, whatever work we do in life, if accomplished from the perspective of doing a good job that will assist and be beneficial to others, becomes a personal ministry. The way we live our lives—how we handle situations, our values and ideals, our goals and the way we strive to attain them, how we treat others—are all aspects of personal ministry. And our world surely needs more ministers of service, happy to dedicate their efforts and energies to the jobs at hand!

Beloved, let us love one another; for love is of God, and he who loves is born of God and knows God. He who does not love does not know God; for God is love.
—*1 John 4:7–8*

As we grow in spiritual awareness, we understand that knowledge brings responsibility as well as certain power; knowledge obligates those who possess it to use it for the good of all. When we choose to allow our lives to be governed by spiritual principles, we may be sure that spirit will sustain us. When we find the kingdom within, the essence of our being becomes a uniting agency, expressing unlimited love. We know that everything productive in life that we accomplish becomes a ministry of loving service. *Every useful life is a ministry.* Our sole thought becomes that of reaching the hearts of others and giving them something of vital value, something that will broaden and enrich their lives. We desire that every person be open and alive to higher inspirations and filled with a beauty and truth so splendid that it elevates his or her soul.

Almost every person is born into the world with many talents that can be developed. Most of us are given more talents than we realize, and it is up to us to utilize those talents to the best advantage. Also, while developing our talents, we perform a ministry of service by helping other people develop their talents. Recognition, praise, and encouragement are powerful stimulators! The intent for a beneficial ministry is not to build yourself as a role model, but to help others discover and develop their abilities. At the same time, you help yourself by helping others.

Some years ago, a young man had a creative idea about the processing of cheese. He started in business by driving a horse hitched to an old wagon, selling his cheese to homemakers door to door. Another young man began his business career by riding his bicycle and selling hand-painted greeting cards to people in his neighborhood. A third man opened what he called his "Golden Rule Store." His business began to prosper because he treated those who came to shop as he would want to be treated. All three of these men had a common denominator. They started their work on a proverbial shoestring and became world-famous manufacturers and merchandisers with enterprises worth millions. But Mr. Kraft, Mr. Hall, and Mr. Penney had something else in com-

mon: they literally took God to work with them and looked to God for help in making business decisions and in conceiving and executing the ideas that led to success. Their useful lives became ministries of service.

Can you imagine the kind of service you can give to humanity through the way you live your life and the manner in which you do your work? I hope that some of the ideas presented in this book will encourage you to explore your possibilities, improve yourself, and experience life to a greater degree of useful purpose. How would it feel to *know* you were making a valuable contribution to your world? What joy would you experience from the awareness that, because of you and your work, someone's life was enriched and blessed? What can you do to become more useful, right where you presently are? We can find satisfaction in many ways.

Perhaps one great truth to be learned is this: there is one desire and one fulfillment—to *practice the presence of God in everything we do.* Is our quest for happiness, for everything good, in reality a quest for God's purpose? When we become conscious of that truth, could we have an answer to every question and the solution to every problem?

◆ Law 4

The more love we give, the more love we have left. —John Marks Templeton

To ALLOW a full and free flow of unlimited love from a sincere heart into your daily life can pave the way for rich, full, and satisfying living. Unlimited, universal love accents the richness and completeness of life. It is the ever-present *potential* through which we can discover beneficial actions and a harmonious attitude. Can you imaging living a life where every thought, feeling, word, and action that flowed forth from you was immersed in

unlimited love? This may sound like a major undertaking, but "with God, all things are possible." The idea of "living in love" may challenge your personal understanding of love, but what tremendous breakthroughs could occur in the way you live day by day if you put it to the test!

Is love the unifying, harmonizing force of the universe—the "spiritual glue" that holds everything together? Does the unlimited love of God give freedom to creation for trial and error and innovation around the foundation of spiritual principles and honesty? This unlimited love may be the basic reality from which all else is only fleeting perception by transient creatures. Could there ever be a situation that cannot be helped or healed by the flowing forth of unlimited love?

Love accepts the completeness of life. It is the ever-present potential through which we can find fulfilling action or harmonious attitude. Through unlimited love, we can enter the dimension of spiritual unity, wholeness, and maturity, where we can be more closely united with everything around us. The universe is not isolated from humanity! And humanity is not isolated from the universe! God's love is expressed through all phases of creation. And the more love we give, the more love we have left.

Perhaps all-encompassing, unlimited love is one of the foremost qualities of divine nature. Can aligning the two sides of our human nature—the visible and the spiritual—be an ongoing creative endeavor that continually moves us in beneficial directions? If we neglect either the heights or the depths of our experiences in life, we may only stagnate. By bringing the two together through attending to the practical details of everyday life, our love can gather power and momentum.

Unselfish, unlimited love that gives unceasingly and expects nothing in return is quite possibly one of the most powerful energies in the universe. It is the love that grows as we give it away! There is never a shortage; there is never a lack of love. *The more love we give, the more love we have left.* We could add to this statement: *continue giving!*

When we practice unlimited love, it becomes easier to love our enemies, to tolerate those who may annoy us, to see God's goodness everywhere, and to find something to appreciate in every being, place, thing, experience, and part of life. The great paradox of unlimited love may be that it calls on us to be fully ourselves and honor our individual

truths, while releasing self-centeredness and giving with nothing held back. Love, as with any other spiritual virtue, does not simply fall into our lives as manna from heaven. Like an inquiring mind, it needs to be cultivated.

So, how can we utilize the abundance of unlimited love to help us build more of heaven of earth? If you find yourself *reacting to* instead of *responding to* another person's words or actions, you can look beyond the appearance of the situation and call forth understanding love. If you feel out of sorts with the world around you, you need only to open your mind and connect with the source of unlimited love to make things right again. When difficult situations arise, unlimited love can guide you through them into a harmonious and beneficial conclusion. Should someone desire your help, unlimited love can inspire you with a useful response to his or her needs. Giving all the love you are capable of feeling may prove to be a powerful turning point for your soul! Surely, most of us would welcome those blessed moments when the hardships of life's adversities give way to greater awakening to our spiritual nature. Can recognizing and amplifying these moments be an important part of your spiritual growth?

A popular song about love includes the words: "It's love that makes the world go around." Elbert Hubbard, a famous American collector of sayings, knows that love does make the world go around. He says: "The love we give away is the only love we keep." Unlimited love has been considered by

Love is like a reservoir of kindness and pleasure.
—*Yehuda Amichai*

Love builds.
—*Mary McLeod Bethune*

Love is above the laws, above the opinion of men; it is the truth, the flame, the pure element, the primary idea of the moral world.
—*Madame de Staël*

some to represent the core of ultimate reality. It is the love that is universal and requires the foundation of integrity, truthfulness, and unity with the spirit. Of all the spiritual practices we bring to any aspect of our lives, the most important is love.

✦ LAW 5

Thanksgiving opens the door to spiritual growth. —John Marks Templeton

Be thankful for the smallest thing, and you will be worthy to receive something greater.
—*Thomas à Kempis*

WHO IN YOUR LIFE have you most admired and from whom have you drawn inspiration? Perhaps someone's words or actions or how he or she handled a situation evoked hope and courage from deep within and brought about beneficial change. To whom do you give credit for the many things you have learned? While we can learn something for ourselves, we also learn from a variety of sources. Who gave you direction and then pushed you forward? From what sources did you draw indispensable insight when you needed it most? How have you converted life situations into learning experiences?

Gratitude originates in spiritual vitality and is its expression.
—*Ferdinand Ebner*

For all the blessings and benefits you received, have you developed the habit of daily giving thanks? Something tremendously powerful and life enriching occurs in the activity of thanksgiving. There is probably no greater inspiration nor a more potent tonic for our spirits than an attitude of gratitude. When we express gratitude for the blessings and abundance present in our lives, we become recipients of a spiritual recharge of energy in our minds, bodies, spirits, and all the activities of our daily lives. Truly, thanksgiving opens the door to increased spiritual growth. In what ways can this growth happen?

We begin where we are and take a good look at our world. Every individual's life contains areas for appreciation and giving thanks. We may need to cultivate counting our blessings constantly and think of our problems as opportunities to learn and to grow spiritually. For example, how can we raise the sacredness of everyday living by being thankful for blessings in areas such as the people, places, and things in our lives; opportunities for service; healing for the body, mind, and spirit; creativity and progress? Every step you take to moderate your lifestyle for the overall betterment of humanity definitely moves you in the direction of spiritual growth and progress. To the degree that we open ourselves to the divine flow of gratitude and thanksgiving, we can change from being "mere mortals" to agents for heaven on earth.

Gratitude is a fruit of great cultivation; you do not find it among gross people.
—*Samuel Johnson*

A woman's daughter was critically ill. As she sat by her daughter's bed in the hospital room, the doctor entered. He quietly told her the coming night would bring a change one way or another. The high fever would break or the child could die. Throughout the night, the woman prayed for the life of her daughter. As early morning light began to break, the child sighed deeply and was still. The mother rang for assistance. The child's doctor had just arrived for early rounds and he and a nurse rushed into the room. The doctor took the child's hand, stood quietly by the bed for a moment, then turned to he mother. "She is asleep," he told the woman. "The child has passed the crisis and is going to be all right!"

Tears of gratitude began flowing down the woman's cheek. She had made a promise that if her child lived, she would create a "gratitude garden for God" on her property to which all people would be welcome. The woman fulfilled her promise. A portion of her property became designated as "God's garden." A small waterfall, stream, and pond were designed and created, becoming focal points for the garden. A flagstone path, interspersed with flowering groundcover, leads the way from the garden's entrance around beautiful shrubs, trees, and flowerbeds, to several comfortable benches surrounding the pond. Over time, the garden has become a place of transcendent beauty. Summer roses and wildflowers bloom in unexpected nooks. Water lilies waft their fragrance from the surface of the pond's transparent water. The waterfall sings its song of joy and praise as it tumbles down the rocks. Birds come to drink and bathe, and from early morning light until evening dusk, melodies of bird song can be heard. Evergreen and deciduous trees surround the garden, and the wind whispers through their branches.

When asked about the garden, the woman shares her story of gratitude. It seems that every aspect of the garden—every plant, tree, shrub, flower, and bench—represents *something* for which the woman is grateful. She continually adds to the garden because, as she explains, her "blessings are never-ending and every *recognition* of a blessing is a step closer to God!"

What a beautiful concept! The more we give thanks, the more we have to give thanks for. To the degree that we can recognize our connection with and open ourselves to the divine flow of thanksgiving, we enhance our spiritual growth. And doesn't it seem logical that all those who come in contact with us also receive benefits from our spiritual joy?

Would you consider creating a thanksgiving "garden" in appreciation for your blessings? An actual piece of ground isn't necessary. What if your garden consisted of a daily journal in which you noted your gifts from the spirit and said "thank you"? Or your garden could be a simple calendar where you record appointments to give a gift to others. Recognize a blessing received, then pass it on by doing something thoughtful and special for another person. There are so many areas where loving service is needed. And thanksgiving definitely does open the door to spiritual growth.

Spotlights ✦ ✦

1. Keep your eye on the vision you hold and continually work toward your goal.

2. Focus on what you want to achieve.

3. Every one of us can be an expression or agent of God through unlimited love and expanding creativity.

4. How can we learn to be helpers in achieving God's purpose?

5. Let's encourage creative thinking within ourselves and others.

6. Have you developed the habit of daily giving thanks for all the blessings and benefits you have received?

7. Every individual's life contains many areas for appreciation and giving thanks.

8. The more we give thanks, the more we have to give thanks for.

9. Love accepts the completeness of life.

10. Could there ever be a situation that cannot be helped or healed by the flowing forth of unlimited love?

11. How can you see your life as a ministry?

12. Everything productive that we accomplish in life becomes a ministry of loving service.

Living the Various Spiritual Laws ◆ ◆

EVERY MAN A MINISTER
—James Dillet Freeman

What does it mean to be a minister?

It means to make yourself small so that others may feel large.

It means to make yourself a servant so that others may feel their mastery.

It means to give so that those who lack may receive.

It means to love so that those who feel unloved may have someone who never rejects them, someone with whom they can always identify themselves.

It means to hold out your help to those who ask and deserve help, and also to those who do not ask or deserve it. It means always to be there when you are needed, yet never to press yourself on another when you are not wanted.

It means to stay at peace so that those who are contentious will have someone to whom they can turn to stabilize themselves.

It means to keep a cheerful outlook so that those who are easily cast down may have someone to lift them up.

It means to keep faith, and to keep on keeping faith even when you yourself find little reason for believing, so that those who have no faith can find the courage to live.

It means not merely to live a life of prayer, but to turn your prayers into life—more life for you, more life for those to whom you minister.

Bibliography

Adams, Brian. *How to Succeed.* North Hollywood: Wilshire Book Company, 1985.

Bahá'í Prayers. Wilmette, Ill.: Bahá'í Publishing Trust, 1991.

Barnet, Lincoln. *The Universe and Dr. Einstein.* New York: A. J. Hoffman, 1973.

Bass, Bernard M. *Leadership and Performance Beyond Expectations.* New York: Free Press, 1985.

Bence, Evelyn, ed. *Quiet Moments with Hildegard and the Women Mystics.* Ann Arbor, Mich: Servant Publications, 1999.

Boldt, Lawrence G. *Zen Soup.* New York: Penguin Putnam, 1997.

Braden, Gregg. *The Isaiah Effect.* New York: Harmony Books, 2000.

————. *Walking Between the Worlds: The Science of Compassion.* Bellevue, Wash.: Radio Bookstore Press, 1997.

Bunson, Matthew E. *The Wisdom Teachings of the Dalai Lama.* New York: Penguin Group, 1997.

Bynner, Witter, trans. *The Way of Life According to Lao Tzu.* New York: Berkley Publishing Group, 1986.

Canfield, Jack and Mark Victor Hansen. *Chicken Soup for the Soul.* Deerfield Beach, Fla.: Health Communications, Inc., 1993.

————. *A 2nd Helping of Chicken Soup for the Soul.* Deerfield Beach, Fla.: Health Communications, Inc., 1995.

Carter-Scott, Cherie. *If Life Is a Game, These Are the Rules.* New York: Bantam Doubleday, 1998.

Childre, Doc Lew. *Self Empowerment: The Heart Approach to Stress Management.* Boulder Creek, Calif.: Planetary Publications, 1992.

Chinmoy, Sri. *The Wings of Joy.* New York: Fireside Books, 1997.

Chittick, William C. *Faith and Practice of Islam.* Albany: State University of New York, 1992.

Chittister, Joan. *There Is a Season.* Maryknoll, N.Y.: Orbis Books, 1995.

Clark, Rebecca. *Breakthrough.* Unity Village, Mo.: Unity Books, 1997.

————. *Macro-Mind Power.* West Nyack, N.Y.: Parker, 1978.

Chopra, Deepak. *The Seven Spiritual Laws of Success*. San Rafael, Calif.: Amber-Allen Publishing, 1994.

Cleary, Thomas, ed. *Further Teachings of Lao Tzu: Understanding the Mysteries*. Boston, Mass.: Shambala Publications, 1991.

Cohen, Alan. *Companions of the Heart*. Kula, Hawaii: Alan Cohen Publications, 1988.

Colton, Ann Ree and Jonathan Murro. *Owe No Man*. Glendale, Calif.: Ann Ree Colton Foundation of Niscience, 1986.

Coomaraswamy, Ananda. *Buddha and the Gospel of Buddhism*. New Hyde Park, N.Y.: University Books, 1964.

Covey, Stephen R. *Principle-centered Leadership*. New York: Fireside Books, 1990.

————. *The Seven Habits of Highly Successful People*. New York: Fireside Books, 1989.

Covey, Sean. *The Seven Habits of Highly Effective Teens*. Salt Lake City: Franklin Covey Company, 1999.

De Bary, William Theodore, ed. *The Buddhist Tradition*, New York: Random House, 1969.

de Châteaubriant, Alphonse. *La Résponse de Seigneur*.

Dennis, Maxine F. *Of Human Hands*. Minneapolis: Augsburg Fortress Press, 1991.

DeVoss, Rich. *Hope from My Heart*. Nashville: J. Countryman, 2000.

Dossey, Larry, M.D. *Prayer Is Good Medicine*. New York: Harper-Collins, 1996.

————. *Recovering the Soul*. San Francisco: Harper, 1996.

Dreher, Diane. *The Tao of Personal Leadership*. New York: Harper-Collins, 1996.

Drummond, Henry. *Natural Law in the Spiritual World*. Santa Fe: Sun Publishing, 1981.

Dunlap, Rebekah and John Marks Templeton. *Story of A Clam*. Philadelphia, Pa.: Templeton Foundation Press, 2001.

Dyer, Wayne W. *Wisdom of the Ages*. New York: Harper-Collins, 1998.

————. *101 Ways to Transform Your Life*. Carlsbad, Calif.: Hay House, 1998.

————. *Manifest Your Destiny*. New York: Harper-Collins, 1997.

————. *Your Sacred Self*. New York: Harper-Collins, 1995.

Easwaran, Eknath, trans. *The Upanishads*. Tomales, Calif.: Nilgiri Press, 1987.

————. *The Dhammapada*. Tomales, Calif.: Nilgiri Press, 1985.

————. *Bhagavad Gita*. Tomales, Calif.: Nilgiri Press, 1985.

Effendi, Shoghi, trans. *The Kitáb-i-íqan: The Book of Certitude*. Wilmette, Ill.: Bahá'í Publishing Trust, 1950.

————. *Gleanings from the Writings of Bahá'u'lláh*, Wilmette, Ill.: Bahá'í Publishing Trust, 1939.

Elgin, Duane. *Promise Ahead.* New York: William Morrow, 2000.

Engstrom, Ted. *Integrity.* Colorado Springs: Water Brook Press, 1997.

Fadiman, James and Robert Frager, eds. *Essential Sufism.* New York: Harper-Collins, 1997.

Fakhry, Majid. *A History of Islamic Philosophy.* 2nd ed. New York: Columbia University Press, 1979, 1983.

Feldman, Christina and Jack Kornfield. *Stories of the Spirit, Stories of the Heart.* HarperSanFrancisco, 1991.

Felleman, Hazel. *Poems that Live Forever.* New York: Doubleday-Dell, 1965.

Fenchuk, Gary W., ed. *Timeless Wisdom.* Midlothian, Va.: Cake Eaters, 1994.

Ferris, Timothy. *Coming of Age in the Milky Way.* New York: Doubleday, 1989.

Ferrucci, Piero. *What We May Be.* Los Angeles, Calif.: J. P. Tarcher, 1982.

Fillmore, Charles. *The Revealing Word.* Unity Village, Mo.: Unity School of Christianity, 1997

Fox, Emmet. *Make Your Life Worthwhile.* New York: Harper & Row, 1942.

Frankl, Viktor. *The Unheard Cry for Meaning.* New York: Touchstone, 1978.

Gaer, Joseph. *What the Great Religions Believe.* Cornwall, N.Y.: Cornwall Press, 1963.

Gandhi, Mohandas K. *Book of Prayers.* Berkeley, Calif.: Berkeley Hills Books, 1999.

Gawryn, Marvin. *Reaching High: The Psychology of Spiritual Living.* Berkeley, Calif.: Spiritual Renaissance Press, 1980.

Hammarskjöld, Dag. *Markings.* New York: Alfred A. Knopf, 1965.

Hanh, Thich Nhat. *Peace Is Every Step.* New York: Bantam, 1991.

Harvey, Andrew. *Teachings of Rumi.* Boston: Shamballa Publications, 1999.

Hawley, Jack. *Reawakening the Spirit in Work.* San Francisco, Calif.: Berrett-Koehler, 1993.

Herrmann, Robert L. *Sir John Templeton: From Wall Street to Humility Theology.* Philadelphia, Pa.: Templeton Foundation Press, 1998.

Hillman, James. *The Soul's Code: In Search of Character and Calling.* New York: Random House, 1997

Hua-Ching, Ni. *The Complete Works of Lao Tzu.* Santa Monica, Calif.: Seven Star Communications Group, 1979.

Huxley, Aldous. *The Perennial Philosophy.* New York: Harper-Collins, 1944.

International Religious Foundation. *World Scriptures: A Comparative Anthology of Sacred Texts.* St. Paul, Minn: Paragon House, 1991.

Kaufman, Barry. *Happiness Is a Choice.* New York: Fawcett Books, 1994.

Kirschenbaum, Howard. *100 Ways to Enhance Values and Morality in Schools and Youth Settings*. Needham Heights, Mass.: Allyn and Bacon, 1995.

Kolatch, Alfred J. *What Jews Say About God*. Middle Village, N.Y.: Jonathan David, 1999.

Kornfield, Jack, ed. *Teachings of the Buddha*. New York: Barnes & Noble, 1993.

Kushner, Harold. *When Bad Things Happen to Good People*. New York: Schocken Books, 1989.

Lau, Theodora. *The Best Loved Chinese Proverbs*. New York: Harper Perennial, 1995.

Leider, Richard J. *The Power of Purpose*. New York: MJF Books, 1997.

Lewis, Jim. *Positive Thoughts for Successful Living*. Denver: Unity Church of Denver, 1979.

Loehr, Franklin. *The Development of Religion as a Science*. Grand Island, Fla.: Gnosticouers, 1983.

Longfellow, Henry Wadsworth. *Selected Poems*. New York: Penguin Books, 1988.

Ming-Dao, Deng. *365 Tao: Daily Meditations*. New York: Harper-Collins, 1992.

McArthur, Bruce. *Your Life: Why It Is the Way It Is, and What You Can Do about It*. Virginia Beach, Va.:A.R.E. Press, 1993.

McArthur, David and Bruce McArthur. *The Intelligent Heart*. Virginia Beach, Va.: A.R.E. Press, 1997.

Moore, Gary. *Spiritual Investments*. Philadelphia: Templeton Foundation Press, 1998.

MSI. *Enlightenment: The Yoga Sutras of Pantanjali*. Waynesville, N.C.: MSI, 1995.

Neville. *Power of Awareness*. Marina del Rey, Calif.: DeVorss & Co., 1952.

Ni, Hua-Ching. *The Complete Works of Lao Tzu*. Santa Monica, Calif.: Seven Star Communications, 1979.

Nicholson, Reynold A., trans. *Tales of Mystic Meaning*. Oxford: Oneworld Publications, 1995.

Novak, Philip. *The World's Wisdom: Sacred Texts of the World's Religions*. Edison, N.J.: Castle Books, 1996.

O'Leary, Brian. *Exploring Inner and Outer Space*. Berkeley, Calif.: North Atlantic Books, 1989.

Olitzky, Rabbi Kerry M. and Rabbi Lori Forman. *Sacred Intentions*. Woodstock, Vt.: Jewish Lights, 1999.

Peale, Norman Vincent. *The Positive Principle Today*. Carmel, N.Y.: Guideposts, 1975.

————. *Treasury of Joy and Enthusiasm*. New York: Fawcett, 1982.

Prager, Dennis. *Happiness Is a Serious Problem*. New York: HarperCollins, 1998.

Ramacharaka, Yogi. *The Kybalion: Hermetic Philosophy*. Des Plaines, Ill.: Yoga Publication Society, 1908.

Rinpoche, Sogyal. *The Tibetan Book of Living and Dying*. San Francisco: HarperSanFrancisco, 1993.

Roberts, Elizabeth, and Elias Amidon. *Earth Prayers from around the World*. San Francisco: HarperSanFrancisco, 1991.

Robinson, James M., ed. *The Nag Hammadi Library*. New York: Harper & Row, 1978.

Ryan, M. J., ed. *A Grateful Heart.* Berkeley, Calif.: Conari Press, 1994.

Samra, Carl. *The Joyful Christ.* San Francisco: HarperSanFrancisco, 1986.

Satchidananda, Sri Swami. *The Golden Present.* Yogaville, Ind.: Integral Publications, 1987.

Schuller, Robert. *Reach out for New Life.* New York: Hawthorne Books, 1977.

Schweitzer, Albert. *Reverence for Life.* New York: Harper & Row, 1969.

Seabury, David. *Your Four Great Emotions.* Los Angeles, Calif.: Science of Mind Publications, 1983.

Shapiro, Eddie and Debbie. *Voices of the Heart.* New York: Penguin Putnam, 1998.

Shah, Indries. *The Way of the Sufi.* New York: E. P. Dutton, 1969.

———. *Tales of the Dervishes.* New York: E. P. Dutton, 1969.

Shanklin, Imelda. *What Are You?* Unity Village, Mo.: Unity Books, 1929.

Simon, Julian L. *The State of Humanity.* Malden, Mass.: Blackwell Publishers, 1995.

Starcke, Walter. *It's All God.* Boerne, Tex.: Guadalupe Press, 1998.

Strauch, Ralph. *The Reality Illusion: How You Make the World You Experience.* Barrytown, N.Y.: Station Hill Press, 1983.

Stephan, Naomi. *Fulfill Your Soul's Purpose.* Walpole, N.H.: Stillpoint Publishers, 1994.

Strong, Mary, ed. *Letters of the Scattered Brotherhood.* San Francisco: Harper, 1991.

Tart, Charles T. *Living the Mindful Life.* Boston: Shamballa Publications, 1994.

Templeton, John Marks. *Worldwide Laws of Life: 200 Eternal Spiritual Principles.* Philadelphia, Pa.: Templeton Foundation Press, 1997.

———. *Is Progress Speeding Up? Our Multiplying Multitudes of Blessings.* Philadelphia: Pa.: Templeton Foundation Press, 1997.

———. *The Humble Approach: Scientists Discover God.* Philadelphia: Pa.: Templeton Foundation Press, 1995.

Templeton, John Marks, ed. *Worldwide Worship: Prayers, Songs, and Poetry.* Philadelphia, Pa.: Templeton Foundation Press, 2000.

———. *Looking Forward: The Next Forty Years.* Philadelphia, Pa.: Templeton Foundation Press, 1998.

———. *Spiritual Evolution: Scientists Discuss Their Beliefs.* Philadelphia, Pa.: Templeton Foundation Press, 1998.

———. *How Large Is God? The Voices of Scientists and Theologians.* Philadelphia, Pa.: Templeton Foundation Press, 1997.

———. *Evidence of Purpose: Scientists Discover the Creator.* New York: Continuum, 1994.

Templeton, John Marks, with James Ellison. *The Templeton Plan: 21 Steps to Personal Success and Real Happiness*. New York: Harper, 1987.

Templeton, John Marks, with Robert L. Herrmann. *The God Who Would Be Known: Revelations of the Divine in Contemporary Science*. Philadelphia, Pa.: Templeton Foundation Press, 1998.

————. *Is God the Only Reality? Science Points to a Deeper Meaning of the Universe*. New York: Continuum, 1994.

Trine, Ralph Waldo. *In Tune with the Infinite*. New York: Bobbs-Merrill, 1957.

Teresa, Mother. *In My Own Words*. New York: Gramercy Books, 1996.

Underhill, Evelyn. *Mysticism*. Venice Beach, Calif.: OneWorld Publications, 1999.

Vaswani, J. P., ed. *The Good You Do Returns*. Liguori, Mo.: Triumph Books, 1995.

Welwood, John. *Journey of the Heart*. New York: HarperCollins, 1990.

Wilber, Ken. *One Taste*. Boston: Shamballa Publications, 2000.

World Scriptures: A Comparative Anthology of Sacred Texts. St. Paul, Minn.: Paragon House.

Yogananda, Paramahansa. *Man's Eternal Quest*. Los Angeles, Calif.: Self-Realization Fellowship, 1975.

————. *Metaphysical Meditations*. Los Angeles, Calif.: Self-Realization Fellowship, 1964.

Zukav, Gary. *The Seat of the Soul*. New York: Simon & Schuster, 1990.

————. *Soul Stories*. New York: Simon & Schuster, 2000.

Acknowledgments

From *The Good You Do Returns: A Book of Wisdom Stories* by J.P. Vaswani, © 1995, reprinted by permission of Liguori Publications.

Excerpt from *What Jews Say About God* by Alfred J. Kolatch, © 1999, reprinted by arrangement with Jonathan David Publishers, Inc., www.jdbooks.com.

Excerpt from *Reaching High: The Psychology of Spiritual Living* by Marvin Gawryn, © 1980, reprinted by permission of Highreach Press.

Excerpt from *Essential Sufism* edited by James Fadiman and Robert Frager, © 1997, reprinted by permission of HarperCollins Publishers.

Excerpt from *Teachings of Rumi*, edited by Andrew Harvey, © 1999 by Andrew Harvey. Reprinted by arrangement with Shambhala Publications, Inc., Boston, www. shamabhala.com.

Excerpt from *Tales of Mystic Meaning* by Reynold A. Nicholson, © 1995, reprinted by permission of OneWorld Publications.

From *Tales of the Dervishes* by Idries Shah, © 1967 by Idries Shah. Used by permission of Dutton, a division of Penguin Putnam Inc.

From *The Way of the Sufi* by Indries Shah, © 1968 by Idries Shah. Used by permission of Dutton, a division of Penguin Putnam Inc.

From *What We May Be* by Piero Ferrucci, © 1983 by Piero Ferruccci. Used by permission of Jeremy P. Tarcher, a division of Penguin Putnam Inc.

Excerpt from *A 2nd Helping of Chicken Soup for the Soul* by Jack Canfield and Mark Victor Hansen, © 1995, reprinted by permission of Health Communications, Inc.

Prayer by Bahá'u'lláh from *Bahá'í Prayers* © 1991 by the National Spiritual Assembly of the Bahá'ís of the United States. Reprinted with permission of the publisher, the Bahá'í Publishing Trust of the United States, Wilmette, IL.

Excerpt from *Book of Prayers* by Mohandas K. Gandhi and edited by John Strohmeier, © 1999, reprinted by permission of Berkeley Hill Books.

Excerpt from *Stories of the Spirit, Stories of the Heart* edited by Christina Feldman and Jack Kornfield, © 1992, reprinted by permission of HarperCollins Publishers.

From *Peace Is Every Step* edited by Arnold Kotler, copyright 1991, reprinted by permission of Bantam Books.

Excerpt from *The Isaiah Effect* by Gregg Braden, © 2000, reprinted by permission of Harmony Books.

From *The Dhammapada*, by Eknath Easwaran, founder of the Blue Mountain Center of Meditation, copyright 1985; reprinted by permission of Nilgiri Press, www.nilgiri.org.

Excerpt from *The Wings of Joy* by Sri Chinmoy, © 1997 by Sri Chinmoy, reprinted by permission of Simon & Schuster.

Excerpt from *The Complete Works of Lao Tzu* by Hua-Ching Ni, © 1979, reprinted by permission of Seven Star Communications Group, www.sevenstarcom.com.

Excerpt from *World Scripture: A Comparative Anthology of Sacred Texts* by A Project of the International Religious Foundation, © 1991, reprinted by permission of Columbia University Press.

From *Enlightenment!: Yoga Sutras of Patanjali* by MSI, © 1995, reprinted by permission of Society for Ascension.

From *The Upanishads*, by Eknath Easwaran, founder of the Blue Mountain Center of Meditation, copyright 1987; reprinted by permission of Nilgiri Press, www.nilgiri.org.

Excerpt from *365 Tao: Daily Meditations* by Deng Ming-Dao, © 1992, reprinted by permission of Harper-Collins Publishers.

Excerpt from *What the Great Religions Believe* by Joseph Gaer, © 1964, reprinted by permission of Brandt & Hochman Literary Agents, Inc.

"That Ye All May Be One," by Hilda Kellis, reprinted by permission of Hilda Kellis.

"Precious Seeds," by Russell A. Kemp from *Weekly Unity Magazine*, May 19, 1963. Used with permission of Unity School of Christianity, 1901 NW Blue Parkway, Unity Village, MO 64065.

"Every Man a Minister," by James Dillet Freeman from *Daily Word Magazine*, October 1966. Used with permission of Unity School of Christianity, 1901 NW Blue Parkway, Unity Village, MO 64065

Excerpt from *Exploring Inner and Outer Space* by Brian O'Leary, © 1989, reprinted by permission of North Atlantic Books.

Excerpt from *Sacred Intentions* © 1999 Rabbi Kerry M. Olitzky and Rabbi Lori Forman (Woodstock, VT: Jewish Lights Publishing). $15.95+$3.95 s/h. Order by mail or call 800-962-4544 or on-line at www.jewishlights.com. Permission granted by Jewish Lights Publishing, P.O. Box 237, Woodstock, VT 05091.

Other Books by Sir John Templeton

Agape Love: A Tradition Found in Eight World Religions

Discovering the Laws of Life

Evidence of Purpose: Scientists Discover the Creator

The God Who Would Be Known: Revelations of the Divine in Contemporary Science

Golden Nuggets

How Large Is God? The Voices of Scientists and Theologians

The Humble Approach: Scientists Discover God

Is God the Only Reality? Science Points to a Deeper Meaning of the Universe

Is Progress Speeding Up? Our Multiplying Multitudes of Blessings

Looking Forward: The Next Forty Years

Possibilities for Over One Hundredfold More Spiritual Information:
The Humble Approach in Science and Theology

Pure Unlimited Love: An Eternal Creative Force and Blessing Taught by All Religions

Spiritual Evolution: Scientists Discuss Their Beliefs

Story of a Clam: A Fable of Discovery and Enlightenment

The Templeton Plan: 21 Steps to Personal Success and Real Happiness

Worldwide Laws of Life: 200 Eternal Spiritual Principles

Worldwide Worship: Prayers, Songs, and Poetry

ORDERING INFORMATION
Templeton Foundation Press
5 Radnor Corporate Center, Suite 120
100 Matsonford Road, Radnor, PA 19087

Tel 800-561-3367 ✦ Fax 610-971-2672
tfp@templeton.org ✦ www.templetonpress.org